FIGHTING FOR CANADA:

SEVEN BATTLES, 1758–1945

BOOKS WRITTEN OR EDITED BY DONALD E. GRAVES

ORIGINAL WORKS

FORGOTTEN SOLDIERS:
THE WAR OF 1812 IN THE NORTH TRILOGY

I: *Field of Glory: The Battle of Crysler's Farm, 1813*
(Robin Brass Studio, 1999)

II: *Where Right and Glory Lead! The Battle of Lundy's Lane, 1814*
(Robin Brass Studio, 1997)

. . .

Century of Service: The History of the South Alberta Light Horse
(South Alberta Light Horse Foundation / Robin Brass Studio, 2005)

(with Werner Hirschmann) *Another Place, Another Time: A U-boat Officer's Wartime Album*
(Robin Brass Studio, 2004)

In Peril on the Sea: The Royal Canadian Navy and the Battle of the Atlantic
(Canadian Naval Memorial Trust / Robin Brass Studio, 2003)

Guns Across the River: The Battle of the Windmill, 1838
(Friends of Windmill Point / Robin Brass Studio, 2001)

South Albertas: A Canadian Regiment at War
(South Alberta Regiment Veterans Association / Robin Brass Studio, 1998, 2004)

Redcoats and Grey Jackets: The Battle of Chippawa, 1814
(Dundurn Press, 1994)

(with Michael Whitby) *Normandy 1944: The Canadian Summer*
(Art Global, 1994)

EDITED WORKS

More Fighting for Canada: Five Battles, 1760-1944
(Robin Brass Studio, 2004)

Quebec, 1759: The Siege and the Battle by C.P. Stacey
(Updated and edited by Donald E. Graves; Robin Brass Studio, 2002)

The Incredible War of 1812: A Military History by J.M. Hitsman
(Updated by Donald E. Graves; Robin Brass Studio, 1999)

Soldiers of 1814: American Enlisted Men's Memoirs of the Niagara Campaign
(Old Fort Niagara Press, 1996)

*Merry Hearts Make Light Days: The War of 1812 Memoirs
of Lieutenant John Le Couteur, 104th Foot*
(Carleton University Press, 1993)

1885. Experiences of the Halifax Battalion in the North-West
(Museum Restoration Service, 1985)

Fighting for Canada

Seven Battles, 1758–1945

Edited by
Donald E. Graves

with

John R. Grodzinski

Robert Malcomson

Ian M. McCulloch

Michael R. McNorgan

Brian A. Reid

and

Maps and illustrations by

Christopher Johnson

ROBIN BRASS STUDIO

Toronto

Published 2000 by Robin Brass Studio Inc.
www.rbstudiobooks.com

Reprinted 2001 (with minor corrections), 2005

ISBN-10 1-896941-16-8
ISBN-13 978-1-896941-16-5

Printed and bound in Canada by Marquis Imprimeur, Cap-Saint-Ignace, Quebec

Canadian Cataloguing in Publication Data

Main entry under title:

Fighting for Canada : seven battles, 1758-1945

Includes bibliographical references and index.
ISBN 1-896941-15-X (bound) ISBN 1-896941-16-8 (pbk.)

1. Battles – Canada – History. 2. Canada – History, Military.
I. Graves, Donald E. (Donald Edward), 1949- . II. Grodzinski, John R. (John Richard), 1960- .

FC226.F53 2000   971   C00-931547-0
F1028.F53 2000

This book is dedicated
To the soldiers who have fought
And died
For
Canada

LEST WE FORGET

Contents

LIST OF MAPS

They fought for Canada

A weary infantry company moves back from the trenches of the Western Front to a rest area in November 1916. The strain of combat is evident on the faces of these men who fought for Canada. (National Archives of Canada, PA 832)

A Soldier

I was that which others did not want to be
I went where others failed to go
And did what others failed to do.
I asked nothing from those who offered nothing
And reluctantly accepted the burden of loneliness.
I have seen the face of terror; felt the stinging cold of fear
And enjoyed the sweet taste of a moment's love.
I have cried, felt pain and sorrow
But most of all ...
I have lived times that others would say were best forgotten
After it all, I will be able to say that
I am proud of who I am ...
A Soldier.

ANONYMOUS

Introduction:
The Central Military Act

Fighting is the central military act; all other activities merely support it.

CARL VON CLAUSEWITZ, ON WAR

Fighting for Canada is a study of seven military actions fought between 1758 and 1945. Although far from a glorification of war, this book is not for the faint of heart because it is a serious investigation into the experience in battle of soldiers who fought, either to defend Canada or on behalf of Canada, during the last two centuries.

In terms of result and scale, the battles examined in *Fighting for Canada* vary considerably. Only two – Queenston Heights in 1812 and Leliefontein in 1900 – can be classified as outright victories, although the latter was barely so. Ticonderoga in 1758, Moreuil Wood in 1918 and the Kapelsche Veer in 1945 were nominal successes won at such terrible cost they might well be regarded as reverses; while Ridgeway in 1866 was a serious and humiliating defeat and the 1944 action at Le Mesnil-Patry can only be termed a disaster. In scale, the actions range from Ticonderoga, with nearly 20,000 men involved, down to Leliefontein, where only a few hundred were engaged. Regardless of the size of the battle, however, the emphasis throughout *Fighting for Canada* is on the tactical level of war.

This phrase, "tactical level of war," requires some explanation – clearly it concerns tactics but it is much more than that. Professional soldiers believe that warfare occurs at three distinct but linked levels: the strategical, operational and tactical. The Canadian Army, like most modern armies, defines the strategical level as the application of all a nation's resources to achieve political objectives critical to that nation. The strategical level (which includes political and economic aspects, as well as military) is concerned with the highest national war aims and provides the direction and the means to accomplish those aims.[1]

The operational level links the strategical and tactical levels and usually occurs within a theatre, or specific geographic area. At this level, commanders decide when, where and under what conditions to engage in battle and attempt to connect tactical actions to achieve operational (and even strategical) objectives.[2]

The tactical level, the focus of *Fighting for Canada*, is defined as that level at which formations (corps, divisions and brigades) and units (regiments or battalions) "plan and fight battles and engagements to accomplish the operational objectives assigned to them."[3] The tactical level is the sharp end, where soldiers kill and are killed, and where personal leadership, training, weapons and experience are of paramount importance.

This is the theory at least but the divorce between theoretical and actual is more distinct in war than perhaps in any other human activity. As a case in point consider the events of 1 August 1944. At the strategical level, the government of Canada had committed all available national resources to the objective of defeating Germany by fighting as a member of an Allied coalition. In August 1944 a major part of the national war effort was vested in General H.D.G. Crerar's First Canadian Army deployed in Normandy as one of the Allied armies under the overall command of General Bernard Law Montgomery. Montgomery's operational objective in Normandy was to defeat the German armies opposing him, an objective that would ultimately be achieved by the breakout of American forces from the western sector of the Allied beachhead, a breakout that had commenced on 25 July. On the first day of August 1944, Montgomery was anxious to keep pressure on the German forces opposing the British and Canadian armies in the eastern sector of the beachhead to prevent them from redeploying against the advancing Americans.

In keeping with this operational aim, Montgomery telephoned Crerar at 9.50 A.M. that day to ask whether First Canadian Army could mount an attack on the village of Tilly-la-Campagne, a German strongpoint on the Verrières Ridge south of Caen. Crerar in turn telephoned Lieutenant General Guy Simonds, commanding 2nd Canadian Corps, which had responsibility for Verrières Ridge, to inquire whether an attack on Tilly might be mounted that night. Shortly after 10 A.M., Simonds ordered Major General George Kitching, whose 4th Canadian Armoured Division was responsible for the front line opposite Tilly, to put in an attack on the village.

At this point the matter descended from the operational to the tactical. A successful attack on Tilly-la-Campagne would achieve Montgomery's objective (and, by derogation, that of Crerar and Simonds) of keeping pressure on the Germans in the eastern sector of the beachhead and thus hastening their defeat in France. It was now up to Kitching and his subordinate commanders to plan and fight the battle to take Tilly.

It is at the tactical level of war that the human element plays the greatest part and this level is most susceptible to the dictates of Murphy's Law that, if anything can go wrong, it will. For reasons which cannot concern us here, but were due mainly to the fact that Kitching's division was grass green, it was nearly fourteen hours after Kitching received Simonds's order that the Lincoln and Welland Regiment, the unit actually tasked with carrying out the attack on Tilly, finalized its plans. Among the last to learn about the business were the men of a tank troop of the South Alberta Regiment who were told by their officer just after midnight that they would help support the infantry in the forthcoming operation. One of these men, Corporal Herbert Watkins, remembered that this officer's briefing was short and to the point: his tank crews were simply told to mount up and follow his vehicle, and that they would receive more detailed orders over the radio while on the move. "What a way to be going into action the first time," commented Corporal Watkins, who had trained for more than four years to help accomplish Canada's national war aims.

The attack on Tilly-la-Campagne was finally mounted between midnight and 2 A.M. on 2 August 1944 and it was a disaster. No information about the strength of the German garrison had been available – only that it was "uncertain." In fact, Tilly was held that night by nine well-entrenched companies of panzergrenadiers from the elite *SS-Panzerdivision Leibstandarte "Adolf Hitler"*, supported by artillery and tanks. An eyewitness remembered watching the single Lincoln and Welland company which made the actual assault moving into what he called a "goddamned sea of fire."[4] It is not surprising that the attack failed, with the loss of fifteen men killed and forty-nine wounded.

The purpose of this digression into the events of a long-ago day in 1944 is not only to provide practical examples of the three levels of war but also to introduce the problems inherent in studying battles. It is a relatively easy matter, using official records and postwar interviews with participants, to trace the sequence of events on 1 August 1944 and analyze and define the various strategical, operational and tactical aims and objectives that caused a rather brassed-off Corporal Herbert Watkins from Edmonton to be bumping about dark Norman countryside in a Sherman tank. It is a far different thing to write about the military action that resulted because battles form one of the most difficult subjects of historical inquiry.

To start with, they are confused events that all too often take place, as a British general once wryly remarked, on the side of a hill in the falling rain at the junction of two maps. They are traumatic (if not terrifying) to the participants, whose personal view is limited (a fighting soldier's war is rarely more than ten yards wide) and who are often tired and hungry, and almost always frightened. Evidence from such eyewitnesses is frequently unreliable and usually biased – particularly if the action is distant in the past as the more opportunity participants have to reflect, the more distorted their recollections are likely to become. It has been said (and said well) that on the "day of battle naked truths may be picked up for the asking; by the following morning they have already begun to get into their uniforms."[5]

Faced with the problems inherent in the study of battles, traditional methods of analysis and explication often prove inadequate and the historian may be forced to fall back on informed conjecture. In doing so, he or she must be very careful as we are warned that the battlefield is "a sombre place for the person with imagination," and the "perils of sentimentality are as grave as those of cynicism."[6] In trying to stay clear of the rock of sentimentality, however, the commentator risks grounding on the reef of sterility and producing a narrative so devoid of human feeling that it might be the work of a highly intelligent alien who has evolved beyond the tedious burden of emotion. Even if the hard pressed mariner avoids these twin navigational perils, there is still no clear passage as even the best effort will lessen the spontaneity of the event and not fully communicate the bedlam that war invariably is at the tactical level. The "problem with all you historians," complains one veteran soldier, "is that you impose order on perfectly chaotic situations."[7] One might reply that imposing order on chaos is what good historians are all about, but what this man meant is that, in attempting to convey to their readers a coherent account of what is almost always a confused and complex sequence of events, historians may fail to convey its true nature.[8]

With such pitfalls waiting to trap the unwary, it is not surprising that most Canadian historians avoid studying battles. Indeed, those few who venture into the field of military history will investigate almost any aspect of armed forces except the purpose for which they exist – to fight. Much of the so-called "military history" produced in Canada is actually concerned with matters on the periphery of the central military act and the study of battles has largely become the province of official historians, popularizers and journalists.[9] The former Army

Historical Section produced histories of the Canadian army in both world wars that remain models of craft, analysis and honesty (certainly honest when compared to their British counterparts). But the Historical Section had an official purpose for their endeavours which, understandably, rarely descended to the lower, human, and confusing tactical level. Some popular writers have produced good work, as have even journalists (when they can overcome a penchant for seeing conspiracies behind every high-level bush) but too often the result has been a species of literature of the type one lucid commentator has called the "Zap-Blatt-Banzai-Gott in Himmel-Bayonet in the Guts worst."[10]

This aversion on the part of Canadian historians to dealing with the real business of war is influenced by prevailing academic and social norms about the unthinkability of armed conflict in a nuclear age, and also by a cherished national myth that Canadians are reluctant warriors. As citizens of a peaceable country founded by confederation not conflict, this myth goes, Canadians will only resort to military force in the last extremity. So prevalent is this myth that one of the most popular surveys of this nation's military past, *Canada's Soldiers* by George F. Stanley, was subtitled "the military history of an unmilitary people." Any reader who quickly peruses the first half dozen titles in the suggested reading list appended to *Fighting for Canada* will realize the irony in Stanley's words and conclude that, whether Canadians like it or not, their nation has been shaped, if not created, by armed conflict or the threat of that conflict. In fact, throughout their history, when required, Canadians have shown themselves to be very good soldiers indeed.

Unfortunately, the same cannot be said of their leaders. No prime minister of Canada since Confederation in 1867 has come from a professional military background, only two have ever donned a uniform for their country, and only one, Lester Bowles Pearson, ever went near a combat zone and Pearson's promising career as a stretcher bearer was cut short when he collided with a London city bus in 1917.[11] With this tradition of determined civilians as national leaders, it is small wonder that military matters are usually at the bottom of any list of government priorities.

This has been particularly so since 1953 when Canadian soldiers were last in sustained combat during the "police action" in Korea. Two generations have grown up in Canada without knowing, as three previous generations did, the experience of war. This long period of peace (actually the longest in this nation's history) is a wonderful thing but it has led to a dangerous belief that, since Canada has not been at war for nearly half a century, it is not likely to go to war again.

Soldiers, unfortunately, do not have the luxury of believing in such cheering, if false, beliefs. The collapse of the former Soviet Union may have reduced the potential for nuclear holocaust but the threat of war is still very much a part of global reality. Since 1991, the Canadian Forces have been continuously deployed in the former Yugoslavia and have played a minor but significant role during the large operations in the Persian Gulf in 1991-1992 and Kosovo in 1999. Armed conflict continues to be one of the most enduring expressions of the human condition, and Canadian soldiers, while praying for peace, must prepare for war. In this respect, the past may hold lessons useful for the future and the distillation of these lessons is the prime purpose of the authors of *Fighting for Canada*.

In doing so, the contributors have taken pains to avoid the negative elements often found in traditional "trumpet and drum" military history. These elements were masterfully delineated by John Keegan in his seminal work, *Face of Battle*, as being extreme uniformity of human behaviour (everyone does his duty bravely or poorly, with no exceptions); oversimplified depiction of that behaviour (everyone conducts himself as he should); abrupt or discontinuous description of movement (the component parts of the battle are choreographed and the outcome is a logical result); and stereotyped characterization (the soldiers or units of one side are named, those of the other constitute a faceless mass).[12] In the seven battles studied below, not all soldiers act as they should (nor do their commanders), the two opposing forces are given fairly equal treatment, and while the events of the action may be presented in a logical fashion (one of the perils of studying battles noted above), it is evident that they were far from logical to the participants on days when Murphy's Law clearly prevailed.

Fighting for Canada does not make for untroubled reading, nor should it, because, stripped to its essentials, the central military act is an exercise in hot- and cold-blooded killing. The soldier's task is to do that awful job as efficiently as possible with the minimum of casualties – anything that works toward that end is a good thing, anything that works against that end is a bad thing. It is the hope of the authors of this book (among whom are four serving or former combat arms officers) that their work will contribute to a better understanding on the part of modern Canadian soldiers and their fellow citizens of the nature of that most terrible of human activities, which, whether we like it or not, is still very much with us.

DONALD E. GRAVES
St. Valentine's Day, 2000
Almonte, Canada

FIGHTING FOR CANADA:

SEVEN BATTLES, 1758–1945

Move Fast and Strike Hard:
Defending Canada to 1758

The aboriginal peoples were the first defenders of Canada. Although divided into a number of linguistic and cultural groups, they possessed warlike qualities strong enough for them, near the turn of the first millennium, to repel the Vikings, the first Europeans to attempt to reach North America in large numbers. Nearly five centuries passed before the nations of Europe again tried to establish footholds in the Americas. Equipped with superior technology, they were able to overcome the resistance of the aboriginal peoples, and by the middle of the 17th century, France had established permanent colonies in parts of the territory that would later form the modern nation of Canada.

Defence was a matter of primary concern in French North America. The infant colony of New France was nearly overrun by hostile aboriginal people and disaster was averted only by the dispatch of regular troops from Europe. Near the end of the 17th century, a new and more dangerous threat arose – the English colonies along the Atlantic seaboard. The rivalry between the North American colonies of Britain and France was fuelled by the desire to dominate the lucrative fur trade, at this time one of the largest commercial activities in the world. To offset the superior numbers arrayed against them and to accomplish their commercial objectives, the leaders of New France developed a practical and effective defence strategy tailored to local conditions.

This strategy relied on small forces, composed of regular soldiers and militia, assisted by warrior allies, which raided and unsettled the outposts of the British colonies. The regulars were drawn from the companies of the *troupes de la marine* stationed in North America. These were not shipboard marines but units of the French Ministry of the Navy which had the responsibility for overseas possessions and were thus the first true Canadian regulars. The militia came from the general population – every male *Canadien* (as the white inhabitants of New France called themselves) was, with few exceptions, compelled to serve. The tactics of these raiding parties were to move fast, strike hard and disappear before the enemy could assemble for pursuit. Invariably successful, they frustrated and annoyed successive English colonial governments and led to the mounting of two major expeditions against Quebec in 1690 and 1711 to stamp out the root of this evil – both failed.

By the early 18th century, Canada, as French North America was now being termed, was a well-established society which had been preserved by good leadership, innovative military tactics and the barrier posed by hundreds of miles of wilderness. In 1713 the Treaty of Utrecht brought to a close the latest round of European warfare that had spilled across the Atlantic Ocean and marked the beginning of three decades of peace. Canada prospered during this period. To the west, the never diminishing European taste for furs led to the creation of a vast inland empire from the St. Lawrence through the Great Lakes and down the Mississippi, and to protect French interests in the Grand Banks fisheries and to serve as a naval and privateering base in time of war, the fortified city of Louisbourg was built at tremendous cost on Île Royale (Cape Breton Island).

But this was the high point and the interlude of peace came to end in 1743 when another European conflict spread to North America and war broke out between Canada and its neighbours to the south. In 1745 Louisbourg fell to an expedition of Massachusetts militia supported by the Royal Navy, and its return to France when the war ended three years later created dismay in New England and, ultimately, led to the establishment of Halifax as a rival base. Although Canada had survived almost unscathed, the decade that followed the end of the war in 1748 was a time of increasing tension as the British North American colonies, by now numbering nearly a million inhabitants, spilled across the barrier of the Allegheny Mountains into the interior of the continent. In 1754 Anglo-French rivalry in the lush fur lands of the Ohio River valley led to an exchange of shots between a detachment of Virginia militia commanded by a young officer named George Washington and a force of *troupes de la marine* and *Canadien* militia trying to establish a post in the area. The result was a diplomatic incident that escalated into a crisis between Britain and France. It was clear to Britain that such local colonial military forces as existed were no match for the French and their allies, and, for the first time, an expeditionary force of regular troops, under Major General Edward Braddock, was dispatched to North America.

War had still not been officially declared in April 1755 when Braddock advanced with 2,200 British regulars and American provincials from Virginia towards Fort Duquesne, the French post in the Ohio Valley that was the cause of the dispute. His was only one of four separate forces dispatched against French frontier posts. Braddock was a veteran soldier but his European experience proved of little use in North America and, on 9 July, his army was surprised near the Monongahela River by a vastly inferior force of *troupes de la marine*, *Canadien* militia and aboriginal warriors. The result was a slaughter with nearly a thousand British and Americans casualties, among them Braddock, who was killed after having had five horses shot out from under him, while French and aboriginal casualties, in contrast, amounted to twenty-three killed and sixteen wounded. The defeat of Braddock's army at the Monongahela and of the three other forces sent against the frontier tilted the military balance in favour of France, and the governor of Canada, François-Pierre de Rigaud, marquis de Vaudreuil, was quick to take advantage. At his urging, offensives were mounted against the borders of the British colonies, in a somewhat larger version of the traditional Canadian raiding strategy. So successful was this policy of "offence being the best defence" that, by the end of 1757, France thoroughly dominated the Lake Champlain, Lake Ontario and Ohio River areas.

One feature of this period was the participation of units of the *troupes de terre*, the regular French army, which had been sent to North America in response to Britain's dispatch of Braddock's regulars. When their original commander, Jean-Armand, baron de Dieskau was wounded and captured in one of the few reverses during this period, a bungled attack on Fort Edward, south of Lake Champlain, in 1755, he was replaced by Joseph-Louis, marquis de Montcalm, who preferred to fight according to European methods and made no secret of his pessimism about the eventual outcome of the war. Vaudreuil and Montcalm grew to hate each and the defenders of Canada divided into two rival factions: on the one side, Vaudreuil, the *troupes de la marine* and the *Canadiens*; on the other the *troupes de terre*. This rivalry, which weakened the French war effort, was not aided by clear evidence of widespread corruption among the civilian administration of Canada.

The reverses experienced by Britain in 1755-1757 led William Pitt, the British Secretary of State for War and the cabinet minister most responsible for military activities, to replace Lord Loudoun, the commander-in-chief in North America, with Major General James Abercromby at the end of 1757. When Pitt turned to devising strategy for the forthcoming year, he adopted a plan that called for three offensives against New France. Louisbourg was to be attacked by an amphibious force from Halifax and an expedition was to be mounted against Fort Duquesne. This latter operation was intended to draw French forces away from the Lake Champlain area, where Abercromby, with the largest army assembled in North America to that time, would carry out a major offensive down the lake. It took most of June 1758 to assemble this army, composed of British and American regulars and American provincials, near Fort William Henry at the south shore of Lake George and to construct the armada to transport it, but by the first week of July 1758 Abercromby was ready to move.

Montcalm, whose intelligence service was good, quickly learned of the existence of this force which was far superior to his own command. Although Vaudreuil counselled raiding the Mohawk River Valley settlements of northern New York as a diversion, Montcalm decided to make a defensive stand at a recently built fort on Lake Champlain which he called Carillon, but which his opponent called Ticonderoga.

1

"Like roaring lions breaking from their chains:" The Battle of Ticonderoga

8 July 1758

The Black Watch attack through the abattis, Ticonderoga, 8 July 1758.

"Like Roaring Lions breaking from their Chains." So an eyewitness described the 42nd Foot, Royal Highlanders (later to become famous as The Black Watch), when they mounted a ferocious assault through the nearly impenetrable abattis in front of the French entrenchments on the Heights of Carillon. The artist has erroneously placed Fort Carillon behind the French position when in fact it was a half mile down the hill and out of sight. (Watercolour by C.C.P. Lawson, courtesy, The Black Watch (Royal Highland Regiment) of Canada Museum)

"Like roaring lions breaking from their chains:" The Battle of Ticonderoga

8 July 1758

Ian M. McCulloch

Vous avez senti les sons
Différents de nos cloches,
Pour en distinguer tous les tons
Vous étiez un peu proches.
Il ne fallait point avancer
Quand vous avez vu commencer
Le Carillon! Le Carillon!
Le Carillon de la Nouvelle-France!¹

At the southern end of Lake George, Major General James Abercromby surveyed his command on the evening of 3 July 1758, a geometric grid of tent lines covering every patch of open ground running down to the water's edge. A golden humid haze had settled on the still water that stretched northwards, flanked on either side by the forested Adirondack Mountains. At the lake shore, sweating men cursed in their efforts to load heavy siege guns onto the cumbersome rafts nicknamed the "Floating Castles." On either side of these ungainly vessels hundreds of loaded batteaux and whaleboats stretched for a mile in each direction awaiting their passengers who, on the morrow, would add their tents and personal kit to the stores and barrels of gunpowder, flour and salt beef loaded that day.

Abercromby, a fifty-two-year-old native of Banffshire, Scotland, was a corpulent man with an affable aristocratic face still pale from the illness that had laid him low over the winter. He had entered the British army at the tender age of eleven as an ensign in the 25th Foot, and after nineteen years service was only a captain, albeit in the prestigious 1st Regiment of Foot.

Despite a lengthy military career, Abercromby had seen relatively little active service by the time he arrived in North America in 1756. He had commanded the 1st Battalion of his regiment in Flanders and on promotion to colonel had served as quartermaster general in an unsuccessful expedition against L'Orient, France, in 1746. Abercromby remained in comparative obscurity until the outbreak of the Seven Years' War when, as a major general, he accompanied Lord Loudoun, the commander-in-chief, to North America to act as his deputy. It was

---

See Appendix A, page 367, for Orders of Battle of Opposing Forces.

Loudoun's opinion that "Abercromby is a good Officer, and a very good Second Man anywhere, whatever he is employed in."[2]

Abercromby's army was growing day by day. His force of 17,000 men was the largest assembled in North America to date, and it was a testament to his administrative abilities that he had concentrated in this spot the necessary troops, guns, firearms, supplies and boats to launch his expedition. Others, however, attributed the results to his able second-in-command, Brigadier General George Augustus, Viscount Howe.[3]

British Secretary of State William Pitt described Howe as "a character of ancient times; a complete model of military virtue." Howe was respected by the men under his command for his no-nonsense approach to soldiering. On his arrival in North America, he had made much-needed reforms to the clothing of his soldiers to permit them to campaign in the heavily wooded terrain of that continent. "You would laugh to see the droll figure we all make," wrote a Massachusetts officer. "Regulars as well as provincials have cut their coats so as scarcely to reach their waists. ... No officer or private is allowed to carry more than one blanket or bearskin. ... No women follow our camp to wash the linen. Lord Howe has already shown the example by going to the brook and washing his own."[4]

General orders, no doubt inspired by Howe, instructed "the Whole Army to have their hats cut down ... that they may know one another from the Enemy," causing Dr. Richard Huck, an army surgeon, to comment wryly that "we are now literally an Army of Round heads" with the brims of the hats worn "slouched about two Inches and a half broad." Further orders stated that regi-

"The Old Squaw:" Major General James Abercromby (1706-1781)

The unfortunate 52-year-old commander of the British-American army at Ticonderoga in 1758, whose reverse at the hands of a smaller French force caused his aboriginal allies to term him the "Old Squah who should wear Petticoats." His own soldiers dubbed him "Mrs. Nabbycromby" after the debacle. (Painting by Allan Ramsay, courtesy, J. Robert Maguire)

"A Complete Model of Military Virtue:"
Brigadier General George Howe (1725-1758)
Beloved by British and American soldiers alike, Lord Howe, Abercromby's 34-year-old second-in-command and *de facto* field force commander, was considered by the Secretary of State, William Pitt, to be the best soldier in the British army, an opinion seconded by most of the officers with whom Howe served. Unhappily for Abercromby's army, Howe was killed in action two days before the assault on Ticonderoga. (Courtesy, René Chartrand)

ments would not "carry their colours, nor camp colours to the field this campaigne" and that "the officers do not carry their sashes, but wear their gorgets on duty." Howe wanted none of his men getting entangled in the woods, or as Dr. Huck put it, "French sticking in our Skirts."[5]

The British regulars, the backbone of Abercromby's large army, consisted of 6,260 infantry, artillery and rangers. His six line infantry battalions and one newly raised unit were an assortment of veterans and units fresh from Britain. Abercromby organized these seven units into three small brigades, each commanded by a lieutenant colonel. Besides a small train of regular artillery, he also had at his disposal 9,000 provincial or North American troops, which he organized into two "wings" or large brigades, one of eight regiments, the other of nine. A special corps of 1,600 "battoemen," expert boatman and frontier fighters, rounded out his forces.[6]

Among the regular units was Abercromby's own regiment, the 44th Foot, which had come out with Braddock in 1754 and been severely blooded at the 1755 disaster at the Monongahela. It had since been rebuilt and numbered many Americans in its ranks. Another veteran unit was the thousand-strong Highland Regiment of Lord John Murray, the 42nd Foot, later to be known as the Black Watch. It still included some 200 veterans of the 1745 battle of Fontenoy when it arrived in 1756. The 27th Foot, the 46th Foot and the 55th Foot had all arrived in America the year before from Ireland and had seen no action until then. All, however, were commanded by veteran officers who were experienced campaigners, albeit on European battlefields. The remaining two regiments were two of the newest on the British establishment: the 60th Foot (Royal Americans) and the newly raised 80th Foot or "Gage's Regiment of Light-Armed Foot," nick-named the "Leathercaps" because of their unique headdress.[7]

Major Robert Rogers's five companies of rangers, a rough and ready "irregu-lar" crowd, were a necessary auxiliary force for patrolling and skirmishing in the wilderness. One ranger in five was a Stockbridge or Mohican warrior, led by a father and son pair accorded officer status, Captain Jacob Cheeksauken and Captain Jacob Naunaumpetonk.[8] Other natives who supported the cause of His Majesty King George II of Britain had also joined the expedition, 400 of the choicest warriors of the Six Nations, "a greater number than ever we cou'd assem-ble together before," noted Captain Charles Lee of the 44th Foot. Led by Sir William Johnson, the superintendent of Indian affairs, these Iroquois warriors gave the entire army such confidence that Lee added: "What a glorious Situation was this! In short everything had so charming an aspect, that without being much elated I should have looked upon any man as a desponding dastard who could entertain a doubt of our success."[9]

One of the most important components of Abercromby's army was also a problematic one – his train of artillery, num-bering forty-four pieces of ordnance and commanded by Captain Thomas Ord.[10] Ord, a veteran of seventeen years, had fought in Flanders and at the Monongahela and was, in Loudoun's opinion, "very Industrious but has no ex-ecution." Ord had sufficient weapons but lacked trained gunners. Of his two companies of artillery, one hundred men of Captain Phillip Webdell's company and their commander had been assigned elsewhere and only Captain William Martin's company remained. Martin was, however, a prisoner of war and so his second–in-command, Captain Lieutenant James Stephens, would

"Royal Highlander:" private of the 42nd Foot, c. 1758
In addition to his Long Land Pattern, .75 calibre "Brown Bess" musket, this private carries a dirk on the front of his belt beside his sporran or purse, his bayonet and basket-hilted broadsword on his left side, and a Highland pistol under his left arm. The 42nd left their swords behind for the Ticonderoga campaign, however, despite all contemporary illustrations to the contrary, and there is an active debate as to whether they wore trousers or kilts on the day of battle. (Author's collection)

The proper Position of a Soldier.

lead the company under Ord's supervision. Because of the critical shortage of artillerymen, on 14 June 1758 Abercromby had ordered each of his infantry regiments to send sixty-three men to Ord to act as "additional gunners."[11]

There were also problems with the engineer department of the army. All winter long, the chief engineer, Lieutenant Colonel James Montresor, had been ill, and he had begged off participating in the upcoming campaign. The next senior, William Eyre, held parallel appointments as a captain and engineer in ordinary in the Royal Engineers and as a major and senior field officer of the 44th Foot. Eyre, an engineer of some note who had designed and laid out Fort William Henry, decided to remain with his regiment during the forthcoming campaign.[12] The engineering responsibilities thus fell to Lieutenant Matthew Clerk, who had four years of experience in the army as an engineer and infantry lieutenant. Recently attached to the 27th Foot, he was an acquaintance of Brigadier General James Wolfe, the future victor at Quebec, who thought him an officer "whom nature has formed for the war of this country." Clerk was assisted in his duties by four foreign officers serving in the Royal Americans.[13]

Abercromby intended using his American provincial regiments for unskilled labour, but he still required experienced sappers and thus was forced to canvas his regulars for men "who have served at sieges" and were "accustom'd to make Gabions, Baskets or Hurdles." Accordingly, four of the six regular infantry regiments were ordered to provide a total of 112 officers and men to serve under the engineers for the duration of the campaign.[14]

Abercromby did not place much faith in the American component of his command. Numbering some 10,600, only the 1,600 river toughs known as "battoemen" under Lieutenant Colonel John Bradstreet were veterans of the frontier. There were some provincial units in the army, such as Major Israel Putnam's Connecticut Rangers and Colonel Oliver Partridge's Massachusetts Light Infantry Regiment, which were experienced in bush fighting, but most were levies of townsfolk and farmers, and their standard of training and expertise ranged from abysmal to fair. The fundamental difficulty was that they simply had not had enough time since their formation to learn or practise the complex drills demanded by the tactics of the period. Many lacked even the rudimentary knowledge of how to handle a firearm, a situation not helped by the fact that some units did not even receive muskets until three days before the army embarked to move up Lake Champlain. The number of accidental injuries and deaths at the Lake George camp when provincial regiments went out to the woods to practice, borders on the ridiculous. Captain Hugh Arnot of the 80th

"Royal American:" private of the 60th Foot, c. 1758

The 4th Battalion and six companies of the 1st Battalion of the 60th Foot fought at Ticonderoga. This "hat" or battalion company soldier is shown in full regimental dress but would have been more comfortably attired on campaign – his coat discarded in favour of his waistcoat, his tricorne cropped on Lord Howe's orders, leaving only the crown and a two-inch brim, his white gaiters replaced with brown marching gaiters, and the whiting scraped off his belt, cross belts and scabbards. (Courtesy, Réne Chartrand)

Foot, an experienced officer, was not amused by the antics of the provincials. "That their numbers did not amount to what they promised is most certain," he observed distastefully, "but the greater their Numbers, the greater the Evil; for of any sett of people in the Universe they are the worst cut out for war, The most stupid and most chicken-hearted sett of Mankind." Little wonder Abercromby did not trust his American units' ability to wage war.[15]

But while Abercromby might find some cause to complain of the quality of some of his troops, he had a well-equipped army by 18th century standards. His infantrymen were armed with flintlock smooth-bore muskets, the most common weapon being the "Brown Bess" or Long Land Pattern musket with a 46-inch, .75 calibre (.75 inch) bore, a walnut stock and a metal or wooden ramrod. A socket bayonet fitted over the bayonet lug and had a triangular blade about seventeen inches long. The Long Land was a heavy weapon and the 80th Foot had cut their barrels down to forty-two inches and carved their stocks to make them lighter, while their irregular counterparts, the rangers, used mostly rifles. In preparation for the campaign, Abercromby had also ordered ten rifles issued to each regular battalion for the "picquet" or company of marksmen he had caused to be formed in each unit.[16] Their opponents were armed with similar weapons. The musket of the French *troupes de terre* was the "Charleville" with a .69 bore while the *troupes de la marine* carried the 1746 St. Etienne pattern of similar calibre.

There was little difference in the performance of the weapons of both armies. British and French muskets were capable of hitting a target the size of a man consistently at fifty or sixty yards range, but their accuracy dropped off beyond that distance unless one was firing at a mass formation. Muskets were difficult to load and fire. The flints wore out after about twenty rounds and had to be replaced.

The bore and vents would quickly foul with powder residue and had to be cleaned after repeated firings. As good reliable ammunition was essential to all infantrymen, quality control was provided by the artillery of both armies, who supervised the mixing of powder and production of cartridges.

Musketry was usually delivered in volleys so that the individual weapon's weaknesses of short range, inaccuracy and low rate of fire (two to three shots per minute) could be overcome by sheer weight of fire. However, the veterans of the line and their various light infantry and irregular comrades of both sides were capable of a certain degree of accuracy. Infantry units usually delivered their fire in lines of three ranks, though Abercromby instructed his battalions to form in two ranks for the upcoming campaign.

Both armies on Lake Champlain also possessed quantities of artillery (see Appendix A for detailed lists of types and calibres). The most useful and numerous type was the gun, which was designed to fire a solid iron ball on a flat trajectory over the greatest possible distance. Abercromby's inventory included weapons of this type, ranging from large 24-pdr. siege guns down to tiny 2-pdr. pieces.[17]

James Abercromby might later claim that he had "had but a nominal army," but it was an army with real teeth, real spirit and sufficient numbers to beat his French adversary, who waited for him at the north end of the lake.

That adversary, Louis-Joseph, marquis de Montcalm, stood gazing intently southwards down the lake the French called St. Sacrement, on the same evening Abercromby was looking northwards. Forty-six years old, short and dark-skinned, Montcalm had been born in 1712 into an old, established family with large estates in southern France. Other Montcalms before him had served their king faithfully, so much so that a local saying went that "War is the tomb of the Montcalms." Montcalm was commissioned an *ensigne* in the Régiment d'Hainault at the age of nine and had had a captaincy purchased for him on his nineteenth birthday, but his active and extensive military career did not start until he turned twenty. Despite his hot temper, sharp tongue and tendency to hold a grudge, the haughty Montcalm did well in the army. By 1744, when James Abercromby was commanding a battalion in Flanders during the War of the Austrian Succession, Montcalm was lieutenant colonel of the Régiment d'Auxerrois and had been made a Knight of St. Louis for gallantry. He was, however, badly wounded at the battle of Piacenza in 1746, where his regiment was virtually destroyed and he was taken prisoner. Peace in 1748 brought his release but also the exorbitant expense of peacetime soldiering. Thus in 1752

The victor — *Général* Louis-Joseph, marquis de Montcalm (1712-1759)

A 46-year-old Provençal aristocrat, the French commander at Ticonderoga was a hot-tempered regular officer who did not have much faith in his colonial soldiers, *Canadien* militia or aboriginal allies and bickered constantly with the governor of New France, the marquis de Vaudreuil, over the strategy to be employed against the British. (Pastel drawing, courtesy, Fort Ticonderoga Museum)

he petitioned the minister of war for leave to retire on a pension to his estates, citing his devoted service of thirty-one years, including eleven campaigns and five wounds.[18]

For the next seven years, Montcalm lived the life of a provincial nobleman, periodically making inspection visits to his regiment. When Baron de Dieskau was captured at Lake George in 1755, King Louis XV of France had to find a replacement. With a major continental war looming, no senior experienced French officer wanted to serve in a country most viewed as "so many acres of snow." The monarch therefore reached lower and appointed Montcalm a major general (*maréchal de camp*) in 1756 and sent him to New France with two battalions of regular infantry to reinforce the eight already stationed there.[19]

Montcalm's small army was a living reflection of the personal antagonism he felt towards the North American-born governor of New France, François-Pierre de Rigaud de Vaudreuil. The two had constantly bickered over control of military affairs. The *troupes de terre*, or units of the regular army, were under the direct command of Montcalm, but the other two components of the defenders of New France, the *Canadien* militia and the *troupes de la marine*, units administered by the ministry of the marine which was responsible for the overseas colonies, were under Vaudreuil's control.

Montcalm's army units were not blessed with good officers. As he soon found out, the battalions in New France had been used as a dumping ground for the cast-offs of their parent regiments in Europe. Montcalm would later be forced to send nine officers back to France, and he was really only happy with one of his eight battalion commanders, Lieutenant Colonel Etienne-Guillaume de Senezergues de la Rodde, whom he deemed fit to withstand the rigours of campaigning in North America. Lieutenant Colonel Jean Dalquier of the Béarn regiment, by contrast, was an officer of "great bravery, experience and knowledge of war" with a body "scarred with the marks of Mars," but he was in his sixties. Moreover, the Chevalier de Bernetz of the Royal-Roussillon was so infirm that he would shortly be forced to resign his commission.[20]

Montcalm also had about two hundred *Canadien* militia at Fort Carillon, which the British called Ticonderoga. These *habitant* soldiers were raised from able-bodied men aged sixteen to sixty and received arms, clothing, equipment and rations from the king, but no pay. The best of them came from the frontier areas, the so-called *coureurs de bois*, well versed in bush fighting or *petite guerre*, whose talents lay in boat work, construction, scouting and raiding. Faced with regular troops firing volleys in the open, they took cover or fled. *Capitaine* Louis-Antoine de Bougainville wrote kindly that the *Canadien* militia possessed "a different kind of courage" in their penchant for concealing themselves and favour-

ing ambush over direct confrontation. Another French regular officer, Pierre-André Gohin, comte de Montreuil, was less charitable. To him the "braggart *Canadiens*" were good skirmishers but "only brave behind a tree and timid when not covered."[21]

Last, but not least, were Montcalm's native allies, who required great tact and diplomacy in handling. He wrote that "one needs the patience of an angel to get on with them," and recognized that their value was more psychological than

North American veteran: private, Compagnies franches de la marine, 1758

The *troupes de la marine*, who, despite their title, fought only on land, were the garrison troops of France's overseas colonies. Their skill in North American bush warfare and movement was superior to that of the *troupes de terre*, their French army counterparts. They employed the same tactics as their aboriginal warrior allies. This private wears the standard grey-white uniform with blue facings and is armed with a .69 calibre St. Etienne Model 1746 musket. (Courtesy, Parks Canada)

Regimental colour: ensign, Régiment de Guyenne, c. 1758

One of the seven regular French regiments represented at the battle of Ticonderoga, the 2nd Battalion of the Guyenne were veterans of North American campaigning, having arrived in 1756. During the battle, they saw some of the heaviest fighting on the northeast corner of the French lines, repulsing numerous attacks and being directly involved in the "surrender" incident in the latter part of the afternoon. (Courtesy, René Chartrand)

real. He had only fifteen Ottawas at Fort Carillon.[22]

Montcalm also had two regular engineers, *Capitaine* Nicolas Sarrebource de Pontleroy and *Capitaine* Jean-Nicolas Desandrouins, and a company of *artillerie de la marine* commanded by *Capitaine* François-Marc-Antoine Le Mercier, comprising eight officers (three of them *Canadiens*), four sergeants, ten cadets and eighty-six gunners. Most of the company was at Carillon and had been augmented by additional gunners taken from the *troupes de la marine* and French naval gunners sent from Montreal.[23]

As dawn broke over the British camp on Lake George on 5 July 1758, the orderly drummer beat the drags and paradiddles of the "General Call to Arms." Every boat was pre-packed except for the tents and the men's personal kit. The sailcloth tents were down in minutes, and the troops marched to their boats. Embarkation was orderly and the immense flotilla of over one thousand whaleboats, batteaux and gun rafts soon covered the entire width of the lake. The *Pennsylvania Gazette* reported that they filled "the Lake from Side to Side, which is a Mile and a half at the upper end; and in the narrower Places, they were obliged to form into Subdivisions to give them Room to row, they extended from Front to rear full seven Miles; and by the time the rear had left the Shore three miles, there was not any of the Lake to be discern'd except that Part that was left behind."[24]

Abercromby's men were "in high Spirits," and, to Major Robert Rogers in the vanguard, the "order of march was a most agreeable sight: the regular troops in the centre, provincials on each wing, the light infantry on the right of the advanced guard, the rangers on the left, with Colonel Bradstreet's battoemen in the centre." In the rear came the stores and baggage batteaux, the heavy flatboats or scows carrying the artillery and a rearguard consisting of Colonel Oliver Partridge's Light Infantry.[25]

The army rowed twenty-five miles to Sabbath Day Point, the light infantry and rangers making a great show of going ashore some two miles to the north of this prominent landing site. The first division of the main body landed on the point and immediately erected tents, made large fires and went through the motions of settling in for the night on the orders of Howe. It was a ruse, however, and appeared to have fooled the French, for by 11 P.M. the army had completely re-embarked and was on the move again, undetected.[26]

At the same time as the British armada departed from the southern end of the lake on 5 July, French detachments had taken post as advance guards at Mont Pélée (now known as Rogers' Rock) on the western side of the lake, 350 men under the command of *Capitaine* le sieur de Trépezac and *Ensigne* Jean-Baptiste Levreault de Langis Montegron, while another force of 300 men under *Capitaine* le sieur de Bernard watched and waited at Mont Agné on the eastern

Cockpit of the war – the southern end of Lake George, 1758

A view looking north on Lake George where the largest army assembled in North America to that date embarked for the attack on Fort Carillon located some thirty miles to the north. (Courtesy, David M. Stewart Museum, Montreal)

shore (see Map T-1). The leading whaleboats, containing Howe, the light infantry and grenadiers, Rogers' Rangers and Bradstreet's battoemen, however, glided past these advance guards, followed by the remainder of the flotilla which stretched back over seven miles.

By 4 A.M. on 6 July, the first boats were three-quarters of a mile from the northern shore of Lake George, in the area known as "The French Narrows." With dawn still a half hour away, Howe and Matthew Clerk in one boat and Rogers in another went forward to scout possible landing sites and check for enemy outposts. They were observed by a French party in a canoe, which turned in the gloom and disappeared. Howe's reconnaissance being successful, he gave the signal for the landing to proceed. When dawn came, the men in the French advance posts saw the surface of the lake covered with whaleboats and batteaux coming toward them and they promptly fled north (see Map T-2 for landing).

The first British troops ashore were rangers, who landed on the far left of the landing place and were followed by the left wing of the provincials, who sent a regiment onto the high western hill that dominated the area. The five companies of the 80th Foot landed in the centre on the main beach with Howe at their head, supported by the grenadier companies of the six British battalions under the command of Lieutenant Colonel Frederick Haldimand, who lined the beach four deep as this was the intended disembarkation point of the greater part of the army.

One of the first men ashore was Captain Hugh Arnot of Gage's Light Infantry. An experienced officer with a good eye for the land, Arnot led his 100 "Leathercaps" briskly forward in skirmish order as the grenadiers formed up behind them and advanced to allow the regular brigades to start landing. All were surprised and in good humour that the landing had been unopposed, since most of the army had expected it would be hotly disputed. One British officer professed that it was here they "had expected to meet with the principal opposition" as it was "a very strong post. But to our great surprise upon our first motions to land, the French deserted their Camp in the most precipitate manner."[27]

Captain Arnot and his company "scour'd" through the 200 yards of open ground to their front, checking out logs and long grass for the enemy before forming "in the Skirts of the wood in a scattered rank & file." Meanwhile, the battoemen under Bradstreet went around the point and landed just three-quarters of a mile south of the main French camp. With its breastworks and cleared fields of fire, the portage camp, as it was known to the French, guarded the bridge of boats straddling the top of the La Chute River and the beginning of the portage road. Two miles to the north along this wide road, which climbed

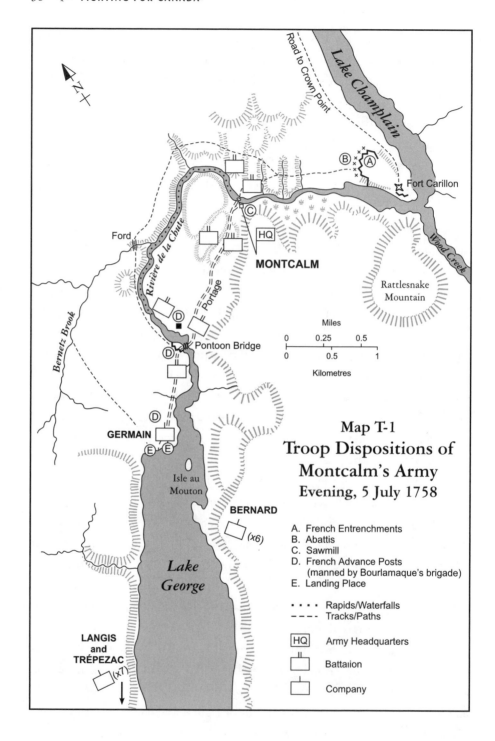

Map T-1
Troop Dispositions of Montcalm's Army
Evening, 5 July 1758

A. French Entrenchments
B. Abattis
C. Sawmill
D. French Advance Posts
   (manned by Bourlamaque's brigade)
E. Landing Place

• • • •   Rapids/Waterfalls
– – – –   Tracks/Paths

HQ   Army Headquarters

Battalion

Company

slightly, then fell more steeply to the river's outlet to Lake Champlain, was a larger entrenched camp guarding another bridge across the winding river and two sawmills garrisoned by four battalions under Montcalm's direct command. At 8 A.M. Bradstreet's men at their landing place saw the French regulars marching away and moved quickly forward.[28]

Two hours later, all his regiments were ashore, and Howe gave them four hours to sort themselves out, cook a meal and stretch their legs after a day cramped in their boats. Abercromby had every reason to be relieved as his first hurdle had been crossed – a major landing had been made on a hostile shore with only a few casualties from skirmishing. It was an occasion that conjured up "a great Part of the Pleasure which Commonly attends the first glimmerings of Success."[29]

Howe's plan now called for an approach march to Fort Carillon (Ticonderoga) on the west side of the hook-shaped river, thus avoiding the most direct and obvious route to the fort – the portage or wagon road (see Map T-2). The British were now in possession of the head of the portage, but they would march instead on the left bank of the river as it curved north and dropped east to Lake Champlain, rendering any French defence of the river line at the sawmill camp and northern bridge untenable. The plan looked good on the map, but would prove extremely difficult to execute on the ground.

At noon, Rogers' Rangers were dispatched to march forward to the Bernetz Brook and seize suitable crossing sites for the army. This stream, which flowed from the west into the La Chute River, was usually fordable at some spots, but heavy June rains had raised the water level to the point where it posed a deep, sluggish obstacle.[30] Bradstreet's battoemen, who numbered many carpenters and shipwrights in their ranks, were ordered to build a boat bridge across the narrow outlet that drained Lake George to the north by means of the La Chute to replace the destroyed French bridge. Five sets of waterfalls and rapids fell 225 feet over a distance of two miles to the short river's egress, a half mile beyond the last set of falls and the sawmills.

Numbering some 7,000 men, regulars and provincials took up their positions in the order of march. From west to east, provincials formed the outer left column and flank guard, regulars the inner left and right columns, while another column of provincials led by Howe would advance along an Indian path that skirted the river, acting as the hinge to the flanking movement that was to swing around and approach Fort Carillon from the west.

They set off at 2 P.M. on 6 July, the battoemen under Bradstreet remaining behind to unload camp stores and provisions. A New York and a Connecticut regiment also stayed to guard the landing site, as well as the artillery, the engineers and commissary staff, who were still unloading their materiel. From the start, the march was slow, except for Howe's column, which made good time. The other three found movement a nightmare; an officer of the 44th Foot described the march through "dark woods and swamps that were almost impassable, till at length, having lost our way, the army was obliged to break its order of march, we were perplexed, thrown into confusion, and fell upon one another in a most disorderly manner."[31] It was not an auspicious beginning.

The head of Howe's column, consisting of Major Israel Putnam's Connecticut Rangers, Colonels Phineas Lyman and Eleazer Fitch's 1st and 4th Connecticut Regiments, Colonel Oliver DeLancey's New Yorkers and the New Jersey Blues, closed up with Rogers at the Bernetz Brook at approximately 3.30 P.M. Howe sent Lyman and Fitch forward to Rogers to locate the best places to build log bridges, then took Putnam's Rangers over to the left to find out where the head of the second column might be.

Rogers had done his work well, sending scouting parties forward to the sawmills, and they had quickly reported that the bulk of the French army was entrenched there, a mere half mile away. As Lyman and Fitch met with Rogers, he informed them "of the enemy being so very near," and when he inquired of the army's progress, "they told me [they] were coming along." Just as the three officers finished their conversation, "a sharp fire began in the rear of Colonel Lyman's Regiment, on which he said he would make his front immediately," reported Rogers. Lyman desired Rogers "to fall in on his left flank, which I accordingly did, having first ordered Captain Burbanks with one hundred and fifty men to remain at the place where I was posted, to observe the Movement of the French at the Saw Mills."[32]

Howe and his group made contact with the "Leathercaps" of the 80th Foot out in front of the right inner column about a quarter mile from Lyman's and Rogers's position, just at the moment they were fired on by a large French force under cover. This was Langis and Trépezac's advance guard from the west side of the lake, which had been skirting the south bank of the Bernetz Brook hoping to return to the main army by means of the ford Rogers now occupied. The French decision to open fire was their undoing.

Captain Alexander Monypenny of the 55th Foot, Howe's brigade major, was right beside him when the ambush was sprung and an unwilling witness to what next occurred.

When the firing began on the left part of the column, Lord Howe thinking it would be of the greatest consequence, to beat the enemy with the light troops, so as not to stop the march of the main body, went up with them, and had just gained the top of a hill, where the firing was, when he was killed. Never ball had more deadly direction. It entered his breast on the left side, and (as the surgeons say) pierced his lungs, and heart, and shattered his backbone. I was about six yards from him, he fell on his back and never moved, only his hands quivered an instant."[33]

Captain Arnot and his men were too busy to see their leader fall, and though he noted Howe's death later in his journal (as did every other officer and man after the campaign), Arnot took a certain professional satisfaction that his men reacted quickly to turn the tables on the French ambushers who, being "so warmly receiv'd by the Lt Infantry," were "oblig'd to retire fighting from Tree to Tree."[34]

Colonel Jonathan Bagley's Massachusetts men on the far left, "at hearing ye first Fire … were ordered to form to ye Right and run up to the enemy." Arnot reluctantly admitted that he could "not give all Favour of that warm little Skirmish to the Lt Infantry" since they "were join'd at the latter end of it by some of the Provincials & a few of the regulars who acted as Lt Infantry." Rogers's Rangers and the 1st and 4th Connecticut Regiments moving down on the brook from the north closed the back door on the unfortunate Trépezac.[35]

Most accounts say that Trépezac's detachment fought grimly for at least fifteen minutes as a formed body before scattering to the four points of the compass. Lieutenant Archelaus Fuller of Bagley's Massachusetts Regiment, moving in with his men from the west, thought it "a very smart ingagment," with "the fire so smart for some time that The Earth trembled." The surgeon of the same regiment wrote "there was near as many Thousand Guns fired, which made a most terriable roreing in the woods."[36]

The French detachment was destroyed: 150 men were shot down or drowned in the swollen stream, while another 151 officers and men were taken prisoner over the next two hours. Only Langis, Trépezac and 100 of their men escaped north across the Bernetz, though Trépezac would die of wounds that night. But the event which Howe had desperately wished to avoid – the stopping "of the march of the main body" had now occurred. Though the "little skirmish" was intense only for fifteen minutes, Abercromby's army spent the next three hours trying to reorganize and absorb the stunning news that Howe was dead. "Bewildered" was the word Abercromby used in his report.

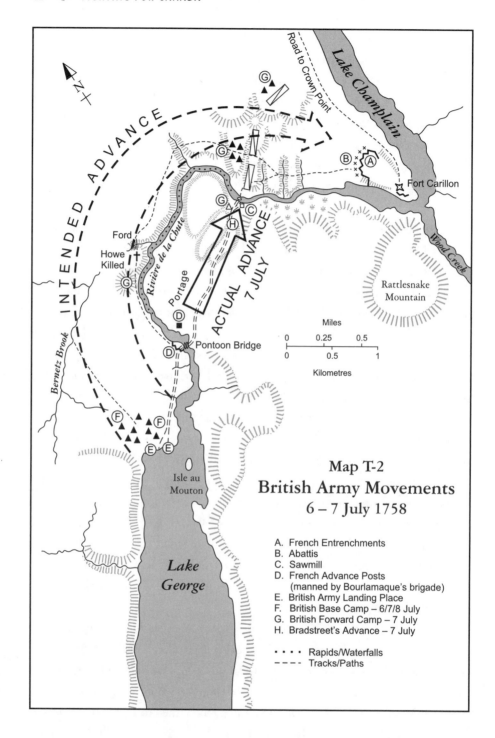

Map T-2
British Army Movements
6 – 7 July 1758

A. French Entrenchments
B. Abattis
C. Sawmill
D. French Advance Posts
   (manned by Bourlamaque's brigade)
E. British Army Landing Place
F. British Base Camp – 6/7/8 July
G. British Forward Camp – 7 July
H. Bradstreet's Advance – 7 July

• • • • Rapids/Waterfalls
- - - - Tracks/Paths

Even worse, troops were so scattered over four square miles or in hot pursuit of Frenchmen, that command and control were virtually impossible.[37] Major William Eyre, leading the veteran 44th Foot, was full of foreboding, and recorded that "this little firing threw our Regulars in to some kind of Consternation, which, tho' ended soon, gave me some uneasyness." A survivor of Braddock's massacre, the perceptive Eyre remarked that the firing, "tho' at some distance, seem'd to Alarm them," which he ascribed to the facts that "where nothing can be Seen, the men fancy the worse, or the Enemy more Numerous than they are" and "Our Irregulers Yelling is believed by those who Are not engaged, to be the enemy: in short, I am more than ever convinced that numbers of our People cannot bear a great deal of firing round them coolly … when they hear & do not See."[38]

By 7.30 P.M., the three marching columns still in the woods reformed as two large divisions, the provincials on the western flank and the regulars between them and the La Chute River. As they approached the Bernetz at dusk with "one column on an eminence of rising ground" and "the other in a valley," Eyre and others heard "a fire in front" which "grew quicker and was followed by a loud heidious Yell." The provincials on the left outer flank started firing blindly towards the centre and the leading elements of the inner column replied in kind. Eyre's worst fear was realized:

> Those in the Front gave Way immediately in the greatest Disorder, and it ran down for two or three hundred Yards along each Column, as it appeared to me; no intreaty could prevail with the men for some time, but in about an hour's time after this, we found out, the fire that began this Confusion in the front was from Ourselves, & by all I could learn Since, not a Single Shot was fir'd against us by the Enemy; by this time it was almost Dark, we were seperated & had som difficulty to Join afterwards but in a very irregular Way, the regts intermix'd with each Other, a most wretched situation.[39]

Eyre was of the opinion that "two or three hundred Indians surrounding us that night" would have completely unnerved the army, and Abercromby by now had had enough. With his "Troops being dispersed, and Night coming on fast, I collected those about me, and they lay on their Arms all Night." Needless to say, few men slept, and a restless Private Garrett Albertson of the New Jersey Blues voiced the thought that was on many soldiers' minds: "the hand of Providence was turned against us in a lonely wilderness."[40]

In the morning, Abercromby discovered that all his regular regiments, except the 44th and half of the 55th Foot, had returned to the Lake George landing place after the first skirmish, as had several provincial regiments after the sunset debacle. Many commanding officers would have some serious explaining to do. Gathering the remainder, some 4,000 tired and hungry troops of the original 7,000, Abercromby marched back to the landing place to take stock and re-organize.[41]

Early on the morning of 6 July 1758, engineer *Capitaine* Jean-Nicolas Desandrouins stood in the wet, knee-high grass of the advance post beside Colonel François-Charles de Bourlamaque watching hundreds of whaleboats round the point. The latter, a forty-two-year-old officer of Italian descent, was the commander of the portage brigade consisting of battalions of the Béarn, La Reine and Guyenne regiments, and it was not difficult to gauge his mood. "The Colonel was furious to see the enemy landing right under his nose," observed Desandrouins. "He wished mightily to throw them back into the water, but it was pointed out to him that 650 of his men were still forward" and that "the English were too numerous for us to even think we could dispute the terrain: to have done so would have led to the defeat of what was left of his three battalions."[42]

Bourlamaque returned to his camp and ordered his grenadiers and light infantry *volontaires* under *Capitaine* le sieur de Duprat to skirmish and buy time for his diminished battalions to pack up and fall back across the pontoon bridge that traversed the river. He waited as long as he dared at the bridge for his advanced detachments to return and was rewarded by Bernard's 300 men marching in at 7 A.M. just as the last of his skirmishers under Duprat were forced back across the bridge. There was no sign of Trépezac or Langis. Reluctantly, he gave the signal to fifty *Canadiens*, who leapt forward to sever the moorings of the pontoon bridge with axes. It swirled away for twenty yards gathering speed then tilted precariously on the edge of the first set of rocky falls and was lost to view.

Bradstreet's battoemen, who had pushed in Duprat's skirmish line, were now firing at maximum range, their balls singing through the treetops. Clipped leaves floated down as French officers mustered their companies and checked their kit. Bourlamaque's reception of the errant Bernard is unrecorded, but the officer and his detachment found themselves detailed with the grenadiers as the rearguard. Bourlamaque then led his battalions north to the sawmill encampment some two miles away.

He found Montcalm waiting there with the other battalion commanders and asked for orders. This request precipitated a small but heated council of war to decide which side of the river the army should defend. Bourlamaque, still angry that he had been humbugged by Howe, was in favour of fighting it out at the sawmills. "All of the officers were fearful of this position," recorded a Béarn officer, "in the bottom of a valley surrounded by hillocks." The commanding officer of the Royal-Roussillon, the older and wiser chevalier de Bernetz, supported by others, prevailed upon Montcalm to withdraw north to the hills that overlooked the open river encampment, and by noon Montcalm and Bourlamaque's troops were entrenching on the north side of the river alongside the Languedoc and La Sarre regiments who had been there since the day before. The sawmills and outbuildings were then put to the torch so they could not be used for cover by the British, but they were damp from the June rains and did not burn. The French dug in, then waited in the heat of mid-afternoon, wondering why Abercromby's army was not following up its landing by pushing smartly down the portage road. Around 3 P.M., the rattle of a great number of muskets sounded a half mile to the southwest. All had been hoping for the safe return of Langis and Trépezac's advance guard, especially the men of the Guyenne, Béarn and La Reine regiments who had friends with that force, but most now knew something had gone terribly wrong (see Map T-2).[43]

Montcalm dispatched *Capitaine* François-Joseph Germain with 150 grenadiers to ascertain what was happening at the Bernetz Brook. Germain returned at 6 P.M. with some of the bedraggled survivors of Trépezac's detachment and reported that the British were in force at the stream and that their "pioneers were in the process of throwing a bridge across it as well as clearing roads and blazing trees." Desandrouins' thoughts mirrored Montcalm's own fear. "The enemy was now able to turn us and envelop us," he stated. "Montcalm had no choice but to order a withdrawal to the Heights of Carillon, where we arrived without incident at seven o'clock in the evening."[44]

Arriving at the heights, the small French army marched past the marked positions of a proposed fortified line staked out the day before and put up tents some 200 yards to the rear of the crest. Here the troops were allowed to prepare food, but were ordered to sleep fully clothed and equipped until called upon to work. Like all infantry, Montcalm's men were not averse to a few hours of rest and, except for the grenadiers and *volontaires* who were excused manual labour to provide guards and sentries, the exhausted troops slept.

At 2 A.M. on 7 July, their officers were awoken and an hour later escorted forward to the proposed defensive position, which was illuminated with large bonfires. The engineers briefed them on the defensive plan and the method of construction of the breastworks, and each regimental group was shown the sector of 127 paces (100 yards) they would be responsible for building.

The heights of Carillon were vital ground for Montcalm, for if the British were to gain them and set up batteries, they would have the advantage of an extra fifty feet of elevation above the small fort, which could hold only one battalion (see Map T-3). Montcalm therefore had to occupy and fortify the high ground to the west to properly defend the fort. The three-year-old rectangular fort to the east of the heights was generally considered to have been poorly sited by its North American-born engineer and protégé of Vaudreuil, the sieur Michel-Charles de Lotbinière. Pontleroy, on viewing Carillon for the first time, declared: "Were I entrusted with the siege of it, I should require only six mortars and two cannon."[45]

The work of fortifying the heights began at 4.30 A.M. on 7 July when Montcalm's drummers beat the *Générale* a half-hour before first light and the regiments marched briskly to the heights with full kit, shovels, picks, axes and hatchets. Montcalm recorded in his journal that the entire army went to work, "officers, axes in hand, set the example and the flags were planted on the works." Out forward, the eight grenadier companies reinforced with the two 100-man companies of *volontaires* provided an advanced guard to protect the army.[46]

The breastworks quickly took shape and *Capitaine* Anne-Joseph-Hippolyte de Maurès, chevalier de Malartic, adjutant of the Béarn regiment, described the pace as one of "incredible vivacity." The front wall consisted of long tree trunks at least three feet thick, laid horizontally on one another. It was placed and then reinforced with packed earth from a trench dug behind. This solid wall, which stretched for 230 yards, had horizontal slits between the logs that were then loopholed using smaller pieces of wood. In some places there were three tiers of loopholes.[47]

The main breastwork's left flank rested on a steep ravine, though additional abattis and breastworks were built farther down the slope to the rear where 200 men would be posted to guard the 130-yard gap between the La Chute River and the heights (see Map T-4). A battery of six guns was started well to the rear of this position to cover the river approach but was not completed before the battle. "The centre followed the sinuosities of the ground," recorded Jean-Guillaume Plantairt, chevalier de la Pause, Montcalm's principal staff officer, adding that "holding to the high ground and all parts gave each other flanking

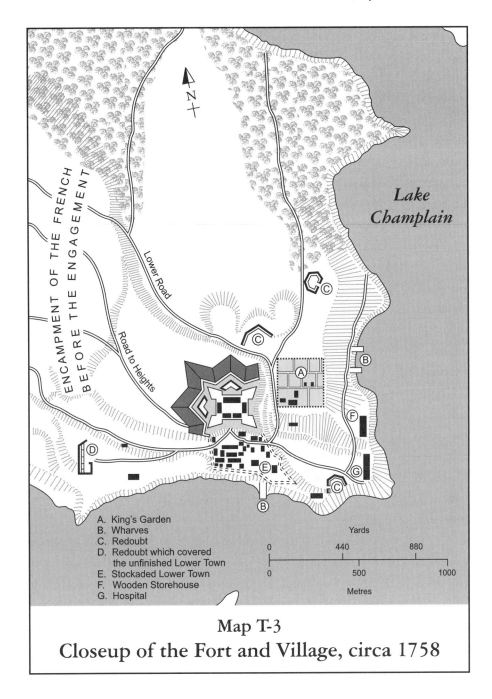

A. King's Garden
B. Wharves
C. Redoubt
D. Redoubt which covered
   the unfinished Lower Town
E. Stockaded Lower Town
F. Wooden Storehouse
G. Hospital

Lake Champlain

ENCAMPMENT OF THE FRENCH BEFORE THE ENGAGEMENT

Lower Road

Road to Heights

Yards

0   440   880

0   500   1000

Metres

Map T-3
Closeup of the Fort and Village, circa 1758

support." Because of dips in the uneven ground, however, there were several places in the centre and on the right "subject to enemy cross-fires; but this was because they did not give us time to raise traverses." Desandrouins acknowledged the breastworks were not perfect, especially without the zig-zag traverses to prevent enfilade fire. "There were complaints that we were enfiladed, that is to say, people were being killed behind the entrenchments," he noted." This is true, but it was because the walls were too low in spots and without "banquettes." In the flanking salients there were some places more elevated than others."[48]

But lack of time was not the only reason for French casualties, according to the young engineer officer. More seriously, the breastwork's weak points were also "the fault of vigilance on the part of officers who had been instructed to give their sectors … their undivided attention" as, despite the "most pressing of circumstances, the majority of officers showed an inconceivable indolence during the work." During the coming battle many French soldiers would be shot in the back or side because of the breastworks' poor construction.[49]

The right flank was the most vulnerable. A plain of about 330 yards of flat, lightly wooded ground existed to the north of the main position and stretched to the shore of Lake Champlain. Here another outwork of abattis and breastworks about 200 yards long was built to prevent this flank from being turned. A battery of four guns was started on the heights to cover and support these outworks with enfilade fire but it was not finished in time, and the guns of the fort were thus the only French artillery able to provide some flanking fire for the forward main position, giving Montcalm some depth of defence. This impressive horseshoe-shaped position, with the exception of the abattis and batteries, was finished by the evening of 7 July. Its completion was due in no small measure to the efforts of the men, who worked around the clock, and the two tireless engineers, Desandrouins and Pontleroy, who were everywhere, explaining the best construction methods and animating the men in the absence of encouragement from their own officers.

At dusk, with no sign that the British army had any intention of advancing further than the sawmills it had seized and occupied at midday, Montcalm let his weary troops return to their tents two hundred yards behind the breastworks to cook soup and sleep. As they moved like dead men, muscles stiff and backs sore from trenching and working with the huge logs, wild cheering broke out at the head of the column and cries of "*Vive le Roi!*" were heard. *Capitaine* Pierre Pouchot of the Béarn regiment and five of the six picquet companies of other regiments, which had been destined for a raid towards the Mohawk Valley, had just arrived as reinforcements, having travelled non-stop from Montreal for two days. "They were received by our little army with the same joy as Caesar's legions were when they relieved Cicero's cohorts besieged by the Gauls," wrote Bougainville, and morale soared.[50]

At short distance to the south, the dawn of 7 July 1758 revealed a dog-tired and dispirited British army at the northern end of Lake George. Abercromby's men had passed two nights with little sleep or food. His regiments reorganized slowly at the landing place. Many soldiers had jettisoned packs containing their provisions in the woods, while others, including the entire left wing of the provincials, had left theirs in their batteaux before they set off. Private Abel Spicer of the 2nd Connecticut recalled that "his regiment was very much broken to pieces and some came in and some was lost in the woods, and came in the next morning." Moreover, several observers noted that the spring had gone out of the army's step. Surgeon Caleb Rea remarked: "I can't but observe since Lord How's Death, Business seams a little Stagnant." Robert Rogers, a good judge of men, recorded that Howe's death "seemed to produce an almost general consternation and langour through the whole."[51]

With Howe's death, Abercromby had no senior officer to turn to for advice. The remaining general officer, and now second-in-command, Brigadier General Thomas Gage, seemed reluctant to step forward and assist. His lack of action at this juncture suggests some form of breakdown and remains one of the mysteries of the campaign. Though a twentieth-century biographer would claim that Gage was lightly wounded, he appears on none of the casualty lists. The panic in the woods on 6 July had all the makings of another Monongahela until it was contained. Perhaps Gage, a survivor of that horrible experience three years earlier, had difficulty in coping with old memories triggered during the previous day's confusion.[52]

Stepping into the leadership breach left by Howe's death was the dynamic and hard-nosed leader of the battoemen, Lieutenant Colonel John Bradstreet. Born in Annapolis Royal, Nova Scotia, to an English officer and an Acadian mother, this forty-four-year old bilingual leader, was in one officer's opinion, considered to be the best man in America "for the battues and expeditions." The night before, Bradstreet and his carpenters had thrown a bridge across the Lake George outlet and relinked the two French entrenched camps, unloaded two 6-pdr. field guns complete with equipment and stores and, early that morning, sent out scouting parties to the sawmills which had been deserted since the previous evening.[53]

When Abercromby called a meeting of his regular commanding officers at 7 A.M. on 7 July, Captain Joshua Loring, a Royal Navy officer and flotilla commander, witnessed a heated council of war. In a letter to Pitt, he recounted how Bradstreet had "begged" Abercromby to give him four or five thousand men to

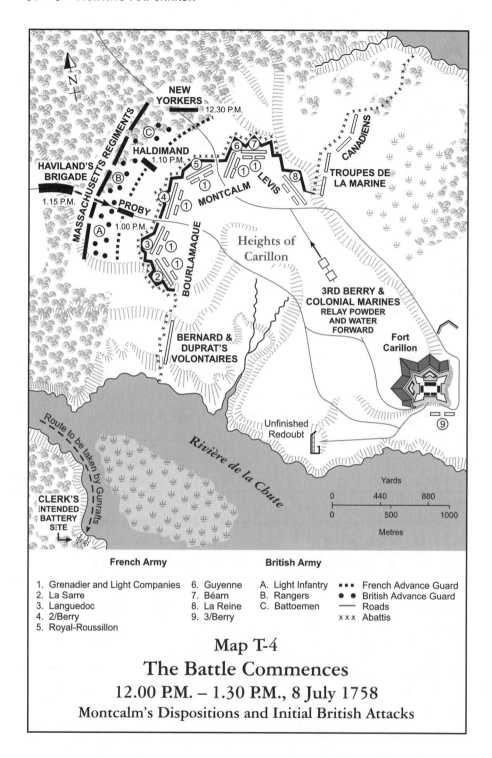

Map T-4
The Battle Commences
12.00 P.M. – 1.30 P.M., 8 July 1758
Montcalm's Dispositions and Initial British Attacks

march directly up the portage road, take the sawmill encampment and rebuild the downriver bridge if necessary. It was only "after Soliciting the thing for a Long time & being Backt by Severall of the Officers in the Army," observed the naval officer, that Bradstreet "was at last permitted to go."[54]

At approximately 10 A.M. on 7 July, Bradstreet's force of 5,000 men, consisting of the 44th Foot, six companies of the 1st Battalion of the 60th, Captain John Stark's company of rangers reinforced by the Stockbridge Indians, two Massachusetts regiments and two light 6-pdr. guns with their detachments and stores, marched north for the sawmills. The destroyed bridge, the encampments on both sides of the river and the partly burned mills were in British hands by 1 P.M. Ben Glasier, one of the carpenters with the force, remembered that his company "took nothing with us Save our guns and axes and went up and Built the Brige and Got Dun just as it was Dark." The river, however, was passable for infantry without a bridge, and Bradstreet sent back word of his unopposed success to Abercromby at about 1.30 P.M., requesting permission to move onwards to Fort Carillon. Abercromby, according to Bradstreet, "took the least Notice" and ordered the rest of his army to move off at 3 P.M. to the captured encampments and consolidate there.[55]

With Bradstreet's column was the most adventurous of Abercromby's three aides-de-camp, Captain James Abercrombie of the 42nd Foot, whom many in the army, as well as later historians, erroneously believed to be the commander's nephew or a direct relation. Captain Abercrombie fancied himself as an engineer but with him was the actual chief engineer, Lieutenant Matthew Clerk, another of Lord Howe's clique of "young Turks." The two officers quickly left the column, Stark's rangers in attendance, and climbed Montagne de Serpents de Sonettes (now Mount Defiance) to get a view of the fort.

Stark, Abercrombie and Clerk had all stood before on Rattlesnake Mountain but none of them had ever seen the heights of Carillon as they now appeared. Some 2,000 men toiled like ants in a clearing about fifty yards wide that snaked from one side of the rocky promontory to the other. Viewing the French activity from an elevation of 850 feet and just over a mile away, the two British officers assumed the construction of some sort of breastworks with an entrenchment was in progress, since they could see some men carrying logs and others digging. By this time, however, the size, shape and exact location of the French breastworks had been cunningly disguised by the addition of living trees and fir boughs entwined throughout its structure of logs to give it the appearance of being "a simple abattis." The main entrenchment with its crowning breastworks, with the exception of some small improvements, was for all intents and purposes finished and hidden from view.

All historians to date have confused this 7 July scouting mission of Clerk with one he conducted the following day. General Abercromby's later statement that the 8 July reconnaissance by Clerk was to confirm the progress of the French defensive lines is a deliberate obfuscation of the facts. The real purpose of the second reconnaissance by Clerk was to find and site a gun battery position to enfilade the French breastworks seen the previous day. The scouting party which reported back to Abercromby's council of war immediately prior to the troops deploying forward for the 8 July battle was not led by Clerk, who was busy arranging artillery and stores for his battery project. Instead it was made by "Broadstreet and an engineer ... sent to reconnoitre the French Lines," wrote an unidentified Highland officer. This separate scouting mission "soon returned with the following account, – that the enemy was encamped on rising ground about a half-mile from the Fort, but not fortified, only a few logs laid on another as a breast Work. Upon this Intelligence it was thought proper to attempt storming the enemy lines, without loss of time, and immediately the whole army marched."[56]

The existence of the Bradstreet reconnoitring party of 8 July is confirmed by Captain William Hervey of the 44th Foot, who, no doubt, heard it from his commanding officer, Major Eyre, who was also at the council on the same day. In his own account, Eyre does not mention that his younger rival Clerk was present, merely stating that "there was a plan of the ground & the Entrenchment given in by Mr Clerk." Hervey hinted darkly that treachery was perhaps involved, as the man accompanying Bradstreet on his reconnaissance was "an Ingineer who was a foreigner." The latter gentleman, probably Lieutenant Charles Rivez, a Huguenot officer in the Royal Americans, made his report at the council of war in these terms: "Je vois tout clair devant moi, et s'il y a un retranchement, il faut que ça soit sous le cannon du fort. (I see everything clearly before me, and if there is an entrenchment, then it must be under the cannon of the fort)."[57]

This foreign engineer's claim not to have seen any entrenchments is most interesting and requires further examination. It is unequivocally true – for how could he and Bradstreet have seen through fifty yards of abattis which, in parts, was as high as a man or have got past the French advance guards posted 150 paces forward of the main position? What Bradstreet and the foreign engineer actually saw was the French advance guards' makeshift breastwork to cover Montcalm's army as it was making its forward abattis and main entrenchment. One New Yorker described this breastwork as "a sort of fence made of loose logs which served to cover the out parties ... with a front extending the whole length ... a little in advance of the principal work." A Massachusetts officer described the position as their "advanced Breast works" and noted that on the day of battle the rangers, light infantry and the battoemen "soon drove them out" of these insubstantial works "and followed them to their Entrenchments which was strongly form'd by art and Nature & fortified."[58]

On 7 July, however, Clerk, Abercrombie and Stark returned from their mountain scout in the failing light, found their general at the sawmills and reported. It was probably at this time that Clerk proposed to erect a battery in the morning after a more detailed scout, an action that Abercromby would seem to have approved. As they completed their report there was much whooping and cheering as Sir William Johnson, dressed as a Mohawk warrior, and 440 Iroquois warriors arrived at the sawmills "in the highest spirits," having passed "the French prisoners on the Lake on their way to Albany."[59]

The portage road behind them was busy as regiments were still marching in from the landing place, Colonel Nathaniel Whiting's 2nd Connecticut Regiment hauled two additional 6-pdr. field guns and their equipment to bring the total number at the mill up to four. Other detachments were already making their way back to the landing place carrying torches to bring up more artillery, stores and entrenching tools.[60]

Rogers' Rangers, Gage's Light Infantry and Bagley's Massachusetts Regiment had been ordered from the portage camp to the sawmills in mid-afternoon of 7 July. But unlike the rest of the army, they were to march the original route chosen by Howe, via the Indian path on the west side of the La Chute River, crossing at the Bernetz Brook ford, until they joined a blazed road that led east to the fort. These 1,200 men led by Rogers, "marched threw a large Brook very bad to pas, " recalled Lieutenant Archelaus Fuller. "About half the Rigement got to the meils. I was last and lay down with the other part of the Reg very wet & cold." Abercromby's men occupied the entrenchments north of the river, lit fires and stood watch in the dark. Private Garrett Albertson of the Jersey Blues passed a restless night, for he could hear "the French all night chopping and felling timber to fortify their breastwork" just a half mile away.[61]

During the evening of 7 July, after some rest and food, Montcalm's men continued the work of fortifying the Heights of Carillon. Axes in hand, they went forward of their main position, built large bonfires, and felled the woods for fifty yards in the direction of the enemy. One Massachusetts officer,

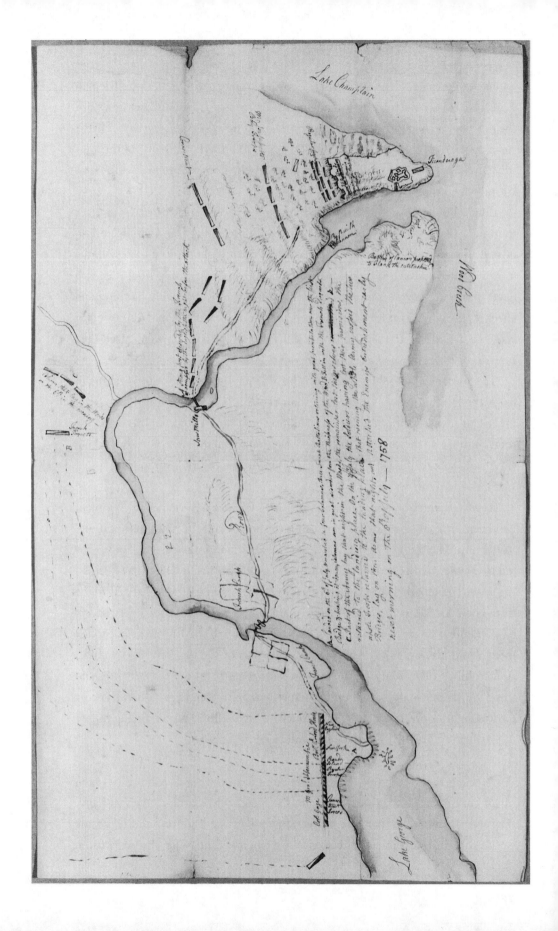

on viewing the result the next morning, said it looked like a forest that had been laid flat by a hurricane. This entanglement of logs and branches not only became a difficult obstacle for attacking forces but provided a natural glacis or shield for the above-ground breastwork against direct artillery fire.[62]

Capitaine Pierre Pouchot highly approved of the measures Montcalm had taken to render the breastwork invisible by camouflaging it with living trees and branches to conceal its shape and true location. He noted that the "parapet was covered with interwoven branches which were disposed in such a way that their prickly sharpened ends were more difficult to cross than palisades & provided better protection from an assault." More importantly, this improvised "barbed wire" concealed "our entrenchments from the enemy who could easily mistake it for a simple abattis," noted Pouchot. There are strong indications that on the following day Abercromby's advance guards had no idea of the main position's exact location until they were virtually twenty yards from it.[63]

Other defensive preparations included constructing small underground powder magazines in the centre of each battalion sector of wall, which was clearly marked by the regimental colours planted on the breastworks. Large hogsheads of fresh water were also placed at intervals behind the wall, not only to quench the soldiers' thirst but also to put out any fires on the parapet or in the abattis. Behind the wall in each battalion sector was a stand of fifty spare muskets, as well as a pile of large logs to be used for shoring up gaps if British siege artillery should be brought up. Small swivel guns known as *pierrettes*, which could fire with shotgun effect, were mounted in pairs in each sector, and the men assigned to them prepared small bags full of musket balls and scrap metal. Others prepared grenades which could be lobbed over the breastworks.[64]

At first light, around 4.30 A.M. on 8 July 1758, the French beat to arms, a "stand-to" rehearsal to ensure that all units would know their exact posts for later in the day if a British attack should come. As Montcalm checked his final dispositions, his rival Vaudreuil's favourite, Brigadier General François de Lévis, and Montcalm's best battalion commander, Lieutenant Colonel Etienne-Guillaume de Senezergues, arrived with the last hundred men of the picquet companies to much cheering and acclaim.

(Facing page) **"Battery with Cannon proposed to Flank the Entrenchment," 1758**
Map drawn by Captain Alexander Monypenny, Lord Howe's aide, to accompany letters home to Britain documenting the death of Howe on 6 July 1758. Note that Lieutenant Clerk's "battery with cannon proposed to flank the entrenchment" is shown on the river shore of Rattlesnake Mountain (now Mount Defiance), opposite the left flank of the French lines. (Courtesy, J. Robert Maguire)

Montcalm's right hand: Chevalier de Lévis (1719-1787)

Montcalm's very capable second-in-command, François-Gaston, chevalier de Lévis, who joined the army with reinforcements early on the morning of the attack and took command of the right flank. Lévis had a good opinion of the colonial troops which endeared him to Vaudreuil, and many historians believe that, if he had been in overall command during the Seven Years War, Canada would still be a French possession today. (Courtesy, René Chartrand)

Montcalm formed his units in three brigades in the horseshoe-shaped defensive position from left to right as follows (see Map T-4): On the left side of the horseshoe was the Brigade of La Sarre, commanded by Colonel Bourlamaque. Next was the centre Brigade of Royal-Roussillon commanded by Montcalm himself, and on the right side of the horseshoe was the Brigade of La Reine under Lévis. In the gap between the river and the left flank, the two *volontaire* companies of Duprat and Bernard were posted. In the larger gap on the wooded plain to the north, Montcalm placed all the *troupes de la marine* or colonial regulars, and the *Canadien* militia under the command of le sieur Florimond de Raymond, the senior captain of the former.[65] Once all troops had become acquainted with their exact positions and duties, they were told that a fort gun would call them to their posts. They then resumed work on the abattis out in front while the grenadiers established a skirmish line 150 paces beyond effective musket range past the edge of the western wood line. They also worked to finish the batteries covering the northern and southern approaches.

At about 10 A.M., according to most accounts, those working on the six-gun battery beside the La Chute River noticed hundreds of Indians on the summit of Rattlesnake Mountain, who began to whoop and fire their muskets in the direction of the battery. Bougainville, on the heights with his general, noted that "they let off a great fusillade which did not interrupt our work at all [and] we amused ourselves by not replying."[66]

But he spoke only for the troops at the main position. Down at river level, the French did respond. *Capitaine* de Maurès de Malartic of the Béarn regiment recorded that British light troops appeared at the same time on the opposite shore at the base of the mountain and Bernard's *volontaires* went down to the shoreline to return fire. Though most of the British fire fell in the water, one of the French lieutenants, the chevalier Darenis, had his arm broken by a lucky shot. Desandrouins remarked that "this affair, no doubt, was a reconnaissance of our position, but perhaps also a diversion to distract our attention from the marching forward of their army." The perceptive Desandrouins was absolutely correct.[67]

In Abercromby's camp, carpenter Ben Glasier and his mates were put to work at first light on 8 July 1758 "to build two floting Baterys" to carry the four 6-pdr. brass field guns which had been brought up the previous day. They were not actually floating batteries, according to Major John Tullikens of the Royal Americans, but "two rafts for the conveyance in each of two 6-pounder guns." These vessels were each to be towed by ten whaleboats to a spot on the south shore at the base of Rattlesnake Mountain. Once there, the guns would be unloaded and positioned to "either take the entrenchments in the rear or enfilade them."[68]

At the same time, Lieutenant Clerk sent two Connecticut regiments back to the Lake George landing place for more artillery, whaleboats and stores. Private Abel Spicer's company of the 2nd Connecticut, however, received a unique task — to act as escort for the engineer who "went on the side of the mountain ... to look and see if he could spy a good place to plant the artillery." While in such an advantageous spot, Spicer and his companions "had a fair prospect at the fort and the men at work ... We could see them drum off their guard and while we was there the Mohawks fired upon them and we seen them run into the fort and within their breastwork. After a small space of time they ventured out to work again. And after the engineer had viewed the fort he ordered them to all return back again." Spicer says that the scouting party returned at approximately 9 A.M. to the sawmills camp, but they were on the mountain when the Iroquois warriors fired on the French from the summit. Their fusillade in fact occurred, according to most British and French accounts, at about 10 A.M., near the time that Abercromby's regulars were forming up to march and the provincials were already on the move. Thus we know with certainty that Clerk was not at the council of war in which the plan of attack was formulated based on Bradstreet's "Intelligence" but was on the side of the mountain.[69]

Abercromby's account of the council bears some scrutiny since his orders would shape the method of attack. It was convened at 8 A.M. and Bradstreet and the "foreign ingineer" reported on the enemy's breastworks. In Abercromby's own words:

> The report made to me, leaving no Doubt of the Practability of carrying those works, if attacked before they were Compleated: it was agreed to storm them that very Day: Accordingly, the Rangers, Light Infantry, and Right Wing of the Provincials were ordered immediately to March, and post themselves in a Line, out of Cannon Shot of the Entrenchments, their right extending to Lake George [La Chute River], & their left to Lake Champlain, in order that the regular troops, destined for the attack of the entrenchments might form in their rear.[70]

Abercromby's subsequent claim that all his "principal Officers were unanimously of Opinion, that the Attack should forthwith be made on the Entrenchments" and "that it was what the whole Officers and Troops earnestly wished for" is an important factor in any serious understanding of the battle. It should not be forgotten that some of these regular battalion commanders, their officers and men had shamed themselves in the woods two days earlier and "earnestly wished" to make up for their behaviour. On the morning of 7 July, Abercromby had come as close as he dared to publicly rebuking his "principal officers" in general orders when he stated that he expected that "better discipline will be kept up, & that the commanding officers will suffer no firing, or any noise to be made in their corps." Abercromby's after-the-fact recollection of what his orders were therefore requires closer examination.[71] The surviving regimental orderly books record the commander's intentions and specific measures for controlling his troops and how they were to fight the battle. They are, however, to say the least, sketchy and vague. A compilation of the records gives the line of battle for the regulars and the following bare instructions:

> Two Regts to be form'd three deep. Short arms in the Front. The March to be made by the Piquets first supported by the Grenrs & they by the Battalions, the Whole marching on Briskly, to rush upon the Enemy's Fire & not give their fire until they are within the Enemy's Brestwork. The Regts to march up silently. The Regts not immediately behind Picqts & Gren to attack at the same Time.[72]

These orders pertained only to the regulars because the provincials, rangers, light infantry, and battoemen had been dispatched earlier to establish a secure screen behind which the regulars were *to form in line of battle*. Captain Peter Dubois of the New Yorkers recorded the provincials' instructions in some detail:

We were commanded to Invest the Enemy's Intrenchments In the Following Order: On the left, the Rangers; The Centre the Battoe men; on the Right, the light Infantry who were 200 yards from the breast Work. In their rear were, on the Left, the first Battalion of the new York Regiment; On their Left in the following order: 1) Bagley 2) William's then Partridges, Dotey's, Ruggles & Prebbles, all Boston Regiments. These were to support the Regulars in their Attack on the Brest Works, In case they were forced to Retire & these were to be followed by the Jersey & Connecticut forces who were posted in the Rear of the Whole.[73]

With the provincials' tasks made clear, and the screening line dispatched, it is interesting to examine what one of the regular commanding officers thought of the plan for the assault. Major Eyre recalled the council as a discussion trying to achieve a consensus on the form of attack rather than a statement of a coherent plan by a decisive commander, until Abercromby became impatient and ordered everyone away to their work. Eyre later wrote:

I remember it was asked whether We should Attack three or four deep, it was carry'd for three, the next question if the Grenadiers & Pickets of the Regulers should attack at the Same time or support each Other, it was agree'd to support each other I was of the opinion we should attack the [Breastwork] in Column, each Regt picking one, or two to support each Other, As we could more easily force Our Way thro' the felled Trees than by making so large Front, but it was said this would cause confusion; in short, it was said, We Must Attack Any Way, and not be losing time in talking or consulting how.[74]

The regulars formed up on the road leading from the sawmill camp to the fort. It was the skirmish line and provincials that moved out first at about 10 A.M., the same time that Johnson's Indians made their demonstration on Rattlesnake Mountain and Clerk was finalizing the location of his battery. The rangers led the skirmishing component, comprising nearly 2,500 men, forward, Rogers placing Captain John Stark's company in the advance guard. They were followed by Bradstreet's battoemen and then Gage's Light Infantry. "I was within about three hundred yards of the breastwork, when my advance guard was ambushed and fired upon by 200 Frenchmen," Rogers recalled. "I immediately formed a front and marched up to the advanced guard, who maintained their ground, and the enemy immediately retreated." Stark's company had bumped into Montcalm's advance guard of grenadiers and *volontaires*, who fired a few rounds and fell back from their advanced breastworks to the main position (see Map T-4). All French accounts note that their picquets returned "in very good order & held the enemy up for a long time," the last being driven in between 12.30 and 1 P.M. By that time, the battoemen had deployed on Rogers's left and the 80th Foot to his right while he and his 600 rangers straddled the road.[75]

The provincials now coming up were in their proper order of march, DeLancey's New Yorkers being the leading unit, moving off the road in column to take up their position on the far left. Well has it been said that in war the plan of attack rarely survives the first shot, for Rogers' unit originally ordered to protect the New Yorkers' front was now, instead, astride the road in the centre. While Rogers exulted that the enemy's ambushing forces did not kill a single one of his men, on the far left the unshielded New Yorkers marched into another ambush.

"The rangers, by some Mistake, instead of taking part to the Left, Employed themselves firing on the Enemy to the Right," stated Captain Peter Dubois somewhat indignantly, "So that when our regiment was going to take post, where we thought to be in the rear of our friends" [we were] "surprized by the enemy, about 300 yards from the breast-works who fired upon us, but they were repulsed and driven [back] by the heat of our people into their trenches."[76] The rangers and battoemen had failed to provide forward security.

Confusion now set in. The New Yorkers reacted quickly, as Dubois relates, swiftly advancing, cheering and firing until they were stopped by the main French position, which opened fire. Dubois's reference to the rangers being out of position is very important since Abercromby and his staff would later encourage the idea that the provincials were partly to blame for the entire army becoming decisively engaged before the designated time.

Captain James Abercrombie later drew notice to the fact that "the Attack [was] not to begin till the whole Army was formed, & then a point of War would be beat for the attack. But, most unluckily this order was not kept up to, for the New York Regt by accident fell upon an Advanced Guard of the Enemy." This was the catalyst that caused "The Picquets who were supported by the Grenadiers & they by the Whole Line" to rush "on to the Attack before any of the army were formed. The eagerness of the troops for the attack was the Loss of that Day & nothing else."[77] General Abercromby's directive of the previous day that discipline was to be better observed had apparently fallen on deaf ears.

Rogers also claimed that the New Yorkers were the cause of the premature attack. At around 12.30 P.M. he noted that the skirmishing "between our flying parties and those of the enemy without the breastwork" was still active when "a

Future Governor-General: Lieutenant Colonel Frederick Haldimand, (1718-1791)
The Swiss-born commanding officer of the 4th Battalion, Royal Americans, Haldimand was selected by Abercromby to lead the grenadier companies of the army
which were mown down at the abattis. Speaking fluent French and German, as
well as English, he became the governor of Quebec in 1778. (Courtesy, René
Chartrand)

smart fire began on the left where Col. De Lancey's [New
Yorkers] and the battoemen were posted." It was at this
point that Abercromby's cautious plan of having his entire
army formed up before advancing, a strong skirmish line to
his front and a wall of provincial regiments to his rear, completely fell apart.[78]

This firing on the left, where Rogers should have been,
prompted Lieutenant Colonel William Haviland, commanding the
right brigade, waiting behind the picquets of the line under Major John Proby
and the grenadiers of the army under Lieutenant Colonel Haldimand, to take
action. Haviland commanded Rogers and his men forward into the thick abattis
to lay down a covering fire against the breastworks and then "to fall down" in order to allow the regulars to pass through (see Map T-4). Rogers obeyed, since this
was his first full-scale battle, though he wrote later he knew the general attack
was commencing "before the General intended it should be" and that Haviland
on his own initiative, "being on or near the centre, ordered the troops to advance, as it were by accident, from the fire of the New Yorkers on the left wing."
Rogers did not mention, however, that it was his command's absence from its
assigned location that had caused the "accident" in the first place.[79] Captain
Hugh Arnot with his "Leathercaps" on Rogers's right, tells a similar tale, though
he mistakenly substituted Abercomby for the over-eager Haviland. He recalled

> a very heavy fire the Irregulars and provincials gave, with a huzza at the same
> time [which] made our Genl believe & so was told (for He could not see
> what was a doing) that some part of the Army had enter'd their Lines, then
> the Whole Army was order'd to March up and attack (quite out of Breath
> from the Distance).[80]

It was clear that Abercromby "could not see what was a doing" as the sound
of musketry rose and fell to his front, which is confirmed by his aide, Captain
James Abercrombie, who marched by his side. The British commander had

given no orders for his regulars to attack, but was amazed, on arriving in some haste at the battlefield where the wood line opened onto the abattis-strewn crest of the heights, that not "only our Irregulars [were engaged] but to his great surprise, when he came up with the Highlanders, he found all the rest of the Regulars attacking the Intrinchment." (see Map T-4)[81]

By not marching at the head of his column of regulars, strung out over two miles, Abercromby had effectively surrendered what little control he had left to exercise over such a large army in wilderness conditions. In his absence, William Haviland, an impetuous brigade and battalion commander, perhaps seeking to restore his good name and his troops' honour for their behaviour on 6 July, took it upon himself to commence the attack without the rest of the army.

Major William Eyre's 44th Foot, the leading regiment of the centre brigade, commanded by Lieutenant Colonel John Donaldson of the 55th Foot, now came up just in time to see Haviland's brigade launching forward in column to support the grenadiers and the picquets. Eyre, like Rogers, knew that someone had disobeyed orders, but he was unwilling to name Haviland directly. Instead, he commented

> Great faults are found with the Method of the attack [which] was made, I am Sorry to Say not in the most Regular Manner, some of the regt beginning before the others were formed, particularly the brigade – I think to the Rt which consisted of the 27th Regt & two Battalions of the Royal Americans. I found the Attack had been begun some time before I could form Our Regt, this being done, all was left for each commanding officer of A Regt to do, was support & march up as quick as they could get Upon the Ground And so on to the Intrenchmnt.[82]

Abercromby's plan to send six regiments forward simultaneously to overwhelm the French lines with sheer numbers at a time of his own choosing thus never took place (see Map T-5). Between 1 and 1.15 P.M., the French regiments in the main position watched silently as four columns of various sizes and compositions approached, while British skirmishers' musket balls slapped viciously against their log defences or whirred overhead to cut leaves and branches from their camouflaged parapets. "This fire hid from us the first movement of their columns," related the chevalier de Lévis, "none of which, I believe, had been given any designated point to attack, other than the right, left and centre."[83]

The first British column to close with the breastworks was in the centre, and consisted of the picquets of the line led by Major John Proby of the 55th. A Royal American officer in Haviland's brigade watching Proby's column go forward wrote afterwards that it was this officer who precipitated the attack, for "instead of making a simultaneous attack as he ought to have done in pursuance of his orders, they attacked in single file." Another officer recorded that Proby, "in too great a hurry, advanced to the attack with small arms, and was followed in a hurry by the rest: The Troops advanced most Courageously but all went to Confusion." Proby was, however, merely following Haviland's orders.[84]

The men of the Languedoc regiment and 2nd Battalion of the Berry regiment waited quietly behind their breastwork until the head of Proby's disjointed column emerged from the abattis then loosed a devastating volley accompanied by fire from four swivel guns. Private William Bremner, a young Scot in Proby's unit, remembered that the men flinched but "orders were well obeyed for 100 men were shot down before they could get near the Trinches as the ground was clogged up by the Enemy with Logs and Trees Intermix'd with Brush which greatly Interrupted the speedy and Regular march of our Troops."[85]

A watching provincial recalled that Proby's men "fell like pigeons," while Colonel Henry Babcock of the Rhode Island Regiment observed, "they were knocked down so fast, it was very difficult for those behind to get over the dead and wounded." Still, Proby led them right up to the foot of the breastworks, but Bremner recalled "they had enough to do to fill up the vacant places made by the Dead and wounded which fell." Proby was shot climbing the breastworks and the column then broke and retreated.[86]

Coming up on the left and slightly behind, the grenadier companies under their Swiss veteran, Lieutenant Colonel Haldimand, fared no better. Grenadier Lieutenant William Grant of the 42nd Foot described the French fire as "exceedingly heavy, and without any intermission; insomuch as the oldest [most veteran] soldiers present never saw so furious and incessant a fire. The affair at Fontenoy was nothing to it." The French fire in fact was murderous, and the reason Montcalm's troops could maintain such an incessant fire was simple. The best shots of every company were manning the loopholes, while their comrades passed loaded muskets to them. An infantryman standing in line in the open was normally expected to fire two or three shots per minute. At Ticonderoga, the French rate of fire was easily doubled to six or more a minute.[87]

While Lieutenant Grant and his grenadiers tried to get over "monstrous large fir and oak trees," Private Thomas Busby of the 27th had "Seven Bullets through his Hat and Seven thro' his Clothes." He emerged from the battle unscathed but forty men out of his seventy-man grenadier company fell dead and dying around him in the space of ten minutes.[88] Grant rightly assessed the French "lethal advantage" to be their abattis for it

> not only broke our ranks, and made it impossible for us to keep our order, but put it entirely out of our power to advance briskly; which gave the enemy abundance of time to mow us down like a field of corn, with their wall pieces and small arms, before we fired a single shot, being ordered to receive the enemy's fire, and marched with shouldered arms until we came up close to their breastwork. If you reflect a little on these many obstacles thrown in our way, you will easily see, that the forcing of the enemy's lines was absolutely impracticable.[89]

Grant did not last long. After the lieutenant had his musket "broke in my hand by a musket ball," he was "shot through the middle of the thigh a little below the groin" and dragged off the field by two grenadiers. The other two subalterns of his company also went down, though their company commander, Captain Allan Campbell, "Eskeap'd without a Scratch."[90]

Haldimand ordered his drummers to beat the retreat and withdrew his shattered column back to the forward edge of the abattis in good order, where the 55th and 46th Foot were forming up to go forward. The wounded were taken to a large breastwork being thrown up by Colonel Timothy Ruggles's Massachusetts Regiment at the head of the road as it left the wood line.

The survivors of the picquets joined the rangers, battoemen and the marksmen of the 80th Foot already in the abattis sniping at the French breastworks. The

Shock troops – Grenadier officer, 60th Foot, Royal Americans, 1758
Regarded as the elite of the infantry, the grenadiers were the largest soldiers in each battalion and wore a distinctive mitre cap. They were usually brigaded into a composite battalion to be used as shock troops. This Royal American officer carries a fusee (a shortened musket) and wears a gorget at his throat, the badge of an officer. Lord Howe ordered that all officers were not to wear their scarlet sashes, as shown here, on campaign and that regimental colours were to be left behind in camp. (Courtesy, René Chartrand)

French, reported Montcalm's aide, started to take casualties as the British "light troops and better marksmen, protected by trees, delivered the most murderous fire on us." This fire, however, came down not only on the French.[91]

The third column, the New Yorkers on the far left, after their pursuit of the advanced guard, found themselves beneath the northern escarpment, below the Béarn and La Reine regiments. There they received "the whole fire of the Enemy on us for near an hour without Succour But received Considerable Damage from our friends in the rear who fired at Random." In an hour's time, the left brigade of regulars had joined them, the 42nd Foot moving forward in such a hurry that an officer of the 44th forming up in the centre reported that "the Highland regiment [ran] along the front of our regiment" in their efforts to get to the left.[92]

The Massachusetts men who formed the main support line, with the exception of the New Yorkers on the far left, watched as the centre brigade "hove down their pak and fixed their bayernits, stod and fit very coragasly." Among them was sixteen-year-old Private David Perry in Colonel Jedidiah Preble's Regiment, who was witnessing his first battle and admitted the "whistling of balls and the roar of musquetry terrified me not a little." His regiment was still in the tree line when the regulars advanced, but some "men kept stepping from their ranks" to shelter behind trees. "Col Prebble, who I well remember was a harsh man, swore he would knock the first man down who should step out of his ranks," recalled the boy soldier, "which greatly surprised me, to think that I must stand still to be shot at."[93]

The fourth column, the 27th Foot and 4th Battalion of the 60th Royal Americans, led by Lieutenant Colonel Haviland, was well forward and on the right trying to turn the French left when the 44th Foot was finally formed and ready to go forward at approximately 1.15 P.M. (see Map T-5). It was at this moment that Abercromby arrived on the battlefield. None of the surviving accounts, or the general's own letters, indicate that he attempted to recall his brigades once he found the attack already launched contrary to his orders. Instead, he moved to the right flank of his army to stand on a knoll marked on one of the French maps as the "rocky outcropping where General Abercromby was during the combat." From there, about 200 yards southwest of the French defensive position, he could look down to his right on the La Chute River, where he expected the battery he had ordered established on the side of Rattlesnake Mountain would shortly commence firing. To his front he could see the fort through the trees and a quarter left could watch as the right brigade under Haviland attempted to storm the left end of the French breastworks (see Map T-5).[94]

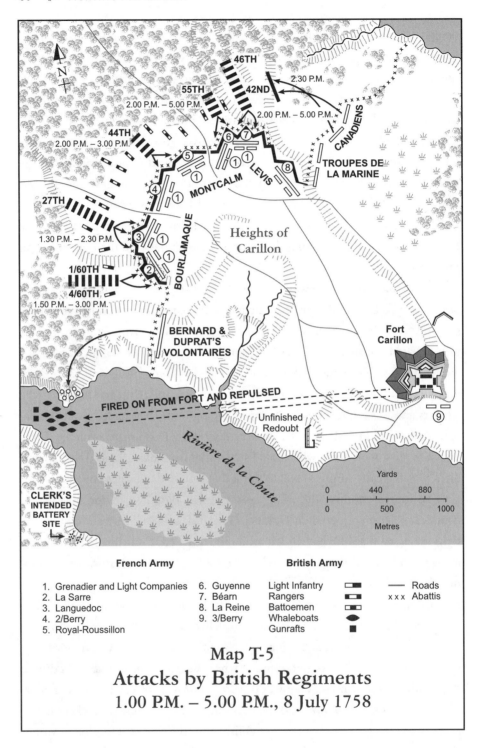

Map T-5
Attacks by British Regiments
1.00 P.M. – 5.00 P.M., 8 July 1758

At no time in Abercromby's pre-battle orders did he tell his commanding officers where he would be. Not that it would have made any real difference: there were no maps, and not one of the British senior officers (including their commander) had ever been on the heights before. Abercromby had, however, ordered one sergeant and corporal from each regiment to travel with his group to act as runners to the battalions and he also had his three aides, to whom he could entrust orders to be delivered. That orders were given during the battle is certain, and these few officers and men were the only means at Abercromby's disposal to make his wishes known to his subordinates. It is also certain that some orders went undelivered when messengers were killed or became lost or, once received, were misinterpreted or ignored.[95] (See Map T-5)

Just after 1 P.M., the British commander would have been joined by his chief engineer, Lieutenant Clerk, who had come forward to the knoll after giving his last instructions to the raft convoys charged with delivering the guns to his battery site. Dr. James Searing of the New Yorkers reported that "at 12 o'clock, by the directions of Mr Clerke, engineer, in pursuance of his reconnoitre, two redeaus with two six pounders, and one royal howitzer, was ordered down the lake towards the fort." The rowers in the twenty whaleboats stroked deeply, while provincials waist-deep in water pushed and heaved the two rafts to give them some momentum. By 1.30 P.M. the lead boats were moving through the bullrush-choked mouth of the La Chute River as it opened into Lake Champlain. Reeds as tall as a man blinkered their view on either side and restricted it to the open space of water ahead. "The orders given to the officer who commanded, were to repair down the lake under cover of the bank, till he came to an open place as described by the engineer," noted Searing. But the tall reeds blocked the officer's view of the large beach where he was supposed to land on the south bank. Instead his lead boats went too far downriver, and emerged in full view of the guns of Fort Carillon.[96]

Lieutenant Jean de Louvricourt, a French army artillery officer, and his gun detachments were waiting, their guns loaded and matches lit. Not only were they ready to fire, but their pieces had been trained and ranged on this exact location days before, and thus his gunners were successful in their first shots (see Map T-5). The two leading whaleboats were swamped, and, adding to the confusion that now ensued among the British flotilla was a brisk musket fire that erupted from the shoreline.[97]

According to Montcalm's aide, Bougainville, "the Sieur de Poulhariez at the head of the Royal-Roussillon's grenadier and picquet companies appeared there and received them in grand style." The officer in charge of the flotilla, according to Dr. Searing, decided that "after going down, till both shot and shells were fired at them from the fort, they could find no such place as described [by Lieutenant Clerk] – so concluding the intelligence to be false, he turned about to regain the lines."[98]

Major John Tullikens of the Royal Americans, who had one of his officers waiting to receive the guns on the intended location (see Map T-5), observed in hindsight that, "unfortunately the duty of reconnoitring [on the river] to ascertain whether the thing was feasible had been forgotten, for at about 1 P.M., after [descending] the stream and passing the point … they immediately came under the fire of the guns of the Fort which opened up on them with so much effect that they were compelled to return to their starting place." The landing site that had appeared so obvious to Lieutenant Clerk 150 feet above the river earlier that morning, was not so apparent to the poor officer placed in charge of conveying the guns at water level to their destination. Abercromby therefore never got his battery established, and without it disappeared the critical enfilade fire that Tullikens was convinced would have ensured the "Fort would have been in our Hands at this moment."[99]

At about the same time the flotilla was retreating, 2 P.M., Tullikens was pulling back his four depleted companies of the 1st Battalion of the 60th intermingled with the eight companies of the 4th Battalion of the same regiment which now came under his command, as their popular American-born commanding officer, Major John Rutherford, lay dead on the field. "A report was made that the entrenchment was impregnable," stated Tullikens, "and that it would be better to retire in good order, but no definite reply was received on the subject."[100] This lack of orders was also noticed by William Eyre on the immediate left of Tullikens. "I could not tell how Matters were going on in the Whole," admitted Eyre, his view restricted to a smoking entanglement full of wounded, dead and dying men. "But it was plain, something should be undertaken," he added.[101] One of Eyre's company commanders after the battle put it more bluntly:

We found that it was not in the power of Courage or even of chance to bestow success unless we alter'd our method,: this was perceived very soon & had we profited of our early discovery, & beat the retreat in proper time, there was no loss sustain'd which was by any means irreparable, but, so far from any order of this kind being taken, that no General was heard of, no Aid de Camps seen, no instructions receiv'd; but every officer left at the head of his division, Company, or squad, to fall a sacrifice to his own good behaviour and the stupidity of his Commander.[102]

Captain Charles Lee went down with "a ball thro' my body" which broke two of his ribs and rendered him "senseless." He lay there for most of the afternoon under a withering fire, one of the luckier "sacrifices" of "good behaviour" as some of his men crawled out and dragged him off before nightfall. At around 2.30 P.M. the centre brigade pulled back.[103]

"We had at last orders to draw off the Regulers," remembered Eyre, "& some Provincial Regts were order'd up." The left and right brigades under Grant and Haviland, however, continued attacking on the flanks, while the provincials, as Lieutenant Archaleus Fuller of Bagley's Regiment recalled, "droed up very near and was ordered to make a stand."[104]

Here then was some semblance of a plan. It might be reasonably assumed that the provincials were not intended to assault and break into the breastworks when the frontal assault of Abercromby's finest regulars had failed. The provincials could have been ordered to maintain a steady pressure against the centre of the French works while the regular brigades on the flanks manoeuvred by or kept on in their attempts to collapse one of the flanks.

However, this clearly did not happen. Private David Perry of Colonel Preble's Massachusetts Regiment remembered "Our orders were *to run to the breastwork and get in if we could.* [Perry's emphasis] But their lines were full, and they killed our men so fast, that we could not gain it." They met the same hail of fire the regulars had encountered, one so intense that "a man could not stand erect, without being hit, any more than he could stand out in a shower, without having drops of rain fall on him, for the balls come like hands full."[105]

Colonel Henry Babcock, commanding the Rhode Islanders, related that at 2 P.M. he "was ordered to march with the regiment, to relieve those who had been engaged." They advanced to "within about forty yards of the breast-work," he recalled. "Soon after I got up, in posting my regiment to the best advantage I could, I received a shot in my left knee; after that finding myself of no advantage, I ordered two men to carry me off and left the regiment warmly engaged."[106]

One of his men, Private William Smith, managed to work himself right up against the wall of the main breastwork unnoticed, where he proceeded to snipe at several Frenchmen at very close range. At length he was discovered by one of the defenders, who fired vertically down at him from the top of the breastworks. Despite being severely wounded, Smith still had enough energy left to brain his assailant with his hatchet. Smith's aggressive spirit was observed by a British officer, who ordered two of his men forward under a strong covering fire to rescue the provincial, which they succeeded in doing. Many letters in Boston and New York papers recounted Smith's adventures. Three weeks later he was reported to be on the mend and swearing vengeance on the French.[107]

Going into action alongside the Rhode Islanders were the Jersey Blues also ordered up from the rear and led by Lieutenant Colonel John Shaw of Perth Amboy, New Jersey. Behind him in the ranks marched a very tired forty-year-old Private Garrett Albertson of Long Island. "When we came near the field of battle, and the bullets began to whistle around us, I felt a tremor or panic of fear," he confessed. "I strove to conquer it, but in vain." When his commanding officer was cut down, the orders given "were then to march on within gunshot of the breastwork, every man to shift and cover himself as well as he could behind trees, stumps, or logs." Albertson took his place beside two of his company lieutenants and others "to make our stand behind a large pine log, where we would drop and load, then rise and fire over the log, until our ammunition was almost spent: my firelock at length so hot I could not handle it."[108]

Indeed, many regulars and provincials ran out of ammunition that day but could not be resupplied because they were pinned down in the abattis. Private Perry described his cover as "a white oak stump which was so small that I had to lie on my side, and stretch myself; the balls striking the ground within a hand's breadth of me every moment." As the seventeen year-old tried to make himself as small as possible, he "heard the men screaming" and saw "them dying all around me."[109]

Though Abercromby directed his regulars to fall back at approximately 2.30 P.M., at least one British regiment on the far left would at least three times ignore the order to withdraw (see Map T-5). The left brigade, commanded by Lieutenant Colonel Grant and comprising the 42nd Highland Regiment and the 46th Foot arrived on the French right at approximately 1.30 P.M. and immediately formed to throw their weight behind the New Yorkers who were caught up in the abattis. The 42nd, according to Captain James Murray, marched up "between one and two, and attacked the trenches and got within twenty paces of them and had a hot fire for about three hours as possible could be, we all the time seeing but their hats and the end of their muskets."[110]

An officer of the 55th Foot on the left watched the 42nd advance, later stating with admiration that "they appeared like roaring lions breaking from their chains." The Highlanders in tandem with the 46th repeatedly attacked the

French right flank defended by the Béarn and La Reine regiments under the command of the Chevalier de Lévis. Lévis, according to Bougainville, "twice ordered the *Canadiens* and the troops of *La Marine* to make sorties and take them in the flank."[111]

The first time the colony regulars went forward with their *Canadien* militia comrades to fire into the rear of the 42nd and 46th column, they were calmly met by some of it detaching and returning their fire, which sent the militiamen running to the rear. The *Canadiens* did not stop at their outworks, according to Montcalm's private report to the minister of war after the battle, but kept on running towards the French batteaux lines on the shore of Lake Champlain. Their own guns at Fort Carillon fired on them, forcing them back to their assigned posts. They would not venture out again from their makeshift breastwork for the rest of the afternoon, leaving the hot work to the colonial regulars under *Capitaine* Raymond.[112]

Like the officer of the 55th Foot, General Montcalm was also impressed by the Highlanders, especially during an attack made at approximately 3 P.M. in conjunction with Haldimand's grenadiers. "This column composed of English grenadiers and Scottish Highlanders returned unceasingly to the attack, without becoming discouraged or broken." The Highlanders, as one of their own officers noted, were beyond discouragement. "They did not mind their fellow-soldiers tumbling down about them," wrote Lieutenant William Grant, but still went on undaunted. "Even those that were mortally wounded, cried aloud to their companions not to lose a thought upon them, but to follow their officers and charge the enemy."[113]

The most furious attack of the day, however, was yet to come, and it followed on the heels of a most bizarre incident. One French officer claimed it was caused by a Royal-Roussillon officer tying a red handkerchief to the end of his sword and waving it back and forth as a target, similar to his men who were placing their tricorne hats on the ends of sticks and holding them up for British marksmen to shoot at. Desandrouins, however, claimed it was merely the colour of the Royal-Roussillon regiment, which was red in the upper right quarter, being animatedly raised up and down by its ensign, who was yelling "*Vive le Roi!*" Whatever it was, it caused the British column advancing in this sector, comprising elements of the 55th Foot, Haldimand's grenadiers, the New Yorkers and Preble's Massachusetts Regiment, to think that the French were surrendering, as a red flag signalled a desire to parley. They started to advance with their weapons held high shouting, "*Bon quartier,*" meaning they were willing to accept their French enemy's surrender.[114]

The probable "culprit:" regimental colour of the Royal-Roussillon, 1758

Late in the afternoon of the battle, British troops thought they saw the French waving a red flag, the period signal for a parley, over their entrenchments. They advanced, with their weapons held over their heads, thinking that the French wanted to discuss surrender terms. The similarly confused French, in their turn, held their fire thinking that the British wanted to surrender. When both sides realized their mistake, the slaughter was awful. The probable cause for this incident was the colour of the Royal-Roussillon, with its red upper right quarter, which may have caused the British to mistake it for the signal to parley. (Courtesy, René Chartrand)

A New York officer wrote that "the enemy Hoisted English colours, Club'd [reversed] their Firelocks & Beckoned to us in that manner very thick on the breastwork on which Major Monypenny order'd the whole to advance cease firing which was done." Meanwhile, *Capitaine* Pouchot's picquet company manning the northern wall was running out of ammunition in firing at the 42nd. The Béarn officer was on his way to the left to ask the commanding officer of the Guyenne for a resupply when he saw Lieutenant Colonel le sieur de Font-bonne yelling to his men on their breastworks to tell the enemy "to lay down their arms & their surrender will be accepted." Pouchot, an experienced officer, could see by the advancing British soldiers' expressions and demeanour that "they had very different ideas in mind & their sole purpose was to reach the entrenchment."[115]

He ran forward shouting excitedly: "Fire! Fire! Can't you see these troops mean to overrun your position! Fire!" The soldiers of the Guyenne realized he was right, and, standing on top of their parapet "poured in a heavy volley which brought down two or three hundred of them," though this is an exaggeration. The New York officer recorded that this "terrible and Heavy fire, such as we had not yet experienced, killed Multitudes and oblig'd us to retire to recover ourselves from the Disorder we were thrown in." Private William Bremner of the 55th remembered that "the Enemy gave us a smart Volley & Hove a great number of grenade shells among us which distroyed a great Number of our Regulars." Bremner and others considered this action a "diceet."[116]

This incident may have been the catalyst which sparked the most determined and furious assault of the battle. The Guyenne and Béarn regiments now found themselves attacked simultaneously by two large columns, one on the high ground against the Guyenne and another on the lower ground against the Béarn and its neighbour, the La Reine regiment (see Map T-5). Ammunition was now low and some French battalions were near breaking point – *Capitaine* Jean-Nicolas Desandrouins, acting as one of Montcalm's orderly officers during the battle, admitted the French defenders "were on their last legs." The 2nd Battalion of the Berry regiment in the centre, tormented by sniping fire from the flanks, for which their entrenchment walls provided little protection due to poor construction, had already had its younger and more inexperienced soldiers bolt from their positions, only to be faced by steely-eyed grenadiers with fixed bayonets who persuaded them to return.[117]

"They [the Highlanders] attacked with the greatest fury," recalled Bougainville, who was standing at Montcalm's side, "and this attack threatened real danger." Montcalm, stripped to his waistcoat and sword in hand, marched quickly at the head of the reserve grenadiers just in time to see screaming Highlanders jumping over the parapet led by a large six-foot Scot who was wielding his broadsword to deadly effect. This small determined band was quickly bowled over and bayoneted in a counterattack led by Montcalm. Lévis sent over half of the La Reine regiment, which was not heavily engaged, to reinforce Béarn's sector.[118]

As the French grenadiers took post between the hard-pressed Guyenne and Béarn regiments, a Massachusetts officer on the other side of the breastworks marvelled at the 42nd Foot's last futile assault: "A part of the Hilanders forcd them Selves within the first lines of ye Enemys Brestwork & But were Soon obliged to quit the Same & Retreat a few yards, Back where they Stood Fast & Faught Like Brave Soldiers with as much Likelyhood of doing Service as if they had discharged so many Rounds into the Lake."[119] Only when the Highlanders were out of ammunition could their officers convince them to leave the battlefield. This one regiment suffered 65 per cent casualties in a single day's action, 647 men out of a total strength of 1,000 all ranks, a loss unsurpassed by any other regiment in 18th century North American warfare.[120]

At approximately 5 P.M., Abercromby made the decision to withdraw. "The general thought proper to order a retreat," remembered Major Rogers, but the order did not reach everyone until approximately 6 P.M. "He directed me to bring up the rear," said the ranger commander, "which I did in the dusk of the evening." The French all noted that the weight of British fire slackened at 5.30 P.M. though "they left their light troops to continue their firing to cover their retreat," observed Lévis. "These light troops also retired around 7.30 P.M."[121]

The French were exhausted and none dared venture out into the abattis to loot the dead and wounded for there were still many men hidden there, alert, alive and waiting for nightfall to descend in order to extricate themselves and their wounded friends. Writing in hindsight, Lévis admitted that "for our part, we were too feeble to pursue the enemy, and in fact, strongly believed they would attack the next day at dawn. Instead we passed the night manning the abattis while the soldiers cleaned their weapons."

Typical of the many men still lurking in the abattis at the onset of dusk on 8 July was Private Perry of Preble's Regiment, who had finally got out from behind the white oak stump and taken shelter behind a large log with several other men. Pinned down since mid-afternoon, "we lay there till near sunset," he recalled. "Not receiving any orders from any officer, the men crept off, leaving all the dead, and most of the wounded, a great many crying for help, which we were unable to afford them. I suppose that soon as we left the ground, the enemy let loose his Indians upon them, for none of those that we left behind were ever heard of afterwards."[122]

The walking wounded streamed back along the single road leading to the sawmills, many assisted by able-bodied men who perhaps should have remained on the field. Abercromby in one of his letters hinted darkly that this was one of the main reasons he decided his army was no longer physically or psychologically fit to stay and fight another day with a reinforced enemy. "After the attack was over, I returned to the Sawmill," he wrote, "as upwards of two thirds of [the Provincials] retired with great precipitation to our Landing Place."[123]

Back at the camp that guarded the northern bridge, Abercromby posted "a Guard at the bridge to stop the Remainder of them" but was also startled to find that "more of the Regulars than was necessary took the same Route." Abercromby, seeing the conduct of his army all around him, brooding on the intelligence extracted from French prisoners that another 6,000 *Canadiens* and Indians were coming to reinforce Montcalm, and reflecting on the loss of so many field officers, came to a fairly quick decision. He deferred to the opinion of his senior aide-de-camp, Captain James Cunningham, who counselled immediate retreat over consultation with any of Abercromby's remaining commanding officers. In one of the general's letters home, he revealed his greatest fear, one which he had already experienced to some degree on 6 July after Lord Howe's death: "If the Trees at some Little Distance from the Breastwork had not concealed our Disorder, we might have suffered much more by the Enemie's being encouraged to follow us." Colonel Henry Babcock, the wounded Rhode Islander, was more blunt: "We became a confused rabble."[124]

The French would not stir in force from their entrenchments for at least another day. On 9 July, volunteers scouted as far as the sawmill camp and reported that the British had apparently fallen back to the portage camp on the northern shores of Lake George. On the following day, Lévis emerged at the head of eight grenadier companies, the *volontaire* companies of Duprat and Bernard and 400 *Canadiens*. Marching down the portage road to the head of Lake George, they found the detritus of a hurried retreat: "wounded, provisions, abandoned equipment, shoes left in miry places, remains of barges and burned rafts; incontestable proof of the great loss our enemy had suffered."[125]

"What will our descendants say when they hear that 14,000 men with heroic courage but hopeless of success, for six consecutive hours sustained a triple fire from an enemy in entrenchments impregnable by small arms?" asked Major John Tullikens of his commanding officer, Henri Bouquet. The surprise and outrage of the army was absolute. The provincials dubbed their general "Mrs. Nabbycromby." The Iroquois warriors told him through their interpreter that "he was an old Squah that he should wear a petticoat" and "go home and make sugar." The outspoken Captain Charles Lee of his own regiment called him "a damn beastly poltroon" and "our Booby-in-Chief" to any who would listen.[126]

Lieutenant Colonel John Bradstreet fumed:

> I must now tell you that after my having transported & conveyed an Army of 16000 Men full of helths & Spirits with every requisit for War and driving 1100 Men from an advanced Guard and one of 1200 from another and the whole Army assembll'd within a mile of the Enemy, the want of knowledge in the Commander-in-Chief has sacrifis'd about 2000 men killed and wounded and shamefully deserted with the remainder that night.[127]

Bradstreet's casualty figures are almost exactly correct, the final total for Abercromby's four-day campaign being 1,967 all ranks killed, wounded or missing out of a force of 17,550 men, a casualty rate of just over 11 per cent. The French, by contrast, had a total of 554 all ranks, killed or wounded over the same period out of 4,236 officers and men, a higher casualty rate of 13 per cent. This anomaly of who suffered the most sets completely on its head the standard historical conclusion that the British were slaughtered and the French suffered very light casualties. Of the two armies, the one which could least afford such a high casualty rate was Montcalm's, which explains why his troops remained in their defensive position long after Abercromby's army had fled down the lake on 9 July.

That the British withdrawal was disorderly is confirmed by Captain William Hervey of the 44th Foot in his journal: "9th. This morning the whole army moved off in great confusion, and regulars, Provincials, Artillery and sick sailed mixed together, not stopping till they came to the end of the Lake, the general among the first." The report of the battle offered to the British public by way of the *Gentleman's Magazine* openly recited the commander's blunders and oversights. It spoke of "pannic at the headquarters," the bad intelligence and ignorance concerning the enemy's breastworks, unsupported frontal assaults of infantry that persisted for most of the action, and the somewhat hasty abandonment of what still could have been a successful siege as an army of "near 14000 men" retreated "from an enemy not above 3000."[128]

Certainly James Abercromby had many options available. The traditional claim, that he did not intend the artillery to come forward is not, however, correct. He had put in train a plan for a battery of four 6-pdrs. to be positioned south of the French breastworks, from where it could easily enfilade the enemy line. Since one French battalion broke during the battle merely from flanking musket fire due to the incomplete breastworks, one might argue that the effect of four field guns raking their positions would have been most influential.

As well, all available evidence strongly suggests that Abercromby's plan of attack was never given a chance to succeed. Rogers' Rangers being out of place set in motion a number of unfortunate events that conspired to destroy all attempts by Abercromby to coordinate and control his troops. Certainly, though, he surrendered what offensive action and latitude he may have had with such a large army by placing himself at the rear of his regulars rather than leading them onto the battlefield. In his absence, an over ambitious brigade commander ordered the regulars to attack before the army was ready. In addition, the traditional charge that Lieutenant Clerk was responsible for the engineering intelligence failure that led to the unanimous decision of the principal officers to attack is not correct. John Bradstreet and the "ingineer who was a foreigner" must share some of the blame for the inadequate ground reconnaissance on 8 July. It was their misleading information that led Abercromby and his officers to believe the French breastwork was so inconsequential that all could "easily get to it and push down with [their] shoulders."

The only things for which Clerk can truly be faulted are his poor navigational instructions and lack of measures taken to ensure that the battery was sited properly on the south bank of the La Chute River. If the battery was truly the key to the entire British attack and its success, he should have placed the guns himself or at least have conducted a water-level reconnaissance that would have discovered that tall river reeds concealed the landing site for the guns.

In the larger scheme of things, Abercromby was guilty of not using his trained scouts from the rangers, Sir William Johnson's Indians or his regular light infantry to probe and determine the size, flanks and approaches to his enemy's formidable position. This would have allowed the British general to make a more knowledgeable and sensible plan of attack rather than the frontal assault *en masse* which he devised. Robert Rogers, his principal scouting officer responsible for reconnaissance, must therefore also shoulder some of the blame for the army's blindness in the battle.

Not unnaturally, despite their heavy losses, the French rejoiced. Montcalm wrote almost incredulously to his friend, André Doreuil, the commissary of stores in Montreal, that "the army, the too-small army of the King, has beaten the enemy. What a day for France!" He went on to claim that if he had "had two hundred Indians to send out at the head of a thousand picked men under the chevalier de Lévis, not many would have escaped." Montcalm's exuberance was apparent in his closing words: "What soldiers are ours! I never saw the like." Three days after the battle, Montcalm sent a brief account of the battle to the minister of war which on several points was not entirely accurate. He claimed that Vaudreuil had deliberately held back the 1,200 *Canadiens* and a large force of Indians he had promised to send to his assistance. The French commander stated that his small army had been attacked by 20,000 British – subsequently changing his estimates in later correspondence upwards to 25,000, then 27,000, and eventually to 30,000 – from 8 A.M. to 8 P.M. on 8 July. Total British casualties he assessed to be at least 5,000 men.[129]

In another letter to the minister of war dated 28 July, Montcalm expanded on the events of the battle and declared he was in no doubt that the ministry of marine would try to enhance the role of the colonial regulars and the *Canadiens* during the battle. He claimed that he and his regulars had single-handedly saved the colony, since only 400 colonial regulars, *Canadiens* and a handful of Indians were present at the battle. He added that the militiamen had behaved badly during the battle, refusing to attack when ordered and abandoning their posts.[130]

It was not long before Montcalm's accusations and deliberate twisting of the facts reached Vaudreuil, who was predictably furious. Reporting to the minister of marine, the governor told of a near-revolt among the colonial regulars "when they learned Monsieur de Montcalm, instead of boasting their efforts, attributed their success to the *troupes de terre*." The participation by the *troupes de la marine* and *Canadien* militia in the action was indeed relatively modest, and the latter group had actually run away at one point. However, Montcalm deliberately downplayed the numbers of *troupes de la marine* who participated in the battle as well as the *Canadiens*. Accounts show that at least 450 colonial regulars and 200 militiamen fought on the northern flank of the battlefield for a total of 750 instead of the 400 that Montcalm claimed. He also deliberately forgot to mention *marine* infantrymen and artillerymen manning the guns of the fort that decisively stopped Abercromby's effort to establish a battery on Rattlesnake Mountain. Many colonial regulars and *Canadiens* also toiled beside the soldiers of the

Victory against superior odds: Montcalm congratulates his troops after the battle.
Montcalm, stripped to his waistcoat, congratulates his victorious but tired men during the evening of 8 July 1758 while, in the foreground, an officer of the Royal-Roussillon joyously waves the regimental colour. Although he had won the bloodiest battle fought in North America during the 18th century, such were Montcalm's losses that he did not attempt a pursuit of the retreating British-American force until two days after the action. (Painting by Harry A. Ogden, courtesy, Fort Ticonderoga Museum)

3rd Battalion of the Berry regiment bringing vital ammunition, water and supplies forward to the defensive position during the battle. Others guarded the batteaux lines and the artillery park.[131]

In sum, Montcalm's attitude can only be termed as uncharitable and to a certain extent vindictive. His actions after the battle were calculated to give Vaudreuil the maximum offence possible and served to further poison the poor relations between his French regulars and Vaudreuil's *Canadiens* and colonial regulars for months to come. The year 1759 would see large British armies and the Royal Navy closing in on all sides at a time when petty rivalries and jealousies should have been put aside to cooperate for the greater good of the colony. But, by then, Montcalm and Vaudreuil no longer talked to one another, using Lévis as a go-between.

Louis-Antoine de Bougainville, Montcalm's principal aide, was sent to France to relate the details of the victory at Ticonderoga to the king. Promoted lieutenant colonel as the bearer of good news, Bougainville asked a revealing question of his wife in 1759 before he returned to Canada: "Can we hope for another miracle to save us? I trust in God; he fought for us on the 8th of July!"[132]

Ticonderoga Today

Fort Ticonderoga and its battlefield have been preserved since 1820 by the Pell family. The restoration of the fort and the development of the museum, which interprets the battle and its subsequent history from the French and Indian War until the present day, was initiated by Stephen H. Pell in 1909. Since 1931, the battlefield, fort and museum have been under the care of the Fort Ticonderoga Association, a private, not-for-profit organization chartered in 1931 by the State of New York.

The battlefield is in pristine condition, though heavily wooded in parts. Those areas open to the public are well signposted with map displays and memorial cairns. The remains of the earth breastworks are clearly visible and are in the process of being cleared of brush and trees on an annual basis.

For a magnificent bird's eye view of the fort, battlefield and surrounding topography, visitors should drive to the top of Mount Defiance which is maintained by the Fort Ticonderoga Association as a picnic area and lookout. The landing sites are clearly visible. One can follow the valley and La Chute River running north and east around to the Heights of Carillon and the fort some 850 feet below.

Detailed tours of battlefield areas closed to the public are available on request for serious historians and students through special arrangement with the Fort Ticonderoga Museum. Its research centre and library preserve an extensive collection of military his-

tory manuscripts, journals and books as well as historical artifacts from both the Seven Years War and Revolutionary War periods. Researchers or visitors requesting special permission to tour the battlefield should contact the curator at (518) 585-2821 or write to: Fort Ticonderoga, Fort Road, Box 390, Ticonderoga, NY, USA, 12883.

To reach Fort Ticonderoga from Canada, take Highway 15 south from Montreal, crossing the border at Lacolle, then proceed on Interstate 87 south past Plattsburgh to the Schroon Lake exit. Fort Ticonderoga is well signposted from this exit. For visitors coming from Albany or New York, take Interstate 87 north and exit at Schroon Lake.

Bird's eye view of Fort Ticonderoga today

An aerial perspective of Fort Carillon (now Ticonderoga) from the south looking toward the north. The actual battle took place a half mile to the west of the fort, just beyond the railway cutting visible on the left of the photograph. The observation tower in the foreground (now replaced) is on the summit of Rattlesnake Mountain (now Mount Defiance) where Lieutenant Matthew Clerk scouted the French position the day before the battle. (Courtesy, Fort Ticonderoga Museum)

"A Mere Matter of Marching:"

Defending Canada, 1758 to 1812

Unfortunately, Bougainville's prayer was not answered. Montcalm's victory at Ticonderoga was one of the last successes enjoyed by the defenders of Canada and, on 27 July 1758, nineteen days after Abercromby came to grief on Lake Champlain, Louisbourg surrendered to a British besieging force. It had held out long enough, however, to delay the implementation of William Pitt's strategy for 1758 but he prepared to renew the offensive in the following spring.

Vaudreuil and Montcalm were at loggerheads on how to meet the attack both men knew was coming. The fall of Louisbourg left the St. Lawrence open to the Royal Navy and Montcalm was certain that Quebec would be the next object of attack. In his opinion it was "no longer time when a few scalps, or the burning [of] a few houses is any advantage or even an object," as the "war is entirely changed in this part of the world according to the manner the English are attacking us."[1] He urged that all available forces be redeployed to defend the area between Quebec and Montreal, the heartland of Canada, but Vaudreuil insisted on "contesting the ground on our frontiers inch by inch."[2] In the end Montcalm prevailed and the result was that the greater part of the regular troops, both of the army and the marine, were shifted back from the borders to the St. Lawrence.

In the spring of 1759, three British armies invaded Canada. In June, Major General James Wolfe, transported by the Royal Navy, arrived at Quebec and laid siege to the capital of New France. The attackers were frustrated throughout the summer by Montcalm's stubborn defence of the city. British arms had more success to the south and west, where a series of victories wrested control of Lake Champlain and Lake Ontario away from France. In September Wolfe, faced with the oncoming winter, tried a desperate gamble and transported his army by night to a landing place above Quebec. Rather than defend the city from its for-tifications, Montcalm opted to attack, and on 13 September the two armies met on a field named after one Abraham, a farmer – the result was a British victory in a bloody action that saw the death of both commanding generals.

Winter brought an end to active operations, but in the following year the British juggernaut advanced slowly but relentlessly on Montreal, the last remain-ing French strongpoint. Despite a notable victory won by the chevalier de Lévis at the battle of Ste. Foy outside Quebec in May, it was all over by September when three British armies overwhelmed the outnumbered French forces. Vaudreuil and Lévis signed articles of capitulation and the war itself was brought to a close by the Treaty of Paris of February 1763 which ceded all French terri-tory in what is now Canada (and 60,000 inhabitants) to the British Crown. The removal of the long-standing French threat caused jubilation throughout the American colonies but, as one historian has noted, it was not the provincials' own military efforts but "British regulars, the Royal Navy, and the British tax-payer that finally defeated the French."[3]

Armies are costly institutions and the financial burden of providing for the defence of North America was a contributory cause to a new threat to Canada. Although Britain ruled unchallenged (except by the aboriginal peoples) over much of the continent in 1763, she was faced with the task defending the fron-tier which, in the decade following the Seven Years War, moved steadily west-ward. Not surprisingly, the British government asked her American colonies to help defray the expense of the large garrison deployed for their protection, but this request met with a firm refusal and the government was forced to impose increased taxation in North America to help pay for its defence. The result was the cry of "no taxation without representation," widespread unrest, civil disobe-dience and occasional outbreaks of violence between the Americans and British troops. The centre of discontent was the city of Boston and, in 1774, the bulk of the British army in North America was shifted to that place to maintain order. Tension in the city led to riots that ultimately evolved into a revolution and, by the early months of 1775, Britain and thirteen of her colonies were on the brink of war.

The defence of Canada in that year was the responsibility of Major General Guy Carleton. In the spring, when British regulars and American rebels clashed at Lexington and Concord near Boston, Carleton had two regular regiments and part of a third to defend an area that encompassed much of the southern part of modern Quebec, Ontario and Michigan. By June he daily expected an invasion, and he complained that "consternation in the Towns and Country was great and universal, every Individual seemed to feel our present impotent situation, for tho' in no Danger of internal Commotions, we are equally unprepared for Attack or Defence."[4]

That attack was not long in coming. The Congress of the rebellious colonies wanted to seize Quebec as the military stores there would augment those already taken from British military posts on Lake Champlain. Two small American armies, one under Brigadier General Richard Montgomery and the other under Brigadier General Benedict Arnold, set out to invade Canada. Montgomery, moving by way of Lake Champlain and the Richelieu River, took the small posts at St. Jean and Chambly, and then Montreal, before proceeding down the St. Lawrence. Arnold, for his part, moved from Massachusetts up the Kennebec River and then down the Chaudière River and ultimately the St. Lawrence toward Quebec. As it had been during the French period, the wilderness proved one of Canada's most effective defences – the invading American forces had lost nearly half their men by the time they joined together before the walls of Quebec.

Carleton defended the city with a polyglot mixture of newly-recruited regular troops, English- and French-speaking militia, and sailors and marines from the Royal Navy. He had been disappointed in his efforts to rouse the *Canadiens* to the British side. They preferred to stay aloof from a quarrel which they saw as being none of their affair and, as Carleton remarked, "there is nothing to fear from them while we are in a state of prosperity, and nothing to hope for when in distress."[5] Some *Canadiens* tried to profit from the business by selling provisions to the half-starved American besiegers at Quebec and were infuriated when the paper money they received in exchange proved to be worthless. Two hundred *Canadiens* did rally to the British cause and helped defeat an American assault on the city launched on New Year's Eve. The Americans, half starved and suffering from smallpox, hung on until spring brought the Royal Navy up the St. Lawrence and they then dispersed.

The danger was over, and for the rest of the Revolutionary War Canada was never again seriously threatened by either the Americans or their French ally. Distance and wilderness proved as effective, however, for the Americans as they had for their opponents when a major British attempt under Major General John Burgoyne to mount an invasion of New York by moving up Lake Champlain came to grief at Saratoga in October 1777 when Burgoyne surrendered his surrounded army to triumphant rebel forces. Except for a number of small raids launched across the border, the scene of major operations now shifted to the south. The war dragged on for another six years but ended when a second Treaty of Paris, signed in 1783, established thirteen of the British colonies in North America as an independent nation, leaving only Quebec and the Maritimes under the British Crown.

This treaty ended the fighting but left disputes unresolved between the signatories, who in any case did not live up to its terms. The new American government failed to compensate the Loyalists, those former citizens of the thirteen colonies who had remained true to the British connection, while Britain, in retaliation, refused to abandon a number of military posts in the northern territory of the new republic. Some of these problems were resolved by the Jay Treaty of 1794 but new sources of tension shortly arose, fuelled by the outbreak in 1793 of the great war with revolutionary and imperial France which raged, with a brief two-year intermission, until 1815.

When Britain and France passed "tit for tat" legislation forbidding ships trading with one nation from trading with the other, the United States was caught in the middle. In response, the American government prohibited its citizens from trading with either belligerent but this harmed the economy of the United States more than it did those of the warring nations. There were also problems on the high seas. British naval officers inspecting American merchant ships often refused to recognize the identification papers carried by the seamen and impressed them into the Royal Navy, and British warships sailed into American territorial waters with impunity. In 1807, when HMS *Leopard* fired a broadside into the unprepared and unresisting American frigate, USS *Chesapeake*, it provoked an incident that nearly brought the two nations to war. Added to these problems were troubles with the aboriginal nations living in the American Northwest (modern Ohio, Michigan and Illinois) who were desperately trying to turn back a wave of white settlement. They expected assistance from Britain, their traditional ally, who did not provide it but nonetheless many Americans became convinced that there would no lasting peace until all of North America was part of the republic.

Britain, preoccupied with the struggle against France, adopted a policy towards the United States that was, at one and the same time, a masterful combination of arrogance, shortsightedness, and stupidity. Receiving no redress through diplomacy, President James Madison decided to seek it through military means and on 18 June 1812 the United States, with the cry "Free Trade and Sailors' Rights," declared war on Britain.

America, one historian has very truthfully written, "swaggered into the War of 1812 like a Kansas farmboy entering his first saloon."[6] A war against Britain could not be fought at sea – the United States Navy was a very professional service but, in numbers, no match for the Royal Navy – and it would therefore have to be fought on land and that meant an invasion of Canada. Madison and his cabinet were gambling that such military strength as they could muster would be able to occupy Britain's North American possessions before that nation, preoccupied in Europe, could redeploy its forces. The American government hoped that Canada would fall without difficulty and then be used as a bargaining chip in the diplomatic negotiations that would follow. It certainly looked good on paper – the population of the United States was about six million, that of British North America about half a million. The Americans were confident, and in the early summer hastily-raised units of regulars and militia began to move north toward the border to participate in what ex-President Thomas Jefferson thought would be "a mere matter of marching."

Standing between the republic and the laurels of victory was Lieutenant General Sir George Prevost, the governor-general, and a force of British regulars. A professional soldier, Prevost had been appointed to his post in 1811 when the threat of war became imminent, and he had no illusions about the difficulty of his task – he had 9,777 officers and men to defend a vast territory and he could expect no rapid reinforcement from Britain. Prevost's plan was to retain the city of Quebec, the only fortified place in Canada, at all costs. As the best route for an American invasion force was down the St. Lawrence, he deployed the bulk of his forces south of Montreal – Prevost intended to fight hard to retain Montreal and block any threat to Quebec, but he was prepared to abandon Upper Canada (modern Ontario) which, bordered on three sides by American territory, he regarded as a military liability. Under instructions from London not to engage in offensive operations "except it be for the purpose of preventing or repelling Hostilities or unavoidable Emergencies," Prevost's overall policy was defensive and it was to remain so almost throughout the war.[7]

This policy did not sit well with his principal subordinate, Major General Isaac Brock, the commander in Upper Canada. Brock was more offensive-minded – far from abandoning that province, he wanted to take the war to the enemy, to attack and seize neighbouring American territory that might serve as a staging point for invasion. Brock obeyed orders, however, and devoted considerable energy to putting Upper Canada in the best possible state of defence. He repaired and strengthened the chain of little forts along the border and he devoted particular attention to the Provincial Marine, a small colonial navy whose warships controlled Lakes Erie and Ontario. This naval force was an asset as it permitted Brock to move and supply his widely-separated forces more effectively than if he were dependent on the primitive road system and it also denied the Americans these same capabilities. Brock reorganized the militia of Upper Canada, basically a levy of every male aged sixteen to sixty, by forming "flank" companies, drawn from the younger and more active men in each regiment, who received extra training. Finally, he secured the confidence and support of the native nations of the American Northwest, who were prepared to fight on Britain's side as allies.

The key to Canada, as British commanders and their American opponents knew, was Montreal. Seize Montreal and cut the St. Lawrence lifeline and, inevitably, all British territory to the west would fall. Despite the strategical importance of that city in 1812, the American invasion plan called for the initial military thrust to be made from the Detroit area against western Upper Canada. It was felt that a victory along the Detroit would crush native military power in the Northwest and thus resolve one of the problems that had prompted the United States to declare war. A Detroit offensive would then be followed by separate attacks in the Niagara area, against Kingston and against Montreal. If all these operations were successful, the invading armies would winter in Montreal and then, in the following spring, move on Quebec. It was an ambitious and complicated strategy, but, unfortunately it was founded on neither common sense nor the realities of the military situation.

The simple fact was that the United States was manifestly unprepared for war. The tiny regular army was deployed along the coasts and frontiers with the greater part (five of ten regiments) stationed in the newly-acquired Louisiana Territory. To conquer Canada the American government was forced to rely on hastily-raised and poorly-trained units of "regulars" commanded by a collection of politicians with a thirst for glory, green militia officers and elderly relics from the Revolutionary War. From top to bottom this army lacked leadership – Secretary of War William Eustis was an alcoholic incompetent, while the senior commander on the northern frontier, Major General Henry Dearborn, was old, sick and tired. Still worse was the fact that the distances, the wilderness, the primitive communications and the weather combined to create a logistical nightmare – not only was it difficult to move large numbers of troops to the northern frontier, it was still more difficult to supply them once they got there.

The result was a fiasco. Brigadier General William Hull, ordered to invade western Upper Canada, crossed the Detroit River in July and spent a few days on

Canadian soil before concern over the threat posed by the native peoples to his lengthy supply line caused him to withdraw to the United States. Sensing an opportunity, Brock used the mobility afforded to him by the Provincial Marine to shift his forces to the threatened area. He invaded American territory in mid-August and laid siege to Hull's superior force at Detroit before convincing Hull, in a colossal act of bluff, to surrender his entire army.

Brock had defeated the first American invasion attempt, and for a while it looked as if the war would soon end. On learning that the British government had repealed its restrictive maritime legislation, one of the major causes of the conflict, Prevost proposed an armistice to Dearborn on the basis that the United States would not want to continue a needless war. Dearborn agreed and the two commanders signed an armistice on 9 August that neither side would undertake offensive measures until their respective governments considered the matter. Madison, however, refused to recognize this agreement and on 4 September hostilities officially resumed.

The aggressive Brock disliked the idea of a ceasefire and, as September 1812 wore on, his attention became focused on the Niagara area, which appeared to be the target of a new invasion threat.

2

"It remains only

to fight:"

The Battle of

Queenston Heights

13 October 1812

The Battle of Queenston Heights, 13 October 1812

View of the action painted by Captain James Dennis, 49th Foot, who depicted in one painting each phase of the battle from the crossing of the first wave of American batteaux, the fighting in the village, Brock's death, Sheaffe's attack, and the chaotic American retreat. (Courtesy, Weir Gallery, Queenston)

"It remains only to fight:" The Battle of Queenston Heights

13 October 1812

Robert Malcomson

The blow must be struck soon or all the toil and expense of the campaign will go for nothing and worse than nothing, for the whole will be tinged with dishonour.[1]

MAJOR GENERAL STEPHEN VAN RENSSELAER, 12 OCTOBER 1812

Those Yankees did invade us,
And to distress our country,
Our peace for to annoy.
Our countrymen were filled
With sorrow, grief and woe,
To think that they should fall
By such an unnatural foe.

Come all ye bold Canadians,
Enlisted in the cause,
To defend your country,
And to maintain your laws;
Being all united,
This is the song we'll sing:
Success onto Great Britain,
And God save the King![2]

During the second week of October 1812, Major General Stephen Van Rensselaer stood at the head of the 5,000-man American army poised to cross the Niagara River into Upper Canada. Aged forty-seven, Van Rensselaer was perhaps better suited to undertake his duties as the patroon of his family's estate along the Hudson River near Albany, New York. He had been born to wealth, educated at Harvard University and elected to the New York State legislature as a representative, and then a senator before accepting the office of lieutenant governor in 1795. He had married the daughter of Major General Philip Schuyler, a veteran of the Revolutionary War, and served in the state militia, rising to the rank of major general, but the extent of his practical military experience was

---

See Appendix B, page 372, for Orders of Battle of the Opposing Forces.

virtually nil. In that respect, one American historian notes that Van Rensselaer had "no training beyond the sanguinary prognosis of a dress parade, or a night attack on the café of the old Fort Orange Hotel at Albany."[3]

How had such an amateur come to command an army intended to mount a major offensive? As a member of the Federalist party, Van Rensselaer had opposed the war policies of President James Madison and his Republicans (popularly known as the "Democratic-Republicans"), among whom was the governor of New York State, Daniel Tompkins. It was widely known that Van Rensselaer meant to challenge Tompkins in the gubernatorial elections to be held in the spring of 1813 – he had unsuccessfully run against Governor George Clinton in 1801. When the overburdened American secretary of war, William Eustis, could not find a general to command the army on the Niagara Frontier after the declaration of hostilities in June 1812, Tompkins obtained permission to offer the appointment to Van Rensselaer. It was a shrewd political tactic because it wedged Van Rensselaer between his political principles and the risk of losing popularity among the electorate by failing to serve his country at a time of need. There was little Stephen Van Rensselaer could do but accept Tompkins's offer; perhaps he hoped that victory on the battlefield would help him in the polls.[4]

Acknowledging his lack of experience, the general invited his thirty-eight-year-old cousin, Lieutenant Colonel Solomon Van Rensselaer of the New York militia, and John Lovett, a close friend, to act as his aide and secretary respectively. The former had seen action as a regular officer during General Anthony Wayne's campaigns against the aboriginal peoples in the Old Northwest in the 1790s, while Lovett was a lawyer with the militia rank of major but not much else in the way of military experience.[5]

Major General Stephen Van Rensselaer (1764-1839)

On the death of his father in 1769, Van Rensselaer inherited Rennselaerwyck, an extensive tract on the upper Hudson River settled by his Dutch ancestors in the early 1600s. He began managing the estate in his late teens and obtained a commission as major in the New York militia at the age of twenty-three. (Courtesy, National Archives of Canada)

Lieutenant Colonel Solomon Van Rensselaer (1774-1852)

The son of a Revolutionary War general, Solomon Van Rensselaer obtained a commission as cornet in the Fourth U.S. Cavalry in 1792 and served in the army until 1800. Between 1801 and 1811 he was the adjutant general for the New York State militia. (Lossing, *Pictorial Field-book of the War of 1812*)

After a month-long tour of the northern frontier from Ogdensburg to the Niagara River, Van Rensselaer and his retinue arrived at Buffalo on 10 August 1812, where he inspected his army in its camps at various points along the length of the Niagara River (see Map Q-1). He found 400 regular troops and 800 militia, the majority lacking sufficient uniforms, muskets, ammunition, tents and cooking utensils. Batteries had been constructed at Black Rock, near Buffalo, and at Lewiston Heights, seven miles south of Lake Ontario, but they had no heavy guns, while Fort Niagara, which commanded the river's mouth at Lake Ontario, was in such a state of disrepair that some officers favoured abandoning it. Determined to turn this ragtag force into an efficient military formation that could invade Upper Canada, Van Rensselaer pitched his marquee in the middle of the camp at Lewiston and issued orders to regulate guard duties, drills and camp discipline. He called in units from scattered bivouacs and wrote to Governor Tompkins and Major General Henry Dearborn, the senior American general on the northern frontier at Albany, for reinforcements.[6]

A three-week armistice arranged in August by Sir George Prevost and Dearborn allowed time for a flotilla carrying artillery, ammunition, stores and several hundred regular troops to reach the Niagara from Oswego during the first week of September, though more reinforcements were still needed before the invasion could be made.[7] While he waited for further units to arrive, Van Rensselaer moved his main camp a mile east of Lewiston and had a road cut to the rear of Fort Niagara, which was improved and armed, as were the batteries at Lewiston Heights and Black Rock. September unfortunately brought bad weather and further delay. An atmosphere of gloom descended and lazy habits began to sneak in; obedience to camp rules faded, guard duty was conducted indifferently and

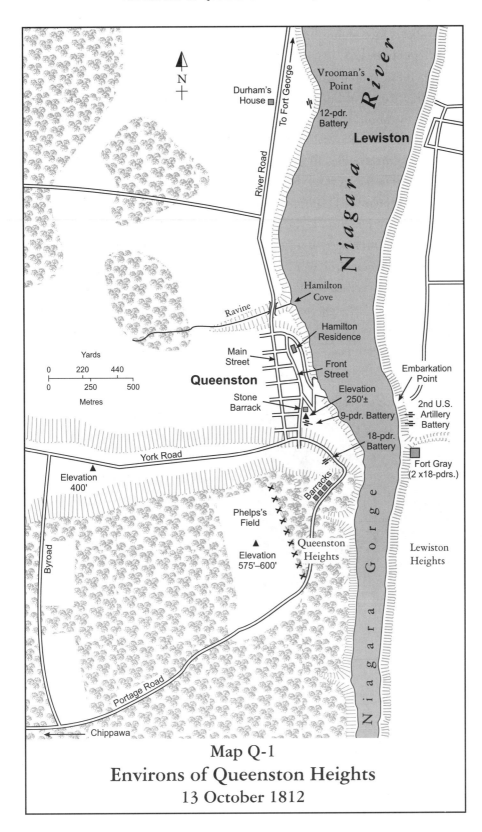

Map Q-1
Environs of Queenston Heights
13 October 1812

some officers missed morning parade. The quartermaster general, Peter B. Porter, a Republican stalwart, performed his duties half-heartedly and openly chastised his commanding general and his motives.[8] There were too many shortages: of hospital stores, of building supplies for the new constructions, of hay and grain for the horses and of straw for the soldiers' pallets. During the third week of September, Van Rensselaer was handed a piece of birch bark bearing a note "from the soldiers to the officers that unless they were paid they would absolutely quit the field in 8 days from that time."[9]

On 27 September Dearborn notified Van Rensselaer that Brigadier General William Henry Harrison was expected to attack Upper Canada from Detroit with up to 7,000 men, that a force of 2,000 had assembled at Sackets Harbor and that a naval squadron would soon be formed on Lake Ontario under Commodore Isaac Chauncey. "We have nothing to fear," wrote Dearborn from Albany, "and much to hope as to the ultimate success of measures now in operation with a view to Upper Canada, but much may immediately depend on what may happen at your post." To emphasize the importance of action on Van Rensselaer's part, Dearborn emphasized, "At all events we must calculate on possessing Upper Canada before winter sets in."[10]

The regulars sent by Dearborn and the militia ordered out by Tompkins began arriving at the Niagara in large numbers late in September, so that by the second week of October Van Rensselaer commanded just over 2,500 regulars and nearly 2,700 militia along the line from Buffalo to Fort Niagara. Brigadier General Alexander Smyth of the United States Army had also arrived and taken charge of the largest camp of regulars (1,650 men) and some militia

New York militia officer, 1812

Militia officers purchased their own uniforms and were usually better dressed than the men they led. This fine painting by H.C. McBarron depicts a captain of the New York militia, c. 1812-1813, in dark blue coatee with red facings. (Courtesy, Parks Canada)

(about 400) at Black Rock, near Buffalo. In search of further support, Van Rensselaer met with the chiefs of the Tuscarora village near Lewiston, but that nation decided to stay neutral in the campaign.[11]

Despite the influx of additional units, the long delay and bad weather had weakened the army's spirit. As Van Rensselaer explained to Dearborn on 8 October: "Our best troops are raw ... many have not necessary clothing. We are in a cold country, the season is far advanced and unusually inclement; we are half the time deluged with rain. ... With my present force it would be rash to attempt offensive operations."[12] Nevertheless he convened a council of war, during which he proposed a diversionary attack on Queenston with the militia while a brigade of regulars, presumably under Smyth, landed on the shore of Lake Ontario west of Fort George to assault it from the rear. Although Smyth had less than four years of military experience and had never seen the Niagara River before September 1812, he was loath to take orders from a militia officer and ignored Van Rensselaer's invitation to the council, instead suggesting in a note that the upper Niagara River was a preferable site for the invasion.[13]

On 9 October an American raiding party cut out two British armed brigs from their anchorage at Fort Erie and sailed them to Black Rock. When news of this event reached Lewiston and Fort Niagara, it "began to excite a strong disposition in the troops to act."[14] Van Rensselaer learned "through various channels" that his troops "must have orders to act or at all hazards they would go home." Painfully aware of what he termed "the obvious consequences to me personally," he discussed with his senior officers the latest intelligence from the British side and made the decision to cross the river. His immediate objective would be "to dislodge the enemy from the heights of Queenston and possess ourselves of the village, where the troops might be sheltered from the distressing inclemency of the weather."[15]

The attack was planned for the early hours of 11 October, with Lieutenant Colonel Solomon Van Rensselaer commanding the assault force of regulars and militia. Rain fell in torrents the day before and into the night as thirteen boats, flat-bottomed batteaux, were brought to a landing above Lewiston. Unfortunately, one craft carrying oars meant for the other boats mysteriously went off course and the mission was cancelled. Drenched and exasperated, the troops who had assembled withdrew from the river's edge to find places to dry out.

"The previously excited ardor seemed to have gained new heat from the recent miscarriage," wrote Stephen Van Rensselaer. "On the morning of the 12th such was the pressure on me from all quarters that I became satisfied that my refusal to act might involve me in suspicion and the service in disgrace."[16] A new plan was accordingly made to send a larger force over the river at Queenston. Once again Van Rensselaer asked Smyth to join him, but the brigadier kept his troops at Black Rock, stating that they would wash their clothing the next day, after which "they might march to the number of 1200 effective men, though imperfectly disciplined."[17]

On the other side of the Niagara River, British Major General Isaac Brock watched the movements of the American army closely. "The enemy … made an attempt last night to carry off the guard at Queenston," he wrote on the morning of 12 October, and the "vast number of troops which have been added … on the opposite side convinces me … that an attack is not far distant."[18]

Brock had been preparing for such an attack since the outbreak of war, although he would have preferred to have taken the offensive. "I firmly believe," he had written to one of his brothers on 18 September, "I could at this moment sweep everything before me from Fort Niagara to Buffalo – but my success would be transient."[19] He grudgingly accepted Prevost's defensive strategy and knew that he must carefully marshal the small army he had to defend the extensive frontier of Upper Canada.

The summer of 1812 presented Isaac Brock with only the third campaign of his twenty-eight years in the British army. Born in 1769, Brock had entered the service as an ensign at the age of fifteen, though it was not until he had risen to the rank of lieutenant colonel in the 49th Regiment of Foot that he saw action for the first time during a brief campaign against the French in Holland in 1799. In 1802 his regiment was sent to Quebec, from where Brock led his troops to occupy garrisons in the province of Upper Canada. With the war against Napoleon raging in Europe, Isaac Brock lamented his assignment to a provincial backwater and the "uninteresting and insipid life I am doomed to lead in this retirement."[20]

Canada, however, was not a complete disappointment for Brock. Under the approving eye of Sir James H. Craig, then governor-in-chief of British North America, Brock was appointed brigadier general in 1809, and two years later rose to the rank of major general. That same year, 1811, he assumed command in Upper Canada and became administrator of the province's government when Lieutenant Governor Francis Gore went to England on leave. As war threatened in the spring of 1812, Brock finally received his long-sought permission to return home, but concluded that his duty was to remain in Canada until the current crisis with the United States was resolved.

"Queenstown," 1794
Elizabeth Posthuma Simcoe, wife of John Graves Simcoe, the first lieutenant governor of Upper Canada, made this sketch of Queenston between 1792 and 1795 when the barracks of the Queens Rangers stood on the bank close to the river. Robert Hamilton's house is the structure on the right. (Courtesy, Archives of Ontario, F47-11-1-0-70, 53a)

Of the 2,500 regulars Brock had to defend the border of Upper Canada in October 1812, 1300 officers and men were stationed along the banks of the Niagara River. He divided this force, supplemented by 900 militia and 300 native warriors, into four small "divisions" stationed at Fort Erie, Chippawa, Queenston and Fort George. Brock's headquarters was in the Canadian village of Niagara, adjacent to Fort George, but since his responsibilities often demanded his absence, Prevost had sent Major General Roger Hale Sheaffe to act as Brock's second-in-command. Aged forty-nine, Sheaffe had served with the 5th Foot in Canada from 1787 until 1797, returning there in 1802 as a lieutenant colonel in the 49th Foot, subordinate to Brock.[21]

Late on Monday, 12 October, Brock received word that the Americans were about to make another attempt on Queenston. This intelligence came from Major Thomas Evans, who had gone that morning to set up an exchange of officer prisoners with Van Rensselaer following the capture of the British vessels three days before. Having made previous trips to the American camp on official business, Evans was surprised when he was directed to remain in his boat and finally told,

Major General Isaac Brock (1769-1812)
Portraits of Brock are speculative at best as he is not known to have sat for a portrait later in life. An American officer who encountered him at Detroit in August 1812 described him this way: "His personal appearance was commanding; he must have been six feet three or four inches in height; very massive and large boned, though not fleshy, and apparently of immense muscular power." (Courtesy, National Archives of Canada, C-36181)

after a long delay, that Van Rensselaer did not have time to meet him. Evans noted the signs of increased activity on the American shore and that evening tried to convince Brock that an assault on Queenston was imminent. Brock, however, believed that such a move would be only a feint and that the main attack would come against Fort George.[22]

Captain James Dennis of the 49th Foot held command at Queenston, a two-street village with 200 people and forty homes.[23] His grenadier company, numbering about eighty officers and men, occupied the village, being billeted in and around a stone guardhouse at the edge of the lofty bank overlooking the landing at Queenston. The light company of the 49th, under Captain John Williams, was housed in a row of huts on the crest of the Niagara Escarpment, where the Portage Road climbed 300 feet from the landing at the river's edge. To support the regulars, Dennis had about 150 militia from the 1st flank company of the 2nd Regiment of York Militia, the 1st and 2nd flank companies of the 5th Lincoln Militia, and the 1st Lincoln artillery company.

Queenston offered several advantages to the Americans besides being a cosy spot to spend the winter. It was situated at the northern end of the Niagara River gorge where the river widened to 350 yards, and was directly across from the Lower Landing on the American portage route around Niagara Falls. The landing at Queenston had marked the end point for British shipping on Lake Ontario for twenty years and provided access to the Portage Road on the western side of the river, the vital link in the highway along the river bank between Fort George and Fort Erie. At the easternmost end of the Canadian portion of the Niagara Escarpment, Queenston Heights was the "high ground," a perfect location for fortifications and observation of the plain below that stretched seven miles north to Lake Ontario.

The defence of the village, however, presented problems. Queenston sat on a steep fifty-foot bank, which made it difficult to cover the most likely landing site with artillery. After consultation with his gunner officers, Brock had decided early in the summer to place three guns at Queenston. The first was an iron 12-pdr. on a garrison carriage at Vrooman's Point, nearly a mile downstream, which was intended to enfilade any crossing; it was served by the 1st Lincoln Artillery under Lieutenant John Ball. The second gun was either an iron 9-pdr. or a brass 6-pdr., also on a garrison carriage, located in the village beside the grenadiers' stone guardhouse. The defenders had also thrown up a crescent-shaped "redan" battery 200 feet above the river on the Portage Road, where an 18-pdr. long gun and a mortar were placed. These weapons covered the American bank and the river crossing but left dead ground (an area they could not reach) directly below the redan battery. Militiamen served these weapons, under the direction of regular gunners.

In total, Dennis commanded about 325 regulars and militia at Queenston on the night of 12 October. Evans had warned Dennis about the signs of attack, and accordingly that night the guard kept their eyes and ears open for the slightest sound of enemy movement.

By midnight on 12 October about 3,000 American troops had assembled near Lewiston (about 200 remained at Fort Niagara), including units from the Sixth, Thirteenth and Twenty-Third U.S. Infantry Regiments, the Regiment of Artillerists (or First Artillery Regiment), the Second and the Light U.S. Artillery Regiments and the Sixteenth through Twentieth New York Militia Regiments. Major General Van Rensselaer had given command of the initial phase of the operation to Solomon Van Rensselaer, an act which ruffled the feathers of Lieutenant Colonel John Chrystie, whose regular Thirteenth Infantry was assigned as part of the first wave – the resulting dispute was settled when the two officers agreed to share command. Van Rensselaer's militia force appears to have been made up of volunteers from the five New York regiments. Unlike the regulars, American militiamen were required by law to take up arms only when there was a need to quell domestic insurrections, to assist local authorities in settling disturbances they could not manage, or to oppose foreign invasions. Although

they outnumbered the regulars at Lewiston on 12 October, the militia's participation in the intended invasion was problematic as, again by law, they were not
required to fight on foreign soil – including nearby Canada.[24]

The thirteen boats from the abortive attempt on 11 October were now properly equipped, but at most they could accommodate 350 men. As a result it was
decided that Solomon Van Rensselaer would take 150 militia and forty men
from the First Artillery in the first assault wave while Chrystie brought 150 of his
regulars. Lieutenant Colonel John Fenwick of the Light Artillery would command the second wave, comprising the rest of the Thirteenth, some of his own
regiment, and regulars from the Sixth and Twenty-Third Infantry. The rest of the
regulars and militia and some field artillery would follow in subsequent waves.

The American artillery available to support the landing was a pair of 18-pdr.
guns and a small mortar, under the command of Major John Lovett, in a battery
on Lewiston Heights named Fort Gray. On 12 October, however, Lieutenant
Colonel Winfield Scott arrived from Black Rock with a company of his Second
Artillery Regiment and two iron 6-pdr. field guns. Scott was too late to be given
a place in the assault but managed to persuade General Van Rensselaer to let him
position his two guns on the American bank above the embarkation point to
cover the flotilla of landing craft.[25]

The Americans were in motion at 3.30 A.M. on Tuesday, 13 October. Solomon Van Rensselaer went to Chrystie's tent and asked him to lead his men to the
Lower Landing. This spot, at the foot of a deep ravine that ran down to the river's edge directly across from Queenston, marked the beginning of the American
portage route up Lewiston Heights and around the falls of Niagara.[26] From the
outset, however, the plan went wrong, with only the forty gunners, commanded
by First Lieutenant John Gansevoort (Light Artillery) and Second Lieutenant
Samuel B. Rathbone (First Artillery), boarding one of the boats as scheduled.
The militia under Major James Morrison were slow in reaching the pathway and
Chrystie's regulars hurried ahead of them to the boats. When Solomon Van
Rensselaer discovered the Thirteenth Infantry clogging the ravine and about to
fill all the assault craft, he called a halt and nearly ordered the regulars to retrace
their steps so that his militia could take their places first. Realizing this delay
might rob him of the valuable minutes remaining before the first glint of dawn,
however, Van Rensselaer told the regulars to carry on. Ordering Morrison to follow in the second wave, he ran down to join Gansevoort and Rathbone. Finally,
just after 4 A.M., they set out to cross the 350-yard stretch of water to the Canadian shore (see Map Q-2).

The Americans did not get far before the sentries at Queenston spotted them, and the still of the night was broken by the crackle of musketry and the dull booming of artillery. Ten of the American boats, with about 270 men, grounded at the chosen spot "in a perfect sheet of fire" where Solomon Van Rensselaer led them ashore to take cover on the narrow beach under a low bank while the oarsmen headed back for the second wave.[27]

Details of how Captain James Dennis of the 49th Foot directed the defence of Queenston at this point are lacking, although it appears part of his force advanced slowly from the direction of the guardhouse while another detachment took post at the landing to fire at the American right flank. His grenadier company was the mainstay of his defence, and while Brock had once commented that the 49th had "been ten years in this country, drinking rum without bounds," it was still "respectable and apparently ardent for an opportunity to acquire distinction."[28] Dennis, whose career had begun with an ensigncy in the 49th in 1796, had drilled his men rigorously and they met the Americans with steady volleys from their .75 calibre India Pattern flintlock muskets. Because their smooth-bore barrels made them highly inaccurate, muskets were most effective if fired in mass, either by the entire company or by smaller fire-units

Flintlock musket

The flintlock musket was the basic weapon of the infantry of both armies. It relied upon a sharpened piece of flint, locked in the hammer, making sparks against a frizzen (shown here in open position) which ignited the powder in the pan whose fire was communicated, via a minute touch-hole, to the main charge inside the bore. The musket shown here is the U.S. Model 1795 Springfield .69 calibre musket, the main weapon of the American army during the War of 1812. (Photograph, courtesy, Parks Canada)

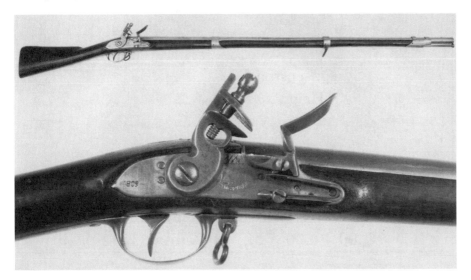

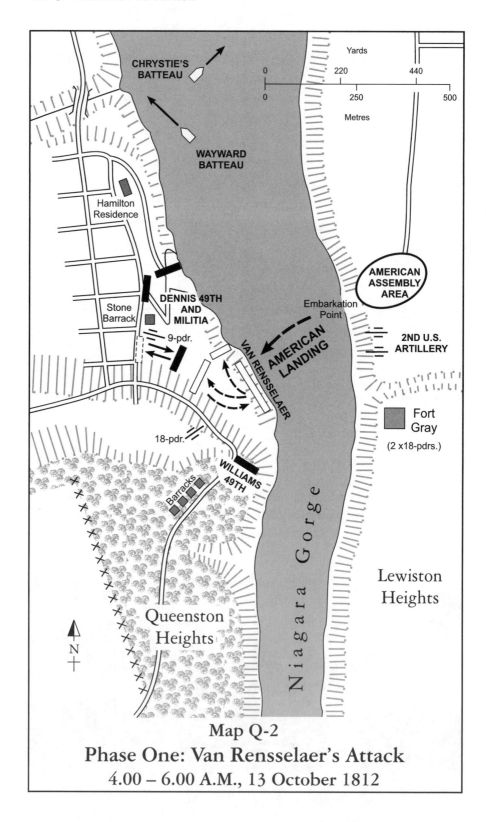

Map Q-2
Phase One: Van Rensselaer's Attack
4.00 – 6.00 A.M., 13 October 1812

called platoons, at a range of 100 yards or less. A properly trained British infantryman could get off four shots in a minute, but such a rate would soon clog the musket with a heavy residue of black powder and too quickly consume his sixty rounds of ammunition. For this reason the rate of fire in battle was usually slower although "a perfect sheet of fire" could seemingly be created by mass volleys. The Canadian militia companies at Queenston, under the command of Captains Samuel Hatt and James Durand of the 5th Lincoln Regiment and John Chisholm of the 2nd York Regiment, were less well trained but they fought bravely alongside the grenadiers to slow the American advance.

With dawn now faintly showing, Solomon Van Rensselaer formed his troops and moved out, scaling the first bank and proceeding up the slope south of the village. Most of his force were drawn from companies of the Thirteenth Infantry commanded by Captains John Wool, Henry B. Armstrong, Richard N. Malcolm and Peter Ogilvie. These officers were all new to the army, having obtained their commissions in the spring of 1812, and the men they commanded were similarly inexperienced. Like the British, they were armed with a smoothbore musket, in their case a .69 calibre weapon. The comparison ended there, however, because the American regular was not nearly as well trained as his British counterpart.

Van Rensselaer called for an advance and the Thirteenth Infantry moved toward Queenston, where "a short, but severe engagement took place, with heavy loss on both sides," Van Rensselaer recollected.[29] Lieutenant John Valleau and Ensign Robert Morris of the Thirteenth Infantry were killed, while Captains Armstrong, Malcolm and Wool suffered wounds. Van Rensselaer was hit no fewer than six times in his lower limbs and borrowed a greatcoat from an aide to cover the stains of blood spreading over his white trousers. During a pause in the fighting, he asked for the whereabouts of Chrystie, but no one could find him. Shortly after this, Van Rensselaer concluded he had succeeded in fighting off the British, who "gave way, and fled toward Queenstown, on our right."[30] Rather than holding his ground or advancing, however, he ordered his men to gather their dead and wounded and fall back to the beach. At this point, as the sky lightened, Major John Lovett, across the river at Fort Gray, concentrated the fire of his two 18-pdrs. on the stone guardhouse. "We raked them severely," Lovett recalled proudly, "and at the eighth shot tumbled up a heap of men, and I believe dismounted the gun."[31]

This bombardment and the fighting took their toll on the British defenders. One gunner was killed and two others wounded, one of them losing his leg to an

18-pdr. shot. Several of the grenadiers of the 49th Foot were killed, while Captain James Dennis and more than a dozen from his company and the 5th Lincoln were wounded. Dennis, however, seems to have maintained his positions at the guardhouse and near the landing waiting for the Americans to renew their attack.

As he waited for his second wave to join him, Solomon Van Rensselaer eased to the ground, urgently repeating his request that someone find Chrystie so that the regular could assume command. Unfortunately the missing colonel was literally "down the creek without a paddle." Through miscalculation or incompetence, the pilot of his boat had failed to follow the main body of the first wave, instead veering downstream with two other craft. An oarlock on the right side of Chrystie's boat then broke, making it difficult to steer and just at that moment all three craft came under musket fire from the defenders and artillery fire from the 12-pdr. gun on Vrooman's Point. As deadly roundshot skipped around them on the surface of the river, Chrystie's pilot steered for the American bank "but, being ordered with severity to make the Canada shore at any point, he made another effort, literally groaning with fear."[32] Concluding he would land too far north to be of any use, Chrystie himself took over the boat and steered it back toward the American shore where it grounded several hundred yards north of the embarkation point.

The men in Chrystie's boat were more fortunate than those in the other two craft. Shot to pieces, they landed just north of Queenston at the mouth of a creek known as Hamilton's Cove and surrendered. As many as five American boats eventually met this fate, "so badly shattered and disabled that the men in them threw down their arms and came on shore merely to deliver themselves up."[33] Lieutenant Colonel John Fenwick was one of them. Assigned to command the second wave, he ended up joining about a hundred Americans who were rounded up and marched to Fort George under guard.

At the lower landing, Chrystie found "a scene of confusion hardly to be described. No person being charged with directing the boats and embarkation or with the government of the boatmen, they forsook their duty."[34] Meanwhile, shots and shells were raining down from the redan battery just below Queenston Heights, inflicting heavy casualties. Chrystie and other officers sought to restore order by withdrawing the men up the ravine and away from the shore.

As Solomon Van Rensselaer grew weak from loss of blood, he came to the conclusion that Chrystie had not crossed the river and turned to his junior officers to save the day. He ordered them "to incline a little to the left, and ascend the heights by the point of the rock, and storm the [redan] battery, which by this time had opened its fire on our place of embarkation."[35] Although Van Rensselaer described the early fighting as brief, nearly two hours had passed since the Americans had landed, because he recollected it was "broad daylight," or past 6.30 A.M., when the detachment of about 150 filed southward along the shore to find a path to the top of the escarpment, following Lieutenant John Gansevoort, who was familiar with the area.

About the same time that Van Rensselaer deployed Gansevoort's party, Major General Isaac Brock arrived at Queenston. A gale was blowing so strongly off Lake Ontario, "one of those uncomfortable, cold, stormy days that … mark the changes of the season," that the sound of the fighting at Queenston was barely audible in Fort George and the nearby village of Niagara; in fact, some residents did not know for hours what was happening to the south.[36] Beacons meant to warn of an attack had been left unlit, but a dragoon shortly arrived at Government House, Brock's residence in the town, with news of the American landing.

Brock was quickly in the saddle and galloping south along the River Road to Queenston. It appears he took no time to consult with his second-in-command, Major General Roger Sheaffe, issuing only a curt order that "no decisive movement by the troops should take place till the enemy's intentions were fully developed."[37] Brock's aides, Lieutenant Colonel John Macdonell from the Canadian militia at York and Captain John B. Glegg of the 49th Foot, also mounted and hurried to catch up with him.

Private soldier, Regiment of Foot, War of 1812
This British private wears a brick red, wool coatee and a black felt shako. The white buff leather cross belts hold his cartridge box (with 60 rounds) on his right hip and his bayonet scabbard on his left. Well trained and well led, the British infantryman was a dangerous opponent for raw and untrained troops as the fighting at Queenston Heights would demonstrate. (Painting by G.A. Embleton, courtesy, Parks Canada)

Brock probably covered the seven miles of muddy road between Niagara village and Queenston in about an hour. On the way he passed the two flank companies of the 3rd York Militia Regiment trotting south toward the sound of the guns and the first group of American prisoners heading north for Fort George.[38] Lieutenant John Beverley Robinson was with the 3rd York and recalled that "the road was lined with miserable wretches, suffering under wounds of all descriptions and crawling to our houses for protection and comfort."[39] There were also civilian refugees from Queenston fleeing the action, carrying blankets and food they had hurriedly grabbed. Other residents of the village, such as Laura Secord, had ventured toward the scene of the fighting to aid the wounded — Secord found her husband, James, gravely wounded and brought him to safety.

As Brock entered the outskirts of Queenston, there was a lull in the exchange of musketry, though the artillery continued to boom. Four boatloads of enemy troops could be seen setting out from the American shore, prompting the order, communicated by bugle, for the light company of the 49th, under Captain John Williams, to come down from its post at the edge of the heights. Whether Brock

gave this order or Dennis did before the general arrived is not known, but the decision had significant consequences, because it uncovered the British right flank at the very moment that the American detachment led by Gansevoort reached the top of a pathway it had found up the gorge wall to the heights.

Captain John Wool, Thirteenth Infantry, at twenty-eight the oldest officer present, assumed command of the party. He found himself in a copse of oak trees traversed by the Portage Road near the row of huts which was the billet of the 49th

United States infantry, c. 1812
American infantryman wearing the dark blue uniform current at the outbreak of the war. The regulars who fought at Queenston Heights had only been in service for a few months. (Painting by Don Troiani, courtesy, Department of National Defence)

The Royal Artillery

The Royal Artillery was an elite corps in every sense of the word. Its officers were better educated than their infantry counterparts and the higher pay of the enlisted men attracted the best quality recruits. RA gunners were usually larger, stronger and more intelligent than their infantry comrades. (Courtesy, Parks Canada)

light company.[40] Wool deployed the first men to reach the summit as cover for the others who were still struggling up the narrow path that rose nearly 300 feet from the river bank. When close to 150 men had arrived, Wool formed them up and quietly advanced through the wood toward the edge of the Escarpment, where he saw the redan battery below in a cleared area (see Map Q-3).

Exact details about Brock's movements after reaching Queenston are not recorded, except for one account penned by Lieutenant William Hamilton Merritt of the Provincial Light Dragoons, who was not then in the village. Merritt wrote that the general, watching the action from horseback and "perceiving our shells [were] not reaching the enemy's batteries," rode up to the redan battery to direct the gunners to use more powder and longer fuses. According to Merritt, Brock's advice was well taken because soon "the mortar threw one or two [shells] with great effect."[41]

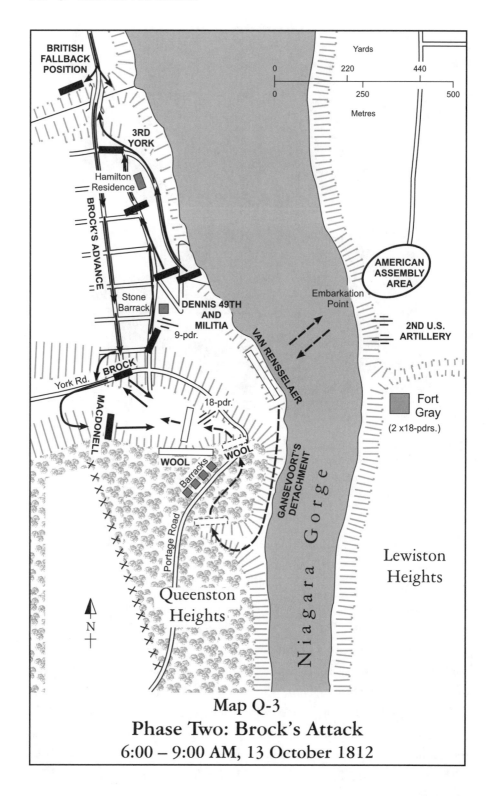

BRITISH FALLBACK POSITION

3RD YORK

Hamilton Residence

BROCK'S ADVANCE

Stone Barrack

DENNIS 49TH AND MILITIA
9-pdr.

York Rd.

BROCK

MACDONELL

18-pdr.

WOOL

WOOL

Barracks

Portage Road

VAN RENSSELAER

GANSEVOORT'S DETACHMENT

Niagara Gorge

Queenston Heights

Embarkation Point

AMERICAN ASSEMBLY AREA

2ND U.S. ARTILLERY

Fort Gray
(2 x18-pdrs.)

Lewiston Heights

Yards

0   220   440

0   250   500

Metres

N

Map Q-3
Phase Two: Brock's Attack
6:00 – 9:00 AM, 13 October 1812

If true, this advantage was abruptly nullified when Wool moved out from the trees at the edge of the escarpment and led his infantry down on the battery. In a mad rush the surprised British gunners abandoned their ordnance and scampered to safety. Wool placed some men at the battery and the rest in a line above it and beside it facing the village. They then began "an incessant and disorderly fire of musquetry" on the enemy in Queenston below, and the British pulled back from their advanced positions, "retiring to the north end of the village on the Niagara road."[42]

It was now about 7.30 A.M. and daylight. Queenston had become a no-man's land, with the Americans in possession of the high ground and the British reorganizing themselves on the other side of the deep ravine at Hamilton's Cove that marked the northern edge of the settlement. Still on horseback and by now attended by Macdonell and Glegg, Brock assessed the situation and decided to attack the Americans before they could consolidate their position. To that end, he gathered up a party of soldiers and at a gallop led them up the main street of Queenston to the foot of the Portage Road. There were barely fifty men with him, mainly members of the 49th light company and some militia, an indication of how the fighting had reduced the British numbers. Brock dismounted by a stone wall and, after a brief pause, scaled it to climb the slope, waving his sword and urging the others to follow him in an attack on the redan battery.

Fifteen-year-old George Jarvis, a resident of York (modern Toronto) who had enlisted as a gentleman volunteer with the 49th Foot, found himself near Brock at that moment. Jarvis remembered that "the top of the mountain and a great portion of its side was thickly covered with trees."[43] The vegetation did not provide much cover for the British advance, however, and Wool's waiting troops opened up at them. The British moved upward "at double quick time," recalled Jarvis, "in the very teeth of a sharp fire from the enemy's riflemen." At the head of his men, wearing a general officer's plumed and cocked hat and a red coat with bullion epaulettes, Brock made a distinctive target.

One version of what happened next was recounted by Robert Walcot, an American gunner who had crossed in Solomon Van Rensselaer's boat. Walcot's post was at the captured 18-pdr., but, wanting to see more closely what was going on, he moved forward to the line of infantrymen and borrowed a musket from an infantryman. Walcot loaded it with two balls and then "went to the edge of the line and, taking aim, fired at Brock. His face was partly turned to the troops as I fired. He fell almost instantly and I hurried back to my post."[44]

George Jarvis saw it this way: "ere long he [Brock] was singled out by one of them, who, coming forward, took deliberate aim and fired; several of the men noticed the action and fired – but too late – and our gallant General fell on his left side, within a few feet of where I stood. Running up to him I enquired, 'Are you much hurt, Sir?' He placed his hand on his breast and made no reply, and slowly sunk down."[45]

Horror-stricken, the British gathered around their fallen general until an officer brought them back to reality and ordered Brock carried off the field. Command now passed to twenty-eight-year-old Lieutenant Colonel John Macdonell, who, following consultation with Williams and other officers, decided to try an assault on Wool's left flank from the top of the escarpment. As Captain Glegg, Brock's other aide, directed the party that removed Brock's body to a building in the village, Macdonell withdrew the remainder of the men from the slope, marched a short distance west on the York Road and then moved up the hillside again.[46]

By this time, the two flank companies of the 3rd York, under the command of Captains Duncan Cameron and Stephen Heward, which Brock had passed, had arrived at the northern part of the village. They were ordered to occupy the grounds of the Hamilton residence, an impressive two-storey stone structure above Hamilton Cove, in order to fire on any American boats that were still crossing, but their presence drew the attention of Lovett's American gunners in Fort Gray. A roundshot took off the leg of militia Private Andrew Kelly and ripped the calf muscle from one of Private Thomas Major's limbs. The militia withdrew to safety, but then an order came to join Macdonell's attack. Cameron and Heward, with Lieutenants Robinson and Archibald McLean, obeyed, but very few of their men seem to have followed them as they ran through the village, dodging shots from Fort Gray before turning up the York Road.[47]

Fewer than seventy men eventually gathered around Macdonell near the upper edge of the escarpment. Since the American fire "was too hot to admit of delay," he quickly deployed his force in a line stretching down the hill and ordered the advance on the American position.[48] Meanwhile, more Americans had scaled the gorge path and Captain Wool used them to reinforce his original line, which had almost used up its ammunition. The Americans, "covered by bushes and logs, were in no kind of order and were three or four hundred in number … and at about 30 yards distance fired," remembered Lieutenant John B. Robinson of the 3rd York.[49] A fierce firefight took place as the British moved toward the redan battery, led by Macdonell who remained mounted – and then disaster struck.

Lieutenant Colonel John Macdonell (1785-1812)
Born in Scotland, Macdonell came to Upper Canada in 1792. He moved to York in
1803 to study law and became the attorney-general of the province in 1811. He was
described by Anne Powell, mother of the young woman whose hand Macdonell
ardently pursued, as "the flower of our youth in talents and manners." (Courtesy,
Toronto Reference Library, T-17053)

A bullet struck Macdonell's horse and when it wheeled about in pain, its
rider received a musket ball in the back that passed through his abdomen. Macdonell tumbled to the ground. Then Captain John Williams of the light company of the 49th went down with a head wound, his scalp so badly lacerated that
everyone thought him dead. Captain Duncan Cameron of the 3rd York ran forward to assist Macdonell, but a ball glanced off his arm and he stumbled, where-
upon Lieutenant Archibald McLean of the same unit tried to drag both men
clear and was shot in the thigh. These three officers struggled off the field, followed by a dazed Williams and most of their men. When young George Jarvis
turned to retreat, he discovered that he and five other regulars plus fifteen militiamen had been outflanked by the Americans – they threw down their weapons
and surrendered.

It could not have been much past 8 A.M. when the Americans took control of
the battlefield. Though only a handful of boats were still in service, they moved
reinforcements steadily across the river, returning with wounded, among them
Solomon Van Rensselaer and John Wool.

The remainder of the Thirteenth Infantry landed next on the Canadian
bank, followed by companies from the Sixth, Twenty-Third and the Light
Artillery. Captain James Gibson of the last unit managed to get an iron 6-pdr.
field gun, and its ammunition wagon and accoutrements, over the river and up
the hill to a position facing Queenston. The largest contingents of New York militia which crossed at this time belonged to the Sixteenth, Seventeenth and
Eighteenth Regiments, with smaller numbers coming from the Nineteenth and
Twentieth. In all, probably not more than 500 militia foreswore their constitutional rights and crossed to Canada, which meant that about 1,800 of their comrades chose to stand on those same rights and remain in the United States. At its
peak strength, the invading American force numbered about 1,300 regulars and
militia.[50]

Lieutenant Colonel John Chrystie of the Thirteenth Infantry finally got over the river and reached the heights not long after the British counterattacks had been beaten off. He assumed command from Captain John Machesney of the Sixth Infantry, who had taken over from Wool when that officer was evacuated after being wounded. Chrystie ordered the British and Canadian prisoners removed to the United States. He then consolidated his position along the perimeter of the oak woods on top the escarpment by maintaining Wool's original line facing north to the village and setting up a second line behind a split-rail fence along the margin of Isaac Phelps's 200-yard-wide cultivated field lying west of the woods. A militia rifle company was deployed on the southern edge of the wood, where the Portage Road angled toward Chippawa. The captured 18-pdr. gun in the redan battery would have been of significant use to Chrystie, but it was unserviceable — the later consensus was that an American had jammed a gunner's spike into the touch hole during Macdonell's attack, rendering the weapon inoperable, to prevent the British from making use of the piece if they managed to recapture it.[51] None of Chrystie's men, it seems, had the knowledge or the tools to unblock the gun which, along with its attendant mortar, remained idle for the rest of the battle.

Brigadier General William Wadsworth, the commanding officer of the Seventh Brigade of New York militia (which included the Eighteenth to Twentieth Regiments), now appeared and asked Chrystie to return to Lewiston and apprise Major General Van Rensselaer of the situation. Curiously, General Van Rensselaer had been absent not only from the embarkation point but also from the battlefield; his time was apparently taken up with expediting the transfer of ammunition across the river and urging the reluctant New York militia on the far bank to join their comrades fighting on Canadian soil. Chrystie crossed the river, found the commanding general on a road half a mile from the river, and made his report. He was told that Van Rensselaer had sent Lieutenant Colonel Winfield Scott to assist Wadsworth on the far shore with an engineer, Captain Joseph Totten, who was to supervise the construction of defensive positions. Van Rensselaer also informed Chrystie that he intended to cross himself. Chrystie did not wait to accompany him. Hearing renewed musketry on the heights over the river, he rushed back to the beach, only to encounter a well-equipped militia company just turning away from the boats. They had been preparing to board when this new firing broke out and the noise reminding them of their legal rights, they resolved to remain in American territory and defend the republic.

Though driven from Queenston, the British were by no means beaten. Reinforcements, dispatched from Fort George by Sheaffe not long after Brock had galloped off, were on the way. The first to set out was a detachment of thirty gunners of the Royal Artillery under Captain William Holcroft with two brass 6-pdr. field guns and a 5.5 inch howitzer. To provide Holcroft's gunners with infantry support, Sheaffe had ordered the light company of the 41st Foot, under Captain William Derenzy, to accompany them. Sheaffe had also met with Captain John Norton of the Indian Department, who agreed to take his warriors to Queenston. Norton's command consisted of 300 men from the Grand River territory representing fourteen different nations: the Mohawks, Oneidas, Onondagas, Cayugas, Senecas, Tuscaroras, Nanticokes, Tutelos, Delawares, Creeks, Cherokees, Moravian Delawares, Munseys and Chippawas. They had been camping at Niagara village since September under their war chief, Norton, the fifty-two-year-old son of a Cherokee father and Scots mother who was the protégé of Chief Joseph Brant.[52]

Sheaffe himself stayed at Fort George, watching the lake for signs of an American landing. Nothing was seen, although the American batteries at Fort Niagara, under the command of Captain Nathan Leonard of the First Artillery, opened fire on the town and fort, hurling hot shot that set buildings aflame and reduced the courthouse, jail and some barracks to ashes. The British guns responded in turn and silenced the Americans around mid-morning. By this time a dragoon had brought word that Brock was dead, so Sheaffe set out for Queenston, leaving Major Thomas Evans in command at Niagara village. Later in the day the American gunners in Fort Niagara renewed their bombardment, but under Evans's direction the British guns forced them to leave their weapons and seek cover.[53]

John Norton's warriors were still on the road to Queenston when Sheaffe galloped by. Soon they met American prisoners marching for Fort George under guard, learned of Brock's death and heard a rumour that the enemy was flanking them by a route through the forest on the west side of the road. Believing this unlikely, Norton nonetheless led his men into the woods, where they came upon militia fleeing the fighting, who warned of six thousand enemies on the heights. Norton divided his warriors into a number of separate detachments and they threaded their way through the dense forest and finally emerged onto the York Road a mile or more west of Queenston (see Map Q-4). Here Norton was disappointed to discover that only eighty men of his command were still with him; the others, "filled with anxiety for the safety of their families," had deserted.

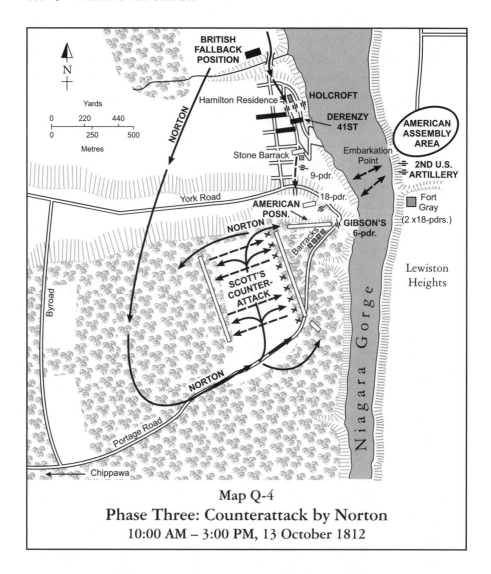

Map Q-4
Phase Three: Counterattack by Norton
10:00 AM – 3:00 PM, 13 October 1812

Nevertheless, those warriors present "burned with indignation," as Norton re-called, "and panted to come in contact with the insolent Invaders." "Comrades and Brothers," he told his eighty stalwarts, "We have found what we came for ... there they are – it remains only to fight."[54]

Under cover of the trees, Norton's party climbed the escarpment and moved south until it came to the upper stretch of the Portage Road. Turning north to approach the Americans from the rear, the warriors encountered a British dragoon who had escaped from the enemy and a mounted militiaman, both of whom rode for Chippawa to hurry on reinforcements from that place. They proceeded a little farther until the ploughed field belonging to farmer Phelps opened on their left and revealed Americans in the copse overlooking the river.

"We doubled our pace to come up with them," recorded Norton. "They fired and ran, and fired again."[55]

These Americans were the riflemen deployed by Chrystie to the south of the main position. They stood their ground briefly and then withdrew. Lieutenant Jared Willson of the militia rifle unit, who participated in this action, later recalled that the British "savages, greedy for plunder, and thirsting for blood pursued us closely, firing and yelling, in a most frightful manner ... I expected every moment to be made a 'cold Yanky' as the soldiers say."[56] The sight of their comrades retreating from Norton's screaming warriors unsettled the men in the second American line stationed behind the split-rail fence. Some men at the south end turned to run, but Lieutenant Colonel Winfield Scott, who by then had assumed command at Wadsworth's request, rallied them "by storming and a free use of the [flat of the] sword," as he recalled, and "brought his whole line to face the enemy."[57] The Americans fired a series of volleys, but the warriors ducked into a hollow that crossed the field and ran more or less unscathed to the northern edge of the Escarpment, where they hid among the trees and tangled undergrowth.

At this point, Norton remembered hearing "Shrapnel Shells fired from a Field Piece," which he at the time mistook for the sound of musket balls clattering among the trees as if the British infantry was advancing, firing by platoons.

Captain John Norton, or the Snipe, War Chief of the Mohawks
The son of a Cherokee father and a Scots mother, Norton first came to Canada as a private in the 65th Foot in 1785. He left the army three years later and, after brief careers as a school master and fur trader, joined the Indian Department at Niagara in 1794, where he became an interpreter for Chief Joseph Brant. (Oil portrait by Thomas Philips, reproduced by gracious permission of the Duke of Northumberland)

Native warrior

This 1804 watercolour shows a Mohawk warrior as he might have appeared in October 1812. This man has painted his face red and black, the favoured colours for battle. Although they were mercurial allies, the presence of aboriginal fighters at Queenston Heights was a positive asset for the British as they represented a psychological threat out of all proportion to their numbers. (Watercolour by Sempronius Stretton, National Archives of Canada, C-14827)

The shrapnel came from the two 6-pdrs. of Captain Holcroft's detachment which had just gone into action from its position at the Hamilton property. Captain William Derenzy deployed his light infantry company of the 41st Foot in a protective screen beyond the Hamilton property. American soldiers still lurking in the village (or plundering as was alleged by some) shortly fled to Scott's position on the northern edge of the Escarpment. Holcroft's gunners, assisted by some militia, including Robert Hamilton, a captain of the Provincial Light Dragoons, kept up a steady fire on the Escarpment and the boats crossing the river. They also duelled with the two 6-pdr. field pieces positioned by Scott above the embarkation point and claimed to silence them several times.[58]

Thinking the British regular troops were going to mount a frontal attack on the Escarpment, Norton moved to distract the Americans. Splitting his force into several small groups, he rushed along the edge of the hill "with more forwardness than our small numbers should otherwise have authorized. ... The Foe raged like a Hive of Bees disturbed."[59] But his warriors, "darting forward and swiftly," changed their firing positions after each round, hid behind trees or lay on the ground, or withdrew rapidly when the Americans seemed about ready to attack. Emboldened, one group of twenty warriors moved onto Phelps's field and threatened the very centre of the American force along the split-rail fence. Scott ordered a counterattack, and regulars and militia climbed over the fence and chased the Indians back across the field, killing two chiefs and a warrior and wounding numerous others. The native fighters dragged their wounded into the trees on the western side of Phelps's field, followed by the Americans, but a party led by Norton had already circled and began to fire on the Americans from the flank. "The Indians here presented no object for a charge," John Chrystie remembered, and "while their fire was bloody ours produced a comparatively small effect."[60] Scott ordered a withdrawal back across the field to the relative safety of the fence on the eastern side. Some of Norton's party retreated in the opposite direction, having had enough of fighting, but their war chief and a few men returned to annoy the Americans. Other small groups of warriors also kept up their attacks, their fire "less general and fatal," as Chrystie remarked, "but it was never intermitted during the remainder of the day."[61]

Badgered from the north by the Royal Artillery and from the west and south by Norton's native fighters, the Americans held their position on the Heights and advanced no farther. Winfield Scott sent repeated requests for ammunition and reinforcements but by this time few on the American bank were willing to cross the river. The sight of the wounded being carried ashore and the unmistakable shrieks and yelps of what Jared Willson called "the inhuman foe" depleted their courage. Willson condemned the militia who refused to cross as "poor, ignoble, base-born wretches."[62]

Among the most wretched was Major General Stephen Van Rensselaer. He had made his way to Queenston Heights near the beginning of Norton's attack but had not taken part in the fighting. Lovett had accompanied him only to be sent right back to urge the reluctant militia on the American side to cross the river. After standing on the edge of the hilltop and seeing no troops boarding on the American shore, Van Rensselaer worked his way back to the beach and boarded a boat. Just before he pushed off, men came scurrying out of the nearby bushes and leapt on board. A new evil had struck the American force – their numbers were shrinking as individuals left their posts and skulked at the river's edge looking for the first opportunity to return to the safety of the republic.

Just past noon the firing died away and the senior American officers gathered on the crest of the heights intently watching the signs of activity north of Queenston. The sky had cleared, and they could see the glimmer of sunlight reflecting off the shako plates and bayonets of a column of red-coated infantry marching toward them.

Major General Roger Sheaffe had now assumed command at Queenston. In the eyes of many he was markedly inferior to Isaac Brock. The fact that he had been born in Boston and spent his early years under American influence is said to have spawned prejudice among his English contemporaries, and he also had a reputation as a martinet. He and Brock served together for many years in the

49th Foot, and Brock both praised Sheaffe, saying "no man understands the duties of his profession better," and criticized him for having "little knowledge of mankind."[63]

On 13 October, however, Roger Hale Sheaffe demonstrated a sound knowledge of tactics and more patience than his late superior. His early decision to order the artillery, light infantry and warriors to Queenston had proved valuable and, shortly after reaching the village himself and assessing the situation, he sent a message to Evans at Fort George to bring up the reserve. This consisted of 140 men of the 41st Foot under Lieutenant Angus McIntyre, two brass 3-pdr. guns in charge of Lieutenant William L. Crowther, 41st Foot, and about 130 militia from five separate units under the command of Captain James Crooks of the 1st Lincoln Militia. Later, the few remaining regulars in the fort and some militia, including members of the Coloured Company (a small collection of black volunteers), moved south to Queenston. Sheaffe also ordered Lieutenant William Hamilton Merritt of the Provincial Dragoons to ride hard to Chippawa and summon Captain Richard Bullock's grenadier company of the 41st Foot and the flank companies of the 2nd Lincoln Militia stationed there, to make a forced march for Queenston.

Like most people living in the village of Niagara, Captain James Crooks was unaware of the intensity of the fighting seven miles to the south and surmised "that the attack at Queenston was a mere ruse de guerre," but shortly after leaving the fort with his detachment of the 1st Lincoln, he heard that Brock had been killed and that the enemy was in the surrounding woods. Crooks's men marched past the militia gunners who had remained at the batteries along the river, and at Brown's Point two officers from the 3rd York warned him against going further. One "said I was mad," Crooks remembered, "and that if I proceeded we would all be taken prisoners, as our people" at Queenston "had been completely routed." Crooks ordered his men to load their muskets and hurried on, until, after nearly two hours of marching, his Lincolns arrived near Vrooman's Point where the Durham family farm was located and which had taken on the appearance of a military camp. Here he paused and, receiving complaints from his men that they were hungry, he permitted them to dig up a nearby field of potatoes, which they soon had boiling in the Durham's kitchen.

Around noon Sheaffe began forming up to attack. His column consisted of McIntyre's regulars from the 41st Foot and Crooks's Lincoln units, elements of Derenzy's 41st light infantry company and some of the militia gunners at Vrooman's Point under Lieutenant John Ball. The column left Durham's and cut

Major General Sir Roger Hale Sheaffe (1763-1851)

Born in Boston, Sheaffe lost his father, the deputy collector for customs, at the age of eight. The future Duke of Northumberland, who resided in the boarding house run by Sheaffe's mother, became the boy's patron, first sending him to sea as a midshipman and then to England to Lewis Lochee's military academy, where he was a classmate of George Prevost. (Courtesy, National Archives of Canada, C-111307)

across the fields in a southwesterly direction, taking down the split-rail fences as it proceeded. Along the way Dennis of the 49th Foot joined with a party of stragglers he had collected. Dennis had been wounded early in the morning and "appeared much exhausted yet he would not leave the field."[64] The guns at Fort Gray across the river fired at them, but the shots ploughed into muddy ground far short of the British as they tramped toward the Escarpment.

Sheaffe reached the York Road about one and a half miles west of Queenston and ascended the Escarpment up a narrow byroad, heading south as Norton had done, until he reached the Portage Road. It was now about 2.00 P.M. He next turned northeast to follow the Portage Road toward the American position on the Heights, and Phelps's field soon appeared on the left, with the woods in which the Americans were positioned right ahead. Also visible through the trees was Fort Gray, and Lovett's gunners again brought the column in the road under fire but "did no harm," noted Captain Crooks, "the shot flying over us as we lay on the ground."[65] Sheaffe now called a halt to wait for the troops from Chippawa to arrive.

While the British were moving in for the attack, Major General Van Rensselaer managed to order over one last boat with ammunition, followed by a note advising Wadsworth that he would send as many boats as he could find and cover a retreat but that Wadsworth should "govern himself according to circumstances under his more immediate view."[66] On Queenston Heights, Wadsworth, Scott and Chrystie were acutely aware that their numbers were falling below 500 as more and more men left the ranks. They discussed their alternatives, with

Fort George from Fort Niagara

Completed in the 1790s, Fort George dominated the American Fort Niagara across the river. While the two armies clashed at Queenston on 13 October, the two forts fought an artillery duel that ended in a British triumph. (Painting by Edward Walsh, National Archives of Canada, C-000026)

Lieutenant Colonel Thompson Mead of the Seventeenth New York Militia arguing "to make a vigorous effort to maintain the ground for which so many of our brave men had bled."[67] Winfield Scott recalled that "the disgrace of Hull's recent surrender was deeply felt ... [and we] resolved, though with but little hope of success, to sustain the shock of the enemy, when, if beaten, the survivors might seek an escape by means of the promised boats."[68] Minutes ticked by, the American senior officers kept conferring, but no firm decision was made about what to do.

Just before 3 P.M. Sheaffe saw a column marching north up the Portage Road from the direction of Chippawa – the flank companies of the 2nd Lincoln Militia commanded by Lieutenant Colonel Thomas Clark, who had been joined by Joseph Willcocks, a well-known local politician and constant critic of the British Crown. When this reinforcement arrived, Sheaffe deployed for the attack, which as Crooks recalled "was done by advancing in line from the left, the light company of the 49th Regiment leading till fairly in front of the Yankees."[69] In this way the general sent the main part of his brigade, about 200 regulars, across the western edge of Phelps's field to its centre, followed by the militia. He also ordered McIntyre's light infantry company of the 41st commanded with Norton's warriors, who had themselves been recently joined by a party of Cayugas from their camp near Fort George, to repeat Norton's previous movements along the slope of the Escarpment. At 3 P.M. as the warriors raised their war cries to full pitch, the "order came for the Regulars to front and attack." The action was opened by the fire of Lieutenant Crowther's two 3-pdrs., probably unlimbered on Portage Road (see Map Q-5).[70]

Just at that point the American commanders decided to withdraw. To do so, it would be necessary to cover the road down the Escarpment so it could be used

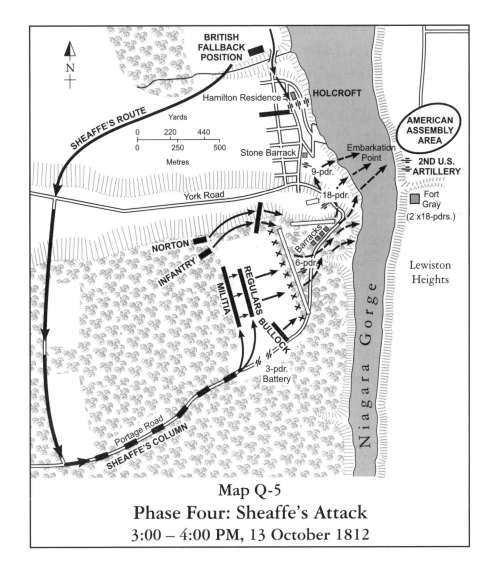

Map Q-5
Phase Four: Sheaffe's Attack
3:00 – 4:00 PM, 13 October 1812

as an escape route to the landing place, where a last stand could be made while an embarkation took place. As the British regulars moved steadily towards them across Phelps's field, the Americans fired a volley from behind the split-rail fence and then began to withdraw unit by unit, but the movement became confused as some of the troops panicked, and then chaos broke out as Norton and McIntyre's men burst in from the right.

According to James Crooks, the British advance was also confused. No instructions had been given for the militia to advance like the regulars, so they kept moving northward until ordered to halt. Crooks took the opportunity to have his men "front and attack," and he then led them toward the woods "and at double quick we soon encountered the enemy."[71] At almost the same time, Bullock arrived with 150 men of the 41st from Chippawa, raising Sheaffe's numbers to 800. They joined in the fighting, which had become one continuous but widespread skirmish. "The musketry made such a noise I heard no order, but as others moved we all followed," recollected Private William Woodruff of the 1st Lincoln Regiment. "As the wind blew from the enemy we had their smoke and ours in our faces," he added, remembering how he emerged from the smoke to find himself staring down the muzzle of the abandoned American 6-pdr., which had been turned to face the British attack.[72] From the safety of Fort Gray on Lewiston Heights, Major John Lovett watched a "furious, obstinate and tremendous conflict" that seemed to cause the "mountains" to "shake beneath the stride of musketry."[73] "I have been in many hail storms," remembered Crooks, "but never in one when the stones flew so thick as the bullets on this occasion."[74]

The British crossed the fence and pushed in the last of the American defenders. A mêlée ensued as most of the Americans fled down the road to Queenston

Winfield Scott (1786-1866)
Queenston was Scott's first battle and he ended it as a prisoner of war. From this inauspicious start, he went on to greater things, ending the war as a 27-year-old major general. Scott remained in service until 1861 and dominated the U.S. Army for nearly half a century. (*Portfolio Magazine*, 1816)

and the river, while a few ran straight off the edge of the cliff, falling to their deaths 300 feet below. Norton's warriors raced wildly among their enemy looking for trophies; Crooks watched one unlucky Canadian, without a uniform as most militiamen were, fall beneath a tomahawk. Winfield Scott came within a hair's breadth of meeting the same end but was rescued by John Beverley Robinson, who escorted him to Sheaffe.

It ended quickly. A half hour or so after the first shot of the attack on the American position, a bugle sounded to cease firing, but it still took time to regain order on the mountainside as British regulars and Canadian militia alike tried to pick off the dozens of Americans swimming across the river. "The English were infuriated because of the death of Brock and showed no mercy," recollected the man who claimed to have shot him, Private Robert Walcot of the First Artillery. "With several others I reached the river and swam across. While swimming three of our party were shot dead and I was wounded in the back of the neck."[75]

The firing gradually died away and the victory was complete when Wadsworth and Scott surrendered their swords to Sheaffe. Dazed, fatigued and famished as the victors were, there was no time for rest because the sun was sinking and the battlefield had to be secured. The prisoners were marched to Niagara, mixed with wagons full of wounded. After dark, Lieutenant Archibald McLean left the house where his thigh wound had been dressed and hitched a ride on a wagon driven by elderly Isaac Swayze. To his horror, McLean realized that the wagon's burden was the body of Isaac Brock, "him whom I had seen in the morning in full health and strength hastening to the scene of Action to meet the Enemies of his country."[76]

The battle of Queenston Heights had lasted about thirteen hours and the losses were heavy on both sides. Much uncertainty prevailed about the American casualties – Stephen Van Rensselaer thought it impossible to provide "a precise account" and estimated that sixty of his officers and men had been killed, 170 wounded and 746 others captured.[77] John Lovett repeated these figures, though others speculated that as many as 500 had been killed, many of them disappearing in the river during the early-morning crossing and the late-afternoon flight to safety. An unofficial tabulation put the figures at 57 regulars and 28 militia dead, 89 regulars and 57 militia wounded. The official casualty lists revealed that the Sixth and Thirteenth U.S. Infantry and the Sixteenth and Seventeenth New York Militia had suffered the most. On the day after the battle,

Van Rensselaer sent a note over the river to ask that his dead be returned, but the efficient Captain James Dennis had already sent his men to inter any bodies they could find. The British ended up with 925 prisoners (436 regulars and 489 militia, of whom 120 were said to be wounded), some of whom were, the following day, flushed out of the vegetation along the gorge where they had hidden to avoid Norton's warriors. All the militia and some of the regulars were paroled or exchanged, and only a small number of regular prisoners were transported to Quebec for confinement.[78]

British casualties were calculated more precisely: 13 dead, 78 wounded and 21 captured, with some of the wounded, such as John Macdonell, dying that night or in the following weeks. The 49th Foot had borne the brunt of the fighting, losing 8 dead, 33 wounded and 6 captured. Next came the various York militia units, who lost 2 dead, 17 wounded and 5 captured, followed by the Lincoln militia with 15 wounded and 10 captured. At least five of Norton's party were killed, but no count of the wounded was made. It had been a hard-fought, successful victory, but Brock's death invoked a gloom that overshadowed any celebration. He was buried with Macdonell on 16 October in the north bastion of Fort George in a ceremony attended by thousands and honoured by salutes from the American batteries across the river.[79]

British spoils from the battle included a stand of colours from a New York militia regiment and an iron 6-pdr. field gun, with its ammunition wagon, accoutrements and two roundshot and fourteen canister rounds, an indication that the weapon had fired more than fifty rounds. Nearly 6,000 rounds of musket cartridges were retrieved, but only 435 muskets and 380 bayonets and half as many cartridge boxes. The British ordnance officers admitted that the weapons had been distributed quickly to the militia after the action, though it is probable that many were removed from the field long before any officials could count them.[80]

A three-day armistice negotiated by Sheaffe and Van Rensselaer was to have ended hours after Brock's funeral, but lasted until 20 November. Stephen Van Rensselaer resigned his command on 20 October, expressing his "extreme mortification at surrendering a victory which had been gallantly won." He blamed his defeat on the fact "that the great body of the militia" could not "be prevailed upon to cross the river."[81] Many criticized his leadership, including Lieutenant Colonel Mead of the Seventeenth New York Militia, who wrote that "the plan was not sufficiently matured" to provide adequate boats or ammunition while "the place selected for the attack was perhaps the most difficult for effecting an landing."[82] For his part, Solomon Van Rensselaer pointed the finger at Chrystie, who he claimed actually ordered his boat and others to turn away from the initial landing. "His return dampened the hitherto irrepressible ardour of the militia," lamented Van Rensselaer.[83] Jared Willson, in his turn, branded Solomon Van Rensselaer as an "ambitious creature" who was "allured by the prospects of acquiring unfading Laurels" but added that Stephen Van Rensselaer was "answerable for our ill success." "Thus has the ambition of one man and the folly of another brought disgrace upon our country" was his feeling on the matter.[84] The *New York Evening Post*, a pro-Federalist newspaper, placed the blame in Washington, asking, "What excuse can be framed for an administration that thus sends a handful of brave and worthy men into a battle, under the delusive expectation of being reinforced?"[85]

Stephen Van Rensselaer returned home and avoided a formal court of inquiry into his conduct, but the court of public opinion judged him, and the next spring Daniel Tompkins was reelected as governor. Instead of having his questionable behaviour examined, Brigadier General Alexander Smyth was rewarded with the command of the Niagara frontier, but his attempts to cross the river in November failed miserably and he, in his turn, rode away from war with a greatly diminished reputation.

The defeat at Queenston combined with Hull's disaster at Detroit to cost Secretary of War William Eustis his position. It was assumed by John Armstrong whose twenty-year-old-son, Henry, had commanded a company of the Thirteenth Regiment during the action. The disaster demonstrated that the American regulars were not able to face a well-trained opponent and until they received better leadership and training. The army's performance improved somewhat in 1813, but it was not until 1814, when Winfield Scott, by then a brigadier general, returned to the Niagara to train Major General Jacob Brown's division, that the American regular was able to fight his British counterpart on equal terms. Queenston was Scott's first action and both he and Captain John Wool would benefit from that experience, for they went on to long and successful careers in the United States Army.

Sir George Prevost, the commander-in-chief of British North America, proudly announced "the brilliant victory achieved on the 13th instant" in a published general order and appointed Sheaffe to replace Brock in Upper Canada.[86] Months later Sheaffe learned that he had been granted a baronetcy by the Crown, but his appointment in Upper Canada was fraught with troubles and ended miserably after he relinquished the provincial capital at York to the enemy in April 1813. For their part in the action at Queenston Heights, Captains

Dennis, Williams, Holcroft and Derenzy all received brevet promotions to major. Dennis enjoyed a long and successful career, rising to major general before his death in 1855. The Canadian militia were exultant about the role they had played standing in the front line of the fight to defend Canada. John Beverley Robinson, Archibald McLean, James Crooks, William Hamilton Merritt and even young George Jarvis would go on to become leaders in the commercial and political circles of Upper Canada.

For the Americans the battle of Queenston Heights ended up by being "tinged with dishonour" as Stephen Van Rensselaer had feared, while for their opponents it was epitomized as a high point in the valiant struggle to preserve Canada waged by the thin red line of British regulars, supported on many occasions by the militia, throughout the War of 1812.

Brock's Monument

Work on the first monument to Brock (135 feet high), shown here, was begun in 1824 and completed in 1827, but a bomb set off by anti-British dissidents in 1840 so badly damaged the column that a more impressive tower (185 feet high) was built between 1853 and 1856. It was officially inaugurated on 13 October 1859. (Courtesy, Ontario Archives, 6326 S8495)

British infantry advance

Modern re-enactors portray a small company of the 41st Foot advancing in line with its Colours. A captain marches in the centre of the line with his sword raised. (Photograph by Robert Malcomson)

Queenston Heights Today

The village of Queenston and the battlefield are situated just north of the Queenston-Lewiston Bridge, one of the major border crossings along the Niagara River and the junction between Ontario Highway 405 in Ontario and New York State Highway 190. To get to Queenston Heights from Toronto, travel via the Queen Elizabeth Way (QEW) to Highway 405 (one mile east of the St. Catharines Skyway); exit at Stanley Avenue (turn left to pass over the 405) or at the final exit before the border (turn left on the Niagara Boulevard to pass under a portion of the Queenston-Lewiston Bridge). From Buffalo, the visitor should take Highway 190 nearly twenty miles north to the Lewiston bridge. This route is also accessible from Interstate 90 via Highway 290.

Brock's Monument (185 feet tall, erected in the 1850s) dominates the battlefield park atop Queenston Heights, which is a favourite place for picnickers from spring to autumn. Parks Canada maintains interpreters at the monument who will provide a history of the structure and the original column that was damaged by a terrorist's explosion in 1840. They will also provide information on the self-guiding battlefield tour, which covers key locations in the battle, such as the redan battery and the ap-

proximate place where the Americans scaled the gorge. Interested visitors should diverge from the tour's beaten path and take time to follow the streets of the village down to the river's edge where sand dredgers unload their burdens at the dock.

At the base of the escarpment and adjacent to the Mackenzie House Museum is a small park with several memorials of the battle, most notably a simple boulder bearing a plaque honouring Captain John Norton's native warriors. Beware of the "Alfred the horse" statuette and the cairn that claims to show where Brock fell – both are based on unsubstantiated hearsay. To properly retrace Brock's last charge, climb from this point diagonally up the hill toward the redan battery, trying to envision the slope with a scattered covering of trees, bracken, weeds and wild flowers, heavily cloaked in white smoke.

If time allows, proceed seven miles north along the Niagara Boulevard to Niagara-on-the-Lake and visit the Fort George National Historic Site, where you will see one of the most comprehensive interpretations of the War of 1812 to be found in North America.

Undefended Borders, Valiant Militia and Other Myths: Defending Canada, 1812 to 1866

British victories at Detroit and Queenston Heights prompted changes in the direction of the American war effort. Fleets were constructed on the Great Lakes to support the land forces in a renewed offensive planned for 1813 by John Armstrong, who replaced the incompetent Eustis as secretary of war. Armstrong's objective was Montreal but he wanted first to take the British naval base at Kingston to gain control of Lake Ontario. His military and naval commanders instead advised attacking York (modern Toronto) before occupying the Niagara area, and Armstrong agreed to this change. In April Dearborn's army took York and then invaded the Niagara, but their advance was blunted by defeats at Stoney Creek on 6 June and Beaver Dams on 24 June. In September Armstrong came north to put some life back into the war. He called for a renewed offensive against Montreal by two separate armies: one moving down Lake Champlain to the city, where it would join with a second, larger force, which would move down the St. Lawrence to the same objective. This operation was delayed until too late in the season and it was brought to a swift end by twin British victories at Châteauguay on 26 October and Crysler's Farm on 11 November 1813.

By early 1814, Lieutenant General Sir George Prevost was confident that he could preserve Canada as a British possession. He had received gradual reinforcements and now commanded nearly 20,000 troops and, better still, Britain and its allies were gaining ground in the war in Europe against France. The successful outcome of that struggle meant that more troops would be available for North America and Prevost could turn from defence to offence.

American leaders, aware of this same possibility, had accepted a British proposal for direct negotiations to end the war. Wanting to have the best possible bargaining position, they decided, however, to mount one further offensive against Canada. In early July 1814, Major General Jacob Brown invaded the Niagara at Fort Erie to begin the longest and bloodiest military campaign of the war. The United States army of 1814 was a far more effective fighting force than it had been at the time of Queenston Heights as incompetent leaders had been replaced by deserving officers who prepared their troops properly for battle. These improvements were apparent at Chippawa on 5 July, where for the first time American regulars defeated British regulars in a major pitched battle fought in the open, and three weeks later at the battle of Lundy's Lane, the bloodiest military action ever to take place on Canadian soil. Although Lundy's Lane was tactically an American victory, Brown withdrew to Fort Erie, where he withstood a British siege of that place that lasted until early September.

While diplomats from the two warring nations met in the Dutch city of Ghent, British reinforcements, available after Napoleon's abdication in April, poured across the Atlantic. Most of these troops went to Canada but others were dispatched on costly and ultimately unsuccessful expeditions in the Chesapeake area and Louisiana. This reinforcement allowed Prevost, on the orders of his superiors, to undertake a major offensive with the purpose of seizing American territory to strengthen the hands of British negotiators. In September 1814 he crossed the border with a large army and moved up Lake Champlain to Plattsburgh. Unfortunately, when his naval squadron on that lake was defeated and captured, he retreated to Canada because (with Burgoyne's 1777 example in mind) Prevost knew he could not sustain his army without the support of a fleet. It was the right decision but it resulted in his recall. On Christmas Eve 1814, Britain and the United States signed the Treaty of Ghent, which restored the *status quo ante bellum* and ended this strange conflict which both sides claimed to have won.

If the War of 1812 provided one lesson for Canadians, it should have been that their independence had been preserved by regular soldiers. Unfortunately, in the postwar euphoria, a dangerous and pernicious belief took root that it was the efforts of the militia, not the regulars, who had saved the country. The origin of this myth can be traced directly to a sermon preached by the Reverend John Strachan at York just a few short weeks after Queenston Heights in which he confidently predicted that it "will be told by the future Historian, that the Province of Upper Canada, without the assistance of men or arms, except a handful of regular troops, repelled its invaders, slew or took them all prisoners, and captured from its enemies, the greater part of the arms by which it was defended."[1] Never, Strachan believed, "was greater activity shewn in any country, than our militia have exhibited, never greater valour, cooler resolution, and more approved conduct; they have emulated the choicest veterans, and they have twice saved the country."

While it is true that the militia had fought well in some of the early major engagements of the war, including Queenston Heights and Detroit (hence Strachan's reference to having "twice saved the country"), their most valuable wartime contribution had been to release regular troops from secondary duties on the lines of communication. It was regular troops, both British and Canadian, who did the bulk of the fighting in the War of 1812 and paid the price – 2,733 dying from all causes defending Canada during the conflict.[2]

This mistaken belief in the valour and effectiveness of untrained militia was dangerous as the threat to Canada's security posed by its aggressive neighbour to the south did not diminish. The half century after 1814 was an uneasy time punctuated by a series of border crises: the 1837 Rebellions in Upper and Lower Canada; the Aroostook "War" of 1839 in New Brunswick; the Oregon boundary dispute of 1846 and the Pacific Pig Island "War" of 1859. Although the United States government never overtly threatened Canada, hotheaded American politicians occasionally proclaimed the republic's manifest destiny to control all of North America and the example of Mexico, which had lost one third of its national territory to the United States by 1848, was a constant reminder of the dangers inherent in the close proximity of the United States.

Despite the evident perils, the governments of the various British North American colonies proved reluctant to spend a cent on defence. It was the British taxpayer who footed the bill for the large program of military construction that saw major fortresses built at Halifax, Quebec and Kingston and smaller works at various points along the border, and the Rideau Canal dug from the Ottawa River to Kingston as a parallel waterway to the St. Lawrence, which was vulnerable in time of war. Britain also maintained a large garrison, rarely fewer than 5,000 men and rising in times of crisis to as high as 14,000 in Upper and Lower Canada. But all British attempts to get the colonial governments to take greater responsibility for their own defence met with protestations of loyalty to the Crown and little else.

The outbreak of the Crimean War in 1854 and the withdrawal of much of the British garrison to fight in Europe provided some incentive for increased Canadian interest in defence. On 1 July 1855 the province of Canada, which at that time incorporated both Ontario and Quebec, passed an important new Militia Act authorizing the organization, arming and training of volunteer militia units.

This new organization, which included infantry, artillery and cavalry units, would number 4,000 men who would train actively in peacetime to fight in war.

This was a step forward and it came not a moment too soon as the outbreak of the American Civil War in 1861 raised the spectre of a new invasion threat. British leaders, noting that the United States was raising large armies to quell the rebellion, became concerned for the security of Canada. They increased the garrison of Canada to a peacetime high of 18,500 officers and men and urged that more volunteer militia units be raised. There were 14,000 in service by 1862 but attempts to increase this strength usually met with resistance on the part of Canadian politicians, whose attitude was expressed by the Toronto *Globe*, which could not "agree to the dogma that Canada should provide entirely for her defence when she is not the author of the quarrels against the consequences of which she is called to stand upon her guard."[3] This attitude puzzled Lieutenant General Sir William Fenwick Williams, the British commander-in-chief in North America, who commented that Canadians "seem to look on their coming dangers with the eye of a child, under the protection of a Parent who is bound to fight, whilst they pursue their ordinary business, or agitate themselves by fruitless party politics and parliamentary conflicts."[4] The British army would have to defend Canada, as it had in 1812-1814, but its senior officers knew that the odds, given the ever greater number of troops being mobilized in the United States, were very much against it.

Numbers were not the only problem; the conflict being waged to the south was the first modern war. It saw the use of railways, telegraphs, iron-clad warships, automatic weapons and aerial observation. The introduction of rifled weapons, both infantry and artillery, increased the range at which forces could engage and tipped the tactical balance in favour of the defence. Attempts to use the massed infantry formations of the Seven Years' and Napoleonic periods only resulted in heavy casualties – in the bloodiest day in American history, 15 September 1862, 23,000 men were killed or wounded at the battle of Antietam, and from that day forward the American soldier began to entrench as a matter of routine. The last campaigns of the war, with trench lines on both sides, heralded the Western Front of 1914-1918, and the forces deployed grew ever larger. By April 1865, when the rebellion was crushed, the American federal army mustered a million men, equipped with the latest weaponry.

It is small wonder that British leaders were concerned that such a massive war machine would roll over British North America. In the event, however, the threat did not come from the war-weary United States (although it was launched from American territory) – it came from Ireland.

3

"Prepare for Cavalry!"

The Battle

of Ridgeway

2 June 1866

THE PORT.

Behind Fenian lines, 1866

One of eighteen paintings by self-appointed Fenian war artist Alexander Von Ericksen, this work shows Fenians engaging Canadian skirmishers from the cover of woods. While his productivity may have exceeded his talent, Von Ericksen's images provide a fascinating and generally accurate depiction of the events of the time. (Painting by Alexander Von Ericksen, courtesy, Fort Erie Museum Board)

"Prepare for Cavalry!"
The Battle of Ridgeway

2 June 1866

Brian A. Reid

We are a Fenian Brotherhood, skilled in the arts of war,
And we're going to fight for Ireland, the land that we adore.
Many battles we have won, along with the boys in blue,
And we'll go and capture Canada, for we've nothing else to do.[1]

In the middle of the 19th century several Irish groups were working to free their homeland from British rule. Chief among these was the Irish Republican Brotherhood (IRB), an Ireland-based organization founded on St. Patrick's Day 1858 to foment revolution.[2] The Irish Republican Brotherhood had an American wing, the Fenian Brotherhood, led by John O'Mahoney, a veteran of the failed 1848 rebellion in Ireland, and a man dedicated to the cause of Irish independence. He named the organization after the *Fianna Eirionn*, ancient Irish warriors, in 1859. There was a key difference between the two organizations: the Irish Republican Brotherhood was a secret society dedicated to revolution in Ireland; the Fenian Brotherhood began life as an organization to raise funds in the United States to aid the cause of independence and evolved into a largely social organization.[3]

In 1865 the Irish independence movement suffered a severe blow when the British crushed the Irish Republican Brotherhood and scattered its leaders.[4] That same year saw the end of the American Civil War and the victory of the Union over the Confederacy. During the conflict the British had been sympathetic to the Confederacy and Confederate agents had operated in Canada.[5] By the end of the war, therefore, there was a considerable amount of bad feeling in the United

See Appendix C, page 378, for Orders of Battle of the Opposing Forces.

States towards Britain, and relations between the two countries were at their lowest point since the War of 1812. Indeed, a Canadian who saw active service in 1866 as a militia officer wrote in 1910 that the period was one of the most dangerous in the history of Canada.[6]

This unhappy situation gave encouragement to the Fenian Brotherhood, and particularly to a more militant faction within it led by William Randall Roberts which advocated striking the British Empire anywhere it could be struck, and soon. The destruction of the Irish Republican Brotherhood increased the importance of the Fenian Brotherhood, and since early prospects for a rising in Ireland were virtually non-existent, the Roberts faction was able to gain control of the Brotherhood at its October 1865 convention. O'Mahoney may have been elected president, but real power lay in the Fenian Senate, headed by Roberts, which controlled policy-making.[7]

The Fenians, or at least the Roberts faction, now began preparations for an invasion of British North America. This required at least the non-intervention of the United States government, if not its active support, and it was encouraging that both President Andrew Johnson and Secretary of State William Seward had hinted at support for the Fenians, albeit in the somewhat obscure language favoured by politicians.[8]

This impression of implied support was fostered when the election of Thomas W. Sweeny, a major general in the U.S. Army volunteers and commander of the regular Sixteenth Infantry Regiment, as secretary of war and head of the Fenian Brotherhood's military arm, the Irish Republican Army or IRA,[9] resulted in no more than his removal from active duty.[10] "Fighting Tom" Sweeny had been born in Cork in 1819 and had come to America in 1832. Despite the loss of his right arm in the Mexican War of 1846-1848, where he had won a battlefield commission, Sweeny continued his military career, serving in Indian campaigns and the Civil War. In the latter war General Sweeny was wounded twice, commanding a brigade at Shiloh in 1862 and a division in General William Tecumseh Sherman's 1864 Georgia campaign. The new Fenian secretary of war wasted no time gathering a staff and beginning preparations to invade Canada.[11]

This activity did not escape the attention of the British and Canadian governments. British diplomats in the United States provided a stream of reports while the intelligence network set up by Prime Minister John A. Macdonald of Canada in 1864 to keep an eye on Confederate sympathizers shifted its focus to watching Fenians.[12] The Canadian government called out the militia twice in response to threats of invasions voiced by prominent Fenians. The first occasion involved relatively small forces in November 1865 to garrison Prescott, Niagara, Windsor and Sarnia but the second in March 1866 consisted of 10,000 troops, later raised to 14,000, who were deployed along the border in anticipation of a St. Patrick's Day invasion.[13]

The expected invasions did not materialize, but in April 1866 the Fenians did strike at Campobello Island, New Brunswick, accomplishing little more than burning a few buildings before the ill-fated enterprise collapsed.[14] The relaxation of tensions after the March scare and the Campobello fiasco of April created a sense in Canada that Fenianism was a spent force. What no-one recognized, however, was that the Campobello raid had been mounted in haste by the O'Mahoney faction in an unsuccessful attempt to regain influence and credibility within the Brotherhood. The Roberts wing was still very much committed to an invasion.[15]

In early May Sweeny ordered a general mobilization of the Irish Republican Army with the aim of invading Canada by the end of that month.[16] His plan saw the Fenians advancing into Canada in three wings (see Map R-1). The left and centre wings, commanded by Brigadier Generals C. Carroll Tevis and William F. Lynch respectively, would mount a diversion into Canada West (now Ontario) to draw the defenders away from Montreal. Brigadier General Samuel B. Spear's right wing, which was nearly twice as large as the others combined, would then strike from Vermont and northern New York State to cut the lines of communications into Canada West and capture Montreal and Quebec City. An enclave in the Eastern Townships would be carved out and held as an Irish republic in exile. The plan reflected the strategic importance of controlling Quebec City and the need to prevent forces in Canada West from interfering with its capture. However, it blissfully relied for its logistical support upon French-Canadian radicals and the large Irish community in Canada – after the French the biggest ethnic community of the future Dominion.[17]

The Sweeny plan had another major flaw – it depended as before upon the support of or at least the turning of a blind eye by the United States government. It is true that this support had been hinted at by the Johnson administration – but in an election year. There was, however, a precedent for believing that it would be forthcoming. The United States government had allowed William Walker to mount freebooting expeditions in attempts to seize power in Latin America and had granted diplomatic recognition to his short-lived republic in Nicaragua in 1856.[18] Tempting though it might have been for the United States to twist the lion's tail, however, it was quite another matter to risk war with the British

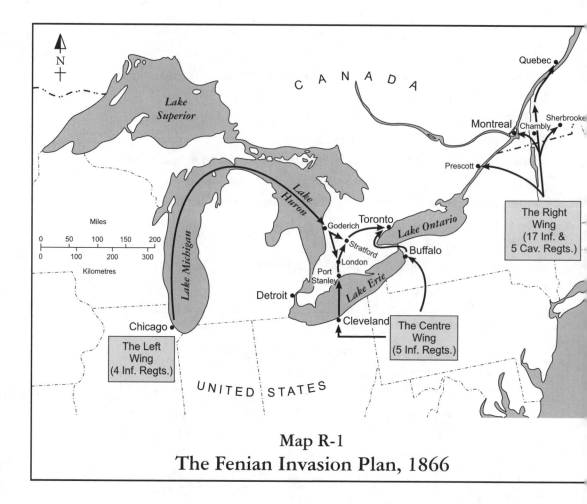

Map R-1
The Fenian Invasion Plan, 1866

Empire. Furthermore, President Johnson and Congress were unlikely to support the Fenians if the invasion of Canada did not meet with early and substantial success. If the British and Canadians had misread the Campobello raid as the death of the Fenian movement, the Roberts wing, with the optimism of true believers, failed to understand the implications of the arrest of the invaders and the seizure of their arms and shipping by the American government in response.[19]

As part of their preparations, the Roberts Fenians had purchased 10,000 surplus Springfield rifles and 2,500,000 rounds of .58 calibre ammunition from federal arsenals and stockpiled it at concentration points near the border. (An attempt to purchase three batteries of artillery was rebuffed by federal authorities but, with their classic optimism, the Fenians rewrote their plan to include the use of captured guns.)[20] The stockpiling of arms did not escape the attention of the Canadian intelligence network, although its implications were misread. Instead, a sense of complacency seems to have affected Canadian authorities. As late as 24 May, Gilbert McMicken, head of intelligence in Canada West, advised Macdonald that the situation was under control – yet within forty-eight hours it would change dramatically.[21]

In late May 1866 groups of men, some wearing military accoutrements and Union uniforms, complete with officers' badges of rank and swords, had begun to move towards the border. When queried as to their purpose and destination, many said they were going west to seek work on the railways. This claim may have masked their intentions for a while, at least until they turned north and east, not west. By 26 May H.W. Hemans, the British consul in Buffalo, had become aware of the proposed attack.[22] This was followed on 29 May by a telegram from a Canadian intelligence agent in Buffalo, John McLaughlin, who reported the presence of "many strange military men" in the city. The next day Hemans wired McMicken that Buffalo was "full of Fenians,"[23] and reports began to come in that more Fenians were en route from Cleveland.[24] All signs pointed towards an invasion.

In the original Sweeny plan, the crossing at Buffalo was a subsidiary of the two-pronged attack on London and Stratford, Canada West, by the left and centre wings. How and why it became the *only* thrust into Canada West requires some explanation. First, men did not arrive at any of the concentration points in the numbers anticipated. Of the left wing at Chicago, for example, only

Fenian soldier, c. 1866-1870

This relatively well equipped Fenian is armed with a .58 calibre Springfield musket and uniformed in a green version of the United States cavalry jacket from the Civil War period with a rather unique kepi. This painting is based on a Fenian uniform captured in Quebec in 1870 which was recently acquired by Parks Canada from the Royal Artillery Institution. (Painting by Ron Volstad, courtesy, Department of National Defence)

1,500 of the expected 3,000 reported. Moreover, to make a bad situation worse, the Fenians were unable to hire shipping for even this reduced strength.[25] The situation at Cleveland, the main concentration place for the centre wing, was not much better. Lieutenant Colonel John O'Neill, the commander of the Thirteenth IRA Regiment, left Nashville, Tennessee, on 27 May with 115 men. Picking up Lieutenant Colonel Owen Starr with 144 men of the Seventeenth at Louisville, Kentucky, and Captain Hugh Haggerty and 100 men at Indianapolis, Indiana, they arrived at Cleveland on the night of the 28th to find – nothing.[26] The commander of the centre wing, Brigadier General William Lynch, suffered from recurring bouts of fever as a result of his Civil War wounds and was too ill to join his command. Furthermore there were no ships waiting to carry the invaders to Port Stanley.[27] On the next day, a Fenian emissary arrived with orders for Lynch to effect a crossing from Cleveland to Port Stanley. Since this was clearly impossible, a wire was sent to Sweeny requesting instructions.[28]

With the operation in a shambles, logic called for scrapping the campaign that year, but there was a political reason why this could not be done – cancellation would doom the Fenian movement since it had nothing to show for several years' efforts but the rebuff at Campobello, and that by the rival O'Mahoney faction. Even if victory seemed out of the question, an "honorable failure in the field" would preserve the organization to fight another day.[29] Sweeny therefore ordered the centre wing to Buffalo forthwith, where Captain William F. Hynes, a member of his staff, would be waiting with orders.[30]

The centre wing, O'Neill's, Starr's and Haggerty's units, as well as Lieutenant Colonel John Grace's Eighteenth IRA Regiment, wasted no time in setting out for Buffalo by train. Arriving in the morning of 30 May, the men disembarked, formed into squads and moved to warehouses and other accommodation throughout the city.[31] The rifles and ammunition to equip them were stored in Patrick O'Day's warehouse. (Canadian intelligence had located this cache in February before the anticipated St. Patrick's Day invasion.)[32] Colonel O'Neill contacted Captain Hynes, who advised him he was looking for General Lynch or some other senior Fenian officer to command the expedition. In the meantime, he solicited the assistance of O'Neill and the other Fenian officers to assist him in completing preparations for the crossing.[33] It soon became apparent that Lynch was too ill to command the expedition, and since Colonel Sherwin, his adjutant, could not arrive before June and Sweeny thought it essential that the crossing be made on the night of 31 May to attract attention away from the right wing, command fell to the senior officer present, Lieutenant Colonel John O'Neill.[34]

Lieutenant Colonel John O'Neill, Irish Republican Army (1834-1878)

O'Neill, who had been a pre-civil war regular cavalryman in the US Army and an officer of volunteers during that conflict, clearly outclassed Booker, his Canadian opponent. No matter what one may think of his politics, O'Neill deserves recognition as an able tactician and commander. As a result of his victories at Ridgeway and Fort Erie, he rose to the top of the Fenian movement, but, with its collapse, his life went rapidly downhill and he died poor and alcoholic. (Courtesy, David Owen)

John O'Neill was born in Drumgallon, County Monaghan, in 1834. He had come to the United States in 1848 and enlisted in the U.S. Army in 1857. After serving in the 2nd U.S. Cavalry in the Second Mormon War in Utah in 1858-59, he had deserted to seek his fortune in California, a common practice at the time. O'Neill had later re-enlisted and was promoted sergeant on the outbreak of the Civil War. During the war he had served in the 7th Michigan Cavalry and the 15th Colored Infantry and was commissioned in 1862. After being badly wounded near Nashville in 1864 he left the army to work as a land claims agent.[35]

O'Neill recorded that Hynes formally appointed him to command the expedition on the night of 31 May, scant hours before the invasion was launched, and that he received no more than a few verbal general instructions as to his mission and tasks. Furthermore, he added, he did not have a map of the country.[36] However, O'Neill must have realized that as the senior officer present he was the leading candidate for the job and surely must have been considering the problem. As for the lack of a map, Major John Canty of the Seventh Regiment had been living under cover in Fort Erie, on the Canadian side of the Niagara, since January, employed as a section foreman on the Buffalo and Lake Huron Railway.[37] If O'Neill did not have a map before he landed, he would have had access to both a map and someone with detailed local knowledge once he did. From the amount and quality of the information he received while in Canada, a network of Fenian agents must have been in place, although O'Neill understandably did not draw attention to it in his report written after the invasion attempt had failed. O'Neill's operation, while substantially altered in form, was not the poorly planned effort his later report seemed to indicate.

By the end of May 1866 sizeable Fenian forces were converging on Buffalo. O'Neill, using the available units, his own Thirteenth, Starr's Seventeenth,

Grace's Eighteenth and Lieutenant Colonel John Hoy's Seventh Regiment from Buffalo as well as Haggerty's two companies,[38] planned to establish a bridgehead in Canada on the night of 31 May/1 June. This would allow Colonel Sherwin's gathering force to cross unimpeded into Canada over the next few days. The re-structured centre wing, more than 5,000 strong, would force the British and Ca-nadian forces to commit large forces against it, allowing General Spear's right wing an opportunity to develop its operations against Canada East.[39]

All this, however, depended on the American government standing aside. Whatever may have been hinted at by the Johnson administration, no direction to allow the invasion to proceed had been passed to local civil and military au-thorities. Both John Wells, mayor of Buffalo, and William A. Dart, the U.S. dis-trict attorney, took steps to warn the Canadian authorities as well as to prevent the crossing. In addition, the collector of customs closed the port of Buffalo to departing vessels between the hours of 4 P.M. and 9 A.M. effective 31 May. Last, but by no means least, the USS *Michigan*, an eight-gun warship, and the armed tug USS *Harrison* were stationed in the area to prevent a crossing.[40]

The Fenian choice of the lower Niagara Peninsula as the invasion site re-flected a sound appreciation of both the strategical situation and the tactical ad-vantages provided by the ground (see Map R-2).[41] The area lying south of the Welland River and east of the Welland Canal measured roughly eighteen miles square. The upper Niagara River could be crossed almost anywhere between Lake Erie and the mouth of the Welland River, at least by small craft. French-man's Creek emptied into the Niagara about two miles north of Fort Erie, while Black Creek did the same about eight miles south of Chippawa and both streams were crossed by bridges on the River Road from Fort Erie to Chippawa. In the west of the area, the Humberstone Marsh lying east of the canal was a major im-pediment to movement while in the east the ground was a mixture of gently roll-ing farmland and woods with a well-developed road network, with one excep-tion. A limestone ridge about thirty-five feet high rose near Frenchman's Creek and ran across the peninsula in a northeast-southwest direction to within a mile of Lake Erie. This ridge dominated the surrounding countryside, especially to the west. A road ran along the west slope near the crest from just north of Frenchman's Creek to Ridgeway on the Buffalo and Lake Huron Railway. On the east side of the ridge the ground gradually dropped away until it neared the Niagara River, where it ended in an escarpment, at the foot of which lay the vil-lage of Fort Erie. Fort Erie was the site of both a passenger and a rail ferry to Buf-falo, as well as the terminus of two railway lines, the Buffalo and Lake Huron

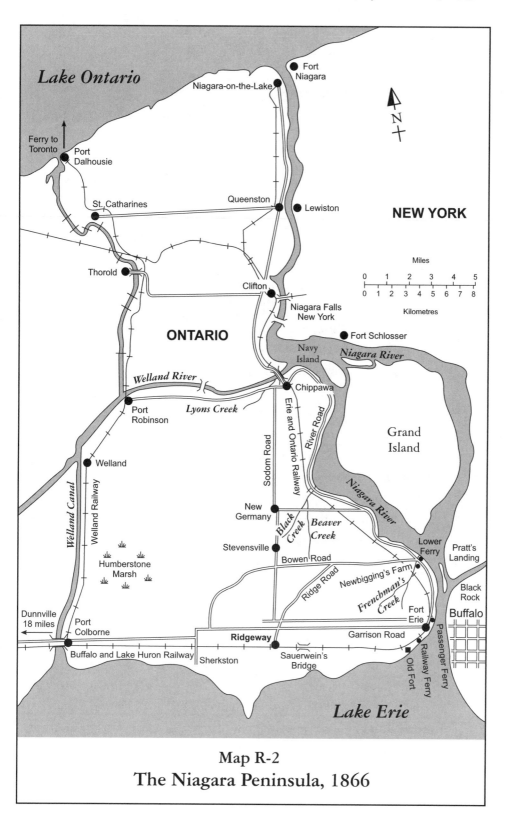

Map R-2
The Niagara Peninsula, 1866

running east–west and the Erie and Ontario running north through Chippawa, Niagara Falls and St. Catharines to Port Dalhousie. Another railway paralleled the Welland Canal, running on its east side from Port Colborne through Welland, Port Robinson and St. Catharines to Port Dalhousie.

If the invaders could advance to the banks of the Welland Canal and River and seize or destroy the bridges, they would have a major advantage, for the canal and the railways were of major economic importance to Canada. Even if the government was prepared to accept the humiliation of an invading army occupying a piece of its territory, it could not ignore the economic turmoil that would result.[42] Moreover, to bring the Fenians to battle, British and Canadian forces would be forced to attempt a water crossing, a difficult and risky operation at the best of times. If unable to hold the waterways, the invaders could occupy a strong defensive position based on the limestone ridge, forcing their enemies to mount a set-piece attack. There were no defending troops closer than eighteen miles to Fort Erie, and these were militia – the Welland Canal Field Battery at Port Colborne and Port Robinson[43] and the 19th and 20th Regiments at St. Catharines.[44] The only British regulars in the western part of the province were the right wing of the 16th Foot at Hamilton sixty miles northwest, while the left wing of that regiment, the 4th Battalion, 60th Rifles and a field artillery battery were at London, and the 47th Foot and another field battery at Toronto.[45] The Fenians could therefore count on several hours in which to consolidate their bridgehead and build up their forces.

On the evening of 31 May the Fenians gathered in Townshend Hall in Buffalo, a popular meeting-place for them. By 10 P.M. they had dispersed, to reassemble on the Black Rock road about half a mile north of the city. John McLaughlin, the Canadian agent, had gone straight from Townshend Hall to O'Day's warehouse, where he observed nine wagons being loaded with boxes of arms and ammunition. He continued to shadow the Fenians, estimating their strength at between 850 and 900 men with 1,200 weapons.[46] This was a commendable bit of espionage. The number actually assembled at Townshend Hall was about 800, although the total strength that would actually embark did not exceed 600.[47] The men made their way to the dock of Pratt's Ironworks at Black Rock, three miles north of Buffalo, where four canal boats and two tugs as well as the arms and ammunition were waiting. By 3.30 A.M. the Fenians had embarked, had received weapons and ammunition, and were crossing the Niagara River in two waves. The first wave, consisting of the Seventeenth and the Indiana companies, was commanded by Colonel Owen Starr. It probably numbered about 185 all ranks, or roughly one third of the force. At 4.00 on the morning of 1 June 1866 Starr's men, their green regimental colour to the fore, landed on Canadian soil at Freebury's Wharf, about two miles north of Fort Erie. The invasion of Canada was under way.[48]

The invaders were not the most enthusiastic of soldiers. The Irish Republican Army was a regionally based organization that had developed as an offshoot of the local chapters of the Fenian Brotherhood. During the later stages of the Civil War the Fenians had operated freely throughout the Union Army, recruiting and preaching the doctrine of freeing Ireland. With the end of the war, and no resettlement program for veterans in place, many gravitated to the IRA as a natural extension of the comradeship of army life and thus regimental organization and tactics closely followed the structure of the Union Army. For many of its members the IRA was more of a social club than a military force in an era when drilling was a popular social activity, and events would show that only a fraction of its membership was willing to risk life and limb for the establishment of an Irish republic in Canada. Still, it possessed a hard core of good, tough soldiers and experienced, capable officers. It should be noted that the IRA had no legal status as a belligerent, especially in the absence of any statement of support from the American government. Therefore, any men taken prisoner would not be guaranteed prisoner of war status but rather were liable to trial by the civil authorities as brigands and faced severe penalties, including execution, if convicted. This was probably known by the membership and no doubt contributed to the low turnout as well as the many men who deserted after the force landed in Canada.

Having come ashore, Colonel Starr led his men south along River Road into Fort Erie to secure the town, cut the telegraph wires and capture the rolling stock at the railway station. His force then split: Captain John Geary of Starr's regiment set off with a small party west along the railway to tear up the tracks and burn Sauerwein's Bridge over Six Mile Creek, west of Fort Erie, while Starr personally led a detachment through the town to "capture" the abandoned War of 1812 fort at the mouth of the river.[49] As soon as he landed, Colonel O'Neill summoned the village reeve, Dr. William Kempson, and requested him to arrange provisions for the Fenians. After a hastily called meeting of the village council, this was complied with.[50] While Fort Erie was being secured and the telegraph wires cut, some early-morning fishermen had spotted the invaders and warned the residents in time for word of the invasion to be passed and a train to raise steam and escape with its rolling stock. Canadian government detective

Charles Clarke cabled McMicken from Welland that "at 5.30 A.M. 1,500 Fenians landed at Fort Erie."[51] While inaccurate in both time and number, this was the first official word that Canada was under attack.

O'Neill set about consolidating his position around the landing place at Freebury's Wharf, although pickets were left in Fort Erie itself. By 10 A.M. his main body was entrenched on Justice of the Peace Thomas Newbigging's farm, on the south bank of Frenchman's Creek, three miles north of Fort Erie on the River Road.[52] The balance of the day was spent resting the men, while the reporters from Buffalo newspapers who visited the camp noted that the Fenian officers were studying maps.[53] Security seems to have been rather lax for, besides the journalists, both Richard Graham, the collector of customs at Fort Erie, and Detective Charles Clarke visited the camp in the late afternoon.[54]

As befitted a pre-war regular cavalryman and wartime officer in General George Armstrong Custer's cavalry brigade, O'Neill understood the value of a mounted force. He managed to collect some horses during the day and sent out parties to patrol the countryside. One party, led by Captain Donohue of the Eighteenth, foraging on the road to Chippawa, encountered another group of mounted men, who promptly fled. This was misinterpreted as an encounter with Canadian cavalry, although they may have been some of the scouts sent out by John Kirkpatrick, the reeve of Chippawa.[55] Certain that British and Canadian forces were assembling, O'Neill sent Lieutenant Colonel John Hoy's Seventh Regiment to secure the approach via the River Road from Chippawa. Six miles from the camp Hoy also bumped into what he interpreted as scouts. He sent word to O'Neill and halted at Black Creek, covering the approach to the camp.[56]

Even before Detective Clarke's alarm on the morning of 1 June, British and Canadian authorities had reacted to the imminent invasion. On the evening of 31 May orders were issued calling out the bulk of the militia infantry and garrison artillery in Canada West, although for some unexplained reason no cavalry or field artillery were included. This oversight was quickly rectified and by 3 June more than 20,000 Canadians were under arms.[57]

The officer responsible for expelling the Fenian invaders was Major General George T.C. Napier, commander of British forces in Canada West. Napier's immediate task was to safeguard the Welland Canal and he reacted accordingly (see Map R-3). He appointed Lieutenant Colonel George Peacocke, the commanding officer of the 16th Foot, to lead operations.[58] Peacocke was a steady, dependable officer, albeit without combat service.[59] This lack of experience and his

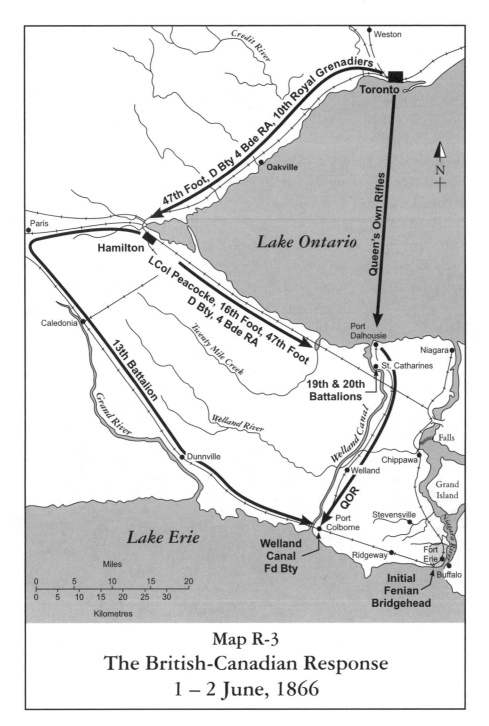

Map R-3
The British-Canadian Response
1 – 2 June, 1866

rather plodding manner would have a major effect on the developing operations. Peacocke's appointment was ultimately to be short-lived, as he was superseded by the more experienced (and senior) Colonel Robert W. Lowry on 3 June, but for the time being Peacocke was in command of the troops immediately available.[60] These consisted of D Battery, 4th Brigade, Royal Artillery; elements of two British infantry battalions, the 16th and 47th Foot; four Canadian militia infantry battalions (the Queen's Own Rifles from Toronto, the 13th Battalion from Hamilton reinforced by the York and Caledonia independent rifle companies, and the 19th and 20th Battalions from St. Catharines); as well as the Welland Canal Field Battery and the St. Catharines Garrison Battery.[61] Both militia batteries were organized and equipped as foot artillery companies, i.e., infantry. Peacocke was reinforced by two more companies of the 47th Foot and another militia battalion, the 10th Royals, from Toronto on the morning of 2 June[62] and by a troop of militia cavalry, the Governor General's Body Guard of Toronto, in the evening of the same day.[63]

Camp scene, 13th Battalion, Thorold, summer 1866

Dressed in a variety of uniforms, soldiers of the 13th Battalion, many of whom had fought at Ridgeway a few weeks before, relax in the much-needed militia training camp established at Thorold in August 1866. They appear to be wearing their full dress uniforms. The bell tents in the background were to be standard issue in the Canadian army for another century. (From *Semper Paratus,* courtesy, The Royal Hamilton Light Infantry)

Full dress for the field, 1866

Sergeant William P. Strickland of the 13th Battalion in full marching order, 1866. As a sergeant he is armed with the 1858 Pattern .577 calibre Enfield Short Rifle and carries a 20-round ball bag on his right hip and his percussion cap pouch on his left hip. He is also wearing his knapsack and just visible behind his neck is the oilskin cover for his mess tin fixed to the top of his knapsack. This uniform can still be seen today worn by the Fort Henry Guard of Kingston in their popular displays of the weapons and tactics of the period. (From *Semper Paratus*, courtesy, The Royal Hamilton Light Infantry)

Before he had appointed Peacocke to command the forces on the frontier, Napier had ordered the Queen's Own Rifles to Port Colborne and the 13th Battalion with the rifle companies to Dunnville on the morning of 1 June.[64] His orders to Peacocke directed him to base himself at St. Catharines and, at his discretion, to advance on Clifton or elsewhere and attack the enemy as soon as he could with a force sufficient to ensure success.[65] At 2 P.M. on 1 June, after being joined by 200 men of the 47th Foot and a British field battery from Toronto, Peacocke with four companies of his battalion, proceeded by train from Hamilton to St. Catharines.[66]

There he received the disturbing information that the Fenians, about 800 strong, were marching towards the suspension bridge over the Niagara gorge at Clifton. They were estimated to be within three miles of Chippawa, in other words somewhere along the Niagara River between Black Creek and Chippawa.[67] This news was probably based at least in part on reports from the scouts sent out from Chippawa by Kirkpatrick. Although the information was inaccurate about strength and intentions, it did provide an indication of where the Fenians were and what they were doing.

Peacocke immediately pushed on by train to the suspension bridge, leaving orders for all troops arriving at St. Catharines to follow him as soon as possible. On arrival at Clifton (now part of the city of Niagara Falls, Ontario) he learned that the Fenians had not yet reached Chippawa and so decided to occupy that village to keep possession of the bridge over the Welland River at that point. After detraining the field battery at Clifton to march by road to Chippawa because there was a lack of platform space at the Chippawa station, Peacocke pushed on with his 400 regular infantrymen and occupied Chippawa without incident about 9 P.M. that evening.[68]

By the late afternoon of 1 June 1866, things were not looking quite so rosy for the Fenians. On the credit side, the crossing had gone well, and O'Neill's force was well positioned to block any advancing force. However, on the debit side, no reinforcements had arrived during the day other than a few small parties who crossed by rowboat, and the late afternoon appearance of the USS *Michigan* off Black Rock effectively cut O'Neill off from any hope of further reinforcement.[69]

In the early evening the Fenian commander evaluated the latest intelligence, considered his options and made his plan.[70] According to his intelligence, 5,000 British and Canadian troops, including artillery, were massing against him. One column would advance from Chippawa, while a second column would move east from Port Colborne to attack from the south.[71]

Any opportunity to hold the British and Canadians on the Welland Canal and River was gone but O'Neill could not just sit and wait for the enemy to come to him, especially as nearly one hundred of his men had deserted or otherwise absented themselves during the day[72] and others would surely follow when rumours of advancing columns spread through the ranks. He had already achieved a major part of his mission – to divert attention from General Spear's right wing – as the reports of troop movements showed. However, to retire without an engagement with the hated redcoats would be premature, and in any case the presence of the *Michigan* threatened retreat to the safety of American territory.

O'Neill probably deduced that, as the British and Canadians had fixed his position at Frenchman's Creek, the two columns would unite near Stevensville to prevent him from advancing any further west. These two columns were of unequal strength and capability. The Chippawa column included British regular infantry and artillery, reflecting the importance given to confining the invaders south of the Welland River. The second column, made up of Canadian militia, although the less formidable of the two, was still nearly twice the strength of the Fenian army. The Chippawa column would probably march from Chippawa through New Germany to Stevensville, a distance of seven miles; the other column would travel by rail from Port Colborne to Ridgeway on the morning of 2

June, then cover the six miles to Stevensville. O'Neill realized that he had been presented with an opportunity to defeat the Port Colborne column before the Chippawa column could intervene. In his words, "my object was to get between the two columns, and, if possible, defeat one of them before the other could come to its assistance."[73]

In his official report O'Neill puts the time he received the intelligence upon which he based this decision as 8 P.M. on 1 June, which seems too early as the Chippawa column was probably still on the road and Peacocke had yet to decide on a plan and issue orders. It was not until midnight that Peacocke despatched an aide with orders for the commander of the Port Colborne column to meet him at Stevensville between ten and eleven o'clock the next morning. As he noted in his own report, this was after the latter had telegraphed him at about 10 P.M. to report he intended to advance to Fort Erie and attack the Fenians in the morning, and not as O'Neill claimed, to meet Peacocke at Stevensville. While O'Neill may have made an intelligent appreciation of the enemy's capabilities and intentions, he may also have deliberately disguised the presence of a Fenian intelligence network, including someone who was intercepting the defenders' telegraph communications. It seems more than a fortunate coincidence that the Fenians intercepted the Port Colborne column where and when they did.

The Fenians broke camp at 10 P.M. and marched north along River Road to join the Seventh Regiment at Black Creek.[74] Before departing, however, there was an unpleasant duty to perform. Eight hundred stands of arms had been brought into Canada but only 600 men had crossed. Now, after a further 100 Fenians had absented themselves, 300 rifles were surplus.[75] Captain John S. Mullen recalled, "We made a big pile of brushwood, threw the muskets on it, poured oil on the heap and set fire to it."[76] Other rifles were smashed, bent and thrown in the river, while men scattered surplus ammunition on the ground.[77]

At midnight the combined Fenian force turned off River Road and moved south towards Ridge Road, halting for a few hours rest en route.[78] After a hurried breakfast, they resumed their march south, screened on their right by Beaver and Black Creeks.[79] It was not an easy march, for the roads were soft from recent rain and badly rutted.[80] At roughly 6 A.M. the advance guard of Starr's Seventeenth Regiment moved up onto the limestone ridge and cautiously advanced south along Ridge Road. O'Neill probably used his mounted scouts to keep him informed of the location and actions of the Chippawa column. By 7 A.M., when it was roughly three miles north of Ridgeway, the advance guard made contact with what they identified as mounted Canadian scouts, who galloped away towards

Ridgeway to pass word of the Fenians' presence. Shortly after that the Fenians heard train whistles and bugle calls from the direction of the village.[81]

O'Neill's plan had worked. He would fight the Port Colborne column on the ground of his choosing without interference from Peacocke's Chippawa column.

As the commander of all the British and Canadian troops on the Niagara frontier, Lieutenant Colonel George Peacocke's orders were to attack the enemy as soon as possible with a force sufficient to ensure success. From information received from the scouts sent out by Kirkpatrick, he knew the Fenians were at Frenchman's Creek and that they had sent a party towards Chippawa. Estimates of their strength varied from 800 to 1,500.[82] While British armies as a matter of course fought superior numbers and won, Peacocke was not a man to take risks and, in this case, if the intelligence was to be believed, he was facing an enemy force up to four times the size of his own.

Peacocke's forces were disposed as follows. First there were 400 regular infantry and the Royal Artillery field battery at Chippawa. Peacocke had ordered the St. Catharines Garrison Battery and the 19th Battalion (actually a composite of the 19th and 20th Battalions)[83] forward from St. Catharines to Chippawa, less two companies left to guard the suspension bridge at Clifton, and sent another company to guard the entrance to the Welland Canal at Port Colborne.[84] He also knew he would be reinforced by two more companies of the 47th Foot and the 10th Royals from Toronto before dawn on 2 June.[85] The relatively small number of troops at Port Colborne was more troublesome, but this was offset

Volunteer rifleman, Canadian Militia, 1866

The dark green uniform worn by the Queen's Own Rifles at Ridgeway is depicted here in a modern painting. This rifleman is armed with the 1858 Pattern .577 calibre Enfield Short Rifle with its attendant sword bayonet and equipped with black leather rifle equipment including a 40-round ball bag on his right hip and a percussion cap pouch on his cross belt. Many of the Queen's Own at Ridgeway were actually armed with the 1853 Pattern Enfield Rifled Musket rather than the Short Rifle. (Painting by Ron Volstad, courtesy, Department of National Defence)

by the lack of any apparent Fenian movement in that direction. The Port Colborne garrison consisted of the Queen's Own from Toronto, who had arrived at about noon after crossing Lake Ontario by steamer to Port Dalhousie and then travelling by train to their destination,[86] and the Welland Canal Field Battery. The latter unit, while not officially called out until 2 June, had mustered at Port Colborne the day before.[87] The commanding officer of the Queen's Own Rifles, Lieutenant Colonel J. Stoughton Dennis, was now the senior officer present at Port Colborne.

Peacocke had already taken steps to reinforce the Port Colborne garrison and to contain the Fenians. While still at Clifton he had ordered Lieutenant Colonel Alfred Booker, the commanding officer of the 13th Battalion, to bring his unit and the York and Caledonia rifle companies forward from Dunnville to Port Colborne.[88] He had also ordered the ferry steamer *International* to steam from Fort Erie to Port Colborne and had directed Dennis to embark a detachment of troops on board. The ferry would patrol the Niagara River to prevent Fenian reinforcements crossing and cut O'Neill's line of retreat.[89] Unknown to Peacocke and Dennis, however, the *International* had left Fort Erie for a safe haven before the Fenians arrived in the village and could not be contacted. This vessel would therefore play no part in the coming battle.

In addition, Peacocke was working at a major disadvantage. His only map was a simple post office map of a scale of ten miles to the inch that showed the post offices and the routes between them but no topographical detail. It seems he was not aware of the existence of the mile to the inch county map that showed all the roads, streams, villages, as well as the name of the owner of every farm. Kirkpatrick, who of course had such a map, assumed that Peacocke had a proper military map and did not presume to offer him what he assumed to be an inferior product.[90] Throughout the campaign, therefore, the British and Canadian forces groped their way about the Niagara Peninsula without benefit of reliable maps and scouts, unlike the Fenians, who had a fairly accurate picture of the region and their enemy's location and movements.

As O'Neill had deduced, Peacocke had decided to concentrate at Stevensville and then attack the Fenians he believed to still be at Frenchman's Creek. Peacocke apparently selected Stevensville as the rendezvous because he felt the Fenians could not reach the village before the Chippawa and Port Colborne columns linked up.[91] It is possible that he thought that, until the two columns joined, they were vulnerable to defeat in detail. Peacocke also appreciated the difficulties that a militia officer experiencing his first taste of command on active service had to be undergoing. He wired the "officer commanding troops" at Port Colborne that he was sending Captain Charles Akers, Royal Engineers, with orders, although the phrase used was "to communicate with you," and that Akers would arrive about half past one. In this message, Peacocke also raised the issue of arming the ferry to emphasize its importance in the mind of the recipient.[92]

The tension at Port Colborne must have eased considerably when the train carrying the Queen's Own Rifles pulled into the village station at about noon on 1 June. This regiment had been called out during the night, paraded at its drill hall in Toronto, sailed across Lake Ontario to Port Dalhousie, then travelled via the Welland Railway to Port Colborne.[93] The battalion commander, Lieutenant Colonel J. Stoughton Dennis, had been ordered to occupy Port Colborne, and if necessary entrench a position there. He was then to wait for reinforcements and further orders before any attack was made on the enemy, who numbered 1,500 men and were advancing on that point.[94] Dennis found things quiet in Port Colborne, no definite news having reached the village after the Fenians had cut the wires from Fort Erie that morning. Although word had arrived of the burning of Sauerwein's Bridge six miles from Fort Erie, parties of scouts sent out during the morning had not reported any contact with the Fenians.[95]

The Queen's Own Rifles was, like other militia infantry units, equipped for the most part with Enfield .577 calibre rifled long muskets. The exception was No. 5 Company, which, while crossing the lake, had been issued Spencer .56-50 calibre seven-shot repeating rifles. Changing weapons on the eve of battle is not sound military practice – as Sergeant Andrew McIntosh of No. 5 Company commented: "I think it was a great mistake, we know our enfield rifles but know nothing of the others, and a very poor thing they turned out to be at any distance over 200 yards."[96] The battalion, dressed in green wool uniforms, carried an average of forty rounds of ball ammunition per man, except No. 5 Company, which had only twenty-eight rounds per man for its Spencers.[97]

Colonel Dennis now began actively to seek information about the enemy. He sent a messenger across country to Buck's Tavern at Stevensville to determine if there had been any Fenian movement in that direction. Then, having arranged for the use of a locomotive with the superintendent of the Buffalo and Lake Huron Railway, he steamed towards Fort Erie, halting when he reached the still-burning Sauerwein's Bridge.[98] Later he despatched a party from Port Colborne by train to repair the bridge. Their task accomplished, they were back in Port Colborne by 11 P.M.[99]

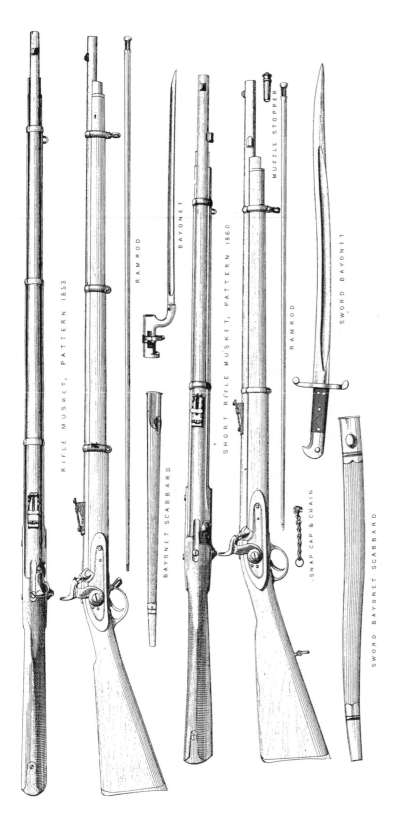

New weapon on the battlefield: Pattern 1853 .577 calibre Enfield rifled musket and Pattern 1858 short rifle

The widespread introduction of rifled infantry weapons dramatically changed the nature of combat in the mid-19th century. With its longer range, better accuracy and higher rate of fire, the rifled musket quickly did away with the massed infantry formations of the Napoleonic period and forced soldiers to disperse to present fewer targets. The Fenians who fought at Ridgeway were almost all veterans of the Civil War and had learned this new way of fighting – their Canadian opponents had not. (From *Equipment of Infantry,* War Office, London, 1866)

John Stoughton Dennis was very much a man on the make. On 31 May Colonel Patrick MacDougall, the adjutant general of militia in Ottawa, had ordered Lieutenant Colonel William G. Durie, the assistant adjutant general in Toronto, to despatch a provisional battalion of 400 men to Port Colborne. Dennis, the brigade major of the 5th Military District, immediately telegraphed Ottawa, volunteering to command the force. Because Dennis was an excellent peacetime officer – hard working, ingratiating and persuasive – MacDougall ordered Durie to appoint Dennis to command the expedition. In the meantime, rather than cobble together a battalion from a number of different units, Durie had called out his old regiment, the Queen's Own, under its own commanding officer, Major Charles T. Gillmor. This move made Dennis's appointment unsatisfactory. First, it was a slap in the face for Gillmor and his battalion, and second, not only was Dennis from another militia district, but he had never served in the infantry and had only commanded a militia artillery battery for two years.[100]

By nightfall on 1 June Dennis must have concluded that the Fenians were not going to attack the southern end of the Welland Canal, indications being that they were entrenched at Black Creek in unknown but sizeable strength. Suddenly, however, he received information that changed the picture dramatically. At 10 P.M. he met Richard Graham, the collector of customs at Fort Erie, in the Port Colborne customs house. Graham had visited the Fenian camp at Newbigging's farm at 6 P.M. that day, and he told Dennis that the Fenians numbered no more than 400, were disorganized and drinking heavily, and planned to retire across the Niagara before dawn.[101] It was Graham's belief that 400 good men would gobble them up before day.[102] Much of this information was later confirmed by Detective Charles Clarke, although he omitted any reference to drinking in his written report.[103] (Possibly O'Neill appreciated that he was likely to be visited by Canadian agents and had deliberately spread the rumour that his force planned to retire – but this is speculation).

By this time Dennis had realized that the ferry *International* was not going to arrive. Therefore, at about 10.30 P.M. he wired Captain Lachlan McCallum of the Dunnville Naval Brigade, ordering him to bring his powerful steam tug, the *W.T. Robb*, forthwith to Port Colborne.[104] Shortly thereafter the train bearing the detachment of the Welland Canal Field Battery returned from repairing the Sauerwein's Bridge at Six Mile Creek, opening the route to Fort Erie.[105] Dennis had already formulated a plan to attack the Fenians at Frenchman's Creek and telegraphed Peacocke to that effect, although evidently omitting any reference to the strength and apparent low morale of the Fenians.[106] Like most Canadians of

Lieutenant Colonel J. Stoughton Dennis, Canadian Militia (1820-1885)
Dennis was an energetic, persuasive and bone-headed officer who not only set the stage for the defeat at Ridgeway but also failed to block the Fenian retreat to the United States. Despite a display of ineptitude rarely equalled in Canadian military history, he escaped censure for his actions at what was widely considered to be a rigged inquiry. Unlike O'Neill and Booker, Dennis went on to enjoy a successful civilian career, proving yet again that who you know is more important than what you know. (Courtesy, National Archives of Canada, C-5490)

the time, Dennis dismissed the Fenians as drunken loafers who would flee in panic at the first sight of a red coat. The reports of Graham and Clarke could only have increased this contempt, which was based on little other than traditional Anglo-Saxon disdain for the fighting ability of both the Irish and Americans.

At 11 P.M. Lieutenant Colonel Arthur Booker arrived and, being senior to Dennis, immediately assumed command at Port Colborne.[107] Booker found himself the commander of a hastily-organized brigade without a headquarters and staff. Moreover, he had no experience nor any qualification for the job other than seniority (but the same could be said of Dennis). Shortly after assuming command, Booker received word from Peacocke that Captain Charles Akers had been ordered to Port Colborne to communicate with him.[108] The use of a trusted aide to pass orders to a subordinate is a well-established military practice, since everyone understands that the officer speaks with the full authority of his commander. The aide can both explain his commander's intentions and answer any questions that may arise, but he does not have the authority to change the orders. This would probably have come as a considerable relief to Booker, if for no other reason than that he would now have a British regular officer as an adviser.

On Akers's arrival, Booker and Dennis were somewhat taken aback to find that they apparently had better information than Peacocke, for Akers told them the Fenian camp was at Black Creek, not Frenchman's Creek. That Akers did not fully understand the situation is evident from his summary of Peacocke's intention in his official report:

a combined attack on the enemy supposed to be entrenched on Black Creek about three miles down the river from [Fort] Erie, seven miles from Chippawa and two from Stevensville. Col. Peacocke was to move on Stevensville so as to arrive there about 9.30 a.m.; Lieut Col Dennis was to move along the railway to Ridgeway as far as the state of the Railway would permit, and march from there to meet Col Peacocke at Stevensville at the above hour, and from there the combined forces were to march on the supposed position.[109]

The distances do not match up. The first, three miles from Fort Erie, is correct for Frenchman's Creek, the second refers to Black Creek, while the third fits neither. Akers's mistake led Booker and Dennis to question Peacocke's selection of Stevensville as the rendezvous,[110] if not his whole plan.

In fact, Booker and Dennis had already made a plan based on the situation as they understood it – that the Fenian invaders, numbering no more than 400 or 500, were drunk and disorganized at Frenchman's Creek. More correctly, perhaps, Dennis had made a plan and talked Booker into it when the latter arrived. When Akers arrived at Port Colborne at 1.30 A.M., he found Dennis itching to attack the Fenians immediately with the Port Colborne column, while Booker was less enthusiastic and would only carry out

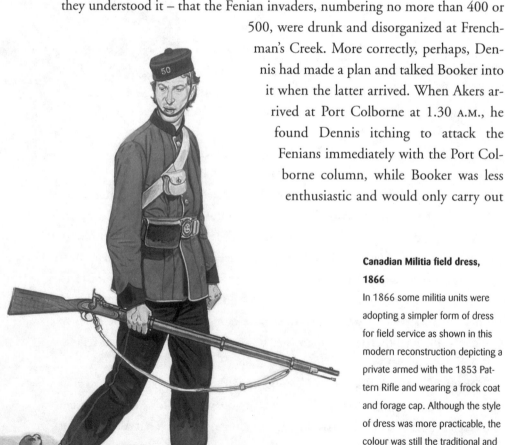

Canadian Militia field dress, 1866

In 1866 some militia units were adopting a simpler form of dress for field service as shown in this modern reconstruction depicting a private armed with the 1853 Pattern Rifle and wearing a frock coat and forage cap. Although the style of dress was more practicable, the colour was still the traditional and highly-visible red. (Painting by Ron Volstad, courtesy, Department of National Defence)

such an operation if properly authorized.[111] Akers refused to sanction it because he did not consider it prudent in the light of information that the Fenian strength would double during the night. Once he "learned" that the Fenians were at Frenchman's Creek and the line to Fort Erie was open, he was persuaded to develop a third alternative.[112] Caught up in the enthusiasm of the moment, the three officers created a new plan, or rather modified the Dennis-Booker plan, that would see the two columns converging on Newbigging's farm via River Road. Dennis and Akers would cruise the river in the tug, cutting off any escaping Fenians and communicating between the forces advancing from Chippawa and Fort Erie.[113]

The conference broke up shortly before 3 A.M. on 2 June after a little less than ninety minutes, and Akers wired Peacocke outlining the proposal, although he later admitted he may have failed to mention the use of the tug.[114] The *W.T. Robb* steamed into Port Colborne shortly after 4 A.M., carrying Captain McCallum and the men of the Dunnville Naval Brigade. No time was wasted loading Dennis, Akers and Captain Richard S. King's Welland Canal Field Battery, and the tug was soon steaming through the pre-dawn fog on the lake towards Fort Erie. The total embarked strength was 110: Dunnville Naval Brigade, 3 officers and 43 men with Enfield rifled muskets; Welland Canal Field Battery, 3 officers and 59 men with short Enfield rifles; and Dennis and Akers.[115]

Before he departed, Akers had provided Booker with a belated explanation of Peacocke's plan and dictated the following instructions:

Move at no later than 5.30; 5 o'clock if bread be ready. Move to depot at Fort Erie and wait till 7. If not communicated with before 7, move to French-man's Creek. If "no" by telegraph, disembark at Ridgeway and move to Stevensville at 9 to 9.30 a.m. Send pilot engine to communicate with Lieut.-Col. Dennis at Fort Erie and with telegrams.[116]

As these instructions, especially the time to arrive at Stevensville, had a major influence on Booker's subsequent actions, it is necessary to examine them more closely. The selection of Ridgeway as the terminus is understandable, especially for someone unfamiliar with the terrain. There was a whistle stop at Sherkston, about halfway between Port Colborne and Ridgeway, where the column could have detrained and the route to Stevensville from Sherkston is direct and avoids the limestone ridge.[117] However, there was no reason for either Akers or Booker to have considered the possibility of Fenian intervention at this time and the

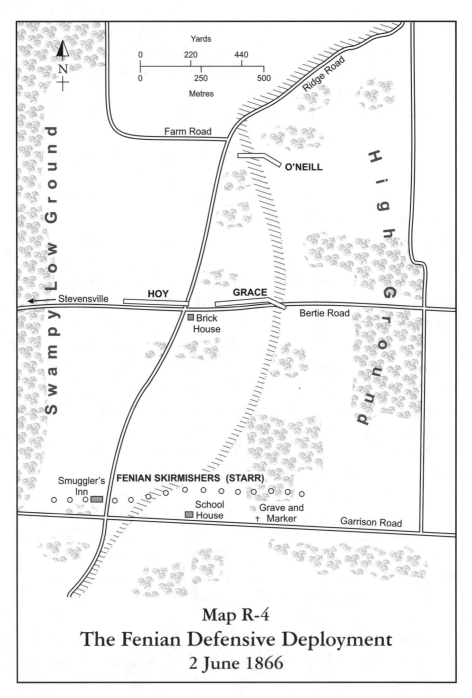

Map R-4
The Fenian Defensive Deployment
2 June 1866

instructions from Akers ruled out this more secure option, even if Booker would
have considered it.

Akers seems to have literally "guesstimated" the time the column was to be at
Stevensville. Peacocke had instructed him to inform the officer commanding at
Port Colborne to meet him at Stevensville between ten and eleven and that he

himself would leave Chippawa at 6 A.M.[118] Akers recalled the estimated time for Peacocke's arrival as being 9.30,[119] but he later testified at the Dennis inquiry that

> I had not been able to ascertain the exact time at which Col. Peacocke would start from Chippawa as he told me he would be detained till the arrival of re-inforcements from St. Catharines or elsewhere. As far as I could make out he would leave Chippawa about six o'clock, and I therefore imagined that he would be at Stevensville from nine to half past nine, and gave instructions to meet him there at that time.[120]

While the issue of the time of arrival at Stevensville may not have affected the battle to follow, the conflicting recollections suggest that Peacocke left too much to Akers's discretion. He should perhaps have given him specific written instructions to deliver to the commander of the troops at Port Colborne – the more in-experienced the subordinate, the greater the need for supervision and encourage-ment. Still, Peacocke could not have imagined that Akers would be foolish enough to allow himself to be talked into altering his commander's plan or that he would abandon Booker, who had the most need of his expertise and advice, to go chasing after glory with Dennis.

Booker must therefore have been taken aback to receive from Peacocke the following short, sharp reply to Akers's telegram: "Have received your message of 3. A.M. I do not approve of it. Follow original Plan. Acknowledge receipt of this"[121]

The train carrying the Port Colborne column steamed out of the station shortly after 5 A.M., preceded by a pilot engine sent a few minutes earlier to con-firm the route was secure. On board were the Queen's Own Rifles (ten compa-nies, 450 officers and men,[122] as the battalion had received reinforcements dur-ing the night); the 13th Battalion (six companies, 265 officers and men); and the York and Caledonia rifles companies (48 all ranks each), for a total strength of 810 officers and men.[123] The 13th wore red tunics, while the others were in rifle green. Booker was accompanied by two Canadian government detectives, a Mr. Armstrong[124] and the ubiquitous Charles Clarke.[125] The only horse on the train belonged to Major James Skinner of the 13th Battalion, who had offered its use to Booker. The colonel had requested the field officers of the Queen's Own to bring their horses, but they had refused, explaining that horses would be useless in the woods where the column would likely be operating.[126] This is another example of British and Canadian lack of familiarity with the terrain. There may have been another reason: Major Charles Gillmor later stated that the station master at Port Colborne had told him he could not detrain his horse at Ridgeway without breaking its legs, there being no platform.[127]

Lieutenant Colonel John O'Neill of the Irish Republican Army, meanwhile, was on the limestone ridge with his men preparing to meet the column from Port Colborne before it could join Peacocke and his force at Stevensville (see Map R-4). O'Neill had chosen a naturally strong defensive position about half a mile wide running from the intersection of Farm Road with Ridge Road, south almost half a mile to the junction of Ridge and Bertie Roads and then about another half mile south to the Garrison Road.[128] The ground here was generally open, gently rolling and divided into fields and pasture by split-rail fences, and there are a number of small woods that would provide cover for the Fenians, especially on the north and east of the position. The Ridge Road runs along the western slope of the ridge and is dominated by the crest within rifle shot to the left, or east. The open fields and orchards to the south of Bertie Road provided a natural trap into which to draw the attackers, while the low ground to the west of the ridge was even more dangerous for advancing troops.

The weakness of the position was that Canadians could outflank the Fenians by moving east onto and along the crest. O'Neill could, however, counter this move by extending his left flank forward and by enticing the enemy into advancing along Ridge Road by engaging them with skirmishers deployed near the intersection of Ridge and Garrison Roads. The skirmish line could give way slowly but steadily, drawing the attackers into the trap. High ground to the northeast of the line of Bertie Road could be occupied by a reserve, reinforced by Starr's skirmishers after they withdrew. The reserve would provide defence in depth, as a force to counterattack or exploit success, or in the worse case, as a firm base for the forward troops to withdraw through back along Ridge Road.

It was a good defensive position and O'Neill knew it. He positioned two regiments forward along the south side of Bertie Road. Lieutenant Colonel Grace's Eighteenth deployed from just left of the crossroads running east for a quarter mile before curving south to partially flank the Ridge Road. Lieutenant Colonel Hoy's Seventh did the same from around Anger's brick home at the crossroads and down Bertie Road to the west into the low ground. Their men improved their position by tearing down the rail fences to the north of the road and placing the rails over the fences on the south side, the butts of the poles on the ground facing south. O'Neill's Thirteenth occupied the reserve position a few hundred yards farther back and up the slope. Lieutenant Colonel Starr took his own Eighteenth and Captain Haggerty's independent companies forward as skirmishers at least as far as the north side of Garrison Road and perhaps even farther.[129]

O'Neill's choice of position and tactics reflected his recent experience in the Civil War. Rather than attempt to attack the Canadian forces on the march, he opted to entice them into attacking his force on ground of his own choosing. While his plan sacrificed the chance for a surprise assault on the enemy spread out in column on the road,[130] it forced the Canadians to fight their way forward against a strong skirmish line and then attack the Fenian main position arrayed where it could bring massed rifle fire to bear on the attackers concentrated in the open. This tactic had worked well for both sides in the Civil War – time would tell if it would prove successful against the Canadian militia.

O'Neill's plan also made use of the recent shift in advantage towards the defence that had resulted from the introduction of the percussion rifled musket. Fifty years earlier armies traded short range volleys from notoriously inaccurate smooth-bore flintlock muskets, but both the Fenian .58 calibre Springfield and the Canadian .577 Enfield rifled muskets were able to effectively engage formed bodies of troops at 800 yards, although the preferred range was 500 yards and below. Not only had the range increased, but the rate of fire had doubled to four rounds a minute, at least for an experienced soldier (the Spencer repeating rifles of No. 5 Company of the Queen's Own Rifles did not play a significant part in the battle, as will become clear.). In fact the ability of the Fenians to deliver rapid, aimed fire led to Canadian claims after the battle that the Fenians had been armed with repeating rifles.[131] Nonetheless, the rifled musket was still relatively inaccurate, especially at longer ranges. In the battle to come, somewhere between 20,000 and 30,000 rounds would be fired, with a total casualty count of under fifty dead and wounded on both sides.

The train bearing Booker's force steamed into Ridgeway station after a slow, cautious trip of more than an hour from Port Colborne.[132] Ridgeway was a small village consisting of a flour mill, twenty houses, two taverns and a few stores clustered around the intersection of Ridge Road and the Buffalo and Lake Huron Railway.[133] As the troops clambered down from the cars and formed into their sections, companies and battalions, Booker attempted to no avail to organize some transport to carry his stores, medical supplies and spare ammunition. Here, once again inexperience and the lack of a staff told – he was largely unsuccessful, although the Queen's Own managed to locate a team and wagon for their spare ammunition, and detective Armstrong acquired a riding horse for himself. Booker therefore arranged to return the surplus stores – tents, blankets and perhaps even ammunition – to Port Colborne by train.[134]

Ridgeway would provide the first real test of a Canadian defence system built on the false premise that militia, not British regulars, had defeated the American invaders during the War of 1812.[135] Acceptance of this "militia myth" had encouraged successive Canadian colonial legislatures to keep defence spending to an absolute minimum while maximizing the political benefits by spreading the money as widely as possible. The results, at least on paper, were impressive – 20,000 militiamen were available to answer a call to arms – but the reality was another matter. Booker's two battalions were probably typical of the militia as a whole: they were deficient in nearly everything except enthusiasm – maps, military boots (many were wearing civilian shoes), water bottles, mess tins, rations, haversacks, stretchers, transport and – most important of all – adequate training for active service.[136]

Despite his lack of qualifications for command, Booker desperately tried to cover as many bases as possible. Before leaving Ridgeway he ordered the 13th Battalion's spare ammunition to be distributed, requesting those who could do so to carry another ten rounds in their pockets. To his astonishment, he found that the Caledonia Rifle Company had no percussion caps and little ammunition. While the deficiency was made up from the 13th's spare ammunition,[137] it is telling that an infantry unit could have been on the verge of going into action without ammunition.

As it was, the amount of ammunition carried varied between units. As members of a rifle regiment, each man in the Queen's Own carried forty rounds per man

Officer, 13th Battalion, 1866

Officers dressed more simply in the field and this modern reconstruction shows an officer of the 13th Battalion as he may have appeared at Ridgeway in 1866. He is wearing a plain blue frock coat, waist belt, sash and a forage cap with his unit's numbers on the front. (From *Semper Paratus*, courtesy, The Royal Hamilton Light Infantry)

(only twenty-eight rounds per man in the Spencer-armed No. 5 Company) while the 13th Battalion and the two attached companies carried sixty rounds, plus whatever the men had stuffed in their pockets. In both battalions more than half the troops were teenagers, although a larger proportion of the 13th were trained and had fired their weapons than was the case with the Queen's Own.[138]

The man leading them into battle, Alfred Booker, a native of Nottingham, England, was a typical militia commanding officer. He was self-made, a wealthy merchant and auctioneer who joined the militia out of a combination of patriotism and civic duty. His militia experience predated 1855, for he had transformed the volunteer artillery company he had organized a year or two earlier into a field battery authorized by the 1855 Militia Act. By 1862 he was militia commandant of Hamilton as well as battery commander of the Hamilton Field Battery. In 1865 he was made commanding officer of the 13th Battalion. His appointment was based more on the outgoing commanding officer's dislike of his own majors than any special aptitude on Booker's part, although he held a first-class militia certificate, which reflected his qualification to command a battalion. In private life Booker was a good-natured, kind man who enjoyed entertaining guests by performing puppet shows and ventriloquism.[139]

As the Canadian force began to form up to march north along Ridge Road towards Stevensville, the riders whom the Fenian advance guard had encountered on the Limestone Ridge, galloped into the village and sought out Booker. To his astonishment, they reported that the Fenians were within a few miles of Ridgeway and moving south. No, they responded to his query, the enemy did not have any cavalry or field artillery. Unfortunately, Samuel Johnson, one of the riders, then presumed to offer Booker some unsolicited military advice.[140] At this perceived insult to his dignity, the colonel angrily dismissed them. Booker later claimed that the information regarding the Fenian location was unreliable and contradictory,[141] which is true if he wanted to believe the Fenians were still at Frenchman's Creek, or if his nose was out of joint.

Although he had largely discounted the reports of Fenians nearby, Booker took reasonable precautions for moving through unfriendly country. He ordered the column to load with ball ammunition[142] and then requested Major Gillmor to deploy an advance guard of the Spencer-equipped No. 5 Company of the Queen's Own. The order of march was that company, the remainder of the Rifles, the column commander, the York Rifle Company, the 13th Battalion and the Caledonia Rifle Company.[143] All of this was accompanied by the usual military ritual of shouted orders, bugle calls, drill movements and so on. The train signalled its arrival and departure with its whistle and may have saluted the Port Colborne column with extra blasts. The whistles and bugle calls were what alerted O'Neill's men shortly after they had encountered Samuel Johnson and the other mounted civilians a few miles north on Ridge Road. Still, it was the way things were done, and Booker and the other officers, with their rudimentary experience, can hardly be faulted for following the standard practice.

It all took a considerable amount of time, and it was probably about 7 A.M. on 2 June 1866 before Sergeant Andrew McIntosh marched his section of No. 5 Company, the point of Booker's column, north along Ridge Road.[144] Their job was not to fight but to detect the enemy before the main body could be lured into a trap, a task which was particularly important because of the absence of cavalry to screen the column's movement. As Booker's troops trudged along Ridge Road, all could tell that it would be a typical hot and humid early summer day in the Niagara Peninsula. Booker's aim was to keep his appointment in Stevensville, about six miles ahead, between 9 and 9.30 A.M., while taking proper precautions to avoid being surprised.[145]

The advance guard had moved about two miles and was nearing Garrison Road when McIntosh's section signalled enemy to their front by waving their shakos on their rifles.[146] At about the same time Private Alexander Muir of No. 10 Company, who was just ahead of Booker in the order of march and perhaps half a mile behind the advanced guard, spotted between twelve and fifteen loose horses near the corner of a wood on the left of the axis, and then a party of dismounted men in the woods. He cried out: "I see the Fenians – there are the Fenians." Booker halted the column and searched the terrain with his field glasses, but could only see the horses.[147]

The advance guard doubled back to join the main body and the Queen's Own deployed as skirmishers, while parties checked the woods which paralleled the road on either side of the column (see Map R-5). The main body of skirmishers was made up of the right wing of the Rifles, with Nos. 1, 5 and 2 Companies forward and 3 and 4 Companies in support. No. 5 Company formed the centre of the line and seems to have been just to the right (east) side of Ridge Road. The left wing supported the skirmishers, with No. 7 Company guarding the left flank, supported by No. 8 while No. 6 flanked to the right. The last two companies, Nos. 9 and 10, remained in reserve.[148] Except for the later deployment of Nos. 9 and 10 Companies on the right, the battalion would retain this general deployment during the battle to come. The Queen's Own advanced steadily until Fenian skirmishers fired a volley from behind a line of rail fences as

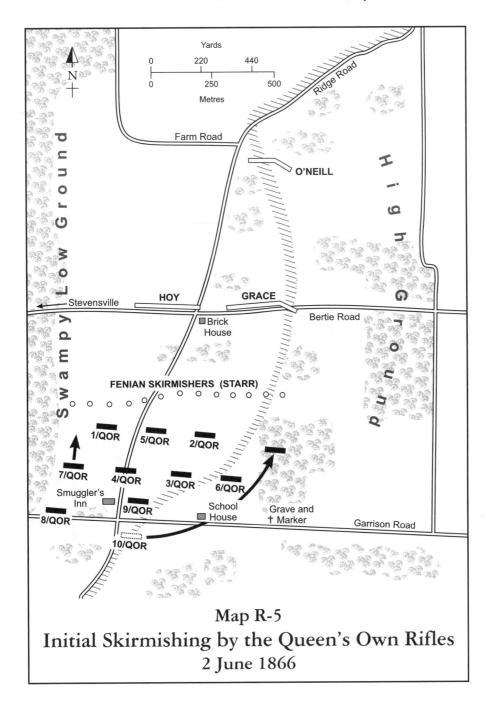

Map R-5
Initial Skirmishing by the Queen's Own Rifles
2 June 1866

the Canadians neared the south side of Garrison Road.[149] As the Rifles came under fire, the men dropped to the ground and returned fire from behind a fence line.[150] Estimates of the time vary, but it was probably about 8 A.M.

What was Booker's plan, other than to attack? He made no mention of a plan either in his written report[151] or his testimony at the later inquiry into his conduct.[152] It is probable that things seemed to be unfolding like an annual militia field or training day and Booker and Gillmor were operating by rote – meet the enemy, deploy the skirmishers, define the enemy's main position, win the firefight, rout the enemy at the point of the bayonet and, triumphant once again, form up and march home to the cheers of the spectators.

The main skirmish lines on both sides were about equal, perhaps 150 men in the three Queen's Own companies and 125-135 Fenians commanded by Lieutenant Colonel Starr. Starr gave way slowly, drawing the Canadians into the trap waiting near Bertie Road, a half mile north. As the Fenians began to drop back, the Canadians followed them. It was at the Garrison Road, or perhaps at the next fence line north, where the first Canadian casualty was suffered. Ensign Malcom McEachran of No. 5 Company was shot through the body while attempting to remove a rail from a fence to get a better shot. He was carried to the rear but died within twenty minutes.[153]

The Canadians advanced slowly, pushing the Fenians back, and as they believed, penetrating their defences. By this time both sides had taken the measure of their opponents. To Sergeant McIntosh and his fellow skirmishers, it was apparent most of the Fenians were old soldiers of the American army by their perfect formation and the position they had taken up.[154] The Fenians were less favourably impressed by the Canadians since, "it was plain that fighting was new to them. They exposed themselves unnecessarily, which trained men never do."[155]

By now the Rifles had advanced no more than three or four hundred yards north along Ridge Road. Major Gillmor moved No. 7 Company onto the left of the skirmish line in an effort to outflank the Fenian skirmishers. On his side, O'Neill felt he was in danger of being outflanked on both flanks, while Starr had been unable to draw out the Canadian centre as much as he wished. In an effort to entice the Canadians forward, O'Neill ordered his skirmishers to retire through the Bertie Road line.[156] The Rifles followed in pursuit but their apparent success was not without a price – they were running out of ammunition. No. 5 Company had fired all the available rounds for its Spencers[157] and had been withdrawn from the skirmish line, while the other companies had been rotated in and out of the line as their stocks ran low.[158] Six and possibly eight companies of the Rifles – at least a third of the Canadian force – were now down to ten to fifteen rounds per man before the main enemy force had been engaged. While the Rifles apparently had reserve ammunition on a wagon in the rear of the column,[159] there is no evidence an attempt was made to replenish the depleted stocks, possibly because events now happened before any resupply could take place.

Lieutenant Colonel Alfred Booker, Canadian Militia (1824-1871)

Booker, who attempted to command a brigade of raw troops in battle without the benefit of training, experience or staff, was ruined professionally and personally by the outrage that followed the debacle at Ridgeway. His direction of the battle, while perhaps uninspired, was steady and workmanlike, at least until he ordered, "Prepare for Cavalry!" Booker was a man in the wrong place at the wrong time. (Courtesy, National Archives of Canada, C-2039)

During the skirmishing Booker had ridden close behind the Queen's Own, where he could observe what was going on without interfering with Gillmor's command of his battalion. Thus when Gillmor reported that his men were running short of ammunition and requested relief,[160] Booker turned to the acting commanding officer of the 13th Battalion and said, "Major Skinner, you will skirmish with the right wing."[161] As the right wing, made up of the York Rifle Company and Nos. 1, 2 and 3 Companies of the 13th, with No. 4 Company in support, began to move forward, Booker ordered Gillmor to seize and clear a wood on the right flank with two of his companies. By this stage, only two Rifle companies, Nos. 9 and 10, were not yet engaged and Gillmor, perhaps wishing to retain at least one company with ammunition, at first sent only No. 10 from its position just east of the corner of Garrison and Ridge roads to carry out the task although No. 9 Company was later deployed on this flank as well.[162]

At about this moment, roughly 9.30 A.M., Booker received two telegrams from Peacocke. The first was a reminder to be cautious in feeling his way, for fear obstacles should prevent a junction, while the second reported that Peacocke could not leave Chippawa before 7 A.M. instead of 5 A.M., which was the time Booker recalled Akers had given him for Peacocke's departure. This information was devastating. Booker had expected Peacocke would be near Stevensville by this time and, hearing the rattle of musketry, would be rushing to his aid. After showing the telegram to Gillmor, who was near, Booker despatched Detective Armstrong with a message to Peacocke that he had been attacked by the Fenians at 7.30 A.M. three miles south of Stevensville.[163] While Booker left no record of

The 13th Battalion replaces the Queen's Own Rifles at Ridgeway, 1866

This painting depicts the passage of the Right Wing of the 13th through the Queen's Own. It is noteworthy that Von Ericksen shows two mounted figures in the foreground, one in uniform and the other in civilian clothes, as the only two Canadians who were mounted during the battle were Lieutenant Colonel Booker and Detective Armstrong. (Painting by Alexander Von Ericksen, courtesy, Fort Erie Museum Board)

his intentions, Gillmor felt that "the situation of the volunteers was then rendered most critical as it seemed improbable we could hold our position for the two hours we were thus left unsupported; however I conceived an advance and repulse of the enemy our only chance."[164] Booker may have shared these views or just have decided to keep fighting for want of any better idea.

Since this event roughly coincided with O'Neill's decision to withdraw his skirmishers, the Canadians were able to pick up the pace of the advance and soon reached the Bertie Road line. The Fenians then abandoned this line and fell back to a barricade a few hundred yards further north along Ridge Road (see Map R-6).[165] The Canadian skirmish line at this time probably consisted of – from left to right – the York Rifle Company, Nos. 3, 2 and 1 Companies of the 13th Battalion, and extending up the hill and inclined towards the crest Nos. 9 and 10 Companies of the Rifles. The line was supported by Nos. 7 and 4 Companies of the Rifles on the left and No. 4 Company of the 13th and No. 6

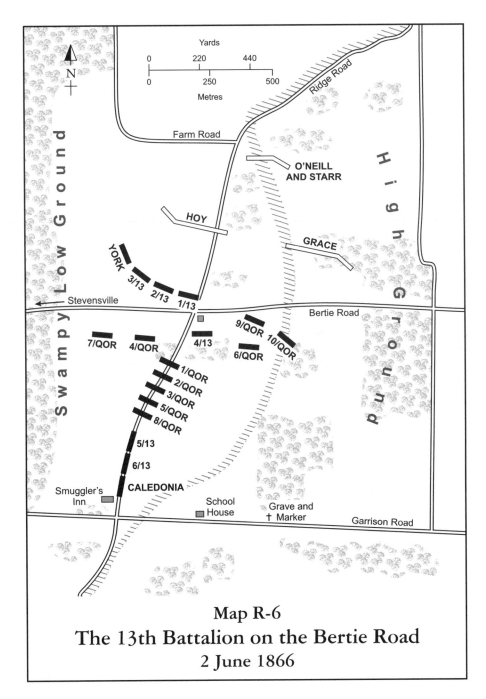

Map R-6
The 13th Battalion on the Bertie Road
2 June 1866

Company of the Rifles on the centre-right, although the skirmish lines and the supports may have been intermingled to some extent. In particular Nos. 6 and 7 Companies of the Queen's Own may still have been on the skirmish line or in the process of withdrawing from it. The remaining Queen's Own companies, Nos. 1, 2, 3, 5 and 8, were formed up in column just to the right of Ridge Road

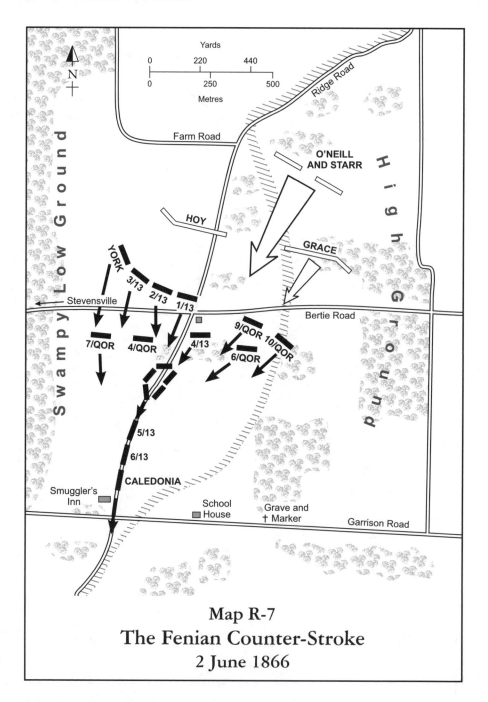

Map R-7
The Fenian Counter-Stroke
2 June 1866

behind the supports. Booker's reserve, Nos. 5 and 6 Companies of the 13th and the Caledonia Rifle Company, was formed in column of companies on Ridge Road just north of Garrison road.[166]

It was at precisely this point, with the two battalions still in the process of switching positions and thus slightly off balance – Captain R.H. Davis of the

York Rifles, having marched his company through the Queen's Own to take up his proper position of the left flank[167] – that disaster struck (see Map R-7). Booker had been concerned for some time that the Fenians might outflank his right and was preparing to alter his deployment to counter such a move when cries of "Cavalry" and "Look out for cavalry" arose from the centre front. Someone on the skirmish line had spotted a couple of horsemen, almost assuredly Fenian scouts returning to report to O'Neill, and raised the alarm. This coincided with the retirement in the centre of a number of relieved skirmishers back on the reserves, as though they were being threatened by a cavalry charge. Booker reacted by rote and smartly ordered: "Prepare for Cavalry."[168] Gillmor in turn ordered the Queen's Own to form square, which was done on the Ridge Road about a quarter mile south of Bertie Road by Nos. 1, 2, 3, 5, and 8 Companies,

"Prepare for Cavalry!" Canadians forming square

The sighting of horsemen, probably Fenian scouts (note the two mounted riders with rifles in the right of the scene), led to the order for the Queen's Own Rifles to form square. This image depicts several Queen's Own companies in square on the road with other men running towards it from the right flank. (Painting by Alexander Von Ericksen, courtesy, Fort Erie Museum Board)

The crest of the ridge from the area of the square

The Fenians attacked down the ridge, roughly between the two modern-day buildings, driving in the Canadian flank guard and forcing the retreat of the troops who had formed square. Despite ample primary source evidence, this attack has largely been ignored by Canadian historians since the end of the 19th century, with the notable exception of David Owen. (Photo by Brian Reid)

although other troops from both battalions, including the 13th Battalion's colour party, also took refuge in the square.[169] Both Booker and Gillmor immediately realized their error and ordered the troops to reform in column. A series of confusing orders and bugle calls ensued, cohesion was lost in a number of the companies, and bewildered and frightened men began to waver.[170]

Most Canadian accounts of the battle, including nearly all secondary sources, claim the Fenians were on the verge of withdrawing and that it was confusion resulting from conflicting orders combined with Fenian rifle fire on the square that sparked the Canadian retreat. While both played a part, evidence from a subsequent inquiry points to a Fenian advance on the right and centre of the Canadian line. Part of that advance drove Nos. 9 and 10 Companies of the Rifles down the slope and back onto the main body milling about near Ridge Road.[171] Captain John Gardner of No. 10 Company testified at the Booker Inquiry that most of his men withdrew towards the square in disarray in the face of a general Fenian advance.[172] Sergeant McIntosh of No. 5 Company felt that the Fenian advance, coming while the men were still in square, caused the retirement, and that if the troops had been in line they could have repulsed the assault with volley fire.[173] Other evidence also pointed to a Fenian charge – No. 9 Company, which had not been heavily engaged up to this point, suffered casualties of three killed and four wounded or a quarter of the total Queen's Own Rifles casualties

Not quite the other side of the hill

This photo taken from just below where Bertie Road crosses the Limestone Ridge shows the route taken by the Fenian attackers as they advanced on the square which was in the centre background. The barn is about one hundred yards south of the junction of Ridge and Bertie roads. These photos were taken in early June and demonstrate how the vegetation masks the view, although the ground was more open in 1866. (Photo by Brian Reid)

at Ridgeway (see Table 1). In fact, all but two of that regiment's casualties were in the companies deployed on the centre and right of the battlefield.[174] Finally the only position that would have allowed the Fenians to take the square under effective fire was the ground vacated by Nos. 9 and 10 Companies. On 30 June 1866, Lieutenant Colonel William G. Durie, the Assistant Adjutant General for Canada West, submitted the results of an investigation and a detailed sketch map he had made of the battle after interviewing participants and local residents and examining the battlefield. After noting that the Fenians had retreated from the Bertie Road line and hastily constructed a second barricade a few hundred yards to the north along Ridge Road, he concluded that a Fenian advance coincided with the cry of "cavalry" and the order to form square. As Durie stated:

> The column had barely been reformed, the officer commanding seeing no cavalry and being aware of the increased risk to his men from this formation, when the running back of the troops on the right followed by the enemy close upon them emparted the panic to those on the road and they also broke and ran.[175]

As for the Fenians, O'Neill reported that when the Canadians "got close enough, we gave them a volley and then charged them, driving them nearly three miles through the town of Ridgeway."[177]

Table 1 – Canadian Casualties by Company, Ridgeway, 2 June 1866[176]

Unit	Company	Killed	Wounded
QOR	1	0	2
	2	1	3 (2 later died)
	3	1	3
	4	0	1
	5	1	2
	6	0	3
	7	1	1
	8	0	0
	9	3	4
	10	0	2
13th	1	0	1
	2	0	0
	3	0	4
	4	0	2
	5	0	1
	6	0	1
Caledonia Rifles		0	0
York Rifles		0	2

In plain words, two militia battalions – first the Queen's Own and then the 13th – broke and ran. But that is perhaps an over-simplification. Some, perhaps most, ran, propelled by fear and panic, casting aside rifles, knapsacks, anything that impeded their flight. Others withdrew, face to the enemy, and paused to fire from time to time. In some cases, primarily in the companies on the left of the line, the officers were able to retain control and their men retired in a body after they observed Fenians to their right and rear. Both Booker and Major James Skinner of the 13th Battalion attempted to rally the men, but troops streamed past them down Ridge Road towards Ridgeway.[178] Gillmor's actions were more ambiguous. At first he seemed to have been unnerved by the sudden turn of events and ordered officers who had rallied their men and turned to face the enemy – in one case a force of between one and two hundred – to resume the retreat as the battle was lost. In fact, by the time the retreating Canadians arrived in Ridgeway, the combination of the muggy June heat and the distance had slowed the rout to a walk. The last troops to reach Ridgeway did so as a formed body commanded by Gillmor who seems to have shaken off his defeatism, and he and Booker only abandoned the little village upon the arrival of the first Fenians.[179]

The Fenian pursuit was not pushed very hard. O'Neill halted most of his force in the area of Garrison Road, ordering Starr to continue the pursuit with his skirmishers, a little less than half the force in all and far fewer in number than the retreating Canadians.[180] O'Neill's men collected the dead and wounded of both sides and O'Neill spoke kindly to a number of the Canadian wounded who were being treated by the Fenian medical officer, Eamon Donnelly, and a local Canadian physician, Doctor N. Brewster, a former medical officer in the Union Army.[181] Some of the prisoners later reported O'Neill told them he was on the verge of ordering a retreat when the Canadians broke. However, his words more likely were an act to comfort wounded captives than an admission of near defeat on his part. This has not prevented Canadian commentators on the battle of Ridgeway from seizing upon his statement in a rather pathetic effort to salvage something from the debacle.[182]

Despite his success, O'Neill was aware that the Chippawa column was only a few miles away and that he was vulnerable to attack from a superior force. He decided that the "best policy was to return to Fort Erie, and ascertain if crossings had been made at other points, and if so, I was willing to sacrifice myself and my noble little command for the sake of leaving the way open, as I felt satisfied that a large proportion of the enemy's forces had been concentrated against me."[183]

O'Neill probably intended to make a last stand in the abandoned and partially ruined War of 1812 fort. The Fenians retreated to Fort Erie in two detachments. O'Neill and his men marched down Garrison Road, while Starr led his down the railway, pausing to set Sauerwein's Bridge alight for a second time. The Fenians almost certainly did not suspect that another Canadian force awaited them in Fort Erie.[184]

About dawn on 2 June, Lieutenant Colonel J. Stoughton Dennis and the troops on the *W. T. Robb* had rounded the point and steamed into the Niagara River. The tug first moved upriver as far as Black Creek without encountering any Fenians and just in time to see the rear guard of the Chippawa column turn inland off the river road.[185] Dennis then returned to Fort Erie, where he disembarked the Welland Canal Field Battery and most of the Dunnville Naval Brigade. Dennis and Akers now took most of these troops on a sweep north along the river, searching for Fenians, until they encountered the abandoned enemy camp at Newbigging's farm. They continued downstream, then reembarked at Black Creek and returned to Fort Erie.[186] The rest of the day was spent rounding up Fenian deserters and stragglers, some fifty-seven in all, who were placed under guard around the village.[187]

Horsemen soon brought word of the approach of more enemy. Instead of standing offshore to prevent their reinforcement or escape, Dennis disembarked his men, secured the Fenian prisoners in the tug's hold, and formed his troops up to meet this new threat.[188] Even if, as Dennis obviously believed, the Fenians had been defeated by Booker and were retreating, it was a foolish move as it not only jeopardized his command for no purpose, but it ensured the Fenians could return to the United States to proclaim a victory.

The Welland Canal Field Battery and the Dunnville Naval Brigade formed on the road in front of the dock with Dennis standing near Captain Lachlan McCallum, the commanding officer of the naval brigade. When Fenians appeared in strength from the direction of both Garrison Road and the old fort at about 4 P.M., Dennis ordered the tug to cast off, thus cutting his line of retreat.[189] A few of the enemy fired long-range shots at the Canadians and, as bullets began to zing around their ears, a number of the troops heard McCallum exclaim, "Where the hell are you going?" Bombardier James McCracken, the British instructor attached to the Welland Canal Field Battery, and Gunner John Graybird later testified that they turned and saw Dennis crouched over and running to the rear.[190]

The ensuing engagement was short and sharp. After firing a volley the Canadians retreated to cover, most of the little party surrendering when their ammunition was expended, although McCallum and a few men escaped downstream to be picked up by the *W. T. Robb*. The tug then steamed towards Port Colborne, thus eliminating the last chance of denying the Fenians reinforcement or retreat.[191]

Dennis managed to evade capture, and after shaving his magnificent sidewhiskers and exchanging his uniform for civilian clothes, slunk through the woods until at first light the next day he contacted the Chippawa column.[192] He initially reported the volunteers had performed badly and had let him down, but later changed his story to one of praise for their performance. For his part, Akers, who had a habit of not being around when he was needed, had taken a horse and buggy on a reconnaissance and was not present during the fight at the dock. Narrowly avoiding capture, he fled west along the railway, pausing to extinguish the fire at Sauerwein's Bridge and then driving to Port Colborne.[193]

Having secured his crossing point to the United States, O'Neill ordered Grace and his Eighteenth Regiment to screen the approaches from Chippawa, while he took the remainder of his force to the old fort. At about 6 P.M. he signalled to Captain Hynes in Buffalo that the gathering British and Canadian forces would surround his command by morning and that he could not hold out for long but, if Fenian offensives were going on elsewhere, he was prepared to stay and fight. On receiving word that no other invasion of Canada had been made, O'Neill requested that his troops be evacuated that night.[194]

The transportation, a large scow towed by a tug, arrived at the wharf of the Buffalo and Lake Huron Railway in Fort Erie at about midnight.[195] By 2 A.M. in the morning of 3 June, or fourteen hours after the skirmish with Dennis's expedition, the Fenians were on their way back to the United States. Before they could reach the American shore, the armed tug USS *Harrison* took them into custody, but after a few anxious days they were paroled and allowed to return home.[196]

The obvious question is how the Fenians managed to escape unchallenged despite the presence of the Chippawa column. The explanation is less than flattering to the commander of that column, Lieutenant Colonel George Peacocke. First, the column did not leave Chippawa for Stevensville until sometime between 7 and 7.30 A.M. on 2 June, or much later than Peacocke had told Akers, or Akers had decided on his own, depending upon which account one accepts. To his credit, Peacocke did telegraph Booker at 5.30, informing him he would be delayed. (As noted, this communication reached Booker when he was already engaged with the Fenians.)[197] Due to a lack of information about the condition of the most direct route to Stevensville, Peacocke took the longer route via Black Creek, which added at least an hour to his march.[198] At 11 A.M. the column was about three miles north of Stevensville when Colonel Peacocke received word that Booker had encountered the Fenians three miles south of Stevensville at 7.30. He also learned that the Port Colborne column was retiring to Ridgeway, not Port Colborne. Apparently not an officer who would "march to the sound of the guns," Peacocke then halted at New Germany, two miles north of Stevensville.[199]

It was not until 4 P.M., after he had learned that the Fenians had retired towards Fort Erie, that Peacocke resumed his march,[200] not towards Stevensville and the Garrison road, but along Bowen Road, which led to the north of Fort Erie. Just before last light, after making contact in close country with what probably were pickets from Grace's regiment, he halted for the night, less than an hour's march from Fort Erie.[201] While the halt may have been justifiable given what Peacocke knew at the time, it allowed the Fenians to escape and to claim the only victory for the Irish independence movement between 1798 and 1919.[202]

The debacle at Ridgeway resulted from a number of causes, some direct and some indirect. Certainly Lieutenant Colonel Alfred Booker must bear the lion's share of the blame for his handling of the battle. Despite his lack of experience and the poor state of his command, the press and the public wanted a scapegoat and he filled the bill. (Many years after the event the author of a particularly virulent attack on Booker confessed that his book had been commissioned by some officers in the 13th Battalion who had resented that officer's appointment to command that unit and took the opportunity to destroy his reputation.) Booker demanded an inquiry. It was held at Hamilton in early July 1866 and found that on the whole he had acted properly, except for the order to form square.[203] This did little to stop the criticism and Booker left both Hamilton and the militia, moving to Montreal, where he died, embittered, on 27 September 1871.[204]

Lieutenant Colonel George Peacocke, as the immediate superior of Booker, Dennis and Akers, bore some share of the responsibility. When asked why he had not placed Dennis and Akers under arrest for disobeying his orders, Peacocke explained, "Dennis is not a soldier and did not know any better, and he is a volunteer officer and it would look as if I was trying to make a scape-goat of him to save myself." Like the unfortunate Booker, Peacocke became a convenient target for an outraged and largely ill-informed public, much, one suspects, to the relief of his British and Canadian superiors.[205]

Captain Charles Akers, who seems to have possessed a uncanny ability for doing the wrong thing at the wrong time, must assume a large part of the responsibility. His disobedience of the spirit of Peacocke's orders and his decision to accompany Dennis rather than the Port Colborne column left Booker out on a shaky limb. That he escaped visible censure was probably because of his junior rank in comparison to Booker, Peacock and Dennis.

If anyone can be said to have set the stage for the Fenian success, it was Lieutenant Colonel J. Stoughton Dennis. His hare-brained scheme, one which defied all sound military principles, undermined the positions of both Booker and Peacocke. His actions at Fort Erie were disgraceful examples of incompetence and outright cowardice. Somehow Dennis managed to escape censure only to display his talents once again in Manitoba, where he played a major part in provoking Louis Riel to rebel in 1870. In 1878 he was named deputy minister of the interior in the second Macdonald government. He resigned on 31 December 1881, was created a Commander of the Order of St. Michael and St. George on 24 May 1882 and died on 7 July 1885 at Kingsmere, Quebec.

The primary cause of the Canadian defeat, however, was Lieutenant Colonel

John O'Neill of the Fenian army. He made few, if any, serious mistakes in the two days he was in Canada. He obtained accurate information on the movements of his enemies and handled his forces in a manner one would expect from an experienced wartime commander. As was to be expected, he reaped the rewards of his success and rose high in the Fenian Brotherhood, but with the decline of the movement, however, his life went sharply downhill, and he died poor, alcoholic and ill on 7 January 1878.[206] This veteran soldier is buried in Omaha, Nebraska, where his name is perpetuated by the town of O'Neill in the same state.

As for the indirect causes, there was little lasting criticism of the British and Canadian civil and military authorities, who proved woefully ill-prepared to meet an invasion. Similarly, little was said of the policy of relying upon poorly trained and ill-equipped militia as Canada's first line of defence. Closer to the event, the decision not to mobilize any cavalry on 1 June doomed Peacocke and Booker to groping their way about the Niagara Peninsula, largely blind to whatever lay on the other side of the hill. (Peacocke at least made use of the information he received from locals at Chippawa, unlike Booker, but neither chose to use these men as mounted scouts during their marches.) The lack of adequate maps was inexcusable, especially as reliable ones were available. The shortages of such basic items of equipment as boots, blankets and the like speak for themselves. Faulty preparation proved disastrous and when all these factors are considered, it can be argued with some justification that the Canadian government stacked the deck against Booker and his men before the first shot was fired.

There are two major lessons to be learned from the battle of Ridgeway in 1866. First, wishful thinking and amateurism disguised as ardour are no substitutes in combat for detailed preparation, hard training and clear-headed thinking. Second, and more important, a government that structures its defences to achieve social and political, not military, ends should not be surprised when its forces fail the test of war.

The Ridgeway Battlefield Today

The Ridgeway Battlefield is easily accessible by road. If approaching from Toronto or Hamilton via the Queen Elizabeth Way, take Exit 16 and go south on Niagara Regional Road (NRR) 116 through Snyder (the name was changed from New Germany during the First World War, but it is still referred to as New Germany locally) and Stevensville until you reach Garrison Road (Highway 3). Turn left and proceed east a few hundred meters to the first traffic light, which is at the corner of Garrison and

Ridge Roads, near the point where the engagement between the Canadian and Fenian skirmishers began. If coming from the United States via the Peace Bridge from Buffalo over to Fort Erie, you may either take the Queen Elizabeth Way towards Toronto and proceed as above, or swing left and follow Highway 3 to the corner of Garrison and Ridge Roads. If in doubt, stop at the Ontario Information Kiosk at the exit from the Peace Bridge and ask for instructions.

At the corner of Garrison and Ridge Roads, turn north and follow the route taken by the advancing Canadian militia. The battlefield has largely escaped development, although because of changes in farming practices it is more heavily wooded than was the case in 1866. The area where the five Queen's Own companies formed square is open, however, as is the ground running north and east from there. One can easily pick out Bertie Road as it crests the ridge – from which the Fenians drove Nos. 9 and 10 Companies of the Rifles and Booker's reputation before them. The corner of Bertie and Ridge Roads provides an excellent view of how the ground drops away to the west as well as a perspective of the Fenian position to the north and east. The brick farm house on the southeast corner of the junction still bears scars from the battle.

If you wish, return along Ridge Road and turn left onto Garrison Road and proceed about 200 yards and turn left into the park where you can visit the Memorial Cairn. You may also opt to drive south along Ridge Road into Ridgeway itself. The Fort Erie Historical Museum in the old Bertie Township Hall at 402 Ridge Road (open only in the summer) has some interesting local displays as well as the complete collection of the works of Alexander Von Ericksen. The latter are not on general display; one should make special arrangements for viewing by contacting the museum at Box 339, Ridgeway, Ontario, L0S 1N0, (905) 894-5322. There is also a battlefield museum which is in the process of being moved to a new location and will re-open sometime in the future.

Pro Patria – The Ridgeway Memorial Cairn
This monument is located in the Ridgeway Battlefield Memorial Park near the junction of the Ridge and Garrison Roads. The inscription reads: "PRO PATRIA. In abiding memory of the officers and men of the Queen's Own Rifles, 13th Hamilton Battalion, Caledonia and York Rifle Companies of Haldimand who fought here in defence of their country against Fenian Raiders, on 2nd June, 1866." (Photo by Brian Reid)

The Creation of a Canadian Army,
1866 to 1899

Ridgeway was not the only Fenian invasion, although it was the most serious incursion. Attempts to cross the Quebec border were stopped in 1866 and 1871 and the final bid, made by John O'Neill at Pembina in Manitoba with only forty men, was brought to an abrupt end by American authorities who arrested the Fenian leader and his followers. The Fenian threat had been serious enough, however, to convince the independent provinces of British North America that there was unity in strength and, on 1 July 1867, they confederated as the Dominion of Canada, the first autonomous state in the British Empire. Defence now became the responsibility of the new Canadian federal government and one of its first steps was to replace the older sedentary militia organization in all provinces with units of volunteer militia.

The leaders of the new nation still expected that British regulars would constitute the first line of defence in event of trouble. They were therefore somewhat surprised when Britain, faced with a growing military threat in Europe from France and Germany, announced that it intended to remove its forces from Canada, retaining troops only in the naval bases of Victoria and Halifax. It was well for the new country that in May 1871 Britain signed the treaty of Washington to resolve its differences with the United States because this document ushered in an era of good relations between Canada and her neighbour to the south. This done, the British army turned over its posts and stores to Canada and evacuated its garrisons – on 11 November 1871 the last British troops marched out of the Quebec Citadel singing "Auld Lang Syne" to board the waiting troopships anchored in the harbour.

The decade that followed saw a decline in the strength of the volunteer militia but also the creation of a permanent Canadian military establishment. In 1871, two small units of garrison artillery, A and B Batteries, were formed to garrison the fortresses at Kingston and Quebec and furnish instructors for the militia artillery. They were followed by a troop of cavalry and three companies of infantry and these "school corps" were later re-organized as permanent military units becoming, respectively, the Royal Canadian Artillery, the Royal Canadian Dragoons and the Royal Canadian Regiment. In 1873 a para-military organization, the North West Mounted Police, was organized to maintain order in the vast western territories turned over to Canada by the Hudson's Bay Company and to prevent the lawlessness common on the American frontier – its members constituted a peaceful reserve in case of emergencies. To train officers for both the regular and militia units, the Royal Military College of Canada was founded in 1876.

The regular units and the training they provided to the militia proved valuable in 1885 during the North-West Rebellion, the first serious threat to the security of the new nation. This insurrection by the aboriginal and Métis peoples of the prairies, whose traditional way of life had ended with the demise of the buffalo, was led by the charismatic Louis Riel and it was not his first effort to proclaim an independent state in western Canada. An earlier attempt in Manitoba in 1871 had been quashed by the dispatch of British troops but the 1885 rebellion was a much more serious affair. In response to the crisis, the Canadian government organized a force of some 5,000 troops composed of regulars, mounted police, militia and volunteers, and sent them west to the Saskatchewan and Alberta territories under the command of a regular British officer, Major General Frederick W. Middleton. In a campaign that involved many lengthy marches but little serious fighting, they put down the rebellion, disarmed the rebels and arrested Riel. A notable feature of this operation was the movement of units from eastern Canada on the new trans-continental railway system. The Halifax Volunteer Battalion travelled more than two thousand miles, the longest military deployment by rail up to that time. It was rather a pleasant journey punctuated by frequent stops for speeches and banquets, but by the time the unit got to the campaign theatre, the fighting was over and the battalion passed its days playing the recently-invented game of baseball.

The last decade of the 19th century was a period of growth and improvement for the Canadian military establishment, with attempts made to improve weaponry, equipment and training. These changes were necessary to keep up with the advances in military technology. Most western armies were now armed with breech-loading magazine rifles, machine guns and quick-firing artillery, and the tactical balance, which had started to tip in favour of the defence during the mid-19th century, was now swinging markedly in that direction. Such was the power of these new weapons that later commentators have stressed that it created a phenomenon of the "empty battlefield" where soldiers were rarely visible because they were forced to stay under cover.

In 1897 Canada's pride in both its military and the imperial connection with Britain was exemplified by the dispatch of a contingent of 200 militia officers and men to London to participate in the celebrations marking Queen Victoria's Diamond Jubilee. It was not the first time Canadians had served overseas. In 1868 a *Canadien* volunteer unit of Pontifical Zouaves, numbering nearly 400, was raised in Quebec to defend the Papal states during the Italian civil war and they returned home in 1870 to an enthusiastic reception by their French-speaking fellow citizens. In 1884, a volunteer force of nearly four hundred Canadian voyageurs was raised from volunteers to help transport Major General Garnet Wolseley's army up the Nile to rescue Major General Charles Gordon, trapped in Khartoum by the fanatical followers of the Mahdi, a religious zealot. They arrived in Cairo in September of that year and quickly gained a reputation as very efficient boatmen but "the hardest-drinking brawlers ever seen by the Sphinx."[1] Unfortunately, their efforts were to no avail as Khartoum fell before Wolseley's army could save its defenders.

The Nile and Zouave contingents were private ventures and not officially backed by the Canadian government, which, while expecting British support in time of need, was always careful to avoid Imperial entanglements. These entanglements were many and varied during the worldwide scramble for colonies waged by the major European states in the 19th century, particularly in Africa. For Britain a particular sore spot on that continent was the existence of two small independent nations, the Transvaal and the Orange Free State, on the borders of her own colonies in southern Africa. These states were peopled by the Boers, a devoutly religious and zealously independent people descended from the original Dutch colonists who had started to settle in Africa in the 17th century. The somewhat stiff-necked Boers were very effective soldiers, as they demonstrated in 1881 when a British attempt to annex the Transvaal resulted in a disastrous defeat at the battle of Majuba Hill. Thereafter, Britain wisely left the Boers to their own devices, but the discovery of gold and diamonds in the republics led to increased pressure being put on them, by various means, to come within the

Imperial fold. When the two republics resisted this pressure, Britain moved troops up to their borders in the autumn of 1899, an explicit threat that led to a Boer declaration of war against Great Britain on 11 October. Britain was confident, as well she might be, and most people in the Empire expected the whole thing to be over Christmas and the troops sailing back home to march in the victory parade.

They were wrong as the war did not progress as planned. In the first three months of the conflict, the Boers took the offensive and advanced deep into the British Cape and Natal Colonies, inflicting a number of bloody, humiliating defeats on British regulars and laying siege to the garrisons of Mafeking, Kimberley and Ladysmith. With Imperial forces in disarray and victory in sight, the Boers paused – a fatal error that allowed Britain time to build up its forces and ultimately doomed the Boer cause, although few realized it at the time.

In the second phase of the war, which lasted from February to October 1900, Britain went on the offensive and rapidly overran the two small Boer republics. With the main population centres and the railways under control, the British declared victory but the Boers refused to cooperate and began to conduct guerilla warfare against British garrisons and their railway-based lines of communications. It shortly became evident that British control over Boer territory extended no farther than artillery range from their garrisons, and fast-moving, hard-hitting Boer mounted forces ranged freely. In an attempt to deny the Boers their source of supplies, British and Imperial forces were organized into mobile columns to pursue their opponents, burn their crops and farms, confiscate their livestock and move their families into hastily-constructed concentration camps.

During one of these operations in November 1900, a British and Canadian column came under attack near a hamlet called Leliefontein – the result was one of the most hard-fought small actions of the South African War.

4

"For God's sake …

save your guns!"

Action at Leliefontein

7 November 1900

BOERS ON THE SKY LINE.

Saving the guns at Leliefontein, 7 November 1900

Sergeant Edward Holland is shown engaging the Carolina Commando with his Colt machine gun as the Boers make a rush to capture No. 5 Gun of D Battery, Royal Canadian Field Artillery at Leliefontein. The events depicted in this painting, while realistic, are compressed in both time and space. (Painting by Peter Archer, courtesy, Royal Canadian Dragoons Archives)

"For God's sake … save your guns!"
Action at Leliefontein

7 November 1900

Brian A. Reid

Lay my rifle here beside me, set my bible on my breast,
For a moment let the wailing bugles cease;
As the century is closing I am going to my rest –
Lord, lettest Thou Thy servant go in peace.
But loud through all the bugles rings a cadence in mine ear,
And on the winds my hopes of peace are stowed;
The winds that waft the voices, that already I can hear,
Of the rooi-baatje *singing on the road.*[1]

The action at Leliefontein fought on 7 November 1900 is unique in Canadian military history. First, it set a record for the most Victoria Crosses – three – won in a single day by a Canadian unit. Second, it shows that God is *not* always on the side of the big battalions. In the detached, computer-driven world of the modern operational analyst, the army that musters superior numbers wins. In the real world, intangibles such as leadership and morale matter, and matter a lot. Leliefontein is a vivid example of a battle between two experienced, well-led forces in which the lesser one averted disaster, by no more than the narrowest of margins, because it plain outfought the enemy.

Nowadays we would look askance at a big power that bullied two small countries whose only sin was a desire to maintain their culture and independence. A century ago the world operated somewhat differently and what we would categorize today as outrageous acts of aggression were carried out with general public support in the name of replacing savagery and regression with enlightenment and progress. Nowhere was this more evident than in the relationship between Great Britain and the two South African Boer republics of the Orange Free State and the Transvaal. The British government had managed to seize the political high ground by downplaying the geopolitical and commercial factors while embracing the plight of the British residents of the two republics, who were denied the franchise and other benefits of citizenship, but not the burden of taxation.

See Appendix D, page 382, for Orders of Battle of the Opposing Forces.

Knowing little and caring less about any issue except Imperial solidarity, English Canada grew more and more enthusiastic towards providing military support for the British cause as the diplomatic situation worsened through the summer of 1899. As usual this was not the case in Quebec, where support for the Imperial cause, not least in the Quebec wing of Prime Minister Sir Wilfrid Laurier's governing Liberal Party, certainly did not extend to an overseas military adventure. In an effort to placate voters outside Quebec, Laurier couched his opposition in fiscal terms, proclaiming on one occasion, "I do not favour at all the scheme for sending an armed force to Africa. We have too much to do in this country to go into military expenditures." He re-affirmed his opposition virtually on the eve of war, this time using constitutional and legal arguments, and departed for a visit to the Chicago World's Fair, confident he had settled the issue once and for all.[2]

If Laurier thought the matter was finished, he was sadly mistaken. The Boer invasion of British territory on 11 October created a massive upsurge of war fever in English Canada. On 14 October, after a hastily called cabinet meeting, the Canadian government announced that the country would send 1,000 infantry to fight beside the British forces in South Africa.[3] The first contingent, which sailed from Quebec on 30 October 1899, was hardly out of Canadian waters when the government offered a second contingent on 2 November, this time consisting of four squadrons of mounted riflemen and three batteries of field artillery. The British politely declined the offer with the *caveat* that, should the situation change, the War Office "will have no hesitation in availing themselves of it." On 16 December, in the aftermath of the devastating "Black Week," during which the Boers defeated three separate British armies, London accepted the Canadian offer, adding, "it is indispensable that men should be trained and good shots and should bring own horses."[4]

After much deliberation the Canadian government decided to organize the mounted rifles into two battalions, each two squadrons strong (A and B Squadrons in the first battalion, and C and D in the second), although the original plan had been to provide a unit made up of three squadrons drawn from the militia cavalry and a squadron of scouts recruited on the prairies. How and why this happened is outside the scope of this study; suffice to say, it was a compromise on the part of the government to satisfy the conflicting claims of the Department of Militia and Defence and the North West Mounted Police. Originally titled the 1st and 2nd Battalions, Canadian Mounted Rifles, the two units were redesignated in South Africa as the Royal Canadian Dragoons and the Canadian Mounted Rifles.[5] For convenience, the latter titles will be used below.

Hurry up and wait – embarkation at Halifax

After an unexpected delay caused by the unavailability of the original troop ship, the Royal Canadian Dragoons embarked on the SS *Milwaukee* at Halifax on 21 February 1900. By this time the horses and baggage have already been loaded and the men are formed in single file by troops, waiting for the order to board the ship. (Courtesy, Royal Canadian Dragoons Archives)

As was the case with the first contingent, these two units were made part of the regular army, the Permanent Force. This was done to provide a convenient repository for any honours won in South Africa and to avoid militia in-fighting over titles and representation. The Permanent Force cavalry, the Royal Canadian Dragoons, provided the cadre, including the commanding officer, second-in-command, both squadron commanders, the adjutant and two troop leaders. Regulars also made up one of the four troops in each squadron and the nucleus of the battalion and squadron headquarters and support staff.[6]

Just as the Royal Canadian Dragoons was an extension of the army, the Canadian Mounted Rifles carried the pride and traditions of the North West Mounted Police to South Africa. In fact, the Mounted Rifles drew on the police even more heavily than the Dragoons did the permanent cavalry, since thirteen of its nineteen officers and more than a third of its other ranks were seconded from the force. While the Permanent Force provided a troop in each Dragoon squadron, the Mounted Police members made up the nucleus of each Rifles troop. This approach was the result of the absence of any extensive militia organization in the North West Territories except the para-military organization of the police which transferred easily into squadrons and troops.[7]

Despite the rigours of a Canadian winter, recruiting was soon under way for both units. In the Annapolis Valley of Nova Scotia, Robert Ryan, a graduate of the Royal Military College and a member of the Reserve of Officers, enlisted in the ranks of 4 Troop, B Squadron of the Dragoons, as did William E. Anderson in Saint John, New Brunswick. Harold Borden, the only son of the Minister of Militia and Defence, left his medical studies to accept an appointment as their troop leader. In Ontario Alfred Ault, a Spanish-American war veteran, decided to join up and caught the train to Montreal from Aultsville on the banks of the St. Lawrence while William Knisley trudged through the snow from his home in Selkirk to Hagersville, Ontario, to catch a train to the recruiting station. In Ottawa Eddy Holland signed on as a private in 3 Troop, A Squadron, as did Plantagenet McCarthy, son of a prominent sculptor. The Manitobans who formed 2 Troop, B Squadron included Francis Young, a veteran of the North West Rebellion, as the troop leader and Albert Hilder, Arthur Roberts and the Carter twins, Arthur and Gerald. In Edmonton William Griesbach gained a place as a private in C Squadron by holding a large lump of coal behind his back when he stepped on the scale during his medical examination. (He passed the minimum weight requirement by half a pound. The mounted police medical officer may have turned a blind eye to this trick for Griesbach's father was Superintendent A.H. Griesbach, holder of North West Mounted Police Regimental Number 1.) Thomas "Casey" Callaghan, a short, muscular Ulsterman from Maple Creek, Saskatchewan traded life as a teamster for khaki drill and seventy-five cents a day. In Macleod, Alberta a twenty-five-year-old Métis cowboy named Jefferson Davis enlisted at the local mounted police post while a few miles farther west in Pincher Creek Fred Morden, a member of the first white family to settle in the area, did the same. Of this disparate group who represented a wide range of social positions and backgrounds, two would be killed in action, five wounded and three decorated, two with the Distinguished Conduct Medal and one with the Victoria Cross.[8]

Canadian planning called for the second contingent (1,320 officers and men) to sail to South Africa as soon as the units were assembled and equipped – at the latest by late January or early February 1900. Two of the field batteries and the Canadian Mounted Rifles left Halifax on schedule, but the departure of the Royal Canadian Dragoons and the third battery was delayed until 21 February because of sickness in the crew of the troopship. While the authorities scrambled to charter a replacement ship, the delay provided a welcome opportunity to carry out a rigorous training program and test the men in riding and shooting. While most were able to make the grade, William Anderson failed his riding test and was ordered to remain in Canada. Anderson, however, was determined to fight with his buddies and stowed away, presenting himself once the ship was safely on the high seas.[9] His ploy worked and he was to see his share of action in the regimental machine gun section.

On 1 May both units joined Major General Edward Hutton's 1st Mounted Infantry Brigade at Karee Siding north of the Orange Free State capital of Bloemfontein, although it should be noted the Mounted Rifles had already seen active service in the Karoo and B Squadron had been in action on 22 April near Leeukop.[10] Mounted troops in South Africa were classed as cavalry, mounted infantry and mounted rifles. In both theory and practice, the two Canadian units were mounted rifles, that is horsemen capable of carrying out all the duties of cavalry except the mounted charge. Mounted infantry, on the other hand, were infantry temporarily mounted on horses, using their improved mobility to cross the battlefield to fight on foot.[11] Because the cavalry rarely had an opportunity to mount a successful charge with sword and lance, the distinction between the arms was blurred, with one exception. The cavalry, British regulars all, enjoyed the pick of the remounts in both size and condition. The other mounted units, both British and colonial, were forced to use animals of inferior quality, which hampered their ability to undertake long marches and carry out prolonged operations.[12]

All Imperial mounted troops used essentially the same tactical doctrine, which was based on the building block of four men. When ordered to fight on foot, three men would dismount and the fourth would lead their horses to a position of safety, so reducing the available firepower by 25 per cent.[13] There was, however, a distinction in Canadian mounted rifle tactics. Unlike the British, who had adopted a system where troops deployed and fought in two ranks, the Canadians, influenced by the experience of the American cavalry, retained the single rank system as "good enough for [J.E.B.] Stuart and [Phil] Sheridan," two renowned American Civil War cavalry commanders.[14] The Canadians were armed with ten-shot .303 calibre Magazine Lee Enfield Mark I rifles and bayonets, and .45 calibre Colt revolvers. The commanding officer of the Dragoons, based on his experience with the British cavalry, saw little use for revolvers and left them in stores. However, the western-Canada-based Rifles found these weapons very useful, particularly for close-quarter work.

For the Canadians the great march to Pretoria, the capital of the Transvaal, that was supposed to end the war, began in earnest on 3 May 1900. Hutton's brigade led the advance of Lieutenant General John French's cavalry column with A Squadron providing the advance guard of the army. The remaining Canadians found themselves near the rear of the mounted column. The advance guard, which was provided on a daily rotation, was a force deployed in front of the main body to provide warning of approaching enemy and to prevent an ambush. It was dangerous work, likened by one correspondent "to hunting for a gas leak with a candle."[15]

Farther back in the main body, it was simply a case of plodding along at a walk, for the column could move no faster than its slowest element, its large baggage train. To the utter disgust of the ex-cow punchers in the ranks of the Mounted Rifles, the routine was to dismount and lead the horses every other hour in an effort to conserve the animals.[16] On this day the march had not progressed very far when the rattle of firing to the front could be heard and orders to prepare to attack were received. The units deployed from "Column of Route" into "Line of Squadron Columns" and began to trot towards the left to take up their positions. In effect, the main body, which had been marching in a long

Mounted infantry crossing a stream

A company of British mounted infantry led by a rather proper officer is crossing a stream, although it was probably classed as a major river in South Africa. A pair of Canadians, who may have been posted as guides, are watching their progress. The soldier on the left has dismounted, observing the golden rule to rest one's horse whenever possible. (Courtesy, Royal Canadian Dragoons Archives)

column changed its formation into a long line of columns, each a squadron strong and spaced about a quarter of a mile apart, perpendicular to and extended to the left of the line of march. It was quite exhilarating and the excited men began to whoop and shout. As the advance progressed, the four troops in each squadron extended into a line of riders galloping towards a long ridge. There the men dismounted and the number 3's in each section held the horses while the remainder doubled forward to form a firing line. As the line crested the ridge the Boers, who were in a draw between two *kopjes* (rocky hills), open a spirited fire upon it. The troops went to ground and returned the fire, while other units arrived and began to extend the line further to the left to outflank the Boers and threaten their retreat. This had the desired effect and the Boers withdrew rather than risk being overrun or cut off.[17]

The tone for the advance to Pretoria was set. The Boers only offered strong resistance on a few occasions, and by the time the British had reached the Transvaal capital on 5 June the Canadians had earned a reputation second to none in the army. An Australian who also served in the 1st Mounted Infantry Brigade devoted considerable space in *Tommy Cornstalk,* his book about the Australians in South Africa, to highly laudatory and colourful stories about Canadians in and out of action. Many observers, including Rudyard Kipling, commented on their picturesque and highly profane language, and they also earned a reputation as enthusiastic and opportunistic foragers (that is, looters). There is little doubt that the Canadians, with their wide-brimmed Stetsons and U.S. Army surplus McClellan saddles, were recognized and respected by Boer and Briton alike.

Their reputation was, in fact, based on more than behaving like escapees from a wild west show, for the Canadians had succeeded by beating the Boers at their own game. As Lieutenant E.W.B. Morrison of the artillery commented:

> I have seen every variety of mounted troops out here – regular cavalry, mounted infantry, regular and irregular, and none of them are in it with the "Canydians" for the sort of work to be done. Their outpost work is the best I have seen by long odds, for the simple reason that they know how to keep under cover. So far, all the British soldier has learned is to keep under cover when he is being fired at. When not being fired at he chooses for preference a conspicuous portion of the sky line or a hill top, and the Boers know just exactly where he is and how many of him there are. The Canadians keep under cover all the time, taking up their position before daylight and the Boers never know where they will stumble on them or how many there will be.[18]

All mounted troops had two advantages. The first, of course, was mobility. Mounted troops could, if the situation in South Africa demanded, move at several times the speed of dismounted troops to strike at the flanks and rear of the enemy. The second advantage was reduced casualties – mounted troops suffered far fewer casualties than did the infantry. The two Canadian mounted units had only five casualties, all wounded, from 22 April to 5 June 1900. In the same period, the infantrymen of the first Canadian contingent, by this time reduced by battle and disease to roughly the same size as the Dragoons and Mounted Rifles combined, lost four killed and eighteen wounded.[19] While part of this was due to their method of employment, another factor was the protection provided to the rider by his horse. Death or injuries to horses from enemy action were many times greater than to their riders. On 22 April, for example, 1 Troop of B Squadron of the Dragoons was lured into a Boer ambush and came under fire from close range, escaping with no human casualties but three horses killed,[20] while at the engagement at Klip River on 28 May, the Rifles suffered two men wounded and five horses killed.[21]

With the capture of Pretoria and the end of the era of highly mobile operations the Royal Canadian Dragoons began a period of semi-static garrison duties interspersed with brief periods of action. In one of these Lieutenant Francis

Three Canadian rough riders
This picture is probably of members of the Canadian Mounted Rifles taken at Cape Town. The term "rough riders" was used to describe men who could ride any horse no matter how wild and had much the same connotation as "commando" does today. Despite their uniforms, the men look more like cowboys than soldiers.
(Courtesy, Canadian War Museum, 75-840)

Young, described as the shortest man in B Squadron, was wounded and evacuated to the United Kingdom, shortly after leading a night raid behind the Boer lines that captured a number of Boers and two guns and earned both Young and Sergeant Robert Ryan praise in the brigade commander's official report.[22] On 16 July, in a hard-fought action against Boer General Ben Viljoen's veteran burghers, Lieutenants Harold Borden and John Burch were killed and two privates were wounded. While there was little heavy fighting, there was a continual series of small clashes and a drain of casualties, including Gerald Carter wounded on 7 October. When not in action, the frustrations of inactivity saw many troops signing up for duties in safer and better paid organizations such as the Imperial Military Railway. The absence of any means of tracking soldiers who were evacuated because of wounds or illness and who simply disappeared into the morass of the lines of communications, as well as the lack of any Canadian reinforcement system, saw regimental strength steadily decrease. By 16 October, with the Dragoons now forming part of the garrison of Belfast in the eastern Transvaal, only 160 effectives remained of an original strength of 375.[23]

The survivors, however, were veterans and made up a highly effective force, probably the best Canadian unit to fight in South Africa, although hardly likely to set an example of parade-square splendour. By this stage the regiment looked like "cowboys, with their shaggy little ponies, prairie hats and rough-and-ready uniform – for their original kit is worn out and they wear any sort of clothes they can pick up."[24] There were a number of reasons for the Dragoons' effectiveness, but two in particular should be noted. The unit was fortunate in having a number of excellent troop leaders to compliment the commanding officer's aggressive spirit; and it had an extremely effective machine gun section led by the

legendary Lieutenant Arthur L. (Gat) Howard, of North West Rebellion fame, and ably assisted by the redoubtable Sergeant Eddy Holland. The machine guns were fought as a manoeuvre sub-unit,

Lieutenant Arthur L. (Gat) Howard, DSO (circa 1846-1901)
Howard commanded the Dragoon machine gun section but was not present at Leliefontein. In an earlier battle, he and Sergeant Eddy Holland had removed the Colt from its carriage and carried it off on foot under heavy Boer fire. Rather than return to Canada, Howard elected to stay behind in command of an irregular unit largely manned by Canadians. He was killed in action on 17 February 1901. (Courtesy, National Archives of Canada, C-26179)

The Colt machine gun on the Dundonald carriage

This may be the actual weapon manned by Sergeant Eddy Holland at Leliefontein. The air-cooled Colt was preferred by the Dragoons over the heavier water-cooled Maxim because of its mobility and speed in and out of action. However, the bouncing and vibrations of day to day operation tended to literally shake it to pieces. In this picture two soldiers are engaged in the ongoing maintenance chores required to keep the weapon in operating condition. (Courtesy, Royal Canadian Dragoons Archives)

not as a support weapons organization, which increased the regiment's punch considerably.

The machine gun section had originally consisted of two horse-drawn guns, a water-cooled Maxim and an air-cooled Colt. Each weapon had its strong and weak points, but the Dragoons' commanding officer considered the Colt superior because it was much more mobile and quicker into and out of action. Furthermore, it was reliable and did not need a supply of water for cooling. He concluded his assessment by noting, "if caught by the enemy at close quarters, the gun can be detached from the carriage quite easily, and carried away on the saddle."[25] Lieutenant Howard agreed:

I find the best machine gun in the field is the Colt automatic. I have only one with me which has been in every engagement, and does exceedingly good execution up to 3000 yds, knocking out of action in one engagement a Maxim 1 pounder (pompom). It is mounted on a Dundonald carriage and with some improvements – which I will suggest, will be adopted by the British Army. It can accompany the cavalry anywhere and can be taken up any kopje, and in competition with galloping and tripod Maxim came into action in 10 seconds (Maxim 55) and out of action 5 seconds (Maxim 55).[26]

By the latter stages of the regiment's tour, the Maxim had been relegated to protection of static installations while the Colt was used as a mobile weapon. With a cyclic rate of fire of 480-500 rounds per minute and manned by skilled and courageous soldiers, it was a very effective weapon.

There was another reason for the regiment's success – its commanding officer. Lieutenant Colonel François Louis Lessard, born in Quebec City on 9 December 1860, had joined the Quebec Garrison Artillery in 1880 and taken several courses at the School of Gunnery in that city. On 11 June 1884 he had transferred to the Permanent Force Cavalry School Corps (later the Royal Canadian Dragoons) and seen active service with that unit in the North West Rebellion of 1885. He had been promoted major in May 1896, received a brevet promotion to lieutenant colonel in 1898 and been promoted substantive lieutenant colonel to command the Dragoons in July 1899.

With the outbreak of war in October 1899, Lessard had gone to South Africa as part of the first contingent and been attached to Lieutenant General John French's cavalry division. Having ridden to the relief of Kimberley. Colonel Lessard commanded the Royal Canadian Dragoons from April to December

1900. During his tour he saw a considerable amount of action and earned a reputation as an aggressive commander, perhaps excessively so.[27]

At this stage it is necessary to address the major reason why the Canadian Mounted Rifles, despite its fine raw material, did not do as well as the Royal Canadian Dragoons. The Rifles were made up to a very large extent of men without military experience

Lieutenant Colonel François Louis Lessard, CB (1860-1927)

This picture was taken when Lessard was a major general. He had seen active service on the lines of communications in the North West Rebellion, but South Africa was his first experience in combat. He proved himself to be an able, if rather impetuous, commander and was both liked and respected by his men – a by no means common state of affairs. (Courtesy, Royal Canadian Dragoons Archives)

and training. This was offset somewhat by the large number of mounted police-men, but police duties do not automatically translate into a military setting. This in turn was exacerbated by the run of incredibly bad luck that befell the unit's senior officers. The second-in-command, Major Sam Steele, had been trans-ferred to command Lord Strathcona's Horse before that unit left Canada, and was not replaced.[28] Another senior officer, Major Gilbert Sanders, had fallen ill en route to South Africa and could not immediately proceed to the front.[29] The Rifles first saw active service in the inhospitable desert-like Karoo of the western Cape Colony and here both the commanding officer, Lieutenant Colonel Law-rence W. Herchmer, the Mounted Police Commissioner, and the last remaining major, Joseph Howe, were incapacitated at various times, prompting Herchmer to request that a senior officer from the Dragoons be posted to the unit. Herchmer was subsequently returned to Cape Town as unfit for duty. It was a bad start, and one from which the Mounted Rifles never fully recovered.[30]

When the Rifles joined the 1st Mounted Infantry Brigade near Bloemfon-tein, the brigade commander took what to him was a logical and necessary step, but one that had unfortunate consequences for the unit. He had Major Thomas Evans, the second-in-command of the Dragoons, appointed as acting com-manding officer of the Rifles. When Herchmer later tried to rejoin, he was examined by a medical board and declared unfit for duty. This prompted Howe to demand he be re-lieved as well, leaving Sanders as the last of the original four senior officers with the unit.[31] This unfortunate situation was exacerbated because Evans was a member of the army and the others were members of the Mounted Police and there was no love lost between the two organizations. Evans's ap-pointment to replace the most senior member of the police was resented by many, if not most, Mounties in the Rifles.

Lieutenant Colonel Thomas Dixon Bryan Evans, born 22 March 1860, had seen active service in the North West Rebellion and then in 1888 joined the Infantry School

Lieutenant Colonel Thomas Dixon Bryan Evans, CB (1860-1908)
This picture was taken while Evans was commanding the Yukon Field Force. In South Africa he earned a reputation as the best Canadian commander of mounted troops. His mild manner and reluctance to get rid of some ineffective subordinates led some to question his resolve and strength of character. By November 1900, any doubts had been dispelled. (Courtesy, National Archives of Canada)

Corps. He later transferred to the mounted infantry school in Winnipeg, which would later be designated B Squadron of the Royal Canadian Dragoons. He had been promoted major on 2 December 1895 and brevet lieutenant colonel on 13 November 1899. Colonel Evans had commanded the Yukon Field Force in 1898-99 and went to South Africa as second-in-command of the Dragoons in March 1900. He was appointed to acting command of the Canadian Mounted Rifles on 5 May and was confirmed in the appointment in August.[32]

Evans earned a reputation as the best commander of Canadian mounted troops in South Africa. If he had a fault, it may have been that he was not ruthless enough in weeding out sub-standard officers. For example he retained Lieutenant Donald Bliss – a fellow veteran of the North West Rebellion and the Yukon Field Force, who had displayed major failings in his personal and professional conduct. In fairness, Evans recommended Bliss be returned to Canada, but in the meantime continued to employ him with the unit. Given the potential for schisms to develop in the Rifles, Evans probably felt he had to tread very carefully. On a happier note, he was followed everywhere by Spud, his Irish Terrier, a veteran of the Yukon Field Force.[33]

Despite its problems the Mounted Rifles did well in the advance to Pretoria and beyond. While the unit was under strength, it managed to avoid much of the siphoning-off of men to other employment that hurt the Dragoons. In terms of performance, the

Canadian Mounted Rifleman, South Africa, 1900

Wearing his khaki field service dress of heavy duck cloth and his tan felt stetson, this rifleman is armed with a Lee Enfield Mk I rifle. His saddle is of the NWMP variety with a horn and lariat. (Painting by Ron Volstad, courtesy, Department of National Defence)

Camp life on the Veld

Scenes from active service with D Battery, Royal Canadian Field Artillery, in South Africa. Below is the officers' mess and at left the officers' sleeping arrangements. Canadian officers shared campaign hardships with their men. (From E.W.B. Morrison, *With the Guns in South Africa*)

Rifles suffered only in comparison to the Dragoons, not to the rest of the Imperial forces in South Africa. While the Dragoons languished near Pretoria, by mid-June 1900 the Rifles were deployed in two-troop detachments along the railway between Bloemfontein and Pretoria. It was a time of patrolling and small clashes that earned Corporal "Casey" Callaghan, who commanded the regimental scouts, commendation for his skilful and aggressive patrolling. In one of the few major actions of the period, Corporal Fred Morden, in command of a small outpost that held off an attack by more than fifty Boers, was killed along with one of his men while the other two Canadians in his party were wounded. All were from Pincher Creek in the foothills of the Rockies. In July the Rifles rejoined the Dragoons and the remainder of the 1st Mounted Infantry Brigade in operations east of Pretoria and by October, with the Transvaal occupied and the war supposedly at an end, were deployed along the railway line from Pretoria to Komati Poort, with a strong detachment of three troops commanded by Major Gilbert Sanders at Belfast.

Besides the two mounted regiments, another group of Canadian soldiers, the left section of D Battery,[34] Royal Canadian Field Artillery, formed part of the Belfast garrison. This unit had arrived in the area on 26 August, just in time to take part in the battle of Bergendal, one of the last set-piece engagements of the war.[35] When the rest of the battery moved on to Lydenburg as part of General Ian Hamilton's division, this section remained behind, attached to the 1st Mounted Infantry Brigade and later the Belfast column.[36] The gunners, a combination of regulars from A and B Batteries of the Permanent Force, militiamen

Lieutenant Edward Whipple Bancroft Morrison, DSO (1867-1925)

Morrison was a member of Ottawa's 2nd Field Battery and a journalist for the *Ottawa Citizen* in civilian life. He was known as "Dinky" because of his size, but his conduct in action had earned him the description of a "fire-eater" by a British general. Here he has managed to bag a springbok, not an easy task at the best of times. (From *With the Guns in South Africa* by E.W.B. Morrison, 1901)

primarily from Ottawa's 2nd Field Battery and a few men enlisted off the street, were, like the other units at Belfast, under strength.

However, the section could still field two 12-pdr. guns, so that its reduced numbers were not so evident. A gun, technically a sub-section, consisted of the artillery piece and its limber (a limber was a two-wheeled trailer loaded with stores and ammunition) drawn by a six-horse team. Accompanying it was an ammunition wagon (a large two-wheeled trailer) with its own limber drawn by another six-horse team. Two such sub-sections (or 2 guns and all their vehicles) made up a section, commanded by a lieutenant. While the basic fighting unit of the field artillery was the six-gun battery, in South Africa sections often operated independently for extended periods of time.[37] The left section of D Battery was commanded by thirty-three-year-old Lieutenant Edward W.B. Morrison, in peacetime a member of Ottawa's 2nd Field Battery and a journalist with the *Ottawa Citizen*. He was nicknamed "Dinky" because of his height, or rather his lack of it, but he would prove at Leliefontein, as he had on other occasions, that size is not a good measure of courage. By late October Morrison's little unit had seen enough action fighting alongside the Dragoons that the gunners "entertain[ed] a sublime conviction that the dragoons, our guns and the Colt could go in one side of the Transvaal and out the other."[38]

Unfortunately, the 12-pdr. was not of the same quality as the standard British field gun, the 15-pdr., and the more modern quick-firing artillery pieces used by the Boers. In particular, it lacked any means of controlling the recoil forces and had to be manhandled back into position after each round. This defect reduced its rate of fire and caused undue fatigue in the under strength gun detachments, which lessened both accuracy and rate of fire. The 12-pdr. gun had an official range of 4,000 yards, the maximum range graduated on the sights. However,

Morrison's gunners were able to engage targets to a distance of 6,000 yards with a practised extra twist of the elevating wheel.[39] Two types of ammunition were used, case shot and shrapnel. The former was an anti-personnel round that operated like a giant shotgun shell, spraying lead balls from the muzzle but case was only effective for about 400 yards and was primarily a defensive weapon to be used at close quarters. Shrapnel, which made up the vast majority of the ammunition load, 132 rounds per gun compared to only eight case shot, was a hollow shell filled with metal balls packed on an expelling charge which was initiated by a fuse set to a predetermined time. When the fuse ignited, the balls were pushed out of the front of the round and dispersed by the centrifugal force of the spinning shell in a cone of ten to fifteen degrees. While shrapnel was effective at short ranges, at longer ranges the drag of the air on the shell so reduced its velocity that the expelled balls did not have sufficient energy to inflict a serious wound.[40]

Belfast, a station on the Pretoria–Komati Poort railway, (see Map L-1) had originally been occupied when the British overran the eastern Transvaal in August 1900. While there was some fluctuation in strength, in late October the garrison, nominally a "movable column," consisted of three and a half infantry battalions, a British cavalry squadron, the Royal Canadian Dragoons and a squadron of Canadian Mounted Rifles, supported by a British field battery of six 15-pdr. guns, a section of pom-poms (automatic weapons that fired one-pound high explosive shells) and two 5-inch guns as well as the two Canadian 12-pdrs.[41]

The town lay on the spine of the high veld, more than a mile above sea level. The altitude and lack of rainfall tempered what should have been a humid, subtropical climate to such an extent that frosts were common at night and sleet, while rare, was not unknown. The ground was open, rolling and covered with short stringy grass that foreign horses, unlike the Boer ponies, found unpalatable, especially after it had been nipped by frost.[42] From the hills ringing Belfast, thanks to the clear air and lack of intervening features, one could actually detect movement around the village of Carolina twenty miles south as the crow flies. The ground gradually sloped away from Belfast down to the edge of the escarpment at Van Wyk's *Vlei* (marsh), where the veld suddenly descended into the valley of the Komati River before climbing again up to Carolina. The Komati valley, which was about five miles wide, was hidden from view from Belfast.[43]

Given its responsibilities to safeguard the town and the railway, the garrison was none too large. Belfast lay in a hollow and the town was about a mile from

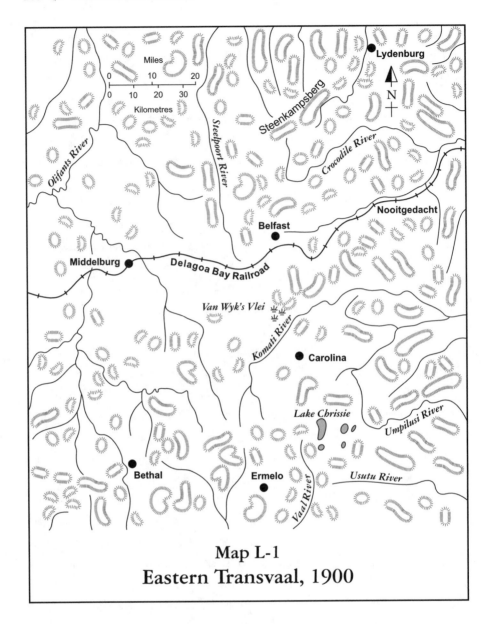

Map L-1
Eastern Transvaal, 1900

the station; to protect both, ridge lines and swells from two to three miles from the centre had to be held and the defensive perimeter measured some fifteen miles. The need to protect Belfast tied down two battalions and severely limited the column commander's ability to mount offensive operations.[44] The latter task was made even more difficult by the low effective strength of the units, since the infantry battalions could only muster about 600 effectives out of an authorized strength of around 1,000. In practical terms, this meant that rifle companies numbered about 50 to 60 men, instead of roughly 100.[45]

The major component of the garrison was British regulars. The opening months of the war had revealed a number of defects in the British army for which it had paid dearly in blood and prestige. Now, after nearly thirteen months of war, it was a different force from that which had first encountered the Boers in October 1899. Lessons had been learned the hard way, and incompetent commanders had been weeded out but, despite the presence of an ever-increasing number of regular and irregular mounted units, the British army still moved, thought and fought at the pace of the foot soldier. In late 1900 it was still "infantry-heavy" in composition and practice, but the British soldier, resolute, well-disciplined and brave, could be counted on not to falter or run away, no matter how desperate the situation.

Command of Belfast had recently been transferred to one of the better commanders of the war, forty-two-year-old Major General Horace Lockwood Smith-Dorrien. First commissioned in 1876, he had seen active service as a transport officer in the Zulu War of 1879 and was one of the few European survivors of the disaster at Isandlwana, having managed to fight his way to safety by a combination of good luck and guts. He had later seen active service in Egypt in 1882 and 1884, the Sudan in 1885-1886, India in 1895 and 1897-1898 and the Sudan again in 1898.

At the outbreak of the South African war Smith-Dorrien sailed from Malta in command of the 1st Battalion of the Derbyshire Regiment. On 2 February 1900 he took command of the newly formed 19th Brigade, which included the 2nd Battalion, Royal Canadian Regiment, and commanded the brigade at the battle of Paardeberg from 18 to 27 February 1900 and in the subsequent capture of Bloemfontein. In the advance to Pretoria he commanded the *ad hoc* infantry division in Sir Ian Hamilton's column. After the occupation of that city, Smith-Dorrien was given responsibility for securing a section of the railway south of Pretoria, and then took part in the advance through the eastern Transvaal. On 13 October 1899 he was ordered to take command of Belfast.[46]

What about the men who opposed the Belfast garrison? The Boer military system had developed in response to the need to rally forces quickly to defend frontier settlements. Every white male between the ages of sixteen and sixty automatically belonged to a local unit, called a commando. He was required to report when called, ready to take to the field armed with a rifle and ammunition and dressed in his normal civilian attire. The individual Boer, especially if he was from a rural district, was hardy, self-reliant, a fine horseman and a

The fighting Boers

A typical group of Boers armed with modern magazine Mauser rifles. These rifles outclassed the Lee Enfields used by the Canadians, establishing a long-standing national tradition of equipping our fighting troops with weapons and equipment inferior to those used by the enemy. (Courtesy, National Archives of Canada, 128778)

good shot,[47] though perhaps not quite as good as legend has it. One Canadian veteran of South Africa described the individual burgher as a compound of all that was unsoldierly in style and soldierly in action.[48]

The commandos were based on the local administrative districts of the Boer republics. Each district had a *landdrost* (magistrate), who handled the civilian administration, and a commandant, who was responsible for military matters and led the commando in war. The districts were divided into *wyke* (wards) with a field-cornet in charge of each ward. In a number of these wards, the field-cornet was assisted by an assistant field-cornet. The field-cornetcies were divided into corporalships of about twenty-five men. All these appointments were elective and the individual burgher could choose the man under whom he was to serve.

The Boers facing the garrison at Belfast were experienced, able and determined. They knew the countryside intimately; in fact, a few were fighting near or even on their own farms, and some had seen their homes burned by Canadians. Initially two commandos, from the Carolina and Ermelo districts, faced the

Boers in battle

A party of Boers fighting from behind the cover of a hastily constructed trench. One Canadian who fought at Leliefontein described his enemy as a compound of all that was unsoldierly in style and soldierly in action. Their system worked well in practice, despite seeming to be unworkable in theory, at least to more conventional soldiers. (Courtesy, Royal Canadian Dragoons Archives)

Anglo-Canadian forces, but around midday on 7 November they were reinforced by a party from the Middelburg commando. While it is impossible to accurately fix the strength of the Boers, it is possible to make an educated guess. The United States military attache with the Boer forces reported the number of men "registered for the field" at the outbreak of the war as follows: the Carolina commando with 427; the Ermelo commando with 963; and the Middelburg commando with 1,550.[49] While there had been casualties and defections and not all the registered men would have reported, it seems that about 300 members of the Carolina commando were present.[50] Probably at least 100 men from the Ermelo commando and perhaps nearly as many men from Middelburg were also present, to result in a force of about 500 men.

The Boers used bolt-action, repeating rifles. Originally most had been armed with German Mausers, although some burghers opted for arms such as British Martini-Henrys, Portuguese Guedes, Norwegian Krags and even sporting arms. As the war progressed and the Boer supply system collapsed, the pragmatic Boers converted to .303 Lee-Metford and Lee-Enfield rifles captured from the British.[51] At Leliefontein, however, many Boers still carried Mausers.

The commander of the Boer forces which would be fighting in the Belfast area at Leliefontein was forty-five-year-old General Joachim Christoffel Fourie. Born at Grahamstown in the Cape Colony on 1 February 1855, he had grown up near Lydenburg in the eastern Transvaal. Fourie had seen previous service in the 1881 Transvaal War as a field-cornet as well as in several campaigns against the natives and in 1899 was the owner-operator of a farm, Welgevonden, close to the Leliefontein battlefield. He had been elected to the *Volksraad* (parliament) in 1893 but reported for duty with his home commando as a burgher on the outbreak of war. Fourie was promoted to assistant-general for Carolina, Lydenberg and Standerton in March 1900. He had seen a considerable amount of service and was an experienced and able commander.[52]

The leader of the Carolina commando was thirty-nine-year-old Commandant Hendrik Frederik Prinsloo. Born near Kroonstad in the Orange Free State on 10 May 1861, he had moved to the Lydenburg area at the age of seventeen. Like Fourie, he had fought in the Transvaal War and several native campaigns. Distinguishing himself in the Mapog War by risking his life to carry a wounded burgher to safety, Prinsloo had fought in the Mpefu War as a field-cornet, and had then become commandant of the Carolina commando in June 1899. He further distinguished himself at the battle of Spion Kop in January 1900 by leading the final charge that led to the British rout. Thereafter he served under Fourie in the eastern Transvaal.[53]

Major General Horace Smith-Dorrien reached Belfast on 14 October 1900 and fifteen days later Lieutenant General Neville Lyttleton, his immediate superior, arrived with orders for him. So far, operations from Belfast had been confined to reconnaissances and raids on farms known to be centres of hostile activity. This was to change. British intelligence had determined that the Boers had taken advantage of the dead ground of the Komati Valley near Belfast to *laager* (camp) at Witkloof, a farm in the valley on the west (Belfast) side of the Komati River. Furthermore, the laager was being used as a base from which to mount raids on the railway.[54]

On the morning of 1 November Smith-Dorrien issued orders to his commanding officers for his first major offensive operation (see Map L-2). His plan was for two columns, one commanded by himself, consisting of the 5th Lancers, 1st Battalion, the Gordon Highlanders, the Mounted Rifles squadron, two

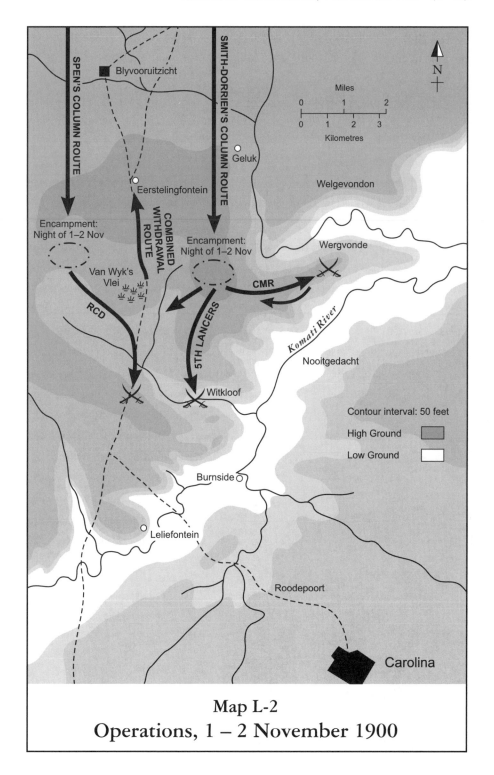

Map L-2
Operations, 1 – 2 November 1900

15-pdr. guns of the 84th Battery, Royal Artillery, and a 5-inch "cow" gun;[55] and the other column led by Lieutenant Colonel James Spens, commanding officer of the 2nd Battalion, the King's Shropshire Light Infantry, consisting of his own battalion, the Royal Canadian Dragoons, two guns of the 84th Battery, Morrison's section of D Battery, a section of two pom-poms and a cow gun. Smith-Dorrien's objective was to attack the laager at Witkloof and he planned to move under cover of darkness.[56]

The day was miserable and cold with heavy rain and sleet in the afternoon that had cleared somewhat towards sunset. At 6 P.M. Colonel Spens's column moved out, making a wide detour to the southwest. An hour later the general's column left Belfast, striking to the southeast. The plan was to link up near the Komati River, about fifteen miles to the south, and then attack the laager. The columns started out under a soft drizzle which shortly turned into a downpour with gusts of wind. The march took place under truly appalling conditions. Visibility was virtually nil, everyone was soaked to the skin and both men and animals were shivering. Mist reduced visibility to sixty yards and direction-finding was only possible by following pieces of glowing phosphorus left by the guides to mark the route. When the columns halted at their predetermined stopping places for the night, orders against lights and fires prevented the men smoking, let alone preparing hot drinks and warming themselves. There was little to do except "walking about to keep warm until you were so

There's no life like it!
The physical and mental strain of active service is obvious. The men are unshaven and haggard and their uniforms are dirty, ragged and probably louse-infested. A number of the men have discarded their holsters and thrust their revolvers into their belts. These are probably members of the CMR as their pistol lanyards are worn NWMP style, looped around their necks and under both shoulder straps. (Courtesy, Canadian War Museum, 82-7624)

Dressed for service not style

By the time of Leliefontein, the Canadians in South Africa had got the matter of clothing and equipment down to the bare minimum: stetson (somewhat tattered), bandanna, shirt, pants, rifle and ammunition bandolier, boots and spurs. (From E.W.B. Morrison, *With the Guns in South Africa*)

tired you couldn't stand; then lie down and take a mud bath under the delusion you were resting yourself, until you got so cold you had to get up and stumble around some more." The only consolation was that the weather was so bad the Boers would surely be at home when the troops came calling in the morning.[57]

With the dawn the advance guard of both columns moved out to find and attack the Boer laager. In Spens's column the Dragoons, supported by Morrison's gunners, led the advance. Shortly after, the advance guard was fired on from the area of a farmhouse on the right flank. Lieutenant Richard Turner's troop of the Dragoons skirmished forward and found the farm unoccupied except for an old woman. As the fire had come from a clump of trees and not the house itself, Lessard ordered that the building be spared. The regiment pushed on to the next ridge, from where the Komati River and the hills beyond were visible. Lieutenant Arthur King's Dragoon troop advanced and came under fire from a hill that was held in strength. Private Angus McDonald was shot in the head, and another man lost his mount.[58]

The Dragoons retreated, followed by the Boers. About this time, word was received that Smith-Dorrien had decided to end the operation and return to Belfast. Morrison's section and a section from the 84th Battery engaged the Boers, enabling the Dragoons to break contact and withdraw. Despite the conditions the gunners did some very accurate long-range shooting, including dropping one round into a gulch full of Boers at 4,000 yards range.[59]

While this had been going on, heavy firing could be heard from the direction of the general's column. Here there was action on two fronts. The 5th Lancers, forming the advance guard, came upon the Boers at some farms south of Van Wyk's *Vlei* and were forced back. Meanwhile a troop of the Rifles surprised some Boers on the left of the direction of advance and opened fire, inflicting a number of casualties. When the troop attempted to rejoin the main body, the Boers followed. Just before reaching the main body, Corporal Joseph Schell's horse was shot and Schell injured his ankle in the resulting fall. Major Sanders and Sergeant Charles Tryon galloped back to his aid and Tryon dismounted, helped Schell onto his own horse and sent him on his way to safety. Sanders then hauled the sergeant up onto the withers of his mount and they galloped away but before they reached their own troops, Sanders's saddle turned, sending both men crashing to the ground. Stunned by the fall and the effect of a bullet wound, Sanders lay in the open and in the process of trying to rescue him, Lieutenant Thomas Chalmers was killed. In all, this affair cost the Canadian Mounted Rifles one killed and three wounded.[60]

The weather had not improved and Smith-Dorrien decided that his troops were in no condition to assault the Boer positions in the Komati valley. He therefore organized a withdrawal to Belfast, deploying a rear guard of two companies of Gordon Highlanders – 100 rifles – and a thirty-man squadron of the 5th Lancers. At one point, the rear guard closed upon the main body when the latter was held up at a difficult crossing of a *spruit* (a small stream). Always quick to take advantage of such a situation, the Boers drove in the lancers and occupied a crest that dominated the crossing. Fortunately, Colonel Lessard had anticipated events and had deployed Sergeant Eddy Holland[61] with his Colt and Lieutenant Arthur King's troop against such an eventuality. The Canadians checked the Boer advance, the Colt being particularly effective because of its mobility and rate of fire. The remainder of the withdrawal was completed without incident, and the column was back at Belfast by five, pretty well done in.[62]

The foray had been an abject failure. It had cost the lives of Lieutenant Thomas Chalmers of the Rifles and Private G. Smith of the Gordon Highlanders, Private Angus McDonald of the Dragoons was missing and three Canadians and eight Gordons were wounded. Many others were soon incapacitated by illness – forty Royal Canadian Dragoons alone reported sick on 3 November.[63] At least some of these men would be unable to take to the field for some time, and their loss would be felt in the days to come. Major Sanders's wound resulted in Lieutenant Colonel Evans moving to Belfast to take command of the Mounted Rifles detachment.

There is one postscript. On 3 November Private Angus McDonald, who had been shot in the head and left for dead in the Komati valley, staggered into camp at Belfast. He had been picked up and had his wound tended to by the Boers. After questioning him, they lodged him in a sheep kraal with a guard posted at the gate. His eye and the side of his head were black and he looked as if he had been beaten with a club. When his guard, who decided McDonald was too sick to escape, left him unattended for a few minutes, the young Canadian stole a horse and made tracks for home. Aided by the bad weather, he cautiously felt his way through country thick with Boers but on the way his stolen horse broke a leg and McDonald had to complete his arduous journey on foot.[64]

Horace Smith-Dorrien was not the type to leave the enemy at Witkloof to their own devices. When the weather finally improved on 5 November, he issued orders for another operation to burn the farms which the Boers had used as outposts, and clear their *laagers* from Witkloof and Leliefontein (see Map L-3).[65] This time he decided to advance on one axis instead of two, thus lessening his problems of security and coordination and allowing him to make better use of his small number of mounted troops. (See Table 1 for the organization of the Belfast column). He also decided to delay departure until well after midnight, hoping to achieve at least a degree of surprise.

Table 1 – The Belfast Column, 6 November 1900

Royal Canadian Dragoons	Advance	
D Squadron, 5th Lancers	troops under	Advance Guard
2 Pom-Poms	Lt-Col Lessard	under Lt-Col Spens
Left Section, D Battery		
4 Companies, KSLI		
Canadian Mounted Rifles	Main Body	
4 guns, 84th Battery		
2 5-inch guns		
Section, Royal Engineers		
4 Companies KSLI		
2 Companies Suffolks		
Bearer Company		
Baggage		
2 Companies Suffolks	Rear Guard	
20 NCOs and men, 5th Lancers		

The advance guard rode out of Belfast at 3.30 A.M. on 6 November, which provided about two hours of darkness. The fog was so thick that special care had to be taken to maintain contact with the various elements of the column. Soon after sunrise, the sun burned the fog away and the weather was delightful.[66] The column contacted Boers near the Eerstelingfontein farm at 7.40 A.M. and from then on was shadowed by parties on the front, flanks and rear. Lessard's men steadily advanced throughout the morning, pushing the Boers across Van Wyk's

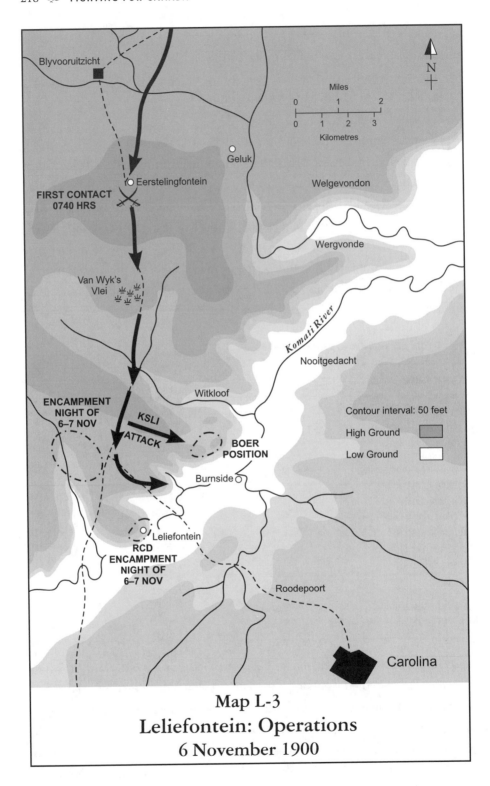

Blyvooruitzicht

Geluk

Welgevondon

Eerstelingfontein

**FIRST CONTACT
0740 HRS**

Wergvonde

Van Wyk's
Vlei

Miles

0 1 2

0 1 2 3

Kilometres

Komati River

Nooitgedacht

Witkloof

**ENCAMPMENT
NIGHT OF
6–7 NOV**

**KSLI
ATTACK**

**BOER
POSITION**

Contour interval: 50 feet

High Ground

Low Ground

Burnside

Leliefontein

**RCD
ENCAMPMENT
NIGHT OF
6–7 NOV**

Roodepoort

Carolina

Map L-3
Leliefontein: Operations
6 November 1900

Vlei. The left section of D Battery kept busy breaking up groups of Boers with long-range shrapnel, in some cases accurately engaging targets more than three miles away.[67]

While this was going on, Lieutenant T.A. Wroughton's troop of the Canadian Mounted Rifles had been burning farms and collecting horses and cattle on the flank of the axis. At one point, after Smith-Dorrien observed a farm that had escaped the torch and Lieutenant J.V. Begin's Rifles troop was despatched to burn it, Lieutenant Colonel Evans noticed Boers gathering on the ridges a few miles from the farm and sent Lieutenant Donald Bliss to warn Begin and have him return at once. Bliss, however, missed Begin, who returned by a different route. In searching for Begin, Bliss encountered twenty Boers, who pursued him and shot his horse. He took off on foot, until he was run down and captured by four burghers, who purloined his revolver, cigarettes and spurs and questioned him regarding the column's strength and intentions. Despite pleas from the owner of the burned farm to be allowed to shoot him, the Boers released Bliss on foot and he joined the column about an hour later.[68]

The Boers, however, had delayed the column enough to allow their comrades to evacuate the laagers and head for safety at Carolina. There also was enough time for Field-Cornet Viljoen and his men of the third ward of the Carolina commando to prepare a strong defensive position on the precipitous, craggy Witkloof.[69]

This feature lay to the northeast of where the British-Canadian column had halted, and the Boers held their fire while the advance guard passed, waiting for a more attractive target. A general movement of troops towards the feature and firing by a section of the 84th Battery signalled to the advance guard that the fight had resumed. The Shropshires began to advance in line towards the river with some mounted Dragoons extending their line to the left. Morrison's section followed the Shropshires. The other section of the 84th Battery came into action to the rear and the baggage train straggled onto the ridge behind the guns. Suddenly Holland's Colt started peppering away and Mauser bullets sang through the air. Lessard shouted, "Morrison – the rocks," and pointed to a low *kopje* to the front.[70]

Morrison's section galloped through the gap between the Dragoons and the Shropshires then wheeled half-right into the open. When well clear of friendly troops, Morrison shouted, "Halt! Action Left!" The drivers hauled back hard on their reins, the 12-pdrs. bounced to a halt and the gunners leaped from their seats on the guns and limbers and swung the two 12-pdrs. to face the rocks, all the while under intense rifle fire from the Boers. The infantry lay down, the dragoons dismounted and sent their horses back and the transport column beat a hasty retreat over the ridge. Morrison misjudged the puffs of dust from two rifle bullets in front of him as spent rounds and ordered an opening range of 2,500 yards. The round sailed over the target to burst in the valley. He dropped the range to 2,200. Still over! William Hare, Senior, the lead driver of No. 6 gun fell from his horse with a Mauser bullet in the shoulder but the centre driver, his son, William, took his place without a word. Another round at 2,000 yards was too long again. Finally, one at 1,800 yards clipped the top of the rocks. Morrison reduced the range to 1,650 and his gunners began to burst shrapnel rounds all along the front of the *kopje*, dampening the Boers' enthusiasm and reducing their accuracy.[71]

The 12-pdrs. and the Colt were doing all the shooting, although at one point the Shropshires stood up and fired three volleys to draw some of the fire away from the guns. A section of the 84th Battery now moved down the slope and joined in the firing from Morrison's left rear. It was soon followed by a 5-inch gun which came into action to the right of the Canadian guns. Morrison was beginning to worry about ammunition, for his guns had done quite a bit of firing. However, whenever he stopped firing, the Mausers opened up again, so he continued, but at a reduced rate. The Shropshires now moved forward to attack the kopje, but were pinned down in the open 500 yards from the Boers for more than three hours, losing six men killed and fifteen wounded. Three men from the 84th Battery, one Suffolk infantryman and Driver Hare from D Battery were also wounded during the day.[72]

So far, Smith-Dorrien had been unable to find a way to outflank the position at the Witkloof since he encountered Boer riflemen whenever he attempted to reconnoitre a likely looking piece of ground. He therefore ordered Lessard to take his regiment, Morrison's section, the pom-poms and two companies of Suffolks and work round the Boer left to threaten their line of retreat.[73] It was 4 P.M. before this manoeuvre was completed. In the meantime, the Boers had been evacuating the farms along the Komati and sending convoys of wagons to Carolina, ready to retreat further south if necessary. The Boer positions along the valley had allowed these convoys to escape unscathed, and now the burghers beat a hasty retreat when their position was turned.[74]

The British-Canadian column moved along the high ground and camped at sundown just west of Leliefontein.[75] Smith-Dorrien reassessed his options and began to firm up a new plan. While he had probably overestimated Boer strength, the intensity of their resistance had come as an unwelcome surprise – all day signal fires calling for Boer reinforcements had been observed in all directions. While he appreciated his force was not strong enough to push on to Carolina, the recent actions had forced the laagers at Witkloof and Leliefontein to withdraw and he could legitimately claim that he had achieved much of his aim. Still, Smith-Dorrien was not one to be satisfied with a half measure and must have considered continuing the push south. In the end, logic won and he decided to return to Belfast. His decision to camp at Leliefontein instead of in the area of Van Wyk's *Vlei* was calculated to convey the impression that he would continue to Carolina in the morning. He hoped the Boers would deploy to counter his advance, thus providing him with a head start in his withdrawal.[76]

That is precisely what happened. During the evening of 6 November, after the British camped in the area of Leliefontein, a council of the senior officers of the Carolina and Ermelo commandos was held at a farm north of Carolina. The Boers concluded that Smith-Dorrien would continue his advance south to Carolina and it was decided to mount an attack on the camp at Leliefontein in the

The enemy: Boer commandos

The Canadian soldier in South Africa had no personal animosity toward his opponent and quickly came to respect his fighting abilities. This photograph, clearly staged for the cameraman, shows a Boer commando on the Veld. Note the sights on the rifles raised to the highest elevation point – the Boers were renowned for their marksmanship. (From E.W.B. Morrison, *With the Guns in South Africa*)

morning to frustrate the British plan. A tentative plan was adopted in which Fourie and Prinsloo, with most of the Carolina commando, would launch a frontal assault. The Ermelo commando under Commandant Hans Grobler would undertake a left flank movement to hit the British from the west, while Field-Cornet de Lange would harass the left flank of the British column.[77]

Smith-Dorrien, meanwhile, faced a number of problems. He was short of mounted troops, the only force which could come close to matching the Boers' mobility. He had a squadron of the 5th Lancers armed with carbines and the two Canadian units, about ninety-five Dragoons with their Colt machine gun, and sixty Mounted Rifles, both armed with rifles. Before the withdrawal could commence, his advance guard had to secure the route onto and across Van Wyk's *Vlei*. His baggage column was far too large, slow-moving and cumbersome – Morrison later claimed that it stretched for six miles along the road.[78] Finally, his column was restricted to the speed of its slowest element, the baggage train, which could make no more than two or three miles an hour over easy ground. It was clear to Smith-Dorrien that his column would be vulnerable during a rearward movement.

He accordingly detailed Lessard and the Dragoons and Morrison's section to form the rear guard, with three companies of supporting infantry. Lieutenant Colonel James Spens, with part of his own battalion, the lancers and a section of the 84th Battery made up the advance guard, while Lieutenant Colonel Thomas Evans and the Rifles and a section of the 84th Battery formed the reserve under the general's direct control. The remainder of the infantry – five companies – and the 5-inch guns would move with the main body and the baggage train.

Lessard had a difficult task. His Dragoons were organized into five sub-units: a scout section commanded by Sergeant Robert Ryan; three troops commanded by Lieutenants Richard Turner, Hampden Cockburn and Francis Sutton; and the machine gun section under Sergeant Edward Holland. A fourth Dragoon lieutenant, James Elmsley, acted as Lessard's adjutant. Lessard was supported by Morrison's two 12-pdrs. which, because of the heavy fighting the previous day, had fewer than 150 rounds of ammunition. There also was the promise of support from three British rifle companies. Morrison described the situation thus,

> In order to understand what followed it is necessary to explain that the country is treeless, with great rolling ridges. It is usually two to three miles from the crest of one ridge to the next, and rocky kopjes are located here and there.

In rear guard work you have to wait until the transport column toils over the far ridge before you abandon the ridge behind and then make a rapid retirement to take up a position on the ridge they have passed over, and so on. Not only have you to wait for the transport, but you also have to wait for your infantry supports too. That means that at one particular period in each successive retirement the guns and cavalry supports are anywhere from two to three miles behind the column and infantry supports and, as it were, isolated for the time being until they can abandon the ridge and retire to the next.[79]

Morrison's memory of the terrain and tactics is clear and concise. However, there were a couple of ridges on the first long slope that could be used as intermediate positions.[80]

Lessard gave his orders (see Map L-4). As the advance guard marched out and the massive transport column tried to sort itself into some semblance of order, his rear guard went into position. He ordered Sergeant Ryan to put out a cordon of scouts to cover approaches where the ground allowed the Boers to approach undetected and then deployed the Dragoons in a screen across the rear of the convoy. Lessard disposed his three troops (although because each troop was subdivided into two small troops of twelve to fifteen men each, he probably fought them as small squadrons) in a curve one and a half to two miles wide. From east to west the troops were commanded by Lieutenants Cockburn, Turner and Sutton with the Colt and the two 12-pdrs. in the middle of the line. To gain as much range as possible, Morrison's guns were pushed forward of the line of dragoons.[81]

Smith-Dorrien wanted to get a jump on the Boers and that is exactly what happened. The burghers were encamped on farms several miles back from the Komati River and therefore would not be able to observe the British camp until they crested the escarpment. Commandant Prinsloo left his farm before sunrise, taking the road to a nearby farm, where he collected the burghers of his commando's second ward. The combined force, approximately 100 men, rode towards the valley, planning to link up with General Fourie. Shortly after sunrise Fourie and his men left their laager and headed down the long, sloping hill toward the Komati. About three miles into his ride Fourie halted to examine the British camp through his field glasses. To his astonishment, he saw that the British had broken camp and were heading back towards the Belfast road. Fourie was outfoxed, but saw an opportunity to regain the initiative. The British column had to pass within rifle shot of the strong position the Boers had held the day before and Fourie led his men northwards along the valley in a rush to re-occupy

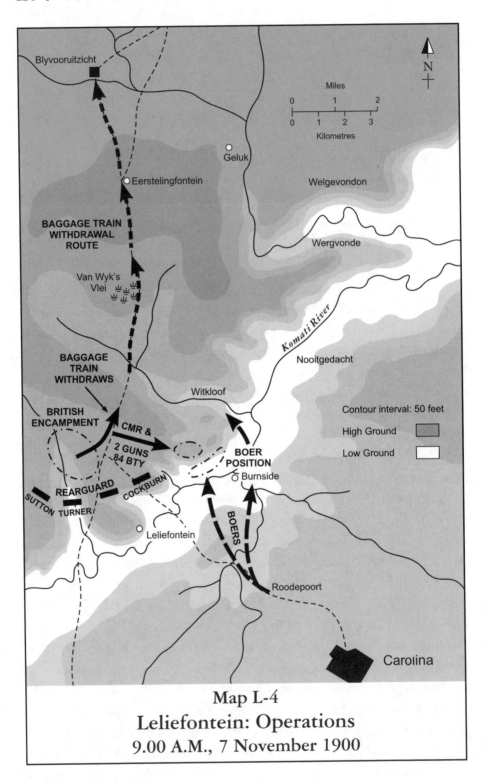

Map L-4
Leliefontein: Operations
9.00 A.M., 7 November 1900

Gunners on the Veld, or how to torture your headgear
Gunners from Lieutenant E.W.B. Morrison's section of D Battery, Royal Canadian Field Artillery, pose for the camera. It is an immutable habit of Canadian soldiers to wear their headgear in any but the regulation fashion and these men have twisted their stetsons into a fantastic variety of shapes according to personal taste. (From E.W.B. Morrison, *With the Guns in South Africa*)

that location, while Prinsloo worked around to cut off the enemy retreat nearer to Witkloof.[82]

Smith-Dorrien quickly grasped the Boers' intent. As was his practice, he had retained a small mobile reserve, in this case the Mounted Rifles, and a two-gun section of 84th Battery. He ordered Evans to gallop straight for the position.[83] If the Boers occupied that kopje, the British would have to repeat the previous day's long, bloody process of forcing them off it before they could resume their retreat to Belfast, this time with other strong enemy forces on their flanks and rear. With the position in British hands, the Boers would be prevented from swarming up onto the plain and the column could cross the ridge and then move up the Witkloofspruit valley to Van Wyk's *Vlei*. In Thomas Evans's economical prose,

a large number of the enemy galloped back over the ridges SE, apparently to occupy the positions of the previous day. I was ordered to occupy the position, if possible, first. One troop being on patrol I had only 35 men left to carry out this order. We galloped for the ridge about 2 miles distant and occupied the two commanding features on it, and at once opened fire on the Boers who were in large numbers in the valley below. Shortly after, 2 guns of the 84th B[at]t[ter]y arrived to support us, and the Boers were forced to retire to the cover of low rocky ridges on other side of valley from which they kept a hot fire in reply to ours.[84]

In the meantime, Morrison's gunners had wheeled their two 12-pdrs. around and engaged the Boers as they galloped northwards along the valley floor. When the Boers began to retire across the valley in small parties, Morrison shelled them again, this time at a range of 5,000 yards.[85]

Smith-Dorrien had also appreciated the threat posed by Prinsloo and his men. He ordered Spens to seize the high ground at Van Wyk's *Vlei*, which he did with the 5th Lancers and the other section of the 84th Battery. He then ordered three companies of the Shropshires (perhaps the ones detailed to support the rear guard) to join Evans on the *kopje* overlooking the Komati valley. The baggage could now move safely back, covered by the rear guard.[86]

At this stage, roughly 9 A.M., the last of the baggage column was still clearing the camp while its head was toiling up the long, open slope to the northeast. The rear guard observed parties of Boers appearing and disappearing in the rolling ground as they moved closer, while others worked their way up the left (western) side of the column. The artillery hammered away at them, but as fast as they drove the Boers from one ridge, more would appear on another. As the Boers were moving closer to the heavily outnumbered rear guard, Lessard sent an urgent request to Smith-Dorrien for reinforcements, to no avail. Meanwhile, Evans sent a message to Lessard, asking if he could spare some men.[87]

It was at this point that Morrison made a decision which would have a major effect on the ensuing battle. His ammunition was running low, so he ordered the gun limbers to be topped up from the section's two ammunition wagons, which he then sent back to join the transport column. This move, which Morrison

The 12-pdr. breech-loading field gun

The Left Section of D Battery, Royal Canadian Field Artillery, manned two of these guns at Leliefontein. Morrison and his gunners were able to keep the Boers at a distance in the initial stages of the battle, buying valuable time for the baggage train to withdraw. (Courtesy, Canadian War Museum, 76-2640)

described as" a bit of luck," took the wagons, which now were a hindrance, out of the range and later permitted the gunners to exchange their exhausted gun teams for the comparatively fresh wagon teams.[88]

By this time the convoy had made enough progress for the rear guard to fall back to an intermediate position part way up the slope (see Map L-5) The procedure was for the artillery to move one gun at a time; when the first gun was back in action, the second gun would limber up and retire. When both guns were in action, the dragoons would mount up and dash for the new position. This way, either one gun and the dragoons or two guns would be in action and firing at all times. Every man knew his job and, just as important, knew that his comrades

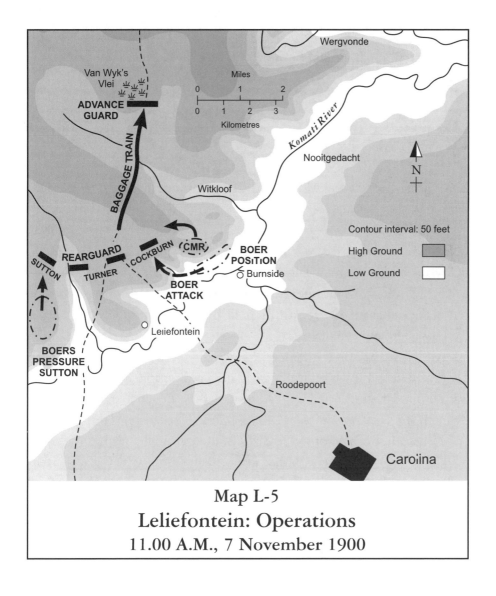

Map L-5
Leliefontein: Operations
11.00 A.M., 7 November 1900

Dragoons resting in the shelter of a kopje

A party of Dragoons halted for a meal in the cover of a low kopje. They have instinctively spread out and blended into the terrain like the veterans they are. A few weapons may be picked out close at hand among the rocks. (Courtesy, Royal Canadian Dragoons Archives)

knew theirs. The problem was that the Canadians were hampered by the slow-moving baggage convoy.[89]

Evans's force meanwhile had abandoned its position overlooking the Komati valley once the convoy passed it and had moved to take another position on the right flank of the column.[90] This move allowed Fourie and Prinsloo's men, who had been driven across the valley, to swarm up onto the tableland to the east and rear of the rear guard. Other Boers from the Ermelo commando were observed creeping up from the southwest.[91]

By 11 A.M. the tail of the transport column and the infantry supports had still not cleared the ridge, while the rear guard had been engaged for three hours and was now in danger of being overwhelmed. A Boer appeared on a ridge to the right rear and began to flash signals with a mirror. He abandoned this enterprise, and his mirror, when Morrison landed a round not twenty yards from him at 3,500 yards range.[92] However, he had managed to pass what the Canadians took to be the order for a general assault on their position. Almost immediately Lieutenant Hampden Cockburn, holding the easternmost portion of the line, reported that the Boers were advancing in force. Lessard ordered Morrison to take a gun to his assistance. The gunner officer ordered number 5 gun[93] to limber up, and together they set off at a gallop to join Cockburn. It was fully one and a half miles and the horses, which had been worked hard on the previous day, were nearly exhausted when they arrived. Morrison found "the Boers were coming on with determination at this point. I went into action and soon scattered mounted men but they dismounted and came on running from cover to cover and my gunners were soon exposed to a sharp rifle fire." Cockburn pushed his men out further to the front to keep the Boers away from the gun. The gunners were beginning to get the enemy under control when Lessard galloped up shouting, "For God's sake, Morrison, save your guns! They are coming down our flank."[94]

This puzzled Morrison as his gun and Cockburn's Dragoons were holding the Boers nicely on his flank. Lessard shouted: "Limber up! They are coming down our on our flank to cut us off!" He gestured towards the left rear and Morrison could see Boers swarming over the hills from the west. Cockburn sized up the situation immediately and led the rest of his men forward against the Boers to buy time for the gun to get away. One of the Dragoons, as he jumped off his horse and unslung his rifle, looked at Morrison with a grin and said, "I guess we can see our finish, sir."[95]

No. 6 gun had already limbered up and was making its way for the ridge. Now Morrison with No. 5 set off at a gallop for the ridge and the infantry support he could see just below the crest. No sooner had he done so than Mauser bullets began to crack through the air, but from a different direction. Turning in his saddle, Morrison saw a long line of Boers 1,500 yards away galloping towards him firing from the saddle.[96] Lessard had ridden back over to the western flank, taking all the available men he could collect along the way to shore up his defences. The centre was now completely open, except for Holland's Colt and a few Dragoons. At the same time, the Boers on the eastern flank rushed forward in an attempt to prevent the gun from getting away, but were halted by Cockburn and his men firing from concealed positions in the grass. In the event, there were just too many Boers and Cockburn and his little party were soon overwhelmed and forced to surrender. But their sacrifice allowed the gun to get away.[97]

By this time, noon or shortly after, (see Map L-6) the Boers on the west flank had been reinforced by the arrival of a party from the Middelburg commando led by Louis Steyn.[98] Lieutenant Francis Sutton and his troop were fighting off parties of Boers in a battle that ebbed and flowed as one side then the other gained the upper hand. To add to the confusion, a number of terrified Canadian horses had escaped and were galloping madly about the plain. One belonged to Corporal Perry Price from Peterborough, Ontario, who later remembered:

When the Boers appeared on the crest of the hill about 800 yards from us, they immediately opened fire on us, we were dismounted and the fire was so heavy on the led horses, they stampeded. My horse was amongst those which stampeded, and I was left to retire on foot; I then ran as far as I possibly could and then laid down behind an ant hill for protection. I then saw No. 185 Private W.A. Knisley RCD come towards me and tell me to get on his horse which I did; he carried me out until I reached another horse.[99]

When Knisley rescued Price, the enemy were within fifty yards of them and the firing was very heavy. Knisley was wounded shortly after picking Price up and lay on the battlefield for several hours before he received medical attention. Price returned to the fighting on a new horse.

The Canadian centre was held by Sergeant Eddy Holland's Colt and a handful of Dragoons, while the east flank was completely open. The line of Boers continued to gallop towards No. 5 gun, still firing from the saddle, although some halted and dismounted so as to be able to fire more accurately. The 12-pdr. had covered about half the distance to the ridge when the horses, poorly nourished and tired, began to falter and slowed from a gallop to a trot and then almost to a walk. Morrison ordered the gun into action and began to engage the enemy with shrapnel. He soon realized that while he could hold off the Boers to his rear, the rest of the line would envelop him, so he limbered up and took off for the ridge again. This brief rest had allowed the horses to recover somewhat, and the team broke into a trot, the gunners running alongside, hauling on the traces. One of the gun horses was hit, but did not drop. With the Boers drawing nearer and nearer, Morrison sent a rider to see if Lessard could spare a few men to come to his assistance.[100]

A number of Dragoons had dropped back under the pressure of the Boer attack and were making their way up the ridge. Private Albert Hilder remembered:

At one period of our retirement, before we finally dismounted in our last stand, A.H. Roberts and I were riding together when a bullet crashed into the underpart of my saddle. Another bullet went through my tunic near my belt. A third bullet hit a drinking cup tied to Roberts's saddle wallet, taking off the cup but leaving the handle in the strap. At that time I noticed L[ance]/C[or]p[ora]l. Anderson shot through his head and fall from his horse … L[ieutenan]t. Turner came galloping towards us, shouting for us to dismount and check the enemy, so that the guns could get away. I remember Turner saying, "Never let it be said that Canadians let their guns be captured.[101]

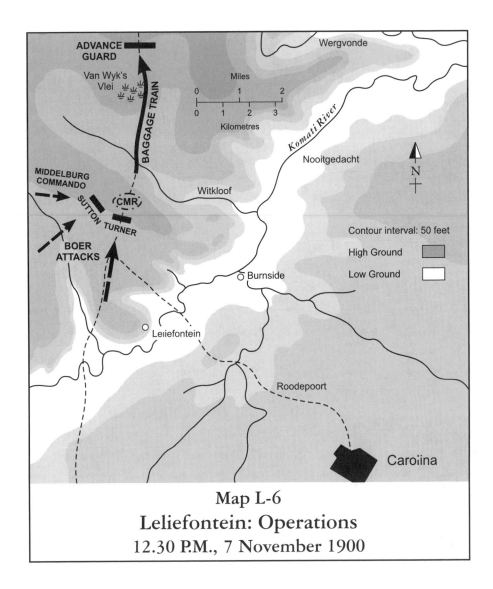

Map L-6
Leliefontein: Operations
12.30 P.M., 7 November 1900

The Dragoons dismounted and took up positions around Sergeant Holland and his Colt. A few men, led by Sergeant Norman Builder, had escaped when Cockburn and his men were overrun. They now made their way along the side of the ridge to join them to buy time for Morrison's guns to escape.[102]

The Boers could see that the guns were nearing the ridge but Fourie decided to make one last effort to capture them, gain the ridge, and attack the baggage train. Gathering about 100 men, Fourie and Prinsloo charged, but ran into the party of dismounted Dragoons clustered around Holland's Colt. The two Boer leaders, who were within a few yards of one another, were both killed by Canadian fire.[103] Suddenly the Colt gun jammed but Holland coolly removed the gun from its horse-drawn carriage and carrying the hot weapon despite burns to his arms, ran to a group of led horses held by Private Hilder. He mounted, a difficult feat when encumbered by a machine gun, and rode off under fire, eventually reaching No. 6 gun and transferring the Colt to its limber. Together Holland and the gunners made their way to the ridge and relative safety.[104]

In an effort to capture the Colt and unaware that Holland had escaped, a number of Boers overran the Canadians clustered around its carriage. Private William Anderson of the machine gun section managed to get away despite a bullet that holed his water bottle before striking his horse in the neck.[105] One Boer shot Sergeant Norman Builder, who was firing his rifle from behind an ant hill, although he believed he had killed the sergeant who had been firing the machine gun.[106] Others attempted to turn the machine gun on the retreating 12-pdrs., and then set fire to its carriage when they realized that they had been foiled. The Canadians fighting around the machine gun carriage, with their ammunition nearly exhausted, reluctantly surrendered.[107] After being disarmed and searched, they were allowed to make their way back on foot, although a young Boer whose brother had been killed in the fighting on 6 November, attempted to shoot Private Albert Hilder.[108]

Meanwhile, Lieutenant Richard Turner had been gamely trying to hold off the Boers with a scratch force. After Holland had escaped with the machine gun and the Boers had overrun the position, he retreated slowly up the hill with no more than a dozen men. Turner, who had been wounded in the arm, met the rider Morrison had sent in search of Lessard. He positioned his men between the gun and the Boers, dismounting them and allowing the gun enough time to escape. In the process, he was wounded again, this time in the neck, and his horse was hit twice.[109] With the Boers checked, Turner went to report to Lessard, who took one look at the blood-soaked subaltern and ordered him to the rear.[110]

Lieutenant Richard Ernest William Turner, VC, DSO (1871-1961)
At a critical point in the battle of Leliefontein, with the Colt out of action and the guns threatened, Turner, who was already wounded and bleeding profusely, rallied his men with the cry, "Never let it be said that Canadians let their guns be captured." (Courtesy, Royal Canadian Dragoons Archives)

Sergeant Edward James Gibson Holland, VC (1878-1948)
Holland had been holding off the Boers with his Colt machine gun, when it suddenly jammed. To prevent the Boers from capturing it, he removed it from its carriage and carried it off on horse back. The staff officer, or perhaps war correspondent, with Holland is unidentified. (Courtesy, Royal Canadian Dragoons Archives)

Morrison was nearing the infantry support and the ridge, when to his surprise and disgust, he saw the infantry suddenly rise and begin to march to the rear. He asked the British officer in command of the troops – about three companies and more than all the Canadians in the rear guard – to turn about and engage the Boers while his gun went into action again to support Lessard and the Dragoons still fighting their way up the slope under tremendous pressure from the Ermelo and Middelburg commandos. The officer's reply was "I can't do anything," and he then hurried his men over the ridge. Without infantry support, it was too dangerous to go into action, so Morrison was obliged to follow the retreating infantry onto the ridge.[111]

All this time Major General Smith-Dorrien had not been sitting idly by. While he was concerned with the return of the column to Belfast as a whole, he was not inclined to leave a rear guard to fight its own way out. When he realized that the Boers threatened to overwhelm the rear guard, he ordered Evans and the Rifles,[112] plus a two-gun section from the 84th Battery and some infantry, onto the ridge. Evans and his men arrived there in time to join in the latter stages of the fighting and helped the Dragoons make their way to safety.[113]

As Morrison and his gun crested the ridge, he was hailed by the general, who asked if he had lost many men. Morrison replied that he had had one horse hit and that both men and animals were exhausted. Now that the enemy had worked their way onto the ridge and were firing into the baggage train straggling across the valley, Smith-Dorrien asked Morrison if he would take his guns to the next crest and engage the Boers who were streaming along the left flank. To gunners imbued with the ethos of their motto *Quo Fas et Gloria Ducunt* (Where right and glory lead) this could merit only one response: the left section some-how managed to stagger to the next crest and drive the Boers back.[114]

The Boer pressure had now slackened. The Canadians had no way of know-ing that the deaths of General Fourie and Commandant Prinsloo had totally un-nerved the Carolina commando which departed, and soon the Ermelo and Middelburg commandos also withdrew from the ridge. For the rest of the day the Boers were content to hang about the column, but came no closer than 2,000 yards.[115]

By noon the next day, 8 November 1900, the column was back in Belfast. The operation had been a tactical failure and Smith-Dorrien realized he would need many more mounted troops before he could hope to advance down the Carolina road and cross the Komati River.[116] Casualties had been heavy for this stage of the war: 9 dead, 31 wounded and 16 Dragoons taken prisoner. The Canadian share was substantial: Driver William Hare of D Battery was wounded on 6 November and the Dragoons lost 3 killed, 12 wounded and 16 captured on 7 November.[117] Lessard was a shaken man. Disaster had struck all at once, virtu-ally on the eve of returning to Canada, and nearly a third of the Dragoons who fought at Leliefontein had become casualties. Of his officers, Lieutenant James Elmsley had been carried off the field apparently dead, Lieutenant Richard Turner was wounded in two places and faced a stay in the hospital and Lieuten-ant Hampden Cockburn was missing, a prisoner or worse.[118] (Elmsley and Turner survived their wounds and Cockburn and his men were in fact released later on the night of 7 November.) The roll of officers was now the colonel and Lieutenant Francis Sutton, with Lieutenant Arthur King back at Belfast and Lieutenant Arthur Howard in Pretoria.

Because Victorian soldiers put a great deal of stock in saving their artillery, the action at Leliefontein resulted in a large number of decorations being awarded to the participants. Of the 78 Victoria Crosses awarded during the South African War, 16 were won for saving guns.[119] Of these, three went to Dragoons,

Lieutenant Hampden Zane Churchill Cockburn, VC (1867-1913)
Cockburn led his men forward to block a Boer attempt to capture a Canadian 12-pounder field gun. All of his men were killed, wounded or captured in the process. He was wounded and taken prisoner but was later released along with his surviving men. (Courtesy, Royal Canadian Dragoons Archives)

The Royal Canadian Dragoons cap badge
The regiment adopted the springbok, a South African antelope, for its hat badge shortly after the South African War. This was probably done in recognition of its tour in South Africa as a whole rather than, as regimental lore has it, because a patrol of dragoons was alerted by some fleeing springboks stampeded by a party of Boers. This is one of few Canadian cap badges that bear an emblem directly related to a battle or campaign. (Courtesy, Department of National Defence)

Lieutenants Turner and Cockburn and Sergeant Holland. Private William Knisley was recommended for the VC for saving Price, but received the Distinguished Conduct Medal instead, while Lieutenant Edward Morrison was awarded the Distinguished Service Order.

It is perhaps trite to add that to win a decoration, one has to be recommended. Smith-Dorrien's nickname of "half rations and full congratulations"[120] reflected his willingness to work his men hard but also to recommend them for decorations. In fact, seven soldiers serving under his command won Victoria Crosses in the eighteen months he served in South Africa. That is not to take away from the achievement of the three Dragoons, or any of the others that fought at Leliefontein.

What lessons can be learned from Leliefontein? First and foremost, leadership and personal example count for much in war. Lieutenant Hampden Cockburn willingly led his men into danger to give Morrison and his gunners a few extra minutes to extricate their gun. Lieutenant Richard Turner, bleeding profusely, inspired soldiers to join him in placing themselves between the Boers and the gun, again to buy time for the gunners. Lieutenant Edward Morrison's energy and zeal were impressive. Last but not least, Lieutenant Colonel Lessard fought with his men throughout the long, desperate struggle up the slope. It was in the best traditions of the military profession that he was among the last of his Dragoons to crest the ridge and it is a pity that, by the convention of the time, commanding officers were deemed ineligible for gallantry awards.

Second, the Boer commanders, who were equally brave, showed themselves to be tactically innovative and flexible. Their mounted charge very nearly succeeded in overwhelming the Canadian defenders and, by the skilful use of ground, they were able to concentrate against the Canadian flanks. That the Boers did not prevail was not for want of trying.

Finally, units composed of soldiers who have served together for a considerable period are an invaluable asset. Fighting units, at all costs, must not be subjected to *ad hoc* organizational changes or undue personnel turbulence. While Leliefontein may be unique in the number of decorations won, it is not unique as an example of what strong leadership and determined men can accomplish in the most desperate of circumstances. Hopefully, this is a lesson that need not be relearned.

The Battlefield Today

Few Canadians have visited the Leliefontein battlefield since that desperate day a century past. To reach it, take the N4, also known as the "Witbank Freeway," east from Pretoria (despite its name, the N4 is a toll road costing 20 Rand or about $4.50 Canadian) past Bronkhorstspruit, Witbank and Middelburg to Carolina (about 190 km). The N4 is a good highway up to the Middelburg turnoff, after which it becomes a four lane road infested with dangerous drivers. Do not take the Carolina exit at Wonderfontein, but continue on the main road. About two kilometres before Belfast, exit right onto the Carolina/Ermelo highway (R33). This road runs right past the battlefield and you should be able to spot the monument raised in memory of Fourie and Prinsloo, which is situated near the point where they fell. At that point, most of the ground fought over by the rear guard is visible, although an impoundment on the Komati River may have flooded parts of it. (The ground between Belfast and Carolina was the site of the Battle of Bergendal (or Dalmanutha) in August 1900, so many of the traces of field works in the area date from that earlier battle.) One last, and a very important, point: South Africans refer to Leliefontein as Witkloof, so one should use that name when seeking information.

From the Veld
to the Fields of Flanders,
1900 to 1918

Although their nation's participation in the South African War was regarded by some Canadians as a backward step, a reversion to pre-1867 colonial status, the majority were proud of the fighting record of their troops in South Africa. As a result, the government became more interested in, and sympathetic to, defence matters, and the military establishment was transformed between 1900 and 1914 through hard work on the part of its British and Canadian senior officers. A higher level of funding – the annual defence budget increased from $1.6 million in 1899 to $11 million in 1914 – fuelled this transformation. The tiny permanent force was increased in strength and provided with the nucleus of a medical, intelligence and signals corps; a staff course was instituted for the advanced training of both regular and militia officers and many were attached to the British army for practical experience; new weapons and equipment were acquired; and better facilities provided for training. The militia was increased in strength from 35,000 in 1901 to 66,000 in 1913 and, more importantly, 55,000 militiamen received extensive training in the latter year.

It was well that these improvements were made as, by 1914, it was clear that Europe was on the brink of war. A complicated system of alliances divided that continent into two armed camps: France and Russia versus Germany and Austria-Hungary. When a Serbian nationalist assassinated the heir to the Austro-Hungarian throne on 28 June, it set off a chain reaction of mobilization and counter-mobilization that impelled these powers, willingly or unwillingly, into war. When German troops advancing on France violated the neutrality of

Belgium, which had been guaranteed by treaty, Britain declared war on Germany on 4 August.

In 1914, when Britain was at war, Canada was at war. The response in Canada was enthusiastic in the extreme for, as one veteran later remarked: "if ever a country wanted war, it was Canada."[1] Crowds gathered in every major city across the land and there were street processions of patriotically decorated vehicles, flag waving and speeches – in Toronto a huge parade made its way through the streets and "hats shot aloft, ten thousand throats boomed out a concentrated roar – a warning to the enemy."[2] Hundreds of men besieged militia units and government offices wanting to enlist, including many Britons living in North America who raised a complete battalion for the British army – Princess Patricia's Canadian Light Infantry – almost overnight.

An agreement was in place between British and Canadian military authorities that in the event of hostilities Canada would dispatch an expeditionary force of one infantry division and a mounted brigade "for active service in a civilized country in a temperate climate."[3] Colonel Sam Hughes, the minister of militia, set about raising this force and there was no shortage of volunteers. By September, 32,655 officers and men had assembled in a vast new camp constructed at Valcartier near Quebec to receive preliminary training. At the end of the month this First Contingent of the Canadian Expeditionary Force boarded an armada of transports to make an uneventful journey across the Atlantic to Plymouth. They were the first overseas troops to reach Britain and a journalist who witnessed their arrival never forgot the sight:

> A big steamship was coming directly shorewards, like a vast phantom emerging from the mist … a great white patch on her bow gave me to believe that she was a transport. …… And then suddenly, it seemed to me like a cinema transformation, her contour seemed to be traced in khaki … then I caught the wavering sounds of a band playing somewhere on board and gave a start as the revelation came upon me that it was "The Maple Leaf For Ever" ……
> A naval petty officer paused at my side and exchanged looks, "The Canadians" he said in a voice tense with pent-up enthusiasm, "Thirty-one transports full of them! That's the tenth which has gone up harbour so far."[4]

The bands stopped playing and the shouting died away when the First Contingent reached Salisbury Plain, its new home, where they spent a wet and miserable winter under appalling conditions. In February 1915, however, spirits were high when the Canadians marched out of their camps bound for France.

By the time the First Contingent, now reorganized as the Canadian Division, reached their destination, the war had become a deadlock. The widespread use of automatic weapons and rapid firing artillery had forced the soldiers of the opposing armies to seek protection in hastily-dug trenches. At first temporary "scrapes," these trenches became gradually more elaborate until Europe, from the English Channel to Switzerland, was scarred with two complete, opposing systems of defensive works with a "no man's land" between them. This was the Western Front and, such was the effectiveness of modern weaponry, that it did not vary more than a few miles in either direction for the next three or so years as any attack was usually brought to an abrupt end at a tremendous cost in human lives.

The reality of this new form of warfare was brought home to the Canadian Division when it participated in the Second Battle of Ypres in April and May 1915. Here it helped to blunt a German offensive launched with the help of a new and terrible weapon, poison gas, but paid an appalling price, losing 6035 men killed and wounded of a total strength of 20,000. Ypres was a grievous introduction to modern war for Canada and her sacrifice will always be remembered in a poem written by a Canadian artillery officer, Major John McCrae, which contains the opening words: "In Flanders fields the poppies blow, Between the crosses, row on row."

The battle did nothing, however, to blunt Canadian enthusiasm for the war and, in the spring of 1915 a Second Contingent of volunteers crossed the Atlantic. Reorganized as the 2nd Canadian Infantry Division, it joined the now renamed 1st Division in France to form the Canadian Corps, which was later augmented by the 3rd and 4th Divisions. Operating at first under British generals until Canadian officers had gained enough experience to command higher formations, it fought in some of the worst battles of 1915 and 1916, actions commemorated by names frequently seen embroidered as battle honours on regimental colours: Festubert, Givenchy, St. Eloi, Mount Sorrel and the Somme. By the spring of 1917 the four divisions of the Canadian Corps, along with their counterparts from Australia and New Zealand, were regarded as the shock troops of the Imperial forces and the Canadians were renowned not only for the fury of their attacks but also for their thorough planning and technological prowess. These attributes were conspicuous on Easter Monday, 1917, when the Corps attacked and captured Vimy Ridge, a German strongpoint that had resisted all previous Allied attempts to eliminate it. It was a proud moment for Canada and it is fitting that her major memorial to the First World War is located on top of that ridge.

But Vimy was only a local success; it did not end the war which dragged on through 1917 as all Allied attempts to break through the German defence lines to the open country beyond were thwarted at bloody cost. Heavy artillery bombardments by hundreds, and later thousands, of guns were tried – the Germans took shelter in deep fortified bunkers to emerge when the bombardment had ceased and scythe down Allied infantry trying to cross ground reduced to a lunar landscape by high explosives. In September 1916, the answer to the tactical deadlock was introduced – the tank, an armoured vehicle impervious to machine gun fire, which could neutralize German defensive positions to allow the infantry to move forward. The concept was correct but the early tanks were primitive and this new weapons system had to undergo a long gestation before it became effective.

The Canadian Corps formed the spearhead of some of the major offensives undertaken by the Imperial forces in 1917, fighting at Hill 70 near Ypres and Passchendaele. The cost was appalling and, as the newspapers in Canada published the ever-lengthening lists of the killed, wounded and missing, the flow of volunteers began to dry up. More than 450,000 Canadians had enlisted by the end of 1917 but such were the casualties on the Western Front that it was proving increasingly difficult to keep front-line units up to strength.

In the opening months of 1918, after three and a half years of the bloodiest fighting in history, both the Allied powers and their German and Austro-Hungarian opponents were exhausted. Russia, weakened by a combination of military disasters and internal revolution, had made a separate peace treaty with Germany and left the war, and for the Allies the only encouraging aspect was the recent entry of the United States into the conflict on their side. Their basic strategy was to hold on until the fresh reserves of American manpower would tip the scale irretrievably in their favour. For the same reason, the German military leaders resolved to use troops switched from the Russian front to launch a final, massive offensive to bring the war to a negotiated end before American troops arrived in numbers. Codenamed Operation MICHAEL, it began on 21 March, and at first the attacking German armies made impressive gains but their advance was gradually slowed down by a number of hard and desperate rearguard actions. One of these actions, which took place in a small wood near Amiens on 30 March 1918, was unusual for the First World War because it was fought by mounted troops, many of them Canadian.

5

"It's a charge, boys, it's a charge!" Cavalry Action at Moreuil Wood

30 March 1918

Fig. 8.

67. *First movements on horseback.*

Soldier, Lord Strathcona's Horse, 1918

On 30 March 1918, at Moreuil Wood near Amiens, C Squadron of Lord Strathcona's Horse (Royal Canadians) under the command of Lieutenant Gordon Flowerdew made one of the few cavalry charges in the history of the Canadian army. (Painting by Ron Volstad, courtesy, Department of National Defence).

242

"It's a charge, boys, it's a charge!" Cavalry Action at Moreuil Wood

30 March 1918

John R. Grodzinski & Michael R. McNorgan

She is watching by the poplars,
Colinette with the sea-blue eyes;
She is watching and longing and waiting,
Where the long, white roadway lies.
And a song stirs in the lane
As the wind blows in the boughs above;
She listens and starts and trembles,
'Tis the first little sign of love.

> *Roses are shining in Picardy,*
> *In the hush of the silver dew;*
> *Roses are flow'ring in Picardy,*
> *But there's never a rose like you,*
> *And the roses will die with the summer time,*
> *And our roads may be far apart;*
> *But there's one rose that dies not in Picardy,*
> *'Tis the rose that I keep in my heart.*[1]

The First World War was not a good war for cavalry. All major combatants fielded mounted troops but advances in technology had conspired to render the cavalry arm more or less impotent on the field of battle. Time after time, during the long years of trench warfare on the Western Front, the cavalry moved up in the hope of exploiting a break through the enemy line, only to be turned back after the failure of the main infantry attack. Even when local success was

---

See Appendix E, page 384, for Orders of Battle of the Opposing Forces.

achieved, horses could not cross through barbed wire, move over ground reduced to the consistency of porridge by artillery fire, or survive sustained machine gun fire. The military tasks of reconnaissance, shock action and pursuit – the staples of cavalry work – were still required, but they could no longer be done primarily on horseback. Technology had created the problem and technology would solve it: the tank and the armoured car began to assume the duties of cavalry.

Nonetheless, once armies were again able to manoeuvre in the open, as they did in 1918, deep exploitation by motorized vehicles remained elusive. Doctrinal development and technological innovation had not yet provided the procedures or equipment to give advancing troops adequate support and reinforcements to maintain the momentum of their advance. As tactical radio communications were in their infancy, coordination between armour, infantry and artillery proved nearly impossible. This dilemma ensured that horsed cavalry remained useful to the very end of the conflict, particularly in the mobile battles that characterized the last months of fighting. It was during this time that the Canadian Cavalry Brigade had a brief, shining moment of glory at Moreuil Wood in March 1918.

Arme Blanche: The Canadian Cavalry Brigade, 1914

Awaiting inspection by King George V in November 1914, the Canadian Cavalry Brigade presents an impressive appearance but, unfortunately, mounted troops had a very restricted role in the trench warfare that dominated the Western Front until the last months of the war. In the foreground are The Royal Canadian Dragoons, the senior cavalry regiment of the Canadian army. (Courtesy, Royal Canadian Dragoons)

This success was all the more remarkable because the Canadian Cavalry Brigade was very much the "poor stepsister" of the army overseas. In October 1914, when the first contingent of the Canadian Expeditionary Force sailed from Quebec for England, the 31,200 soldiers on board the transports were drawn largely from militia and volunteers. The only elements of the Permanent Active Militia, or regular army, with this force were two cavalry regiments, the Royal Canadian Dragoons and Lord Strathcona's Horse (Royal Canadians), and two batteries of the Royal Canadian Horse Artillery. Upon arrival in England, the Expeditionary Force moved to Salisbury Plain to begin training but in early 1915 when the bulk of the contingent, now named the 1st Canadian Division, crossed to France, the regular cavalry units were left behind. It was decided to group these units into a Canadian Mounted Brigade, which was organized in February 1915.[2]

At this time, a mounted brigade consisted of a headquarters, three cavalry regiments, an artillery brigade and administrative units. Joining the Dragoons and Strathconas to create the new formation was a unit known as 2nd King Edward's Horse. Raised in July 1914, this regiment of Britain's Special Reserve was recruited from residents of Canada, New Zealand, Australia and South Africa living in England. Its unusual recruiting pool was the reason for its subsequent demise as it quickly ran out of "colonials" and in 1916 it had to be replaced with an up-to-strength Canadian unit, the Fort Garry Horse from Winnipeg. The addition of the Fort Garry Horse completed the formation of the Canadian Cavalry Brigade, as it now became known.

Each of the three cavalry regiments in the Brigade had an authorized strength of 526 officers and men while the Royal Canadian Horse Artillery (which was an integral part of the formation) had 500. The RCHA component comprised two batteries, each with four 13-pdr. guns. Some 2,200 pounds for gun and carriage, the 13-pdr. was lighter than the 18-pounder, the standard field piece, and the ideal weapon for mobile horse artillery. Each gun was manned by nine men and capable of hurling a 13-pound shell to a maximum range of 6,300 yards.

By January 1916, the Cavalry Brigade also included a 24-man Signal Troop and No. 1 Canadian Machine Gun Squadron with some 230 personnel and six Vickers .303 machine guns. No. 7 (Cavalry) Field Ambulance, with some 200 soldiers, collected, treated and evacuated wounded soldiers, while horses and other animals were cared for by the 27 members of 'A' Mobile Veterinary Section, Canadian Army Veterinary Corps. Lastly, the 1st Canadian Cavalry Brigade Supply Column, with about 100 officers and men, ensured that all units received the necessary supplies.

Quick-firing 13-pdr. field gun
The Royal Canadian Horse Artillery Brigade had eight of these powerful guns in two batteries supporting the Canadian Cavalry Brigade. Unfortunately during the hectic fighting leading up to Moreuil Wood, the brigade was detached to the British and French, leaving the Brigade without its integral fire support. These guns would have been very useful on 30 March 1918 but the RCHA did not rejoin until 1 April. (J.R. Grodzinski Collection).

Although it had been intended to place a Canadian in command, Colonel J.E.B. Seely, a British officer, was appointed by Lord Kitchener with the rank of brigadier general. Seely commanded about 2,700 officers and men, with 2,634 horses. Not all the members of the formation were mounted, however, and, on the march, the Brigade presented a curious collection of horses, wagons, bicycles, cars and lorries. Its cutting edge was its three mounted regiments and their tactics were based on the mounted soldier armed with a rifle and sword who used the speed and mobility of the horse to move around the battlefield.

This ability to cover long distances in a comparatively short time gave the cavalry the power both to obtain information and to combine attack and surprise, particularly in mass, to the best advantage. To do all these things, equitation – namely training the recruit to ride, and the horse to know what was required – was the guiding principle. The rider had to develop a symbiosis with his four-legged partner and gain an appreciation as to how that partner thought and felt, and how to communicate with him. The cavalry soldier was taught to regard his horse as his best friend, to take pride in his mount's appearance and to look after his "long-nosed" comrade's needs before his own.

Cavalry training progressed from learning how to saddle and bridle the horse properly, through mounting and dismounting, to controlling the mount through increasingly complicated manoeuvres in response to the numerous commands possible on parade or in the field. Training continued progressively to include manoeuvres within the section, five to eight men, then within the troop of four sections, the squadron of four troops, and finally as part of a regiment of three squadrons. A thorough understanding of watering, feeding, bedding, grooming and foot care of the horse, the fitting and care of saddlery and the prevention and cure of minor ailments was part of the lengthy curriculum. In peacetime, a cavalry recruit required six months of equitation instruction before he was considered fit for active service but, in war, this was reduced to make the mounted soldier into a good practical horseman in the shortest time possible.

The cavalry recruit was also instructed to use his weapons. When dismounted, his primary arm was the Short Rifle, Magazine, Lee Enfield Rifle Mark III, a cut-down version of the standard infantry rifle. The SMLE, or "Smelly," as it was called, weighed about eight pounds and fired a .303 calibre round from a ten-round magazine. The mounted soldier was also armed with the Sword, Cavalry, Pattern 1908 Mark I, a straight-edged weapon weighing about three pounds, with a slim, tapering thirty-five-inch blade and a leather-covered grip surrounded by a guard to protect the hand and it was designed for thrusting rather than slashing. Training with the sword was initially conducted dismounted with the recruit facing an instructor or partner carrying a stick.

Through a series of prescribed movements, the recruit learned how to engage, point, hilt and parry to the left and right side – he then learned

Position of "Attention" mounted.

"On side" view of Private H.C. Francis shows the proper stance of attention and some of kit worn by mounted troops and placed on the saddle. The left side of the horse was known as the "on side," while the right was called the "off side." This soldier carries a bandolier, rifle and water bottle, while his saddle holds the 1908 Pattern Sword and scabbard and a canvas bucket used for watering his horse. At the front arch of the saddle is one of two "wallets" for storing equipment. His mount has been "clipped" to reduce sweating, the hair being left on the horse's legs. (J.R. Grodzinski Collection).

to do the same movements while mounted. The 1908 pattern cavalry sword had replaced a thoroughly bad predecessor and gained a reputation as the finest edged weapon in the British army. Ironically, it appeared just as the weapon ceased to have any practical use.[3]

The cavalryman sat on the 1912 pattern saddle, the last model of saddle designed for use in the British and Imperial forces. Aside from providing a comfortable seat for the rider, it also held the items needed for both the soldier and his mount, in a number of pouches, bags and straps: iron rations consisting of a tin of bully beef, two biscuits, tea, sugar and Oxo cubes (these were not the normal ration and were only to be consumed in emergencies); mess tin, corn ration, hay net, canvas water bucket, two blankets, a greatcoat, picketing peg, shoe case with two extra horse shoes, rifle, bayonet, sword with scabbard and 140 rounds of ammunition. Then there was the bridle, worn around the horse's head, which helped the rider in controlling the horse's movement. The horse was always mounted or dismounted on the "near side," that is on the left of the horse looking forward, whereas the right side was known as the "off side." With all the kit suspended from the saddle, mounting and dismounting were often awkward actions. The sword was carried in a scabbard on the near side and drawn by the rider reaching over with his right hand, while the rifle, when not slung, was kept in a leather "bucket" on the off side of the horse.[4]

In action, the basic fighting element of the cavalry was the squadron. Commanded by a major or captain, it had four troops, each led by a lieutenant assisted by the troop sergeant. A troop had four sections, with each section having seven privates[5] led by a corporal

Last of the line
Like the 1908 Pattern Cavalry Sword, the Universal Pattern Saddle of 1912 was the last saddle developed for the British and Imperial Forces, and is still used today. The design allowed it to be fitted to any size horse, thus replacing three earlier types of saddles. Care and maintenance of the saddle was a primary duty of the cavalry soldier. (J.R. Grodzinski Collection)

or lance corporal. At full strength, the squadron had six officers and about 144 men. Commands were passed verbally or by using a trumpeter, who employed a number of standard "calls" to pass on the squadron commander's instructions. With the din created by machine gun fire, artillery, shouts and other noise on the battlefield, it was often difficult to hear either verbal orders or calls. As the squadron approached an objective, the squadron commander would move it through a series of formations depending on the tactical situation. These were practised repeatedly to ensure both horse and rider responded automatically on hearing an order. Movement was generally at the "walk," about four miles an hour, but in an attack or to hasten an approach, the pace was increased to the "trot," "canter," "slow gallop" and then the "gallop." [6]

In the attack, there was no rule governing the use of any particular pace. It was generally left to the commanding officer or squadron commander to determine this, basing his decision on the evenness of the ground, natural or man-made obstacles, surprise and experience. The main thing was not to tire the horses too quickly.[7]

The day of cavalry may have been about to pass, but being the recipient of a cavalry attack, even in 1918, was an impressive and frightening experience as a mass of galloping horses and men with drawn swords bore down at you. This mass flowing towards you, at some 400 yards per minute, the ground vibrating from the horses' hooves, which also threw up a cloud of dust, mud and dirt – not to mention the shouts of the riders and glinting steel of their blades – was enough to frighten all but the steadiest veterans.

The squadron

A plate from the manual *Cavalry Training 1912* showing the main formations used by mounted squadrons. Each rectangle represents a troop of about 35 men at full strength. Each troop would have been in two ranks. Squadrons were continually drilled in these formations to ensure rapid movement from one to the other. At Moreuil Wood the three understrength troops of C Squadron probably attempted to move into line, but given the short notice and speed of the operation, it was likely an irregular line.

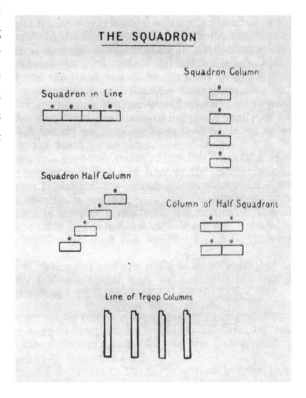

THE SQUADRON

A manpower crisis brought on by heavy Canadian losses at the Second Battle of Ypres, in April 1915, provided the opportunity for Seely's brigade to go to the front in a dismounted role, serving as infantry in the trenches. They served in this capacity under the title of "Seely's Detachment." After a year of intensive lobbying by Seely, they were reunited with their mounts, and retrained as horse cavalry in expectation of the breakthrough that would result from the Somme offensive in July 1916. That offensive was a catastrophic and bloody failure but the Brigade continued preparing for a breakthrough, with the occasional tour in the trenches to relieve the infantry. This relative lack of activity affected morale, causing many officers to satisfy their need for adventure by transferring to the newly-formed Royal Tank Corps or the Royal Flying Corps.[8]

The Cavalry Brigade again saw mounted action during the spring of 1917 when it harried German rearguards conducting a fighting withdrawal to the Hindenburg Line. In March 1917 Lieutenant Frederick M.W. Harvey of the Strathconas won a Victoria Cross for capturing a German machine gun position near Guyencourt, while in November Lieutenant Harcus Strachan of the Fort Garry Horse won the same award when leading his squadron against a German gun battery. A year later came the supreme crisis of the war, the German offensive of 1918.[9]

By January of that year, the war was midway through its fourth terrible year. The intense, mobile battles of the opening months had deteriorated into a static slugging match which gave little advantage to either side, while casualty rates soared. In 1917 alone, the British lost 860,000, the French 590,000 and the Germans 850,000 men killed and wounded. Nearly ex-

Early days, 1915

Officers of The Royal Canadian Dragoons photographed in the spring of 1915 before the unit went into action. From left to right: Lieutenants Jarvis, Fisher and Williams, Captain V.A.S. Williams, Lieutenants T.R. Newcomen and R.S. Timmis. By the time of the battle in March 1918 Timmis was a major commanding B Squadron of the Dragoons and Newcomen was a captain commanding C Squadron. (From Greenhous, *Dragoon: The Centennial History of the Royal Canadian Dragoons, 1883-1983*)

Valour is no stranger here.

The officers of C Squadron of the Strathconas in March 1917, one year before Moreuil Wood. In the front row, left to right, are Lieutenants H. Campbell, S. Williams, R.V. Torrance, Major D.J. Macdonald and Lieutenant G.M. Flowerdew. In the back are Lieutenants J.C. Attwood, F.M.W. Harvey and H.R. Harrower. At Moreuil Wood, Macdonald commanded the regiment; Atwood was second in command of A Squadron; Flowerdew was commanding C Squadron with Harrower, Harvey and Williams as three of his troop leaders. When this photo was taken, only one of the officers, Major D.J. Macdonald, had been decorated. By 1918, these eight officers had amassed two Victoria Crosses, four Distinguished Service Orders, four Military Crosses and one Croix de Guerre (French), perhaps a record unequalled for a sub-unit during the First World War. (Courtesy, Lord Strathcona's Horse (Royal Canadians) Regimental Museum).

hausted, the French army was on the verge of mutiny while Russia, shaken by an internal revolution, withdrew from the war. Allied offensives in Italy had been stymied and, on the Western Front, Britain was the only power strong enough to prevent collapse. To the German high command, it thus seemed that there was a possibility of achieving a single, decisive blow using fresh troops transferred from the east. This attack had to be made before the United States, which had declared war in April 1917, exerted its manpower to tip the balance decisively in favour of the Allies.[10]

The German plan was drawn up in late 1917 by *General* Eric Ludendorff, the German Army Chief of Staff. Code named Operation MICHAEL, it called for three armies to advance on a forty-mile front from Arras in the north to St.

"Long-nosed chums:" Picket line of the Fort Garry Horse, First World War

The care and feeding of his four-legged comrade, the source of his mobility, was one of the primary duties of the mounted soldier. Although envied by his infantry comrades because he rode, the cavalryman daily spent many hours ensuring his "long-nosed chum" remained fit for service. (National Archives of Canada, PA 51)

Quentin in the south (see Map M-1) and break through the British sector. Two more armies would pass through the gap and wheel north, and "roll up" the British line from behind. From his study of recent battles on the Western Front, Ludendorff had concluded that he should concentrate his forces and reinforce success rather than failure (reserves would only be committed where the attack was succeeding), an innovation that still eludes some modern commanders. The point selected for the initial attack was the junction between the Third and Fifth British Armies. Most of the twenty-nine divisions holding this area were severely under strength and were defending longer than normal frontages while few reserves were available. Opposing them were three German armies with seventy-six divisions, supported by 7,000 artillery pieces — twice as many as their opponents. The Germans also concentrated their air force, deploying 730 aircraft against the 579 planes of the Royal Flying Corps. Overall, Ludendorff's plan called for the commitment of one million men to his offensive.

At 4 A.M. on 21 March 1918, a thunderous, surprise artillery bombardment was brought down on the British sector chosen for the attack. The infantry then moved forward. General Sir Julian Byng's Third British Army was struck, but the main blow hit the Fifth Army, under General Sir Hubert Gough, which collapsed quickly. Recently given an additional twenty-five miles of front to defend, Gough's forces were stretched and unable to resist the onslaught. Sensing Ludendorff's intent, the commander of the British Expeditionary Force, Field

Map MW-1
The Western Front
March – April 1918

German gains

Miles

0   10   20

0   10   20   30

Kilometres

Marshal Sir Douglas Haig, sent most of his strategic reserve of eight divisions to the Third Army. Lacking any substantial reinforcement, Gough was forced to rely on his only reserve – the three mounted divisions of the Cavalry Corps. Suddenly, cavalry became vital to the survival of Fifth Army.[11]

At this time, the Canadian Cavalry Brigade was attached to the 3rd British Cavalry Division and on the day Operation MICHAEL commenced, was southwest of St. Quentin. After a short move, portions of the division's three brigades were dismounted, formed into three battalions and grouped into an *ad hoc* dismounted brigade. The Royal Canadian Horse Artillery Brigade was detached to support other British and French artillery and did not return to Seely's command until 1 April. For the next week, the dismounted brigade supported several British and French units who struggled to turn back the German juggernaut. They filled gaps and collected stragglers and on 25 March were attached to the French 125th Infantry Division. When the Germans captured Noyon, the Canadian battalion held a bridgehead further to the east, allowing the French to withdraw their artillery.

Following the creation of the Canadian dismounted battalion, the remainder of the Brigade moved to the area of the Somme Canal. When the Germans broke through to the canal on 23 March, another *ad hoc* force was created from elements of the 2nd and 3rd British Cavalry Divisions, which included the remaining Canadians. This force fought mounted and dismounted actions and conducted patrols and rearguard actions. On 27 March the separate elements of the Brigade were ordered to concentrate near Compiègne and were remounted.

Early on 28 March, reports of a gap in the line south of Montdidier had the Canadian Cavalry Brigade on the move. While leading a patrol, Lieutenant Harvey of the Strathconas and his men charged a group of Germans but, after withdrawing, were taken prisoner by the French, who were convinced they were Germans. Following an interview with the French divisional commander, Harvey and his men were released – he would later receive the *Croix de Guerre* for his pains.

The German offensive achieved spectacular success, advancing almost thirty miles in some areas. However, as the days went on and the supply lines got longer and the troops more tired, the momentum slowed. On 28 March, the same day that Harvey was winning a medal, Ludendorff decided to shift his main effort towards Amiens to force a gap between the British and French armies. He allowed a brief pause for some units to rest, then brought up thirteen more divisions and resumed the advance on Amiens. This pause, necessary because the German forward troops were exhausted, gave the Allies time to regroup and reinforce.

By 29 March, nine days of almost constant fighting and movement had taken their toll on Seely's command. All three regiments had suffered heavy casualties and were weak, averaging only 250 men each, or about half their authorized strength. Heavy officer and NCO casualties meant that, throughout the Brigade, junior ranks had gradually taken over more senior positions. But the formation had performed well, displaying a versatility in mounted and dismounted patrols, skirmishes, and rearguard actions.[12]

The constant "stand-to's," however, had placed considerable physical and psychological stress on all ranks and the Brigade was close to being worn out when it went into a bivouac at Guyencourt Wood, a few miles northwest of the village of Moreuil. They were therefore not very happy to receive yet another order to "stand to the horses" in the early hours of 30 March 1918,

The weather was no more cheerful that Easter Sunday morning: cold and dull with a heavy mist that burned off slowly as the sun rose higher. The men of the Brigade waited patiently by their mounts but the only order that came through was: "Move postponed two hours." Private John Willoughby of Lord Strathcona's Horse and his mates took advantage of the delay to get a hot breakfast of bacon and tea. Meanwhile, Brigadier General Jack Seely, the Canadian commander, was conferring with his immediate superior, Major General Thomas Pitman, commander of the 2nd British Cavalry Division.[13]

Seely, a Briton by birth and a politician by trade, had been the British Secretary of War until the spring of 1914 when an unfortunate blunder involving Irish Home Rule forced him to resign his office. The man at the centre of the affair that had cost Seely his portfolio was a certain Brigadier General Hubert Gough. Not wanting to waste the war away in some minor position, Seely had used his powerful political connections to lobby for an active field appointment. He had been given command of the Canadian Cavalry Brigade, primarily in order to keep him away from senior British officers like Haig, the commander-in-chief, and Gough, who had little use for him. Seely's appointment was protested by the Canadian Prime Minister, Sir Robert Borden, who wanted a Canadian officer in command of Canada's only cavalry formation. Thin, energetic and astute, Seely was a popular and respected commander and he was thoroughly enjoying the irony of the situation as Gough, the man responsible for his political demise, was now a desperate army commander relying on Seely and his fellow cavalry commanders to save his army from disintegration.

Pitman informed Seely that the situation was grave. The Germans had captured the eastern part of Moreuil ridge, which overlooked the Avre River, and enemy troops were pouring into Moreuil Wood, which lay just east of the point where the two men were talking (see Map M-2). He ordered Seely to "Go to the support of the infantry just beyond Castel, this side of the Moreuil ridge. Don't get too heavily involved – you will be needed later." Seely returned to his formation,

Not Canada's first choice: Brigadier General J.E.B. Seely

In 1915 the Canadian prime minister, Sir Robert Borden, opposed the appointment of a British officer, Brigadier General J.E.B. Seely, to command the Canadian Cavalry Brigade, claiming there were Canadian officers suitable for the job. Seely (with riding crop) is shown here talking to the Canadian Minister of Militia, Major General Sam Hughes (large man facing Seely). Borden finally got his wish in 1918 when a Canadian replaced Seely. (Courtesy, National Archives of Canada, PA 599)

briefed his regimental commanders accordingly and then, with a small party, left on a personal reconnaissance, taking with him one of the two available maps of the area. A few minutes later the Brigade mounted and made ready to follow.[14]

Riding in their customary pairs, the soldiers left their camp. The lead unit was the Royal Canadian Dragoons, followed by the Strathconas. Behind them came the Canadian Cavalry Brigade Machine Gun Squadron, while bringing up the rear was the Fort Garry Horse. The column was about 1,200 yards long and took ten minutes to pass any given point, and about twice as long to cross a bridge since this was normally done in single file. Generally the commanding officer of each regiment rode at the front of his command with his trumpeter. Behind him, in the assigned order of march, would be the three squadrons, each of three troops. As all instructions for movement were given verbally or by trumpet, the squadron commanders would position themselves to hear the commanding officer or adjutant's commands, or the trumpet, which in turn might be repeated by themselves or their troop commanders if the orders were difficult to hear. Scouts were usually sent forward to ensure the route was clear and markers, selected detached men, were posted to guide the following elements along the correct route.[15]

The mood of the men as the Brigade rode out of its bivouac was sober, but not depressed. They had more than a week of tough fighting behind them and knew that, if given enough time to select their ground, they could handle anything the Germans might throw at them, short of a full-scale assault supported by heavy artillery. This upcoming operation looked to be yet another delaying action, work that had become entirely too familiar in the last ten days.

Leaving the Guyencourt Wood, the Brigade trotted east across the Noye River, stopping to water their horses and top up their canteens. They then continued on to the tiny hamlet of Castel and its bridge over the Avre, where they encountered troops and vehicles of the Canadian Motor Machine Gun Brigade. The "Motors" were Canada's first armoured unit and had been fighting rearguard actions alongside the Cavalry Brigade for the past ten days. These two formations, in fact, were to be the only Canadian units involved in stopping the German offensive as the four divisions of the Canadian Corps, sitting in defensive positions on top of Vimy Ridge, would see no action. Equipped with armoured cars, the Motors had learned about mobile warfare the hard way – on the job – and had lost many of their lightly-armoured vehicles, which possessed no off-road capability. The motorized vehicles of 1918 simply did not have the mobility of the cavalry and they were not fast enough to get out of the way of the German juggernaut; during the course of the German offensive the Motors would lose half their strength killed, wounded or missing.[16]

While the Canadian Cavalry Brigade was riding east, German troops from 23 (Sachsen) Infanterie-Division were hastily occupying the northern portion of Moreuil Wood. The Saxons discovered that entering the wood was like poking a hornet's nest as they shortly suffered bombing and strafing attacks from low-flying squadrons of Allied aircraft. Despite being initially outnumbered in aircraft, the British had quickly reinforced their air units and the presence of the Royal Flying Corps was increasingly felt by the Germans as their operation progressed. After ten days of continuous offensive operations the Germans were as tired as their opponents – and they had paid a stiff price for their successes – but their casualties had not been replaced and supply lines were stretched to the breaking point.[17]

Also advancing on the wood (but to the east of the Saxons) was the 243 (Württemberg) Infanterie-Division. This formation was moving in two columns.

The right-hand column consisted of *Fusilier-Regiment* 122 and *Pionier-Bataillon* (Engineer Battalion) 306 with the 1st Battery, *Feldartillerie-Regiment* (Field Artillery Regiment) 238, in direct support. The left-hand column comprised *Infanterie-Regiment* 479 and *Pionierkompanie* 253 equipped with a mobile bridge, while in reserve was the *Infanterie-Regiment* 479 and the remaining two batteries of *Feldartillerie-Regiment* 238. The objective of the left-hand column was to secure the village of Moreuil and force a river crossing in order to eventually pass over the divisional reserve. The right-hand column was to secure Moreuil Wood and the high ground overlooking the Avre.[18]

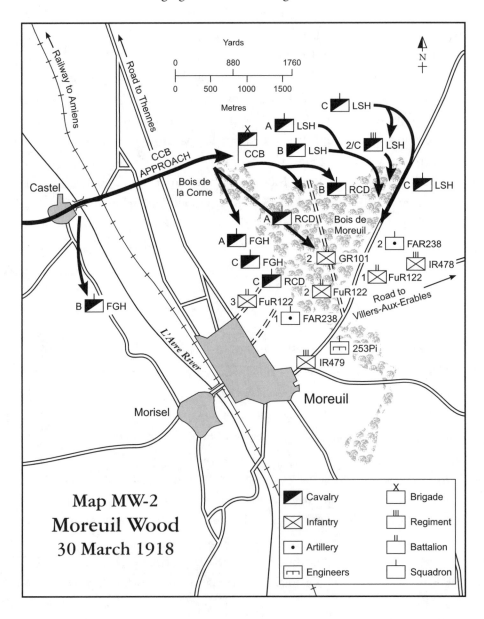

Map MW-2
Moreuil Wood
30 March 1918

When Seely and his advance party arrived in Castel they found French troops, infantry and artillery, about to withdraw to the west bank of the Avre. Only a thin French skirmish line now remained between Moreuil Wood and the river but Seely persuaded the French commander to stay put, telling him that he was going to counterattack the ridge and would need supporting fire.[19]

Seely assessed the terrain and the situation. Moreuil Wood, mainly beech trees in early bud, had a roughly triangular shape with one side facing north, another west and the third southeast. There was a small outgrowth at the northwestern point called the Bois de la Corne (Horn Wood). As the enemy apparently had not yet occupied it, Seely selected this as the site for his headquarters and quickly devised a plan to send a Dragoon squadron around each side of Moreuil Wood and one through the centre. The Strathconas, dismounted, would then clear the feature from north to south, with the Machine Gun Squadron providing covering fire from their Vickers machine guns on the flanks. The Fort Garry Horse would remain in reserve.[20]

Seely gave his orders to his newly appointed brigade major, Major Charles "Con" Connolly, a thirty-year-old Irishman who had served in the ranks of the British army and as regimental sergeant major of the Strathconas before receiving a commission in August 1915.[21] It would be Connolly's task to brief the units as they arrived at the Castel bridge. Then, accompanied by his aide-de-camp, Captain Prince Antoine d'Orléans,[22] his orderly, Corporal King, and the Brigade Signal Troop, Seely galloped up the crest of the ridge toward the Bois de la Corne. The party immediately came under German fire from the wood but seven of the twelve signallers survived to reach the wood, dismount, and returned the enemy fire. Corporal King jammed the staff of a red pennant into the ground at the northernmost point of the wood to mark the location of Brigade Headquarters and Seely turned in his saddle to watch the Royal Canadian Dragoons galloping up the hill along the route he had just taken. It was 9.30 A.M.[23]

The lead Dragoon squadron, A Squadron, about 100 men strong, and commanded by Captain Roy Nordheimer, rode past Seely at a gallop for the northwest corner of Moreuil Wood. Their exact point of entry was not in fact the precise northwest corner, but it appeared to be when viewed from Seely's position. Heavy machine gun and rifle fire forced Nordheimer to dismount his men and order them forward with fixed bayonets. He was soon wounded, shot through the right knee, but the squadron carried on and Lieutenant Eric Cochran of 1 Troop personally killed five Germans while leading his men to the eastern edge of the wood line. The Dragoons drove an estimated 300 enemy soldiers out of the wood in this action.[24]

An unenviable position: Major Charles E. Connolly, Lord Strathcona's Horse

Connolly was the brigade major of the Canadian Cavalry Brigade at Moreuil Wood. He functioned as the brigade commander's key staff officer and was responsible for all training and operational matters within the brigade. During the action, Connolly had to translate Brigadier General Seely's hasty verbal orders into clear and workable instructions and issue them to all units. Connolly rose to command the Strathconas after the war. (J.R. Grodzinski Collection).

Next came C Squadron under Major Terence Newcomen. They were sent south, past the west face of the wood, to occupy the southwest tip and establish contact with those French still in the village of Moreuil but they never reached this objective. As the squadron came over a rise of ground it was hit by heavy machine gun fire from the 3rd Battalion, *Fusilier-Regiment* 122, trying to fight its way into Moreuil. Behind the fusiliers were their close support battery from *Feldartillerie-Regiment* 238, with six horse-drawn field guns. Faced with this heavy concentration of fire, Newcomen chose to turn left into the wood.[25]

Simultaneously, the German battery commander, a *Leutnant* Gottschid, ordered acting *Stabsfeldwebel* (Sergeant Major) Brehm's Number 2 Section into action. The German artillery regiment's historian described the moment:

> Then, in peace so often practised, and in war so rarely used, command "attacking cavalry to right" could now be used. As if electrified, the gun trails flew to the left, and with lightning-like quickfire, the two guns opened fire at a range of 400 metres at the attacking squadrons.
>
> In a few minutes one could only see a few riderless horses heading toward our gun lines. The greatest part of the riders lay dead or wounded on the ground. A few lucky ones were able to escape this fate through quick retreat. The drivers of the 1st Battery were able to capture about 20 horses that were very welcome as replacements for the many horses lost by us. As expected, these horses that had been bred on the Canadian steppes, distinguished themselves from our horses, because of their superior nutritional condition.[26]

B Squadron of the Dragoons, under Major Reginald Timmis, was next on the scene. The squadron's orders, as explained to Timmis by Connolly at the Castel bridge, were to pass around the northeast tip of Moreuil Wood and down the eastern side to the southern end. Instead, B Squadron went halfway across the north face of the wood, and finding themselves under heavy machine gun fire, turned and charged into the tree line. Here it encountered more machine gun fire, as well as rifle fire from snipers located in the upper branches of trees. Unlike Nordheimer's A Squadron, B never received an order to dismount and many of its horses were killed. The situation became confused as knots of mounted and dismounted men became isolated in confused fighting.[27]

The men of B Squadron had understood that their comrades of C Squadron would support their attack.[28] This incorrect impression had probably resulted from the Connolly's hurried verbal orders issued in his thick Irish brogue, when he said that C and B Squadrons would meet on the opposite side of the wood. C Squadron, of course, was not in sight and some men from B Squadron were sent to look for them. Arriving at Brigade Headquarters one dazed man told Connolly that "the squadron was cut up" and it was obvious to the brigade major that B Squadron could not complete its task.[29] Among the casualties was the squadron commander, Major Timmis, who was suffering from shell shock. The only other officer in the squadron, Lieutenant Victor Nordheimer,[30] was dead. He had been shot while advancing on foot, sword in hand, after his horse had been killed.[31]

These northern attacks by A and B Squadrons of the Dragoons had encountered the 2nd Battalion, *Grenadiere-Regiment* 101, of 23 *(Sachsen) Infanterie-Division*, head-on inside Moreuil Wood. Meanwhile, to the south, C Squadron of the Dragoons was struggling with *Fusilier-Regiment* 122. The 3rd Battalion of this German unit was under great pressure. Bombed and strafed by British aircraft, it was still engaging French infantry fighting from positions inside Moreuil village and was also being pressed by C Squadron. The battalion commander, *Major* Graf Zeil, appealed to his superiors for support and the regimental commander, *Oberstleutnant* (Lieutenant Colonel) Von Alberti, was about to order his 2nd Battalion to debouch from the wood to put in a flanking attack on Moreuil from the north when a breathless artillery liaison officer cried out: "Enemy in the rear! Help!"[32]

Von Alberti's response was to order his 2nd Battalion to turn and face the new threat. He had no sooner done this when his 1st Battalion, which had been following the 2nd Battalion up to the wood accompanied by 2 Battery, *Feld-Artillerie Regiment* 238, reported enemy cavalry threatening its right flank.

This cavalry was Lord Strathcona's Horse. While the Dragoons were engaged inside Moreuil Wood, the Strathconas had crossed the Castel bridge. They formed up to the north of the wood about 1,000 yards from the point where the Dragoons' B Squadron had entered the tree line. Seely, through Connolly, ordered their commanding officer, Lieutenant Colonel Donald MacDonald, to attack dismounted and Connolly had arranged for the Machine Gun Squadron (less one section, which was supporting the Dragoons) to provide covering fire. The plan was for A and B Squadrons of the Strathconas to advance on foot to support B Squadron of the Dragoons in their unequal struggle with the Saxons in the wood while C Squadron remained mounted in reserve.[33]

The two squadrons dismounted and had just started to move forward when MacDonald received an order from Seely, again through Connolly, for the Strathconas to supply a mounted squadron for a separate task. C Squadron, led by Lieutenant Gordon ("Flowers") Flowerdew, was the only one available so MacDonald and Connolly rode over to Flowerdew and Connolly briefed him on his mission. Flowerdew was to complete the job that B Squadron of the Dragoons had started – he was to take his squadron around the northeast corner of Moreuil Wood and attack the enemy trying to enter the tree line at that point. Once this enemy was dispersed, Flowerdew was to occupy the southeast face of the wood. As the thirty-three-year-old Flowerdew moved off, he was joined by Seely, who later remembered that as he rode beside the young officer, he told Flowerdew that his was "the most adventurous task of all; but I am confident you will succeed." Flowerdew, a British Columbia fruit farmer in civil life, replied with a smile: "I know, sir, I know, it is a splendid moment. I will try not to fail you."[34]

Seeing that the northeast tip of the wood was occupied by the enemy, Flowerdew ordered Lieutenant Harvey, commanding 2 Troop, to secure that point and Harvey immediately moved off with his command. While riding toward the objective, 2 Troop encountered and killed five Germans soldiers looting a French transport wagon. On reaching his objective, Harvey dismounted the troop and was about to attack a large group of enemy infantry in the wood when Flowerdew galloped up. Harvey explained the situation to his squadron commander who ordered him to attack the enemy with his troop while Flowerdew and the remainder of the squadron "will go around the end mounted and catch them when they come out."[35]

While this conversation was taking place, Flowerdew's remaining three troops, with Private John Willoughby in their ranks, were waiting in a draw somewhat to the northeast of the wood. On returning to C Squadron, Flowerdew led them up out of the draw towards his objective. As the three troops came around the northeastern tip of the wood, Flowerdew saw Germans to his front and decided to charge to maintain the momentum of his advance and exploit whatever element of surprise the squadron's appearance had created.

Flowerdew's formation for this charge has never been satisfactorily described. Cavalry doctrine for this period called for different tactics when facing other cavalry, artillery or infantry. In all cases, the tactics were based upon the time available and the cover afforded by the ground. When the enemy was suddenly encountered, it was considered best to attack in whatever formation the cavalry happened to be in, so a favourable moment would not be missed for the sake of parade ground precision. Only when time allowed was the attacking force to be arranged in several lines with varying distances between each line. As C Squadron rode around the edge of the wood, Flowerdew, realizing contact with the enemy was possible, may have arranged the three troops in column by sections, that is by fours, to allow him to adopt one of a number of other formations should that contact be made. A later painting of the action by Sir Alfred Munnings shows the squadron in line (three troops side by side, each troop in two ranks), the second rank being about two horse lengths from the first with Flowerdew himself located in the centre of the first line. As Flowerdew appears to have immediately ordered a charge, this formation, known as half-squadron, may have been adopted, but would certainly not have been as neat as it was portrayed by Munnings.

While forming his squadron, Flowerdew saw two lines of German infantry, about 300 yards to his front, accompanied by artillery. The front line of this force consisted of 8 *Kompanie* from *Grenadier-Regiment* 101, which had been placed to the east of the wood in anticipation of a rumoured tank attack: (a deployment perhaps inspired by German sightings of the armoured vehicles of the Canadian Motor Machine Gun Brigade). Behind the Saxons were the Württembergers of 1st Battalion, *Fusilier-Regiment* 122, with their attendant battery of six 150 mm guns from *Feldartillerie-Regiment* 238 and a machine gun company armed with Maxim 08 7.92 mm machine guns.

It was an impressive force for three small troops totalling about seventy-five men to take on – but Gordon Flowerdew was not daunted. Half turning in the saddle he shouted: "It's a charge boys, it's a charge!"[36] His boy trumpeter, Reg Longley, riding directly behind Flowerdew, raised his trumpet to sound the charge, but no call was made as Longley and his horse were immediately cut down by German fire. It took just over thirty seconds for the leading Strathconas to cover the 300 or so yards before they hit the enemy infantry. For the riders and the horses, this must have been both exhilarating and frightening. Riding at the gallop, each rider was trained to instinctively keep only a few inches from the next rider. As he advanced in the face of German machine gun and small arms fire – with artillery rounds exploding around them – each rider drew his sword, leaned forward into his saddle, extending his right arm in front of him with the sword pointed slightly downward. As the charge gathered momentum, the hooves of the horses threw up clods of mud from the wet field. The mounts, sensing the frenzy of their riders, became unmanageable, several of them bolting out of control. A man from 4 Troop later recalled:

> There is not much I can tell of the actual charge, because everything happened with such speed and fury. I have a hazy recollection of seeing Flowerdew and his horse falling as we swept by. Everything seemed unreal – the shouting of men, the moans of the wounded, the pitiful crying of the wounded and dying horses. When I woke up I was pinned under my horse which was mercifully dead.[37]

The charge was a spectacle that lasted only a few brief moments before the Strathconas were decimated by German rifle, machine gun and artillery fire. Flowerdew, at the centre of the Strathcona line, was one of the first to be hit, rider and horse tumbling to the ground. The Strathconas streamed past him straight into the German Maxims. The Canadians were cut down in numbers before they covered one third of the distance to the enemy. Sergeant Tom Mackay, leading 1 Troop that day because his troop leader, Lieutenant Hamilton Harrower, had been detached for patrol duties, was later found to have fifty-nine bullet holes in one leg – those in his other leg could not be counted as the wounds ran too close together.[38] Twenty-four of the seventy-five men in Flowerdew's command were killed outright while fifteen later died of their wounds. Most of the remainder – exactly how many is not known — were wounded.[39]

The history of the *Grenadier-Regiment* 101 tells the story from the German perspective:

> Lance-Corporal Kiessig, the dispatch bearer of 7 Company, reached the battalion command post after a desperate struggle with an English officer whom he shot. Kiessig brought word of enemy tanks. Since the terrain was not unfavourable for such an attack, Captain Jungnickel stopped a battery of the heavy Württemberg Foot Artillery and requested that they take up a position on the [2nd] Battalion's right flank. A 15 cm gun succeeded in taking up

position by 8 Company, when approximately two squadrons [sic] of the Lord Strathcona's Horse emerged from the hollow north of the great forest, and in sight of the highway still tightly packed with columns [of German infantry]. They [the Canadians] received the well-aimed fire of 8 Company and a platoon of the 2nd Machine Gun Company. The aimer of one machine gun, Lance-Corporal Hertwig, continued to handle his machine gun resolutely, although he had been seriously wounded. Two direct hits from the 15-cm gun tore enormous gaps. The last horses collapsed 200 metres in front of the Company. Only one horse and two wounded troopers reached our line.[40]

Although only 8 *Kompanie* and the Machine Gun Company are mentioned here, it should be noted that Flowerdew's squadron rode into the combined fire of five infantry companies, an artillery battery with six guns, and assorted mortars. They inflicted a withering cross-fire on his three troops and the result was an outright slaughter.

Those few Strathconas who survived the charge still had to make it back to safety. Only one man from Flowerdew's three troops is known to have returned unharmed – Sergeant Frederick Wooster of 1 Troop. Finding himself alone, with enemy to his front, Wooster turned about and retraced his steps to Brigade Headquarters, where he met Seely and reported the charge and destruction of C Squadron before returning to the wood to join Harvey's 2 Troop. Also joining Harvey's troop were the twenty surviving men of B Squadron of the Dragoons, and Lieutenant Harrower, who had not been used for the planned patrol.[41]

It was Harrower who, with the aid of a sergeant, retrieved the badly wounded but conscious Flowerdew, who was found lying near the tree line. As they carried him into the wood a burst of machine gun fire struck Harrower in the foot and Flowerdew told his rescuer: "You had better get under cover Hammy, or they will

The modest hero: Lieutenant Gordon Muriel Flowerdew
Born in Billingford, Norfolk, in England, Flowerdew became a rancher in British Columbia before the war. Enlisting as a private in 1914, he was commissioned in 1916 and by January 1918 was commanding C Squadron of the Strathconas, which he led at Moreuil Wood. Flowerdew succumbed to his wounds and died on 31 March 1918. (Courtesy, Lord Strathcona's Horse (Royal Canadians) Regimental Museum).

Loved son, brother and comrade
Lieutenant Flowerdew's grave marker at Namps-au-Val, France. Although the marker shows him as captain, no evidence of promotion to this rank has been found and the reason for it being inscribed on the marker remains a mystery. (J.R. Grodzinski Collection).

shoot your head off next."[42] Four men took over the task of carrying Flowerdew back to the first aid post, which was located near the Brigade Headquarters. The Field Ambulance evacuated him to their advanced aid station at Namps but he died of his wounds the following day.

Before continuing with the story of the battle, it may not be out of place to consider the experience of the four-legged warriors. As terrifying as Flowerdew's charge may have been to his men, the reaction of their mounts may have been quite different. Veterinary tests and battlefield experience have shown that horses do not suffer to any great degree from reaction shock. Unless a vital organ is struck or a leg bone broken, a horse wounded in a charge is likely to survive the attack. Many of Flowerdew's animals did in fact do so, only to collapse after the action was finished.[43]

As the medical personnel of the Brigade went about their task of collecting and treating wounded men, their counterparts in A Cavalry Mobile Veterinary Section also moved onto the battlefield to deal with the "long-nosed" casualties. Horses so badly wounded that they could not recover were destroyed, while those with lesser injuries were collected, given rudimentary treatment and evacuated directly to veterinary field hospitals that provided more advanced treatment. Captain J.R.J. Duhault, the commanding officer of the veterinary section, and former veterinary officer for the Strathconas prior to the war, worked with eight of his soldiers, collecting a "great number of wounded horses" that day, and established an animal Casualty Clearing Station on 31 March at Saleux to aid evacuation. This station operated for ten days during which 500 wounded horses were treated and passed through, in addition to another 300 which were placed directly on trains for animal hospitals in the rear.[44]

A terrible price had been paid to gain Moreuil Wood but the sacrifice was not in vain. In the wood itself, the hard-pressed Dragoon squadrons noticed the Germans gradually beginning to give way. The sound of the hooves of the Strathconas' horses caused the Saxons opposing them to look over their shoulders in expectation of an attack from the rear and they started to edge back.

"But what of the poor dumb heroes?" The men who cared for the four-legged troopers

Like modern armoured vehicle mechanics, the work of the Canadian Army Veterinary Corps was critical to keeping the army mobile, the only difference being that they cared for animals, not vehicles. Shown here are members of A Cavalry Mobile Veterinary Section, which provided care for sick, lame and wounded horses of the Cavalry Brigade. For ten days following Moreuil Wood, members of this section had the grim task of collecting, evacuating and disposing of some 800 horses. (Courtesy, National Archives of Canada, PA 4166)

Flowerdew's charge also stopped the 2nd Battalion of *Fusilier Regiment* 122 from taking Moreuil, preventing the Germans from making their planned river crossing over the last natural defence line before Amiens. If the Germans had been successful, the way to Amiens, a vital communication centre, would have been open to the enemy. Although the German momentum had been stopped, the enemy were still fighting. Moreuil Wood was only one of many small actions fought on 30 March that slowed and finally stopped Operation MICHAEL.[45]

Following the charge, at roughly 11 A.M., the sun broke through the mist and illuminated the battlefield. The fighting continued in the wood with A and B Squadrons of the Strathconas, dismounted, trying to push the Germans from north to south. C Squadron of the Dragoons being still heavily engaged on the western face of the wood, Seely sent B Squadron of the Fort Garry Horse back across the Castel bridge and southward along the west bank of the Avre. From the top of a high hill at that point, they could bring long-range fire to bear on the enemy flank in the southwest tip of the wood. As the struggle inside the wood remained in doubt, Seely committed his last reserves, A and C Squadrons of the Garrys, into the battle at the western face of Moreuil Wood.[46]

The Canadians now held all of the wood except the southernmost tip. Both sides had brought up their artillery and a steady stream of shellfire was added to the perils of the combatants. A British artillery battery, deployed to the west of the wood, constantly dropped their rounds short – on top of the Canadians – but after Lieutenant Luke Williams of the Strathconas expressed a few sharp and well-chosen words to the battery commander, the problem ceased. Williams then rode to Brigade Headquarters where Connolly asked him how the Strathconas were getting on and received the reply: "We are getting whittled down gradually. If we don't get relieved soon there won't be anybody left to get relieved."[47] A message was therefore passed to Pitman's 2nd British Cavalry Division that the Canadians required assistance. Pitman responded by sending his 3rd Brigade to their aid.[48]

It was well he did because by this time the three Canadian regiments had lost between one-third and one-half their strength. The fighting in the wood was very bitter; the Germans rarely surrendered, even those mortally wounded preferred to fight to the end. The Cavalry Brigade was clearly unable to hold the position and only the timely arrival of the British 3rd Cavalry Brigade preserved what the Canadians had won. The 4th Hussars and the 16th Lancers, riding down from Castel, charged into the wood in the area where C Squadron of the Dragoons was fighting. The commanding officer of the Lancers, Lieutenant Colonel Geoffrey Brooke, had been Connolly's predecessor as Seely's brigade major and Seely placed C Squadron under his command. Together, the British and Canadians formed a long line and prepared to advance to clean out the area. Because visibility was limited among the trees, the men were informed that the orders to advance, halt and fire would be given by

Lieutenant Colonel R.W. Paterson, only Canadian commander of the Canadian Cavalry Brigade
Lieutenant Colonel R.W. Paterson raised the Fort Garry Horse in 1912 and commanded them until May 1918, when he was promoted to brigadier general and succeeded J.E.B. Seely as brigade commander for the remainder of the war. He is shown here as a brigadier general. (J.R. Grodzinski Collection).

whistle blasts. Not everyone in the combined force was enthusiastic about this operation although it appeared by now that the Germans were losing the struggle.[49]

Brooke later recalled that he

had just passed the word down the line to advance when a soldier, who had temporarily lost his nerve, started to run back. I had a large pair of wire cutters which I hurled at him and hit him on the knee. This may have restored his equanimity as he then carried on – or it more likely may have been due to the remark of an old soldier seeing the German machine guns ripping up the grass in front of us. "God," he said, "It reminds me of old Nobby cutting up the billiard table."[50]

Every fifty yards or so, the Anglo-Canadian line halted and fired "five rounds rapid" into the underbrush before advancing another similar distance. In this way the Germans were gradually pushed back out of the wood with the exception of its southernmost tip, where they stubbornly resisted. At this point, early afternoon, the battle became a stalemate but the Canadians, with British help, held their gains throughout the day against repeated German counterattacks. The fighting in the afternoon took place under a heavy fall of rain that commenced at noon and continued throughout the next day.[51]

When British infantry relieved the Canadian Cavalry Brigade at 9:30 that evening, it proved difficult for the remnants to move back. Horses and riders had become separated during the day and since riders could not find their own mounts, or positively identify them in the dark, they took whichever horse was closest to hand. Finally, the tattered formation then rode back to Castel and watered their horses in the Avre before moving on to Senécat Wood to bivouac. As the medical and veterinary personnel continued their labours, the soldiers of the Brigade went about tending their horses, cleaning their kit and getting some food and rest. The officers of the units involved in the fighting began compiling their casualty lists for transmission to Brigade Headquarters so that replacements, both men and remounts, could be requested.[52]

Those casualty lists were long. Losses on 30 March 1918 from the three cavalry regiments, the machine gun squadron and the field ambulance totalled 305 all ranks killed, wounded and missing, plus 800 horses. The Strathconas had suffered the worst, with 157 killed and wounded. The 3rd Cavalry Brigade also lost heavily – the commanding officer of the 16th Lancers noted that one of his squadrons had been reduced to a single officer, a non-commissioned officer and six men.[53]

The following day the Germans counterattacked and retook Moreuil Wood. They were, however, unable to exploit this success as they were too weak to continue. The Saxon 23 *Infanterie-Division* is reported to have lost 70% of its fighting strength between 29 March and 3 April 1918 while 243 *Infanterie-Division* reported losing 50% in the period 26 March to 4 April.[54]

When the Germans occupied Moreuil Wood on the 31 March they also captured a wooded hilltop north of it nicknamed "Rifle Wood" by the British, honouring the rifle battalions of the 20th Light Division which had defended, but lost, this feature during the fighting of the previous day. (In a similar fashion the British also gave the name "Cavalry Wood" to the forest at Moreuil. This term, however, never caught on.) The Canadian Cavalry Brigade was ordered to recapture Rifle Wood with a dismounted assault, which was accomplished on 1 April. After that, its weary members were finally allowed to rest.

Although Operation MICHAEL had resulted in impressive territorial gains, the Germans failed to capture any significant cities or to split the Allied armies. The operation also cost 250,000 casualties and valuable material resources – they could not be replaced. On the Allied side, 160,000 British and 80,000 French soldiers were lost but the arrival of 318,000 American soldiers over the next few months was a valuable boost to the Allied cause. The overall situation now tilted against Germany and just over seven months later the fighting ceased.

Thousands of acts of individual heroism, mostly unrecorded, helped halt the German offensive of 1918. Of the hundreds of decorations for bravery, only twenty Victoria Crosses were awarded during this period and two went to Canadians: one to Second Lieutenant McLeod of the Royal Flying Corps and the other to Lieutenant Gordon Muriel Flowerdew of Lord Strathcona's Horse. His citation reads:

> For most conspicuous bravery and dash when in command of a squadron detailed for special services of a very important nature. On reaching his first objective, Lieutenant Flowerdew saw two lines of enemy, each about sixty strong, with machine guns in the centre and flanks; one line being about two hundred yards behind the other. Realising the critical nature of the operation and how much depended on it, Lieut. Flowerdew ordered a troop under Lieut. Harvey, VC, to dismount and carry out a special movement, while he led the remaining three troops to the charge. The squadron (less one troop)

passed over both lines, killing many of the enemy with the sword; and wheeling about galloping on them again. Although the squadron had then lost about 70 per cent of its members, killed and wounded from rifle and machine gun fire directed on it from the front and both flanks, the enemy broke and retired. The survivors of the squadron then established themselves in a position where they were joined, after much hand to hand fighting, by Lieut. Harvey's party. Lieut. Flowerdew was dangerously wounded through both thighs during the operation, but continued to cheer his men. There can be no doubt that this officer's great valour was the prime factor in the capture of the position.[55]

The medal was presented to Flowerdew's mother (who lived in Norfolk, England) by King George V on 29 June 1918 in the quadrangle of Buckingham Palace. It now resides at Flowerdew's former school, Framlingham College in England.

The Moreuil and Rifle Wood battlefields remained an attraction for members of the Canadian Cavalry Brigade. Five months after the action, in August 1918, the Brigade was again in the area, preparing for their part in the forthcoming offensive at Amiens. Parties of officers and men from the Dragoons and the Strathconas visited the battlefield and discovered the graves of many of their fallen comrades, buried by the enemy and marked with swords or rifles thrust into the ground. The human remains in some of these graves had been disturbed by shellfire and were re-interred.

On 13 August 1918, Moreuil Wood was visited by four Strathconas: Captain S.H. Williams, Lieutenant A.E. Chapman, Sergeant Walter Land and Private Joe Yans. They rode through the village of Castel, now showing few marks of the war, crossed the Avre River and rode around the northern face of the wood to the eastern side. There they found skeletons of several horses killed in the charge, which were bleaching in the sun. They also found and re-buried the body of Private David Dobson of Flowerdew's squadron. Near Dobson lay the body of a horse from 4 Troop of C Squadron and Williams picked up one of its hooves, marked with the number "122." Williams kept the hoof as a souvenir and later had it made into a pin cushion, with the engraving "Moreuil Wood March 30th, 1918." The hoof is now on display in the office of the commanding officer of Lord Strathcona's Horse. Williams's party also found several Strathcona graves, some marked by sabres and others with steel helmets. One had a crude cross on it with the inscription *ein tapferer Englander* ("a brave Englishman").[56]

In the years following the war, the Royal Canadian Dragoons and Lord Strathcona's Horse lobbied hard to have the action at Moreuil Wood included as an official Battle Honour. Their efforts were to no avail as the British War Office, which administered the award of honours for all the military forces of the Empire, would not support the application, nor would National Defence Headquarters in Ottawa. In February 1931, the Adjutant General of the Militia Service, Brigadier A.H. Bell, wrote to the District Officer Commanding Military District No 13, which at that time included the Strathconas, that

> Whilst the information obtained bears out the importance of the moral and practical results of the actions of the Canadian Cavalry Brigade in recognition of which, the proposed battle honour "Moreuil" has been under review, it is considered it does not reveal circumstances of a sufficiently special nature to make it desirable for the Canadian government to be approached with a view to recommending to His Majesty, for approval, the award of a battle honour which would not be within the general policy governing the award of Great War Battle Honours, it is regretted that no further action can be taken in this matter.[57]

Despite this reversal, the Strathconas have ensured that the memory of the action will never fade. Following a suggestion by Major General Sir Archibald Macdonell, a former commanding officer, that the regiment institute an annual day of commemoration, "Moreuil Wood" Day was initiated on 30 March 1927. The usual activities on this day included a regimental sports competition, a memorial service and parade, reception and mess dinners. On this day, the Regimental Sergeant Major of the Strathconas carries a pace stick made of wood from a tree in Moreuil Wood. For many years after the inception of this celebration, veterans of the battle came to visit their old regiment. Since 1927, Moreuil Wood Day has been held annually by the Strathconas in garrison in Canada, overseas during the Second World War and the Korean Conflict, during service with NATO in Europe and Bosnia and on United Nations peacekeeping missions. It is still observed today.[58]

Over the years, Moreuil Wood has gained near mythical status, which in some ways has perhaps blurred the action's true significance. Commenting after the war, *Maréchal* Ferdinand Foch, the supreme commander of the Allied forces, hailed the offensive dash of the Canadians as they first held and then broke the enemy, thus saving the situation. Foch's acclamation has led some to claim that the First World War was won at Moreuil Wood. Placed in the context of one million men locked in a massive struggle, this conclusion is patently false. What is true is that during a two-week period the Canadian Cavalry Brigade underwent long marches and counter-

A piece of Canadian cavalry history

During a visit to Moreuil Wood on 13 August 1918, Captain S.H. Williams found a horse's hoof, marked with the number "122," which belonged to a horse from Williams's own troop — 4th Troop, C Squadron. Williams had it made into a pin cushion, which now rests on the desk of the commanding officer, Lord Strathcona's Horse in Edmonton, Alberta. The metal rim bears the inscription "Bois de Moreuil March 30th 1918." (Courtesy, Lord Strathcona's Horse (Royal Canadians) Regimental Museum)

marches, often without food, rest or resupply, and fought dozens of actions in the trenches or the open. They never faltered and continually displayed the best attributes of the cavalry spirit: determination, bravery, flexibility and robustness.[59]

At Moreuil Wood, the Canadian Cavalry Brigade won the day by stabilizing a seemingly lost tactical situation. Faced by a brave and determined enemy, the Brigade fought in the most difficult of circumstances. The close terrain, machine gun and artillery fire, limited communication and uncertainty over enemy strength and dispositions compromised the Brigade's advantages of mobility and shock action. The lack of accurate intelligence meant a simple plan was needed. Seely's plan to isolate the wood and then force the Germans out was probably as good as any but inadequate communications (the Brigade had no tactical radios) made it difficult to control once it began and as the battle progressed it became a series of isolated engagements. Despite these conditions, the units of the Brigade managed to keep fighting.

On Easter Sunday 1918, the officers and men of the Canadian Cavalry Brigade showed that, in the confusion of combat, disciplined leadership, good training, initiative and experience can compensate for doctrinal, technological or command and control limitations. The pivotal importance of that "unknown factor," the common soldier, as the Duke of Wellington once remarked, cannot be underestimated. This is one legacy of the battle that must not be forgotten.

Moreuil Wood Today

The battlefield at Moreuil Wood looks very much as it did in 1918. The traveller coming from Amiens, the nearest large city, and following Highway D 934, will first see the wood from the northwest, just as Seely did. The tiny bridge at Castel, where the Brigade crossed, is still there and, once across it, the traveller can follow a secondary road, a lane really, that leads up to the Bois de la Corne, site of the Brigade Headquarters and the first aid station. The sight of numerous "No Hunting" signs posted on the trees may bring a smile, but along the tree line of the wood one can occasionally see caches of unexploded ammunition of various calibres uncovered in the nearby field by local farmers which they pile up for removal and destruction by French army explosive ordnance units.

The wood itself is much thicker than it was in 1918. The unexploded munitions make it a dangerous place to walk and so secondary growth has been allowed to flourish. Geoffrey Brooke, who fought in the battle, visited the wood and "could not believe that it was possible to traverse the wood on horseback – the fact being that a wood with trees blasted and stunted by shell-fire grows such thick undergrowth that it becomes almost impenetrable."[60]

From time to time, other, perhaps more grim, reminders of the action come to light. In 1977, a French souvenir hunter searching the edge of Rifle Wood stumbled across human remains. The presence of a Fort Garry collar badge and buttons revealed them to be from one of two men of that unit listed as missing in action. Unfortunately a positive identification was impossible as the skull was missing, and no distinguishing marks were found. Thus the body of Sergeant William Willis, DCM, MSM, or Private Harry Hancock was consigned to a grave in the Commonwealth War Graves Commission cemetery at Terlincthun near Calais, and the marker carried Kipling's traditional words: "A Soldier of the Great War – Known unto God." A decade later, the remains of Private John Willoughby of Lord Strathcona's Horse were located on the battlefield. Found nearly seventy years after he had fallen in the charge of Flowerdew's squadron, he too was laid to rest in Terlincthun, far away from the beech wood near Moreuil.[61]

On the east side of the wood, a modern highway (D 23) has been built along the route followed by Flowerdew's squadron. Near the highway is a large monument to the French division that fought near here in August 1918 but it carries no reference to the events of March 1918. The only memorials to the battle of Moreuil Wood are the Commonwealth War Graves Commission Cemeteries. One, lying in the northern end of the prosperous town of Moreuil, contains the bodies of most of those killed in the battle, including Lieutenant Victor Nordheimer. The other cemetery, a few miles further west at Namps, was originally the site of the field hospital where the battle's wounded were treated. Here lies the grave of Lieutenant Gordon Muriel Flowerdew. To visit these cemeteries, from Amiens take Highway D29 southwest to Quevauvillers. Turn left (east) onto highway D38 and drive to Namps-au-Mont. The green signs for the Commonwealth War Graves Commission cemetery are the best guide to find it, in a secluded spot in the countryside outside of Namps-au-Mont.

Finally, if the interested traveller visits the magnificent Cathedral of Amiens, which miraculously survived fire and bomb in two world wars, he or she will find a small brass plaque on one of the pillars, the only monument of its type in this ancient structure. It contains a testimony to the sacrifices of the Royal Canadian Dragoons in the action that saved Amiens.

From the Western Front to Normandy, 1918 to 1944

The First World War dragged on for more than seven months after the action at Moreuil Wood. Shaken by the fury of the German offensive, the Allies appointed *Maréchal* Ferdinand Foch as commander-in-chief of all their forces and Foch managed to ward off a series of smaller German attacks launched by Ludendorff in the early summer. The German 1918 offensive had failed and, beginning in early August, the Allies rolled the German army back to its own frontiers in a series of major operations.

The Canadian Corps, which had been held in reserve during much of the fighting of the previous four months, played an outstanding role in what were to be the last months of the war. On 8 August, the Corps spearheaded a major offensive, supported by tanks and aircraft, near Amiens and advanced seven miles. This day, 8 August 1918, Ludendorff later commented, was "the black day of the German army" as it marked the beginning of the end for his country, which no longer had the reserves to fight off a series of Allied attacks that broke through successive German defensive lines. By early November, the Allies were advancing all along the Western Front and Germany requested a ceasefire until peace terms could be negotiated.

The fighting ceased on 11 November 1918 and on the following day the 1st and 2nd Canadian Divisions were ordered to occupy German territory on the Rhine. They spent three weeks marching across old battlefields on roads choked with civilians returning to their ruined homes and liberated prisoners of war trying to get back to their own forces. On 4 December, when the vanguard of the 1st Division, formed by the 2nd Battalion, Canadian Expeditionary Force, crossed the German border near Cologne, the battalion band proudly played "O Canada."[1]

There was reason for that pride. The Canadian Corps had "achieved a reputation unsurpassed in the Allied armies" because it had

emerged successfully from every test, no matter how severe, and its professional ability had proved second to none. Canada had begun the war with little military experience and with practically nothing in the way of a standing army; she ended it with a superb fighting machine.[2]

The cost of that achievement had been heavy. During the First World War, of a total population of just 7 million, 619,636 men and women served in the Canadian Army with 59,544 losing their lives and 172,950 being wounded. Canada had entered the war because Britain had entered the war but it emerged as an independent nation, a status recognized by its separate signature on the Versailles Peace Treaty of 1919. In the eighty intervening years, Canadian politicians and diplomats have often reaped the advantages of that status but it should never be forgotten that it was purchased with the lives of Canadian soldiers.

The war to end all wars being over, that magnificent fighting machine, the Canadian Corps, was disbanded and the country's military establishment lapsed into a moribund state. Defence spending was cut to the bare minimum (or less), particularly during the economic depression that began in 1929, and by 1935 the chief of the general staff was forced to warn the government that Canada did not possess a single modern aircraft and that there was only enough artillery ammunition on hand for about one hour of firing at normal rates. This was the low point and defence spending was increased over the next four years. This improvement came not a moment too soon as international stability was threatened by the territorial ambitions in Europe of a resurgent Germany led by Adolf Hitler in Europe and a militaristic Japan in Asia. On 1 September 1939, German forces invaded Poland, and when Hitler made no response to a British and French ultimatum to withdraw, those two nations declared war on Germany. Ottawa followed suit on 10 September 1939 but in Canada there was little of the exhilaration that had marked the outbreak of hostilities in 1914.

The mobilization plan for the Canadian Army called for the dispatch of an overseas expeditionary force to Europe consisting of two infantry divisions. These formations were duly organized from the three infantry regiments of the regular force and selected militia units across the country, and the 1st Canadian Infantry Division sailed from Halifax during the winter of 1939 and was followed shortly by the 2nd Infantry division. These divisions expected to be deployed in France after training in Britain in a re-run of the First World War but this plan disappeared in April and May 1940 when Germany launched a major offensive in the west and, in a matter of weeks, overran the Low Countries and France. This offensive, styled "blitzkrieg" or "lightning war" by foreign commentators (the term is not German), was characterized by the concentrated employment of tanks in panzer or armoured divisions. The tactical balance in warfare had now swung in favour of the offence.

Over the next eighteen months the conflict widened as Italy and Japan entered on Germany's side while Russia and the United States joined Britain. American industrial might shifted the tide against the Axis powers and by 1943 they were on the defensive. During these years, the Canadian forces in Britain were gradually built up to a strength of five divisions and two independent armoured brigades, organized as the First Canadian Army. Although one division saw action briefly in the disastrous 1942 raid on Dieppe, Canadian government policy, which insisted that this army would only be committed to battle as a complete and independent force under Canadian generals, condemned it to years of inactivity. In 1943, public opinion forced the government to permit the dispatch of two divisions to the Mediterranean, where they participated in the Sicilian and Italian campaigns, but the remainder of army remained in Britain training for what was seen as its major role – participation in the cross-Channel invasion planned for 1944.

Between 1940 and 1944, armoured forces had dominated land warfare, and to be successful the Allied forces invading Europe would require tank support. For Canadian soldiers, this support would be provided by units of the Canadian Armoured Corps, a new organization. Before 1939, the Canadian army had little experience with tanks: a few interested officers had contributed articles on armoured warfare theory to professional journals and a Fighting Vehicle School had been created at Camp Borden in Ontario to offer basic training, but in September 1939 the nation's tank inventory consisted of a pitiful collection of about three dozen obsolescent vehicles. The successful deployment of German panzer divisions in the French campaign of 1940 sparked the creation of a Canadian Armoured Corps which, although hampered by shortage of just about everything required, grew rapidly until by the spring of 1944 units of the corps comprised about 40 per cent of the combat units in the overseas army.

The plan for Operation OVERLORD, the Allied landing in Normandy, called for a Canadian contribution of one division to the initial assault. This formation, 3rd Canadian Infantry Division, would land on JUNO Beach in the centre of the British sector and would be supported by Brigadier R.A. Wyman's 2 Canadian

Armoured Brigade, equipped with Duplex Drive or amphibious tanks. Both the 3rd Division and 2 Armoured Brigade trained hard for their role in the landing but concentrated on the problem of getting ashore and surviving on D-Day. Comparatively little thought was given to what would happen after the beachhead had been secured and the troops would move inland where, inevitably, they would encounter German armoured reserves brought forward to throw the invaders back into the Channel. In the months preceding the landing, 3rd Division and 2 Armoured Brigade devoted only three days to training in tank/infantry co-operation, a skill necessary for the battles beyond the beachhead.

Given the tremendous technical difficulties inherent in an amphibious operation, this emphasis on the landing itself to the detriment of what would happen later was understandable. In any case, even if the two Canadian assault formations had wished to devote more time to preparing for mobile warfare, it would have been difficult as training facilities in Britain, which had become one large armed camp in the months preceding OVERLORD, were extremely limited, particularly for armoured forces. Perhaps worse still, although an attempt had been made to transfer officers with combat experience from Italy to provide a leavening of expertise in the assault forces, the majority of unit commanders and their subordinates were going into their first battle. In the words of a Canadian lieutenant who fought in Normandy, "the greenest bloody army that ever went to war" was about to go into action against the German *Wehrmacht*, a professional and determined opponent.[3]

In the event, the initial landing on 6 June 1944 went relatively well for 3rd Canadian Division as, despite taking heavy casualties in some sectors, it achieved more of its D-Day objectives than any other Allied assault formation. Their problems began in the three days immediately following the landing when the 3rd Division, assisted by 2 Armoured Brigade, tried to expand its bridgehead and encountered the 12. *SS-Panzerdivision*, a very tough and well-led formation. Ferocious fighting occurred as the division tried to push forward while 12. *SS-Panzerdivision* tried to drive it into the sea. The result was a stalemate with neither side able to advance and neither side willing to give up ground.

Three days of fighting on 7-9 June 1944 left a gap between two of the brigades of 3rd Division along the valley of the little Mue River. On 10 June, the First Hussars, an armoured regiment from London, Ontario, with infantry support from the Queen's Own Rifles of Toronto, were ordered to clean up this area. To do so, the Hussars and the Queen's Own would first have to take a little Norman village called Le Mesnil-Patry.

6

Black Sabbath

for the First Hussars:

Action at

Le Mesnil-Patry

11 June 1944

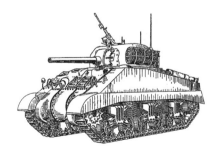

Canadian armour, Normandy, 1944

A Sherman 75 mm of the Canadian Armoured Corps, Normandy, 1944. A robust, reliable tank, the Sherman was outgunned by its German counterparts and, as the action at Le Mesnil-Patry demonstrated, Canadian armoured units, although well trained by Allied standards, still had much to learn. (Department of National Defence, Negative ZK-859)

Black Sabbath
for the First Hussars:
Action at Le Mesnil-Patry

11 June 1944

Michael R. McNorgan

The old First Hussars are a'riding again,
A new breed of steeds, but the old breed of men,
The foe know us of old and they still bear the scars,
If they're wise they'll walk wide of the gallant Hussars.

There are loved ones who miss us, but glory to know,
That the men that they cherish are death to the foe,
For Truth, Justice, and Freedom, we march to the wars,
And more laurels we'll win for the gallant Hussars.[1]

After three years in Britain, including one year spent in intensive training for the invasion of France, Trooper Athelstan Owen Dodds (known to one and all as "A.O.") landed on JUNO Beach in the morning hours of 6 June 1944. In the intense fighting for the Allies' first toehold in Normandy, his regiment, the First Hussars from London, Ontario, lost forty-three men and many tanks, the worst casualties of the three armoured regiments in 2 Canadian Armoured Brigade, which supported the infantry ashore.[2]

Two days after D-Day, the commanding officer of the Hussars, Lieutenant Colonel Ray Colwell (a Great War veteran who had been posted into the Hussars when his own regiment, the Halifax Rifles, was broken up) was forced to amalgamate two of his three armoured squadrons. On 10 June, thanks to the loan of seven tanks and crews from the Hussars' sister regiment, the Fort Garry

See Appendix F, page 385, for Orders of Battle of the Opposing Forces.

Horse, and the arrival of twenty reinforcement tanks and crews, Colwell was able to reorganize his regiment on a three-squadron basis again. In order to ensure that each crew in the unit had at least some veteran members, the crew rosters of the entire regiment were shuffled. Trooper Dodds now found himself the loader-operator in the tank of B Squadron's new commander, Captain Harry Harrison. The changes to the crew rosters, breaking up men who served together as a team for some time, was not a matter of concern for Colwell as he had been promised by his superior, Brigadier Robert Wyman commanding 2 Armoured Brigade, that the Hussars would be able to enjoy twenty-four much-needed hours of rest and relaxation after four days of continuous fighting.[3]

Unfortunately, this promise was not kept. During the advance from the beaches a salient had formed between Major General Rod Keller's 3rd Canadian Infantry Division's two forward brigades along the valley of the Mue River (in Canadian terms it would be described as a creek). Accordingly, Wyman received orders to clear this area and then advance to the village of Cheux, his brigade's original D-Day objective (see Map LMP-1). At 9 P.M. on 10 June Wyman held a planning conference with his senior officers to discuss the forthcoming operations. He informed them that the brigade would be making two attacks on 12 June: the Fort Garry Horse would clear the Mue valley, on the left flank, while the Hussars would capture Cheux and the steep hill behind it that dominated the surrounding area. The commanding officers of the two units paid close attention, because these would be the first operations that 2 Armoured Brigade would conduct on its own – up to this point all of its activities had been in support of infantry operations.[4]

Unknown to Wyman and his unit commanders, General Sir Miles Dempsey, the commander of Second British Army, under which 2 Armoured Brigade and 3rd Infantry Division were serving, had other ideas. Dempsey had also held a conference with his senior officers on 10 June and the topic of discussion was a major operation he was planning for the next day to seize the city of Caen.[5] Wyman's Cheux operation was discussed and its value as an adjunct to the British attack considered. Dempsey therefore ordered the Canadian operation moved forward by twenty-four hours so as to have it conform with an attack to be made by the 50th British Division on the Canadian right flank. Tragically, for reasons which have never become clear, Dempsey's order moving forward the timing of the operation would take fifteen hours to reach its intended recipients, including the First Hussars.[6]

Lieutenant Colonel Colwell returned to his regiment from Wyman's Orders

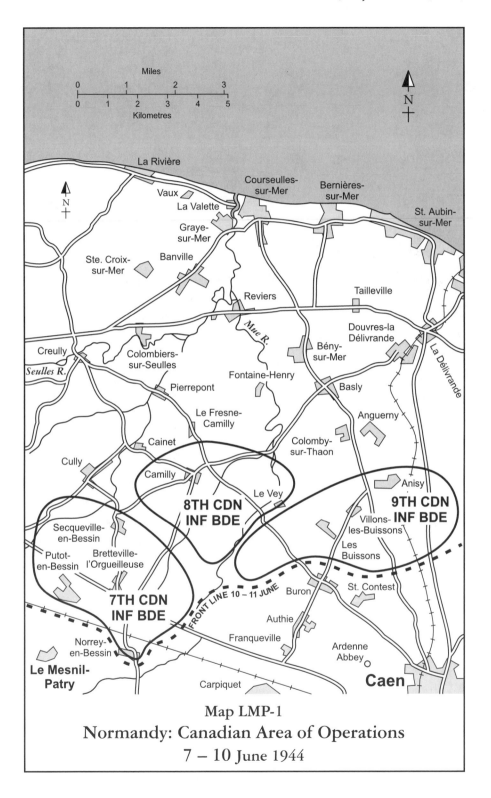

Map LMP-1

Normandy: Canadian Area of Operations
7 – 10 June 1944

Canadian Sherman in a Norman village, 1944

A Canadian tank is moving through a typical Norman village with its narrow streets consisting of well-built stone buildings. This photograph was taken shortly after the D-Day landings as Canadian armoured crews quickly learned to paint out the Allied white star on their vehicles because it made a convenient aiming mark for German gunners. (National Archives of Canada, PA 136846)

Group at 4 A.M. on Sunday, 11 June. He found many of his men alert as, during the first part of the previous night, they had been kept awake by German planes that droned back and forth across their position dropping bombs but inflicting no casualties. He told his staff about the forthcoming Cheux operation but added that they would have twenty-four hours to prepare for it. However, at 7.30 A.M., Dempsey's orders to make the attacks a day earlier than planned were received at brigade headquarters. This change in plan was passed on by Wyman to the Hussars within thirty minutes, causing the unit to go into a frenzy of preparation as the operation's start time was now only five hours away.[7]

Trooper Dodds, as the squadron commander's operator, had the responsibility for ensuring that all the wireless (radio) sets of the tanks in the squadron were tuned into its communications net. This was a complicated procedure that involved his sending out a netting call while the operators in the other tanks tuned their sets to his frequency. Occasionally Dodds would stop chanting into his microphone to ask all the other stations if they were receiving him. If not all answered affirmatively, the netting process had to continue. With many green operators in the squadron using new and unfamiliar equipment (the No. 19 radio set was a notoriously delicate mechanism) it was a long and frustrating business. It was also dangerous because netting calls could be heard by anyone, including the enemy troops the Canadian were preparing to attack. Repeated netting calls simply gave the Germans more time to locate the Canadians radio frequency and permit them to listen in on their conversations. This process was, of course, repeated by all the other squadrons in the regiment and also by the Hussars' Regimental Headquarters (RHQ) in establishing its own communications net.[8]

While Dodds and the other operators were busy netting, the gunners and co-drivers of their tanks were loading and storing ammunition, ensuring that a full complement was on board. The heavy, awkward 75mm rounds, each as thick as a man's arm, would be passed into the turret, past the sweating operators, and placed in the ready racks around the turret and under the floorboards. It was a tricky job as even experienced soldiers would pinch fingers or snag clothing on the many hard projections to be found in a tank turret. Meanwhile, the tank driver was checking the suspension, ensuring that none of the end connectors was loose, for throwing a track in the middle of a battle would immobilize them and leave their vehicle vulnerable, which, if hit, might turn into a flaming torch, incinerating all on board.

Because of its propensity to burn easily, the Sherman was known to the Germans as "the Tommy cooker" while the British and Canadians called it the Ronson after the popular cigarette lighter advertised with the slogan: "Lights every time!" As a result, the one drill that tank turret crews (the commander, gunner and loader-operator) practised until it was second nature was the bail-out. The turret crews' only escape route was the commanders' hatch on the top of the turret. If the commander was incapacitated, the gunner sitting at the commander's feet and the loader-operator, on the opposite side of the 75mm gun from the other two, would have to push him up and out of the hatch – not a simple matter. The two crew members lower down in the hull, the driver and the co-driver, had their own individual hatches. If, however, the barrel of the gun happened to be positioned over one of these hatches, it could not be opened and the driver or co-driver faced the prospect of being burned alive.[9]

While the remainder of Dodds's crew carried on with their preparations, Captain Harrison, their crew commander, was at RHQ trying to get some indication of what would be required of him in this, his first action as a squadron commander. With no time to personally check on the preparations of the vehicles, he could only hope that Captain John Smuck, his second-in-command, had ensured that the squadron's tanks had been refuelled and that rations and ammunition had been distributed.[10]

At 11 A.M., the Queen's Own Rifles from Toronto, the infantry battalion tasked with supporting the Hussars, received the change in plan. Like the Hussars, the Queen's Own had been unlucky during the D-Day landings, suffering the heaviest losses of all the Canadian infantry units on 6 June – 143 casualties,

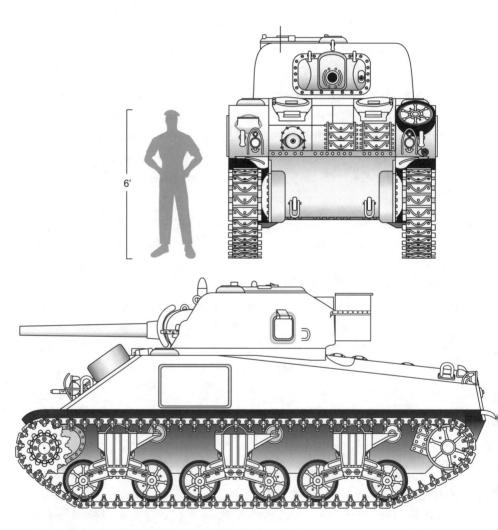

Sherman III (US M4A2), Normandy, 1944

The workhorse of Allied armour units in the last years of the war, the Sherman was a robust, mechanically reliable tank but was out-gunned by its German opponents. The 1st Hussars were equipped with the 29-ton Sherman III variant with a five-man crew, a diesel engine capable of maximum speeds of 29 mph, and armed with 75 mm main gun and two .30 calibre machine guns. (Drawing by Chris Johnson, courtesy of the artist).

61 of them fatal. Only one company, Major Neil Gordon's D Company, which had encountered little opposition on 6 June, was close to its full strength of 120 men. The soldiers of the Queen's Own were enjoying a relatively quiet day on 11 June, cleaning up and digging slit trenches in their area at Neuf Mer about a half mile north of Bray. All that changed late in the morning and, as with the Hussars, the Rifles' area became a scene of frantic activity as soldiers hurriedly packed up their kit and fell in on the road for the march to Bray. It being a warm day

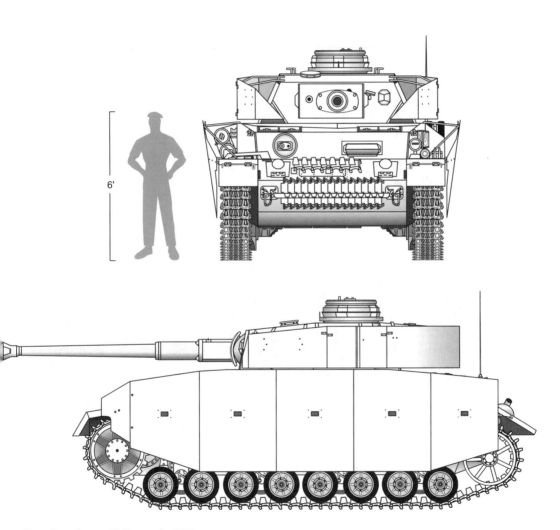

Panzerkampfwagen IV, Normandy, 1944

A prewar design that was progressively upgunned, the Pz IV was the German counterpart of the Sherman. The 12th SS Panzer Division was equipped with the Model H with a five-man crew and a diesel engine capable of 22 mph on level roads and armed with a high-velocity 75 mm gun, and two 7.92 mm machine guns. Note the skirts or aprons attached to the turret and hull as added protection against Allied hollow charge anti-tank weapons such as the bazooka or PIAT. (Drawing by Chris Johnson, courtesy of the artist)

they were in shirtsleeve order with a minimum of equipment: web gear, small packs, entrenching tools, weapons and ammunition.[11]

At about the same time, Brigadier Wyman gathered the commanding officers of the units involved in the forthcoming operation in his headquarters at Bray to issue his orders (see Map LMP-2). A and D Companies of the Queen's Own would travel with the Hussars as the lead assault element while the two remaining rifle companies would move with B and C Squadrons of the Fort Garry Horse in the second wave. In reserve was the 2nd Armoured Brigade's third regiment, the Sherbrooke Fusiliers. The Hussar order of march would be B Squadron, C Squadron, Regimental HQ, with A Squadron bringing up the rear. In order to get to the objective as quickly as possible, the village of Norrey-en-Bessin, a mile and a half south of Bray and three miles north of Cheux, would be bypassed and then the village of Le Mesnil-Patry, a little over a mile southwest of Norrey, would be secured by B Squadron of the Hussars and D Company of the Queen's Own, who would be supported on their right flank by the Hussars' C Squadron.[12] Once Le Mesnil-Patry was taken, D Company would be joined by the Queen's Own Mortar and Anti-tank Platoons. The remaining Hussar squadrons and A Company of the Rifles would then bypass Le Mesnil-Patry and

Officers of C Squadron, First Hussars, before the battle, 1944

This photograph, taken before the Normandy landing, shows many of the officers who would play a prominent part in the action at Le Mesnil-Patry on 11 June 1944. From left to right: Lieutenant G. Stoner; Lieutenant G. Henry; Lieutenant F. Allen; Major D'Arcy Marks, Officer Commanding C Squadron; Captain Harry Harrison, second-in-command; Lieutenant "Rip" Gordon. Not shown is Lieutenant William McCormick, who took the photograph, and Captain A.B. Conron. (Courtesy, Gerry Stoner)

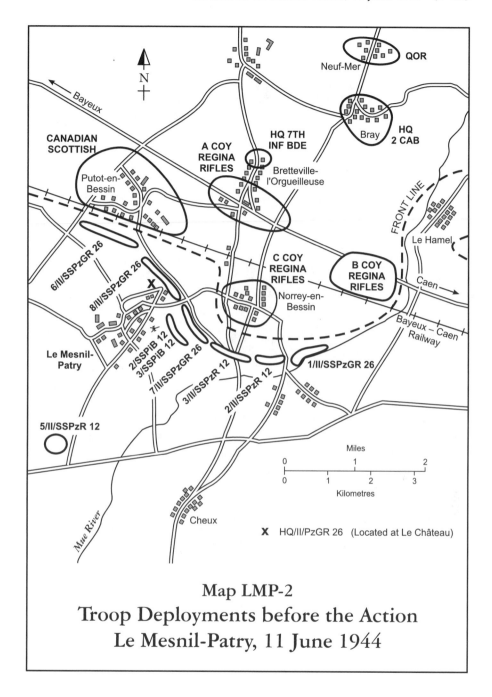

Map LMP-2
Troop Deployments before the Action
Le Mesnil-Patry, 11 June 1944

continue on to occupy the final objective. "Occupy" seems to have been the operative word because 3rd Division's daily intelligence report indicated that little enemy opposition was to be expected.[13]

The countryside these Canadian soldiers would be crossing was rich Norman farmland, fields of wheat and sugar beets interspersed with apple orchards, the

The infantry's best friend: 25-pdr. gun detachment, Normandy, 1944

Although they were facing overwhelming air and land power, the one weapon the German soldiers feared
most in Normandy was the Allied artillery, as illustrated here by this hard-working Canadian gun detachment.
Well-trained, numerous and powerful, it inflicted the greatest number of casualties on the *Wehrmacht.* The
lack of effective artillery support at Le Mesnil-Patry doomed the First Hussars and their attendant infantry.
(National Archives of Canada, PA 115569)

source of Normandy's famous Calvados apple brandy. The weather was beauti-
ful, a warm, sunny June day that made many soldiers think of summers at home
in Ontario. Five days after the landings, the war was still new here and the civilian population had largely remained in place, going about their daily tasks. The
most obvious sign of conflict was that the church steeples, possible observation
posts for artillery observers, were being progressively demolished by HE (high
explosive) rounds. One of those artillery observers was forty-year-old Captain
Charles Rivaz, formerly a lecturer at Ontario Agricultural College in Guelph,
Ontario, now a FOO (Forward Observation Officer) with 12 Field Regiment,
Royal Canadian Artillery. It was Rivaz's job, aided by his observation party of
three other gunners, to bring down the firepower of his regiment, and any other
artillery units in range, on whatever targets he could see. His available selection
of weapons was large, for among the indirect fire systems (weapons whose operators cannot actually see the target they are shooting at) there were naval guns,

heavy and medium artillery, and light and heavy mortars. Potentially the selection was wide, but because the forthcoming operation had been moved forward a day, there had been little time available for detailed planning on the part of the artillery and it would be up to Captain Rivaz to get support, if and when it was found to be necessary.[14]

Lieutenant Colonel Jock Spragge, the commanding officer of the Queen's Own Rifles, had taken some steps to arrange his own fire support. Immediately after receiving the new time of the attack that morning, Spragge had sent his mortar platoon commander, Lieutenant Ben Dunkelman, a thirty-one-year-old former football player from Toronto, forward to meet with his counterpart from the Regina Rifles, the battalion holding the front line. Together they selected potential targets and calculated the number of rounds they could expend on each of them.[15]

For his part, Lieutenant Colonel Ray Colwell of the Hussars did not issue his final orders until 12.15, forty-five minutes before the operation was due to start. There was just not enough time for all the necessary preparations and this deadline was not met – the operation was therefore put back ninety minutes. The plan was now to cross the start line, the point after which the enemy could be expected to be met, at 2.30 P.M. Due to the lack of time, very little information reached the men who would be doing the actual fighting; the lieutenants commanding the tank troops and infantry platoons received only the outline plan and the direction of advance. While they were taking in this information, the Queen's Own Riflemen had completed their short march from Neuf-Mer to

Lethal killer: PAK 40 75 mm anti-tank gun

Although Allied tank crews feared the German 88 mm gun above all else, it was the smaller 75 mm PAK 40 gun, the standard divisional anti-tank weapon of the *Wehrmacht* in 1944 that caused the greatest number of casualties. Easily concealed and powerful, it was a very dangerous opponent. (Photograph by Dianne Graves)

Bray and climbed awkwardly onto the tanks' suspension to reach the Shermans' back decks, Major Neil Gordon's D Company being mounted on top of the vehicles of Harrison's B Squadron. Carrying infantry on tanks was (and still is) a recognized procedure, but it is never used if there is any possibility of contact with the enemy as the tanks cannot fire their weapons and the infantry are very exposed. However, on Sunday, 11 June 1944, this precaution was disregarded in order to get to the start line, the elevated east-west Caen–Bayeux railway running just north of Norrey-en-Bessin, as quickly as possible.[16]

Unfortunately, the departure was further delayed when Lieutenant William McCormick of 2 Troop, C Squadron, discovered a leaking fuel line in his tank and exchanged vehicles with his troop corporal. This caused a gap to open up between the two lead squadrons as Harrison and B Squadron rumbled off with squealing tracks in a cloud of dust along the dirt road leading to Norrey-en-Bessin.[17]

Almost immediately they encountered a problem. Just as the lead elements of B Squadron were approaching the front line, the Regina Rifles informed the Hussars by radio that they had laid a minefield on the ground between Bretteville-l'Orgueilleuse (a large town just southwest of Bray) and Norrey-en-Bessin. This forced the Hussars' tanks to stay on the road and move through Norrey-en-Bessin instead of bypassing it by going cross-country as had been planned. Indeed, at 1.20 p.m., a frantic message went from 2 Armoured Brigade to 3rd Division asking if there were any other minefields laid in this area, since even that basic information had not reached the brigade. The existence of the unsuspected minefield caused the start line to be changed from the Caen–Bayeux railway line to a north-south track west of Norrey-en-Bessin, with the result that the axis of the advance shifted ninety degrees.[18]

Even worse, Norrey had been heavily shelled, leaving only the gaunt remains of the church steeple rising from the centre of the ruins. The narrow width of the streets meant that the tanks had to proceed in single file, and near the centre of the village, a ninety degree right turn was required near the church, but the area was so confined that each tank in turn had to back and fill to negotiate the corner, imposing further delay[19].

As B Squadron's lead tanks moved through Norrey-en-Bessin, Lieutenant Dunkelman ran over to meet them. He naturally expected the assault force to stop in order to be briefed on his fire support arrangements, but instead the squadron swept by him, leaving him standing by the roadside, dumbfounded and angry. Of course, Dunkelman had not been advised of the last-minute

The infantryman's home: A slit trench in Normandy, 1944
An infantryman's war was ten yards wide and his home was his slit trench or fox hole, two feet by three feet, and as deep as he could make it. (Editor's collection)

change of start line. The new start line was crossed at 2.37 P.M., seventeen minutes after the revised start time.[20]

Throughout the approach march a B Squadron officer maintained a running commentary on the regimental radio net so that the Hussars RHQ could follow its progress. One of Harrison's crew commanders, Sergeant Leo Gariepy of 2 Troop, a prewar regular from the Royal Canadian Dragoons, who had transferred to the Hussars in 1940 when the dragoons were made a motorcycle unit, grew tired of this non-stop travelogue and switched off his radio that was on the RHQ net. That action left him with only the set on the squadron net.[21]

Unfortunately, the Germans were also listening to the travelogue and tracking the progress of the Canadian advance. The Hussars and Queen's Own were moving toward positions held by 12 *SS-Panzerdivision (Hitlerjugend)*. Like the Hussars and Queen's Own, most of its soldiers were new to combat as this division had only been formed the previous autumn from teenagers, seventeen to nineteen, recruited from the ranks of the Hitler Youth. There the comparison stopped as it was led by a large cadre of tough and experienced officers and non-commissioned officers, most being veterans of the Russian Front. Although the German and Canadian formations were fighting their first battles, the conditions they fought under were not equal. The Allies had air superiority, a priceless asset, and they were also able to call on naval gunfire support from battleships and cruisers anchored off the landing beaches. For their part, the Germans had superior tanks and anti-tank guns but their most valuable asset was the combat experience of their officers and NCOs.

There was little to choose between the young men of the opposing sides. Although the private German soldier was, on average, several years younger than his Canadian counterpart, both were physically fit, well trained in their individual skills and motivated to risk death or disfigurement for the cause they

Officer and soldier of the Waffen SS
At Le Mesnil-Patry, the First Hussars ran into units of the 12th Waffen SS Division, *Hitler Jugend*, composed of determined young soldiers led by veteran officers and NCOs – the result was a vicious battle. Throughout the campaign in Normandy, Canadian soldiers were matched against the Waffen SS far more often than were their American and British counterparts. (Editor's collection)

served. Where they differed most was in their approach to combat. The Canadians, coming from a far distant land, respected but did not hate their foe; battle was, for them, analogous to a hockey game where one played hard, even ruthlessly, but once it was over one could leave the rink behind and resume a normal existence. The young men (boys really) of 12 *SS-Panzerdivision* had absorbed from their veteran instructors the much different attitudes of the Russian Front, where quarter was rarely asked and just as rarely given.[22]

While the Hussars moved toward and through Norrey, the German division's radio monitoring service, already forewarned by the netting calls that an operation was going to take place, picked up the Canadian frequencies and listened to the coded message traffic. On 9 June, a Canadian tank knocked out near Authie had been found to contain copies of radio procedures and codes, and the English-speaking operators of the monitoring service had no difficulty in comprehending the Hussars' radio traffic. It quickly became clear to the German commanders that an attack was about to take place in the area of Norrey-en-Bessin and preparations were made to shell and mortar the village.[23]

Because of the gap between B and C Squadrons, caused by the delay imposed by Lieutenant McCormick changing tanks, Harrison's B Squadron had already cleared Norrey when the first German shells began to land. Major D'Arcy Marks's C Squadron, followed by RHQ, was just entering the village when Lieutenant Colonel Colwell's tank ran over a Canadian mine left at the side of the road and lost a track, a mishap that impeded the advance of both RHQ and A Squadron behind it.[24] Colwell dismounted and, in the midst of the shelling, tried to sort out the traffic jam. He decided to pull the remainder of his regiment out of the village and back up the road toward Bretteville to a position from which they could support those tanks that had got through Norrey.[25]

Harrison's B Squadron carrying Gordon's D Company of the Rifles was not affected by the German artillery fire, most of the enemy rounds landing behind them. As he left Norrey, Harrison ordered his crews to close their hatches and assume the box formation normally used for movement in open country. He deployed his 1 Troop (three tanks to a troop) on the left and 2 Troop on the right, with squadron headquarters and 5 Troop behind them while bringing up the rear were 3 Troop to the left and 4 Troop to the right. Gordon had one of his platoons mounted on 5 Troop's decks and two others on the decks of the rear troops. To facilitate communication and control, Gordon travelled on the back deck of Harrison's Sherman.[26]

Harry Harrison was young and energetic. A graduate of the Royal Military College at Kingston, he was seen as an officer with a bright future. Employed until now as the second-in-command of C Squadron, he had been somewhat contemptuous of his superior, Major D'Arcy Marks, believing that this older officer, from a militia background, did not understand how to use armour properly. Harrison regarded Marks as too cautious and it would appear that he was determined to show everyone how the job should be done.[27]

The lead element of the Canadian advance had now crossed the revised start line, the north-south track on the western edge of Norrey-en-Bessin (see Map LMP-2). Their direction so far had been to the south but the turn in the centre of Norrey-en-Bessin had caused the axis of advance to be changed to the west. As a result

PBI – Normandy, 1944

The "PBI" (Poor Bloody Infantry), like these men of the 3rd Canadian Infantry Division waiting to move up in Normandy during the summer of 1944, did the worst of the fighting and most of the dying. Note the dust from the passing vehicles; it attracted enemy fire and led to the saying current in the summer of 1944 that "dust means death." (National Archives of Canada, PA 129128)

the unsuspecting Canadians were now driving into a pocket formed by enemy positions. To their right (the north), No. 5 and No. 6 Companies of the 2nd Battalion of *SS-Panzergrenadierregiment* 26 were dug in, while to their front, 7 *Kompanie* held the Château du Mesnil-Patry, a two-storey mansion that was the home of the Bunel family, with battalion headquarters further back in the village of Le Mesnil-Patry. To the south and left of the Canadians were Nos. 2 and 3 Companies of *SS-Panzerpionierbataillon* 12, the divisional engineer unit. Further away, several miles southwest of Le Mesnil-Patry, was *Sturmbannführer* (Major) Karl-Heinz Prinz's 2nd Battalion of *SS-Panzerregiment* 12. Prinz, a charismatic and aggressive leader, had two of his tank companies (squadrons) with him, Nos. 5 and 6, commanded respectively by *Untersturmführer* (Second Lieutenant) Willi Kandler and *Hauptsturmführer* (Captain) Ludwig Ruckdeschel. Both companies were equipped with Mark IV tanks armed with 75mm guns.[28]

B Squadron's right-hand lead troop, 2 Troop, continued down the main road toward Le Mesnil-Patry, while the others swung left into a large wheat field estimated at five acres in area with standing grain about three feet high (see Map LMP-3). Unencumbered with infantry, Harrison's two lead troops laid down speculative fire on likely enemy positions in the hope that the Germans would betray their exact positions by returning fire. Sergeant Leo Gariepy later recalled his progress through the wheat field, head out of the hatch (despite Harrison's order to his squadron to close down their hatches) scanning the ground ahead of his tank for signs of mines, only to find himself staring into the tense faces of youthful panzergrenadiers.[29]

Other B Squadron crews had the same experience and the first report of contact with the enemy was made at 2.52 P.M. Almost immediately, fighting broke out in the wheatfield. It had lasted fifteen minutes when the Hussars reported to 2 Armoured Brigade that they were being held up midway between Norrey and Le Mesnil-Patry. At that point, B Squadron seems to have surged forward in a lunge for Le Mesnil-Patry. It is probable, although not certain, that Harrison's plan called for half the squadron, 2 and 4 Troops, under Captain Richard Wildgoose, to enter Le Mesnil, while he outflanked the village to the south with the remainder of the squadron.[30]

Faced with this charge, the German tactic was simple: separate the tanks from the infantry, then destroy each element separately. The panzergrenadiers therefore stayed in their slit trenches in the centre of the field and held their fire until the armour had passed them by so that they could take on the following

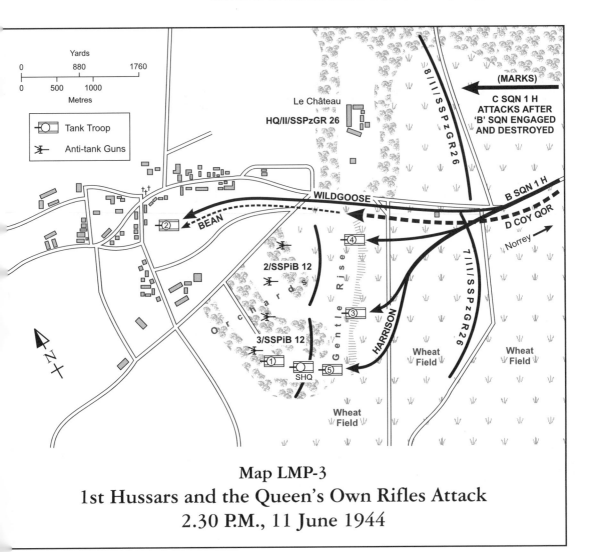

Map LMP-3
1st Hussars and the Queen's Own Rifles Attack
2.30 P.M., 11 June 1944

Canadian infantry. They were somewhat disconcerted to find Canadian infantry on the decks of the tanks moving around them but recovered quickly and engaged the infantry and armour together. The tanks carrying infantry stayed to fight it out and as a result the panzergrenadiers took a terrible beating. German self-propelled anti-tank guns, positioned in depth behind Le Mesnil-Patry, did not come forward to support the infantry but stayed put, waiting for the Canadian armour to advance further.[31]

Sergeant Leo Gariepy of 2 Troop remembered that, as his troop "proceeded about 1,500 yards from town [Norrey] and deployed as arranged, covering [the] infantry," the German resistance "was tremendous, enemy infantry in great numbers were lying in fields on the centre of advance." The Hussars fired HE

Infantry position, Normandy, 1944

The infantrymen of both sides used slit trenches for defensive purposes. The panzergrenadiers of the Waffen SS at Le Mesnil-Patry, concealed in positions like these in the middle of a ripe wheat field, were almost impossible to spot until the tanks of the First Hussars were literally on top of them. (National Archives of Canada, PA 129043)

shells into the German trenches and sprayed them with .30 calibre fire from the two machine guns mounted on each tank. "We were doing good work of annihilation," Gariepy remembered, "when the order to hurry on came over the [radio] set."[32]

This order came from Harrison. In that officer's tank, the loader-operator, Trooper A.O. Dodds, recalled that the squadron commander "gave orders to speed up the attack." Dodds "could hear Jerry machine guns going" but, "from the wireless [radio] messages no one could locate it" and his tank "fired H[igh] E[xplosive] and co-ax [a machine-gun aligned with the main gun] at some haystacks and other points – hedges etc."[33]

Receiving the order to speed up the attack, some B Squadron tanks left their infantry behind and moved toward Le Mesnil-Patry. Not having more than the most elemental information, they had no idea of the plan of attack. As they neared the village the Shermans topped a small rise in the ground, thus presenting easy targets for the waiting German anti-tank guns. These weapons, self-propelled *Jagdpanzer* IVs, heavily armoured and equipped with 75 mm high velocity guns, were from *SS-Panzerjägerabteilung* 12, the *Hitlerjugend* anti-tank battalion. As the Shermans lumbered toward them, they opened fire from well-camouflaged positions. Many Shermans were hit, but even so several tanks and

some accompanying infantry, including a small party led by Lieutenant George
Bean, with Sergeant Samuel Scrutton and seven riflemen, succeeded in entering
the eastern end of Le Mesnil-Patry. The tanks now fired smoke in an effort to
screen their movements from the enemy and at 3.15 P.M. a message was sent an-
nouncing that the village was taken. Within minutes, however, Captain Wildgoose reported enemy armour approaching from the west (see Map LMP-4).[34]

This German armour consisted of 5 and 6 *Kompanies* of *SS-Panzerregiment*
12 led by *Sturmbannführer* (Major) Karl-Heinz Prinz. No. 6 *Kompanie* roared
through Le Mesnil-Patry while 5 *Kompanie* went around its northern side in order to take B Squadron in the right flank. Within minutes of Prinz's attack only

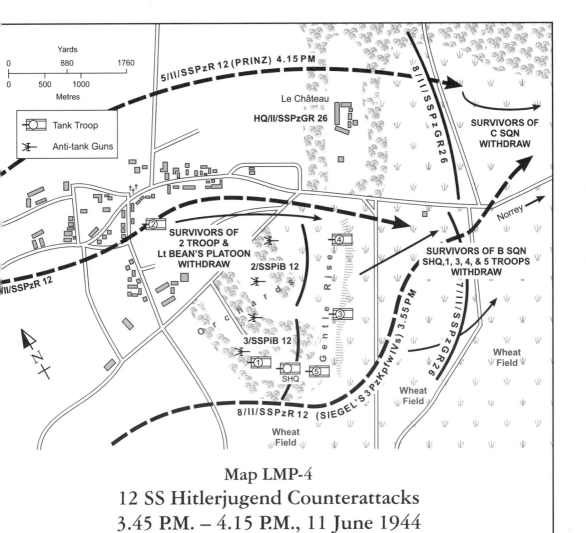

Map LMP-4

12 SS Hitlerjugend Counterattacks
3.45 P.M. – 4.15 P.M., 11 June 1944

four Shermans were still mobile and able to pull back from the village – and one of these was burning as it went along.[35]

Some of Harrison's B Squadron tanks had remained with the infantry in the wheat field firing into the grain in an effort to neutralize a well concealed enemy. Major Neil Gordon the modest, popular commander of D Company, had jumped from the back deck of Harrison's tank and attempted to arrange supporting fire using his own radio operator in order to advance but was frustrated by poor radio communications. He was shot through the face but persisted in his attempts to co-ordinate with the armour. Corporal James Simpson from Windsor, Ontario, a crew commander in 2 Troop B Squadron, watched as Gordon tried to communicate with Simpson's troop leader, Lieutenant James Martin, by shouting to him from the ground. When Martin, a young reinforcement officer who had only joined the Hussars the night before, leaned out of his hatch to hear what Gordon was saying, he was shot through the head, and his body fell back inside the turret. His radio operator went into shock and jammed the squadron net with pleas for help for Martin, who was quite dead. A few minutes later, Martin's tank left the fight, retracing its way back to Norrey.[36] A few moments later, Gordon was felled with a bullet in his left leg. As he lay in the field, his brother-in-law, Lieutenant Robert Fleming of the Queen's Own, came over to give first aid, and Gordon told him to assume command of the company. Fleming left to carry out this order but was quickly killed, leaving D Company without a leader.[37]

Meanwhile, those tanks on B Squadron's left flank which had surged ahead, including Harrison's own vehicle, found themselves in a large orchard that formed part of a farm on the southeastern corner of Le Mesnil. Defending the orchard was 3 *Kompanie* of the *SS-Panzerpionierbataillon* 12, backed up by the battalion's reconnaissance platoon. Although the pioneers were aware of the battle in the wheat field from the noise, their positions were quiet.[38]

One German, *Pionier* (Sapper) Horst Lütgens, was sitting in his trench writing a letter home when the Hussars' Shermans rudely interrupted him. It all happened so fast that, to Lütgens, it seemed that

the Canadians were on top of us. Now I was suddenly very calm, but a rage quelled inside me. I asked myself what had happened to my comrades up front. Were they dead or had they let the tanks roll past? I crawled back to my hole and grabbed my first Panzerfaust and made it ready. I had three of them in my foxhole. Then I looked for a victim. There it sat, the Sherman, huge and mighty. Its turret was pointed in the direction of our battalion command post. Its gun fired round after round.[39]

Trooper Dodds, in Harrison's tank, remembered moving "into an orchard" where the enemy infantry were "apparently quite thick." Dodds's crew fired HE into the German trenches and dugouts, "at times having to back the tank up to get sufficient depression for the 75 gun. We ran out of HE in the turret twice and the Capt[ain] ordered us to 'let him have an A[rmour] P[iercing round] down the dugouts.'"[40]

Things shortly got worse for Pioneer Lütgens:

Now, there were even more tanks! One, two, three, four, five of these Shermans could be seen in the blue haze of the air saturated by gunpowder smoke. When I was within 20 metres, I aimed and fired. But nothing happened. Jam! Just what I needed! ... I cocked the weapon again and this time it roared off. I could not watch the hit. The tank providing cover had spotted me and was firing on me. I did hear the explosion, and then ran in zigzagging jumps back to my foxhole.[41]

His target may have been A.O. Dodds's tank. Dodds remembered that:

We moved ahead a few hundred feet as near as I could tell, I was kneeling on the flooring re-arranging the ammo when the tank was struck. The driver's hatch was knocked off and the 75 knocked out, the breech etc, shook violently and went skyward, Sgt Johnstone [the gunner] said "bail out," the Capt[ain] gave one hesitant look skywards and then both were gone.[42]

There were soon six knocked-out Canadian tanks in the orchard, including those of Harrison and his second-in-command, Captain John Smuck.

Not all the damage had been done by German infantry. Three Mark IVs from 8 *Kompanie* of *SS-Panzerregiment* 12 also counterattacked. The company commander, *Obersturmführer* (Lieutenant) Hans Siegel, had been on his way to an awards ceremony when he encountered his battalion commander, Prinz, southwest of Le Mesnil. Prinz told Siegel that the commander of *SS-Panzergrenadierregiment* 26, *Obersturmbannführer* (Lieutenant Colonel)

Wilhelm Mohnke, had requested tank support to counter an armour/infantry attack against Le Mesnil and directed Siegel to clarify the situation and clear it up if necessary. Siegel departed, taking with him only three of his company's Mark IVs.[43]

As the German tanks approached the southern edge of the orchard, Siegel encountered Harrison. *Untersturmführer* (Second Lieutenant) Jeran of 8 *Kompanie*, who was with Siegel, later recalled the action in the orchard:

> The enemy was still obscured by a hedge. When the hedge ended abruptly and the lead panzer fortuitously found himself among our infantry, several Shermans could be seen in dangerous proximity ... Enemy tanks on the left at 9 o'clock – 200 – engage! ... Within a good minute four or five Shermans were on fire. Only the one farthest to the left, which had worked itself in to a range of 100 metres, caused the Commander to break into a sweat. It had just been noticed as it was training its turret on us. "Enemy tank on the far left at 10 o'clock – 100!" And now barrel trained on barrel, muzzle on muzzle, until they had each other in their cross-hairs for a further instant. – then an explosion, a flame from the breech of the gun, the cartridge falls into the bag, the opponent blows up![44]

After destroying six Canadian tanks, Siegel continued on to the edge of the orchard followed by counterattacking pioneers. He engaged two more Shermans at a range of 1,100 yards, stopping both. Under the mistaken impression that there were cut-off German infantry farther forward in the wheat field, Siegel now gave orders to his other two tanks to accompany him forward. As Siegel's three MK IVs moved north, the far edge of the wheatfield was nearly 1,500 yards

Sherman Firefly, Normandy, 1944

Armed with the powerful 17-pdr. (76.2 mm) gun as opposed to the 75 mm of the standard Sherman, the Firefly was effective against German armour at long range. Each troop in the First Hussars possessed one Firefly but it was no better armoured than the standard Sherman and easily identified by its long gun barrel, which made it a highly-visible priority target for German anti-tank units. (National Archives of Canada, PA 131391)

away. They had, however, presented themselves as perfect side-on targets to the Hussars' C Squadron tanks positioned north of Norrey. After a few rounds from C Squadron, Siegel ordered a right turn and halt. A duel began which was won with a shot from a 17-pdr. gun in the Sherman Firefly commanded by Sergeant Arthur Boyle of C Squadron. One of Boyle's rounds went through the right front of Siegel's tank, killing the radio operator and setting fire to the Mark IV. Siegel and the remainder of his crew bailed out. The other two tanks were destroyed at the same time.[45]

When Siegel had got clear of this burning vehicle, he found himself alone and ran, "in headlong dashes of no more than 10 paces at a time" toward cover.[46] He had lost his cap and pistol and was wearing only a pair of black coveralls devoid of any insignia. Siegel suddenly found himself staring with shock "down the barrel of a rifle pointed straight at him" by a Canadian infantry corporal. The Canadian hesitated to fire and then both men hit the ground as a shell burst near them. The two enemies were now "Eye to eye. Neither ventured to say anything. Breath panting, temples throbbing." Siegel noticed that the Canadian was slightly wounded and dressed his wound with the shell dressing in the man's helmet net, an act that "created trust" and then the German officer urged the corporal to head south to safety with him. The two moved through the wheat field, crouching when shells burst nearby, until Siegel was "able to make out German steel helmets in fox holes." He thereupon

> grabbed his companion, who had in the interim practically become a friend, with his right arm and raised his left one shouting, "Don't shoot, German tank troopers!" The Canadian faltered, stunned, but then followed his example, threw his rifle away and likewise raised his free arm, the right one. The Grenadiers jumped and took him prisoner in my presence. Sorry, my brave Corporal.[47]

Meanwhile, at the eastern end of Le Mesnil, Lieutenant George Bean of the Queen's Own had been wounded in the leg. Still under fire, his party had reached the edge of the built-up area but found themselves alone – the rest of Gordon's D Company was nowhere in sight. Faced with the decision to push on or pull back, Bean turned to his men and said, "Let's go in and take it ourselves." He led them up a sunken road into the village. Coming out of the cover of the sunken road, the men occupied a large crater while Bean went forward to contact two Canadian tanks (part of Captain Wildgoose's command) that he had spotted, but while advancing he was hit again, this time in the back. He attempted to return to his men but was hit a third time and knocked to the ground about fifty yards from the crater. Bean motioned to Sergeant Samuel Scrutton to take command but Scrutton decided it was time to withdraw since they appeared to be the only Canadian infantry in Le Mesnil. The riflemen flagged down one of the Shermans, placed Bean on board and turned back toward Norrey.[48]

On the return journey they suffered more casualties from close-range machine-gun fire and grenades. Of the initial group of nine riflemen who reached Le Mesnil, two were killed, two were wounded and one was missing. The Canadians fought back and the citation for Scrutton's Distinguished Conduct Medal states he "showed no regard whatsoever for his personal safety" but "accounted for and killed 12 to 15 Germans."[49] Bean's initiative and courage would result in the award of a Military Cross.

Sergeant Gariepy also reached the northern edge of Le Mesnil only to encounter German infantry. He opened fire with his Sherman's two .30 calibre Browning machine guns. They soon "went out of action" (probably overheated by continuous firing) and "the only small arm I could bring on [the] enemy was [a] Sten gun." He was firing this from his hatch when his tank's "power traverse and radio and remote firing control failed so I ordered my driver … to reverse and rally" or draw back out of action. It was only then that Gariepy realized that the back of his tank was on fire and ordered his driver "to speed up but it got so I had to abandon it."[50]

As Gariepy and his crew walked back, they passed by Corporal James Simpson's tank from 2 Troop. Out of ammunition, except for some AP (armour-piercing rounds), and with the tank's power traverse unserviceable, Simpson had also decided to turn back. His would be one of only two B Squadron tanks to return with an intact crew. Before leaving the field he stopped to pick up a load of wounded Queen's Own which he delivered to an aid station in Norrey.[51]

At 4:15 p.m. a German armoured counterattack was mounted on the wheat field from the southwest. This was Prinz and his 5 *Kompanie* of Mark IV tanks. Taking up position at the edge of the field, Prinz's tanks fired at the Canadian infantry moving through the grain. The Queen's Own riflemen who, left without tank support, could not overcome the entrenched Germans in the grain, now came under heavy fire from Prinz's tanks. Meanwhile, the surviving

B Squadron tanks that had moved closer to Le Mesnil-Patry without the close-in protection of infantry, were easy prey for the German anti-tank guns. The lack of time to prepare and the failure to brief those involved had led to the most basic tactical rules being ignored, and the price for these mistakes was now being paid – in blood.[52]

Prinz shortly encountered Major D'Arcy Marks's C Squadron of the Hussars. Moving behind Harrison's B Squadron, Marks was unaware of the disaster that had befallen the lead elements. He encountered the first signs of trouble when he arrived at Norrey – a commanderless B Squadron tank being driven back to the village. On the far side of Norrey, Marks deployed with his 4 Troop left, 2 Troop in the centre and 1 Troop to the right and ordered an advance into the wheat field. It was a terrible sight: the crew commanders were staring into a field of burning Shermans but there was nothing to shoot at because there were no enemy visible. Over the radio, Marks again ordered the squadron to advance but his crews remained put, frozen at the ugly scene in front of them. For a third time, Marks ordered an advance – but nothing happened. This quiet, mature, long-serving militia officer, criticized by Harrison for his lack of dash and thrust, had a serious problem on his hands; how to motivate his soldiers to advance using only his voice and the force of his personality. He therefore changed his tack and asked for volunteers to move forward – this broke the spell and the three leading troops deployed in a rough line and moved into the wheat field, opening fire as they advanced.[53]

C Squadron's battle was progressing satisfactorily; Marks's tanks were chewing their way through the panzergrenadiers in the grain when they began to receive fire from their right flank. Marks had recently been warned about the British operation taking place to the west, and made the incorrect assumption that the fire was from the British 50th Division. Messages were sent back to 2 Armoured Brigade, then through 3rd Division, then to corps headquarters asking the British to stop firing on the Canadians. Marks ordered friendly recognition signals to be displayed and then dismounted to personally brief all of his crew commanders, but when the fire did not cease, he gave permission to return it.[54]

The fire, of course, was from Prinz's 5 *Kompanie*, but Marks's troops could not identify its source. Sherman after Sherman of C Squadron was hit. By this time Marks had lost communication with RHQ and sent his second-in-command, Captain Gerry Stoner, back into Norrey to reestablish contact. Picking his way through the ruined village on foot, Stoner passed the Ram OP tank of the middle-aged, very frustrated FOO, Captain Charles Rivaz who was trying, without success, to get artillery support – his radios had failed him at the moment of crisis. When Stoner arrived at Colwell's tank, the Hussar commander gave him a scout car and sent him back to brigade headquarters with instructions to brief Wyman on the situation, to obtain artillery support, and to have the Fort Garry Horse move forward to support the Hussars.[55]

In Norrey, meanwhile, Lieutenant Ben Dunkelman, the Queen's Own mortar platoon commander, had placed his No. 3 Section in a farmyard, where they were protected by an eight-foot-high fieldstone wall. The mortar men could hear the sounds of battle but could not see much. Rifleman John A. ("Jack") Martin, a twenty-year-old member of 3 Section, recalled the action: "Off to our right, about 50-60 yards away, an AP shell (armour piercing) burst through the wall tearing a large chunk out of it. Then we could hear shrapnel and small-arms fire hitting the wall in front of us. The order came for us to range in on a target with HE (high explosive) and then came an order for smoke bombs."[56]

Lieutenant George "Rip" Gordon of 1 Troop C Squadron turned back toward Norrey carrying wounded. Gordon had the well-earned reputation of being someone who would attempt almost any stunt with a Sherman and he lived up to it on 11 June as, while trying to turn about to return to the wheat field, he

Lieutenant Bill Little, First Hussars, Normandy
Little is shown in the ruins of Norrey after the battle wearing the armoured corps model steel helmet.
(Courtesy, Roy Leslie, First Hussars Museum)

managed to roll over his Sherman at the end of a narrow lane way leading out of Norrey. (The marks of a Sherman's tracks are still visible on the wall of the building on the northeastern end of this lane called the Rue de la Vergée.)[57]

In the wheat field, C Squadron continued to lose tank after tank from heavy and accurate German fire. Lieutenant William McCormick's tank took a round through the right rear that killed two of the crew and severely wounded the young officer in the legs. He somehow managed to dismount and was lying dazed in the field when two of his men appeared and dragged him back toward Norrey while mortar rounds burst around them. He was hit again, by a rifle round, before eventually reaching the shelter of a Regina Rifles slit trench. In the midst of C Squadron's fight, Captain Cyril Tweedale, commanding a detachment of the Fort Garry Horse attached to Marks, saw one of his Shermans with its turret swinging around in circles – its crew commander, Sergeant William Hussen, had been knocked unconscious. Another C Squadron tank, commanded by Sergeant H.E. (Foo) Simmons, was knocked out at this point. As its crew worked their way back toward Norrey-en-Bessin one of Prinz's Mark IVs overtook them. Sergeant Simmons, ordering his men to scatter, ran in front of the enemy tank to draw its fire. He was never seen again.[58]

It was now about 4.30 P.M. and it was clear to Colwell that the operation was a disaster. Fearing a German counterattack in strength, he ordered the surviving Shermans of B and C Squadrons to withdraw. Marks acknowledged the order but there was no reply from Harrison. Sergeant Gariepy later admitted that he might have received the message had his radio set on the RHQ net not been turned off. Most survivors, however, now pulled back. Marks personally covered the withdrawal of his squadron to Norrey. Tweedale remembered that "Major Marks and I found our tanks to be the only ones left, so we laid smoke and retired but the road was blocked by an over turned tank [Gordon's]; with [Trooper D. T.] Briggs' skill as a driver, however, we did a skid turn on a dead cow, ploughed through several walls in the village and got out." [59]

Over the radio Wyman ordered Colwell to hold his ground so that reinforcements could be sent up but Colwell did not receive this message. He was now 1,000 yards north of Norrey with nine tanks – the survivors of C Squadron – that he had retrieved from the village. He was only able to do this with great difficulty because, as Colwell had feared, the German shelling had brought down more buildings and totally blocked the streets and lanes of Norrey. The withdrawing C Squadron tanks were instructed to knock down walls to find alternate exits.[60]

One did so, and immediately crashed into a basement. As Rifleman Jack Martin of the Queen's Own Mortar Platoon recalled, another Hussar tank came close to ending his section's day:

> Just after firing a few smoke bombs, off to our right, about 25 feet away, a Sherman tank from the First Hussars, burst through the wall scattering stones and mortar all over the place. A few feet to the tank's right and we would have been crushed and mashed like potatoes. However, we continued to fire the smoke bombs until our smoke ammo was exhausted, at which time we were ordered to withdraw.[61]

The only supporting fire available for the withdrawal came from Dunkelman's mortars – Rivaz had been killed and there was no communication with the artillery. Rifleman Martin remembered what happened when the order to leave arrived:

> After loading the mortars back on the [Bren Gun] carriers, we found that because of the huge mounds of stone, etc., from the damaged wall, it was impossible to turn the carriers around so we had to withdraw up the narrow road in reverse. When we reached the main road, pandemonium was at its highest. All vehicles trying to withdraw at the same time. A Canadian Provost was standing in the cross-roads directing traffic when he was hit by shrapnel. Corporal Gordie Sullivan jumped off our lead carrier, dragged the Provost to the side of the road and took over the job of directing traffic. Sadly, he too was killed.[62]

Once C Squadron had pulled out of Norrey, Major Frank White, the second-in-command of the Hussars, stationed 1 Troop of A Squadron and the surviving C Squadron tanks along the Caen–Bayeux railway line in defensive positions and awaited the expected German onslaught. If the Germans were to come, the elevated railway line would be a good position to resist their advance.[63]

Wyman also feared a counterattack. He called his unit commanders to his headquarters and informed 3rd Division that "considerable numbers of enemy tanks are moving north-east from Le Mesnil-Patry." But in 7 Canadian Infantry Brigade there was a clearer view of events and they informed the division that the tanks moving north-east from Le Mesnil-Patry were Canadian, not German. A half-hour after Wyman's call for the commanding officers to gather, Colwell arrived at brigade headquarters to report in person.[64]

The battle was over but the killing had not yet stopped. In the orchard, the Canadian crewmen who had evacuated their vehicles gathered in small groups to discuss their next move. Some wanted to go on fighting with weapons taken from the tanks while others wished to escape back to their own lines, and still others were preoccupied with their wounds or those of their comrades.

One of these men was Trooper Dodds. Harrison's tank had run out of ammunition for its 75 mm main gun and Harrison, wounded in the head, had been throwing hand grenades at the Germans from the turret when their vehicle was hit. Sherman tanks, which were thinly armoured, were very flammable. When one was hit, every crewman instinctively bailed out as quickly as possible. In their haste to leave the vehicle, Harrison's crew had lost touch with each other and Dodds found himself alone in the lane that led out of the orchard. As he worked his way toward the rear, he encountered other Canadians, among them his best friend, whom Dodds did not recognize, so badly had the man been burned, until his friend spoke. Hiding in a thick hedgerow, Dodds heard shouts and the noise of spaced rifle shots – the SS panzergrenadiers were executing some of the Canadians who had surrendered.[65]

Farther away from Dodds, Sergeant Ernest Payne, along with Troopers Lee Preston and R.C. McLean, had been captured. While they were marched away from the battlefield, their escort opened fire on them, killing Preston and wounding Payne in the ear. Running from their executioners, Payne and McLean hid in a nearby ditch for three days until the Germans pulled back, allowing them to return to their own lines. They were the first eyewitnesses to bring back information about the murder of prisoners.[66]

The killings continued. On 17 June, six days after the battle, a group of seven prisoners, six Queen's Own and one Hussar, were taken into a field near the village of Mouen and shot by a German firing squad. The following day some French civilians were taken to this site and ordered to dig a mass grave.[67] It appeared that they searched the victim's pockets before they buried the dead, as some weeks later, Mrs. Ernest Cranfield, the wife of one of the victims, received in the mail an unfinished letter from her husband with a bullet hole through it. With no explanation for the origin of the letter, nor any other markings on the envelope, she forwarded it to Ottawa as the Department of National Defence, when notifying her that her husband was missing, had asked that she pass on any information she learned as to his fate. Mrs. Cranfield sent the letter to Ottawa with a request that it be returned. It never came back.[68]

Murdered at Le Mesnil-Patry, 1944

Rifleman Ernest Cranfield of the Queen's Own was captured at Le Mesnil-Patry on 11 June 1944 and was one of the many Canadian soldiers who fought in the action who were murdered by the Waffen SS after the battle. (Courtesy, Mrs. M.J. (Cranfield) Stonehouse)

After hiding for three days, A.O Dodds returned to the Hussars' lines with another man. Neither could give much information on the other missing soldiers; in fact it would not be until the war had been over for a month before the fate of some came to light. Only eleven captured Hussars lived long enough to see a prisoner-of-war camp, among them Captain Harry Harrison, the commander of B Squadron. Captured in the evening of 11 June, he later escaped but was recaptured. Threatened with death during his interrogation, he was nevertheless spared. Also captured was Trooper Larry Allen, who was flushed from a hiding spot in a hedgerow and fortunate that three of his captors prevented their more aggressive comrades from killing him outright – even so, he was severely beaten. A third soldier, Trooper Les Soroke, lay unconscious in a ditch for three days. After regaining consciousness, he was picked up by some very surprised Germans while searching for food in a French farmyard.[69]

Not all the Germans behaved in such a brutal fashion. As dusk fell, Canadian ambulances drove out of Norrey flying Red Cross flags. "Orderlies carrying stretchers jumped out, the flag bearers kept waving their banners, and for about a half hour wounded and dead were searched out and gathered, as if this were a peace time exercise. Not a single shot disturbed these events."[70]

He fought and died for Canada.

First field grave of Rifleman E.W. Cranfield, Queen's Own Rifles of Canada, Normandy, 1944. This photograph was sent to his widow in Canada. (Courtesy, Mrs. M.J. (Cranfield) Stonehouse)

For the First Hussars and the Queen's Own Rifles the evening of 11 June 1944 was a grim time. Only eleven unwounded men from D Company of the Rifles initially came back from the wheat field, although others turned up later while only four of B Squadron's twenty-one tanks returned from the action. Moreover only two, those of Corporal Simpson and Sergeant Gristey, had full crews. Just before the action was joined, Gristey had been ordered back by the squadron second-in-command when his tank lost one of its five motors. By the time he returned to the battlefield, now mounted on a 17-pdr. Firefly, B Squadron had ceased to exist. The other two returning tanks, those of Lieutenants Bruce Deans and James Martin, had lost their commanders. Corporal Simpson and his crew helped to pull the dead officers from the turrets and replenish the ammunition so the tanks could go back into action.[71]

To man these four vehicles B Squadron had two sergeants, one corporal and a handful of troopers – no officers had survived the action. Because the squadron had been recently reorganized there was considerable confusion as to who was missing. The only complete nominal roll was in the pocket of the second-in-command, Captain John Smuck, whose body lay in the orchard. The unpleasant job of searching for and identifying the dead fell primarily to the two padres, Honorary Captains Currie Creelman of the Hussars and J.C. Clough of the Queen's Own. As Sergeant Gariepy later noted, it was a terrible task. "In some cases the bodies were indistinguishable from one another, simply a mass of cooked flesh welded together in the great heat; we had to sift through this for identity tags. Each tank told the same story – broken legs, broken arms, open-chest wounds, and so on, had trapped many, so that they had burnt alive. The screams I thought I had heard during the action had not been imaginary after all."[72]

The debacle at Le Mesnil-Patry cost the First Hussars 45 fatal casualties: 7 officers, 6 non-commissioned officers and 32 men. In addition, 1 officer and 1 NCO were wounded and 1 officer and 10 men were prisoners of war. A total of 51 tanks were destroyed while 13 were repairable – this is a record for tank losses in a single action suffered by a Canadian armoured regiment. The Queen's Own losses were also devastating: 1 officer and 54 men killed in action or dead from wounds; 3 officers and 30 men were wounded, and 11 taken prisoner. The total Rifles casualties for the day were 98. The total Canadian losses at Le Mesnil-Patry were 148 men.[73]

In all, 61 Hussars were killed or missing as a result of the battle, a figure that represents one third of the regiment's total wartime fatalities. D Company of the Queen's Own Rifles lost 98 killed, wounded and missing, out of a total of 120.

Human and vehicle casualites, Le Mesnil-Patry, 1944
The tank park at Bray. After the battle, the remains of those crews killed in the action were removed from their vehicles and buried in nearby field graves (note the white cross in foreground). Once this was done and the interior of the vehicle hastily scrubbed, those tanks that were still serviceable or easily repaired were shortly put back into action. (Courtesy, Roy Leslie, First Hussars Museum)

The number deliberately murdered cannot be accurately established, but likely includes a large percentage of the fatal casualties. The murders at Le Mesnil-Patry led to the *Hitlerjugend* being nicknamed "the murder division" by their Canadian opponents.[74]

For its part, that division recorded that the 2nd Battalion of *SS-Panzergrenadierregiment* 26 had 2 officers, 1 NCO and 15 men killed; 6 NCOs and 26 men wounded and 1 man missing. *SS-Panzerpionierbataillon* 12 lost 1 officer, 1 NCO and 27 men killed; 1 officer (the medical officer), 3 NCOs and 45 men wounded, along with 5 men missing. Prinz's 2nd Battalion of the *SS-Panzerregiment* 12 lost 1 killed, 7 wounded, 1 officer and 4 men missing for total German casualties of 198. Three tanks been knocked out, one of which was later returned to action.[75]

The action at Le Mesnil-Patry was a disaster of the first order. So great was its magnitude that many survivors had difficulty in comprehending what, to the Hussars' regimental historian, seemed "an unequal show, in which many brave men died accomplishing what at first glance seemed to be nothing." The ferocity of the enemy resistance and the viciousness of the fighting led some Hussars to conclude that the regiment had run into a full scale German attack by a full armoured division. This mistaken conclusion was not aided by a statement made by Lieutenant General Guy Simonds, the commander of 2nd Canadian Corps, on 12 June 1944 that: "While the battle yesterday seemed futile, it actually put a Panzer Division attack on the skids, thereby saving" 7 Canadian Infantry Brigade "from being cut off."[76] These were kind words but they were not true words.

It is not difficult to find reasons for the catastrophe. The original plan to clear the Mue valley on the 11th and then seize the high ground at Cheux was feasible but the operation failed because 2 Canadian Armoured Brigade had tried to do too much too quickly. The brigade, however, had no choice because the army commander, Dempsey, had ordered the operation advanced twenty-four hours, but this order, for reasons that have never been made clear, did not reach Wyman until the early morning of 11 June. The result was inadequate time for preparation.

This set the stage but four other factors combined to create a tragedy. Lack of accurate intelligence about enemy strengths and positions; that provided by 3rd Infantry Division did not prove accurate. There was also a lack of reconnaissance on the brigade's own front, as exemplified by the minefield fiasco, which was

After the battle

A Sherman 75 of the First Hussars at Bray, Normandy, after the battle. This vehicle has been hit repeatedly by 75 mm rounds – there are at least seven penetrations visible in the photograph. (Courtesy, Roy Leslie, First Hussars Museum)

Elephants' graveyard

After the action at Le Mesnil-Patry, wrecked but recovered First Hussar Shermans were towed to Bray for repair or salvage. Those vehicles which remained in German-held territory at the end of the battle were still there as late as 1947. (Courtesy, Roy Leslie, First Hussars Museum)

attributable to a failure to properly use the brigade's own recce troops and inadequate liaison with other units and formations. Inadequate liaison was also the cause of the minefield fiasco and the confusion over the source of Prinz's fire. Finally, the operation was doomed by the absence of artillery support which might have prevented the disaster or at least mitigated it.

The end result was total confusion, resulting in a breakdown of command and control at the regimental level. The operation was not conducted as an attack but more like an approach march, the result being that the force was defeated in detail.

Le Mesnil-Patry, and other actions like it in Normandy, led to the introduction of tank telephones later in the war. These devices, attached to the rear of the tank, allowed an infantryman to shelter behind the vehicle while speaking directly with the crew commander, even if his hatch was closed. Ironically, Le Mesnil-Patry also led to a somewhat belated instruction from 21 Army Group dated 30 September 1944 that directed higher formations (divisions and brigades) to refrain from arbitrarily assigning H-Hours for lower units which did not leave them adequate time to plan and prepare for operations. These developments were the positive legacy of Le Mesnil-Patry – but they lay in the future.[77]

Le Mesnil Patry Today

To visit the battlefield of Le Mesnil-Patry today, take the N13 Highway either west from Caen or east from Bayeux and turn south onto the D83, which will bring you into Norrey-en-Bessin. At the church in Norrey, turn right on the D172 to exit the town in the direction of Le Mesnil-Patry. As soon as you reach the southwestern edge of Norrey, you are on the original battlefield.

A half-century has passed since that grim Sunday afternoon and the area is once again a prosperous farming district. The roads are now paved and the villages have been rebuilt, their streets widened and straightened. The church in Norrey-en-Bessin has been restored with original materials but still lacks a bell tower. Thought to be a German observation post, that part of the structure was shot off on 9 June 1944 and, due to the expense involved, it was never replaced. The route through Norrey taken by the Hussars, the Rue de La Vergée, has only one wartime building on it. It stands at the corner where Lieutenant Gordon rolled his tank and there are marks from his tank tracks on one of its walls.

The wheat field is still used for growing crops. As one looks at its open rolling features, imagination is required to picture the battle as no physical traces remain; the burned-out hulks of the Hussars' Shermans were removed in 1947. Across the field to the west lies La Ferme de la Château. It was destroyed during the war and its owners, the Bunel family, have rebuilt it on a nearby location but the brick foundations of the original structure can still be clearly seen. Near the entrance to the Bunel farm stands a twenty-foot high calvaire, temporary burial site of many of the Canadian casualties. A farm track leads south from the crucifix toward the Mue valley. Near the area where the dirt track enters a small wood on the banks of the Mue, the traces of the trenches of SS-Pioneerbataillon 12 are evident on the ground. Most of the apple orchards around the village have been cut down, however, and, consequently, the location of Harrison and Seigel's encounter is difficult to find without local knowledge.

The church of Le Mesnil-Patry was blown up by the pioneer battalion during the summer of 1944 but has been replaced by a more modern structure. Outside the church is a memorial plaque bearing the badges of the First Hussars and the Queen's Own Rifles and dedicated to the men who fell on 11 June 1944. Those men, for the most part, are buried in the Commonwealth War Graves Commission cemetery at Bény-sur-Mer near Reviers, a community liberated by B Squadron of the Hussars on D-Day. The majority of the 11 June casualties are together in two very long rows near the rear boundary.

In this cemetery lie Lieutenant James Martin, his headstone bearing the name of his original regiment, the 7th/11th Hussars. Here also is the gunner Captain Charles

Rivaz, who left behind a wife and two daughters. Nearby is the grave of Captain John Smuck, a former sergeant major in the Royal Canadian Dragoons who was the second-in-command of B Squadron. Burnt and twice wounded he was callously murdered in the orchard by the Germans. Near him is Sergeant Tom McLaughlin of the Queen's Own Rifles who was wounded in the action, captured and executed by the SS beside his men in a lonely field days after the battle.

The memory of these men is still cherished by the surviving veterans of the battle. Over the next fifty years they seldom spoke of Le Mesnil-Patry, convinced that they were somehow to blame for their disastrous defeat. This chagrin was mixed with a desire to see the murders of their comrades avenged. Not all those guilty were brought to justice but the sense of failure has been banished for, as we have seen, the defeat at Le Mesnil-Patry had nothing to do with the bravery of the men who fought in that unfortunate action.

On the Left Flank:
Normandy to the Maas,
June 1944 to January 1945

More than two months of heavy fighting in Normandy followed the tragedy at Le Mesnil-Patry. Canadian troops spent most of June and early July 1944 trying to take the crucial city of Caen and, once this place fell on 8 July, most of the remainder of July trying to break out of it. The *Wehrmacht* fought with great determination and skill to prevent this happening and a series of attacks on the Bourguébus and Verrières Ridges resulted in small gains and large casualty lists. The sheer weight of Allied superiority finally told and, at the end of July, the Germans gave way in the American sector to the west and the First and Third U.S. Armies broke through into open territory to begin a rapid advance that rolled up the enemy flank. In August First Canadian Army mounted two major offensives, Operations TOTALIZE and TRACTABLE, in an attempt to break through to Falaise but, although both made initial gains, they failed against inferior but well-commanded German forces. In the end, threatened with encirclement, the Germans were forced to retreat and on 25 August Paris was liberated. Everyone expected the war would be over by Christmas, if not before.

For Canada, the Normandy campaign was a grim introduction to battle. It cost First Canadian Army 18,144 casualties and revealed defects in weapons, training, doctrine and commanders, but, in this, First Canadian Army was no worse off than its American and British counterparts, who experienced similar problems. In the end, the Allies were forced to grind the *Wehrmacht* down in a battle of attrition that the Germans could not refuse, but which they could not win.

In the heady days of late August and early September 1944, however, the victorious Allies pressed steadily east across the Seine and into Belgium. While American and British armies made headline-grabbing advances that promised a quick resolution to the war, First Canadian Army received the unglamorous but necessary task of clearing the Channel ports of Boulogne, Calais and Dunkirk which occupied it until early October. The very swiftness of the Allied advance became a problem as it outstripped the supply lines which ran back to Normandy and the pace began to slow. The solution to the supply problem was the port of Antwerp, which fell to the British 11th Armoured Division on 4 September – but Antwerp lies on the Scheldt estuary fifty miles from the sea, and the Germans had to be cleared from the estuary to permit shipping to enter the port. This job went to First Canadian Army and, throughout October and early November, it fought across the half-flooded polder lands of north Belgium and south Holland, perfect defensive ground for the Germans, in a long and difficult operation to clear the estuary.

By mid-November, Antwerp was open but Allied logistical problems and the onset of winter had permitted the Germans to stabilize their front by withdrawing behind the lines of the Maas and Rhine rivers. It was now clear that that the war would not be over by Christmas and, as Allied leaders made plans to renew the advance as soon as the weather improved and supplies were available, First Canadian Army took up its by now traditional position on the left flank, guarding a sector along the southern bank of the Maas River in Holland.

On 16 December, Allied soldiers had just nicely settled in for the winter when Hitler launched a surprise offensive in the Ardennes, eighty miles to the south of the Canadian position on the Maas. Intended to capture Antwerp and split the American and British forces, it at first made good progress but was stopped after three weeks of heavy fighting that cost the *Wehrmacht* 100,000 casualties, 800 tanks and 1,000 aircraft. First Canadian Army, in positions along the Maas, had no part in halting this offensive and for Canadian soldiers the last weeks of 1944 and the first of 1945 were relatively quiet. At the end of January, however, the war began to heat up again as newspapers across Canada carried reports of heavy fighting on an island in the Maas with the foreign sounding but not unpleasant name of Kapelsche Veer.

7

"If only we had

the wisdom

of our generals:"

The Kapelsche Veer

26–31 January 1945

FIG. 1.—ON GUARD

Canadian Sherman and infantry on the Veer, January 1945

A Sherman V of the South Alberta Regiment and a Bren section of the Argylls on the Kapelsche Veer. Note the tank tracks welded on the Sherman – they provided extra protection but their weight increased the problem of trying to move in the mud. Trooper Cliff Allen (left) and Corporal Jake Wiebe (right) are the drivers of this vehicle. (Courtesy, Jake Wiebe)

"If only we had the wisdom of our generals:" The Kapelsche Veer

26-31 January 1945

Donald E. Graves

When this bloody war is over,
Oh, how happy I will be,
When I get my civvy clothes on,
No more soldiering for me.

No more church parades on Sunday,
No more begging for a pass,
I will tell the sergeant-major,
To stuff his passes up his ass.[1]

Canadian infantry have driven the Germans from their last bridgehead south of the Maas River after five days of vicious fighting around the tiny but strategic ferry harbour of Kapelscheveer.

Nazi paratroopers ordered to hold at all costs this base ... were finally cleared out early on the morning of Jan. 31 from dug-outs in dikes and rubble-filled cellars. It was the third assault in a month on Kapelscheveer by Allied troops. ......

Canadian casualties were not light.

NEWS ITEM, CANADIAN PRESS, 7 FEBRUARY 1945

See Appendix G, page 387, for Orders of Battle of the Opposing Forces.

T he Kapelsche Veer is a low, flat, treeless island in Holland near the mouth of the Maas River. Formed by the division of that river into two channels, a wide northern branch called the Bergsche Maas and a narrow, southern branch known as the Oude Maasje, the Veer is a boggy spit of land, about four miles long and a thousand yards deep at its eastern extremity where it becomes a double dyke. These dykes protect the south bank of the Maas from the current, which is very strong in this area. On the north side of the island is the small ferry harbour that gives it its name, for *veer* is Dutch for "harbour" and, thus, Kapelsche Veer means "the harbour of Capelle," a nearby village.

When the Wehrmacht withdrew north of the Maas in November 1944, Allied troops did not occupy the Veer (see Map KV-1). It was felt it could be easily dominated by fire and the units responsible for this sector of the river contented themselves with occasional patrols. This insignificant piece of water-logged ground only became important in late December 1944 when Allied intelligence anticipated that, in conjunction with the German offensive taking place in the Ardennes to the south, the enemy would also attempt an assault across the Maas. Such an attack was apparently planned, but it remains unclear whether the German intention was serious or simply a ploy to distract Allied intelligence.[2]

In any case the projected attack was cancelled, much to the relief of German *General* Eugen-Felix Schwalbe, whose corps had been tasked with carrying it out. Schwalbe had been disturbed to learn that, in the face of not only Allied air and artillery superiority but the massed firepower of two armoured divisions, his troops were expected to cross the river in rubber assault rafts and civilian ferries armed with 37 mm guns. In fact, Schwalbe was so distressed that "he awoke the day after he had been told of the plan" to ask himself, "Are we really going to cross the Maas or did I merely dream it all?"[3]

There was one outcome from this stillborn operation. In mid-December the Germans established an outpost on the Kapelsche Veer and retained it as a forward position to give "battle inoculation" to green troops who were regularly rotated onto the island from the north bank of the Maas.[4] Late that month General Stanislaw Maczek's 1st Polish Armoured Division took over the area around the Veer from 4th Canadian Armoured Division and the Poles quickly discovered the German presence. During the night of 29 December a Polish patrol exchanged shots with the enemy and confirmed that the Germans were entrenched on the island near the ferry harbour. Maczek disliked having a German observa-

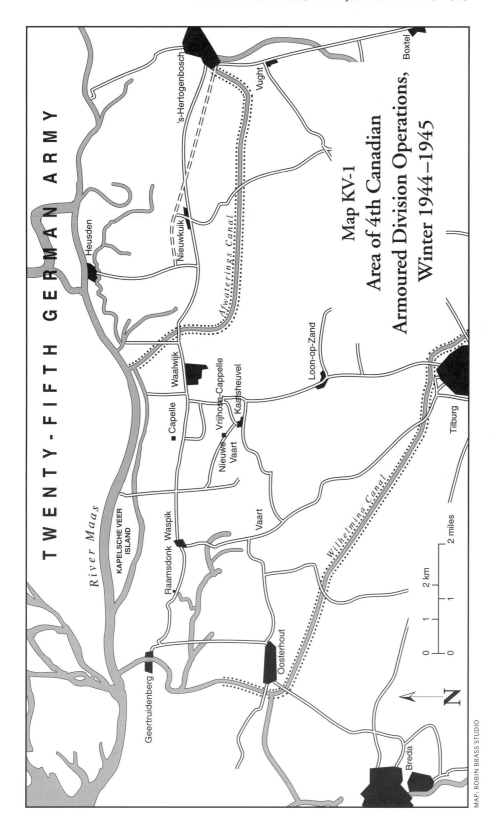

Map KV-1
Area of 4th Canadian
Armoured Division Operations,
Winter 1944–1945

MAP: ROBIN BRASS STUDIO

tion post on his side of the Maas and, on New Year's Eve 1944, he mounted an attack against the Veer with three companies of infantry, supported by tanks. The defenders beat it off at a cost of forty-nine Polish casualties.[5]

Maczek spent a week preparing for his next attack, code-named Operation MOUSE, which went in on the night of 6 January 1945. This time the Polish commander threw elements of two infantry battalions, supported by tank and artillery fire, against the island but was again rebuffed at a cost of 133 killed and wounded.[6]

Lieutenant General John Crocker, the commander of 1st British Corps, which at this time controlled 1st Polish and 4th Canadian Armoured Divisions, wanted the Germans off the Kapelsche Veer. A dour, somewhat humourless officer who had begun his military career as a private soldier in the First World War before being commissioned, Crocker had a distinguished record in the French campaign of 1940, the Tunisian campaign of 1942-1943 and the recent fighting in Normandy. He was not the kind of general to waste his men's lives so, before issuing orders for a new assault, he investigated other possibilities. Unfortunately, as Major Hubert Fairlie Wood, a staff officer with 4th Armoured Division, later wrote, Crocker's efforts "to have the area drenched with heavy bombers and set alight with the new Napalm bombs developed by the U.S. were unavailing."[7] The corps commander therefore turned to the Royal Marines, amphibious light infantry, and on 13 January 1945, the men of 47 Royal Marine Commando mounted Operation HORSE, a nighttime assault that was plentifully supported by artillery. The Marines too were beaten back with a loss of 49 casualties.[8]

Crocker ordered another attack. He was not concerned that the Veer would be used as a bridgehead for an enemy offensive south of the Maas because First Canadian Army intelligence officers had concluded, almost wistfully, by early January 1945 that such a threat no longer existed.[9] Although he may have been wise in retrospect, Hubert Fairlie Wood concluded after the war that there were three reasons for a third attack to be made against the island. The German position was a thorn in the side of the troops guarding the Maas as the enemy "could observe movement, direct fire and mount patrols to harry our forward localities." Second, a determined assault might convince the Germans that the direction of the forthcoming British and Canadian offensive would be in Holland rather than to the south in the Rhineland where it was actually scheduled to take place. The third reason, and most "dangerous of all" according to Wood, was the question of Allied prestige, since to allow the Germans to remain south of the Maas would have "engendered in the troops of 1st British Corps a belief in the superiority of the German soldier." Prestige is about the worst possible reason to mount a military operation but, as Wood noted, after the first attempts to take the island were unsuccessful, "the liquidation of this sore spot became unavoidable." On 14 January, the day after Operation HORSE had failed, Crocker gave Major General Chris Vokes and his 4th Canadian Armoured Division the job of taking the Kapelsche Veer.[10]

This was not good news for the Green Patch Division.[11] It was proud "to have the distinction of being a pinch hitter," its War Diarist commented, "but the pleasure, if NOT the distinction is a dubious one."[12] Crocker emphasized to Vokes that the island was to be taken as soon as practicable but speed was not to be the ruling factor in the operation, which was to be conducted so that the Kapelsche Veer was "thoroughly tied up," and Crocker suggested that Vokes inject some "new element or method" into his own plan so that surprise might be achieved.[13] The staff of the 4th Division spent two days working out a detailed plan for the assault, and on 16 January Vokes passed it along to Brigadier Jim Jefferson of 10 Canadian Infantry Brigade with an order to prepare for an attack.

The assignment was no more welcome to the 10 Brigade staff than it had been to their 4th Division counterparts. Jefferson, a decorated veteran of the battle of Ortona in Italy in 1943, commanded a formation consisting of three Ontario infantry battalions – the Lincoln and Welland Regiment, the Argyll and Sutherland Highlanders and the Algonquin Regiment – which were normally supported in action by the tanks of the South Alberta Regiment and the 25-pdr. gun/howitzers of 15 Field Regiment, Royal Canadian Artillery. His brigade had first entered action in Normandy in early August 1944 and had led the advance of 4th Armoured Division through the Low Countries during the previous autumn, suffering heavy casualties in the process. Since late November it had been stationed along the Maas and brought up to strength with reinforcements whose training left much to be desired, but its only serious action had occurred in a number of fighting patrols dispatched across the river on Vokes's orders. These patrols, which cost heavy casualties for the results they produced, were not popular with the men of the brigade, who would have much preferred a "live and let live" attitude toward the enemy.

It was clear to Jefferson and his staff that the Kapelsche Veer was going to be a very hard nut to crack. The main German defensive position was at the ferry harbour itself, centred on two houses, code-named RASPBERRY and GRAPES by some fructally-minded staff officer. The cellars of these buildings had been reinforced to serve as bunkers, and around them the defenders had constructed "a system of

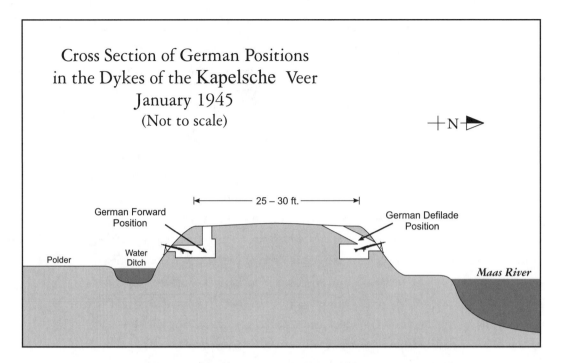

Cross-section of German positions on the dykes of the Kapelsche Veer, January 1945

This drawing illustrates the most common type of German position on the island. The forward position can sweep the top of the neighbouring dyke while the defilade positon covers the approach from Maas. Other positions were situated on the top of each dyke to fire directly down its length. These positions, reinforced with concrete and with 5 to 10 feet of overhead cover, were extremely difficult to neutralize with artillery fire. (Drawing by Chris Johnson after Hubert Fairlie-Wood, "Operation Elephant")

interlocking positions, linked by tunnels in the dykes and commanding every approach."[14] The island was so wet and boggy that the only way to approach the harbour was along the tops of the two dykes that formed the central spine of the island. The northern dyke near the main channel was about ten feet high and the southern dyke about twelve, and both were between twenty and thirty feet wide with steep sides that sloped at a forty-five-degree angle. The dyke tops, which could be swept by automatic weapons fire from the harbour area and mortar fire from the north bank of the Maas, formed perfect killing grounds for the German defenders.

The divisional staff believed that their plan, which employed many of the considerable resources available to an Allied commander in the last months of the war, would overcome the considerable advantages enjoyed by the enemy. Code-named Operation ELEPHANT (the size of the code-names escalating, it appears, in direct proportion to the size of the operations), the assault would be supported by no fewer than 300 artillery pieces ranging from the 75 mm tank guns of the South Alberta and British Columbia Regiments to medium 5.5 inch and heavy 155 mm weapons. According to the 10 Brigade War Diarist, it was the "heaviest concentration of artillery ever allotted to the Brigade, or perhaps to any similar formation, for a single action."[15] No one at 4th Division headquarters actually expected artillery alone to bring victory, however, and, indeed, the plan contained the comforting statement that, when "considering the bombardment of the bridgehead position it should be borne in mind that the extraordinarily good f[iel]dworks of the German g[ar]r[iso]n are practically impervious to neutralization or destruction."[16] This was a cheerful thought but if all that artillery wasn't expected to have much effect, what was going to work?

Despite the fact that three major attacks on the Veer had failed and the Germans defenders were obviously going to be alert for another, the planners of Operation ELEPHANT, following Crocker's suggestion, thought that a surprise assault might just work. They therefore called for a daylight advance by three infantry companies under cover of a heavy smoke screen but with no preliminary bombardment; two companies would attack from the right and move west against the central position at the harbour while the third would attack from the

A fine field of fire

View from the German position on the Veer looking east along the dyke over which the Argylls had to advance. The dyke tops offered the only firm footing for men and vehicles but they provided excellent fields of fire for the defenders. The Argyll & Sutherland Highlanders spent four miserable winter days on top of this dyke. (Photograph by Dianne Graves)

left and move east against the same objective (see Map KV-2). To get the Germans out of their "extraordinarily good fieldworks," the planners wanted to use flamethrowers. Crocodile flame-throwing tanks would have been ideal for this job but since the ground on the island was "only thinly frozen and churned up very quickly into seas of mud," the employment of armoured vehicles was not seriously considered.[17] Instead, six Wasps (flamethrower carriers) were allotted to the companies attacking from the right while twenty-four portable flame units were distributed among all three assault companies. The most amazing part of the scheme was the provision of canoes for a third force that was to seal off the harbour from the north. Setting out from the eastern tip of the island, this waterborne force would paddle under cover of smoke down the main channel of the Maas and land on both sides of the ferry harbour to prevent the Germans being reinforced from the north bank.[18]

The canoe party was General Chris Vokes's personal contribution. Vokes was not happy about his orders to take the Kapelsche Veer because, as far as he was concerned, "the Germans could have stayed there for the rest of the war" as they were doing no harm.[19] Although he thought that the operation would be "a great waste of young lives," Vokes felt he "had to do it – you just can't say no when an order comes down" – but only took the job "if two weeks were granted to him to conduct special training and rehearsals for one of his battalions, plus adequate supplies." Crocker gave the Canadian commander everything he wanted except time as the Lincoln and Welland Regiment, the unit that made the initial attack, received only six days to prepare for the operation. In a postwar statement Vokes implied that his request for canoes was actually a ploy to get the operation cancelled:

> When the action was first suggested to me, I said I would take it on, very reluctantly, if they could provide me with twenty-eight Peterborough canoes, because I had visions of sending the troops down the river in those silent craft under the cover of darkness. For a while I thought that by asking for the canoes, I might have turned the whole thing off. Well, it wasn't. The canoes were provided – flown in specially from Canada – and I had to go ahead.[20]

If Vokes was so unsure about the prospect of success, he should perhaps have tried harder to call off the operation. His reluctance to do so, despite his personal qualms, may have been due to the fact he had only recently been transferred from Italy; Operation ELEPHANT would be the first time he commanded 4th Division in battle and as the new boy Vokes did not want to make waves.

Unfortunately, the command situation at the top was mirrored at the lower levels. The veteran commanders of the South Albertas, the Argylls and the Lincoln and Welland Regiment, the three units that would eventually be involved in the forthcoming operation, were absent when the plans for ELEPHANT were made. Lieutenant Colonel Gordon Wotherspoon of the South Albertas was supervising the divisional battle school and his second-in-command, Major Albert Coffin, had that unit. Vokes had removed the commanding officer of the Argylls, Lieutenant Colonel Dave Stewart, after Stewart had protested the unnecessary casualties Vokes's vigorous patrol program was costing his battalion, and the Argylls were now led by Major R.D. McKenzie, the second-in-command. Finally, the Lincoln and Welland Regiment, which had been chosen to make the assault, had recently lost its superb commanding officer, Lieutenant Colonel Bill Cromb, who had returned to Canada on leave after five years overseas, and were under the temporary command of Major James Swayze. When it comes to protesting orders or getting them changed, new or acting commanders don't have the influence that veterans do. As Swayze remarked, "You only demand so much" and then "you only do what you're told."[21] He recalled that the plan for Operation ELEPHANT was "laid out" and it was simply a case of "take this" and do it.

The ill-fated canoeists

Men of the Lincoln and Welland canoe party train with their unwieldy craft prior to the attack. Due to frozen weapons and lack of smoke cover, they suffered heavy casualties on the first day of Operation ELEPHANT. (National Archives of Canada, PA 114067)

The Lincoln and Welland Regiment worked hard during the six days it was granted to prepare for the operation. Wearing newly-issued white snowsuits, the infantry of the assault companies practised on dykes similar to those on the Veer while the canoe party learned to handle their somewhat unwieldy craft. The appearance of the canoes – exotic equipment in Europe – attracted a Canadian army film unit which shot footage of the canoeists paddling about local waterways. After the operation was finished, this film appeared in a newsreel accompanied by the usual dramatic commentary:

> Even the North American canoe becomes an instrument of war in Canadian hands. Canoe commandoes form one arm of the double-pronged attack on the island. With their smallarms in the bottom of the canoes, clad in snow suits for camouflage purposes, they close in on their objective.[22]

Major Ed Brady of the Lincs' B Company recalled that Vokes showed up one day to watch his men going through their paces using smoke and flamethrowers. At the end of the drill, the divisional commander commented that "I think you've got things pretty well in hand here" and strode off but had an afterthought and returned to tell Brady that he should order his men to fix their bayonets when they actually landed on the island.[23]

The sappers of 9 Field Squadron, Royal Canadian Engineers, were more helpful. While the Lincoln and Welland infantry practised their assault tactics, the engineers built a bridge over to the eastern spit of the Veer (which was held

Lincoln and Welland veterans of the Veer battle

From left to right, Private F.L. Russell, Private J. Sneddon, Corporal R.S. Marshall and unidentified soldier. Note the moccasins worn by two of the men and the white snow suits issued shortly before the operation began. They proved useful garments until the weather warmed up and the snow on the island melted, leaving the wearers highly visible to the enemy. (National Archives of Canada, PA 144706)

by friendly forces) using the footings of a previously-demolished structure as a foundation. This bridge was only 500 yards from the German positions, and although it was under the cover of a dyke, the enemy could bring down fire on all the approaches. The sappers therefore had to work at night and, lest the noise of heavy trucks draw fire, they brought all their materials in by water on man-propelled rafts, or by land on a two and a half ton trailer, also man-propelled, down the icy dyke roads. The bridge, completed the day before the attack, was such a twisted, cobbled-together, unsteady-looking structure that someone dubbed it the "Mad Whore's Dream" and that was the name that 9 Field Squadron neatly lettered on the sign they erected beside it.[24]

All this activity did not go unnoticed by the defenders of the Veer, who were composed of a company of *Fallschirmjägerregiment* (Parachute Regiment) 17. This unit had been formed, along with its parent formation, *Fallschirmjäger-division* (Parachute Division) 6, in September 1944 from comb-outs from Luftwaffe ground crews and anti-aircraft units, stiffened by veterans. Its men were paratroopers in name only but they were relatively young and healthy, and imbued with a faith in ultimate German victory that had not been shaken by recent defeats on both the eastern and western fronts. The commander of *Fallschirmjägerdivision* 6 was *Generalleutnant* Hermann Plocher, a veteran who had first seen combat in Spain in 1936. Plocher wanted to evacuate the Veer but all his requests to withdraw were met with flat refusals by his superior, *General-leutnant* Kurt Student, who told him bluntly to hold the island "at all costs."[25] It would seem that a concern with prestige was not restricted to the south bank of the Maas.

Orders being orders, Plocher maintained the position and rotated the garrison on a regular basis. In the last week of January 1945, the Veer was held by the reinforced 10 *Kompanie* of *Fallschirmjägerregiment* 17, about 150 strong, with a dozen machine guns. The island was not a comfortable post and its garrison suffered from wet entrenchments and frostbite. All their supplies had to be brought over from the north bank by rubber rafts in the darkness hours and this meant that the defenders' food was usually late and almost always cold.[26]

Despite their problems, the paratroopers on the Veer were an aggressive lot. In the week before the attack they sent out nighttime patrols which resulted in a number of small firefights when they encountered similar Canadian patrols. This German activity concerned the 10 Brigade War Diarist, who noted that the enemy's "persistent patrolling" in the area where the attack was to take place was "rather disquieting."[27]

Operation ELEPHANT got under way at 7.15 A.M. on Friday, 26 January 1945. Ninety minutes before, "in the half-light of the setting moon and the rising sun," the first smoke rounds came down as the artillery started to build up a diversionary screen across the Maas to confuse the defenders.[28] The main screen on the island was laid just before the attack began and it was thickened by smoke pots and artificial smoke generators dispersed around the island in locations thought most likely to blanket the defences. Within a few minutes, one onlooker reported, the entire area "was clouded out and there was nothing we could see."[29] The engineers held their breath as the first vehicle, a half track loaded with smoke containers, crossed the "Mad Whore's Dream." It "hit the steep ramp at about 30 MPH and came down with a tremendous crash," but as "nothing gave way" the relieved sappers exhaled and declared their rickety span to be structurally sound.[30] Under the cover of billowing thick, oily grey chemical smoke, the men of the three Lincoln and Welland assault companies clambered into white-painted Buffalo LVTs (Landing Vehicles, Tracked) and crossed to the island (see Map KV-2). To a watching war correspondent, "it was a ghost-like sight as the soldiers set out in these amphibious tank-like vehicles."[31]

The right hand attack went in first. At 7.25 A.M. Major James Dandy's C Company of the Lincoln and Welland Regiment, debussing from their Buffalos, prepared to move along the dyke to link up with Major Owen Lambert's A Company, which crossed about a mile and a half to the west. Dandy quickly discovered that he had a major problem – his Wasp carriers, intended to neutralize the German defensive positions, were unable to climb the slippery sides of the south dyke because of the weight of their flamethrowing equipment. This problem would have been discovered earlier and a solution likely found if the Lincoln and Welland Regiment had been given enough time to make a proper reconnaissance of the area over which they had to advance but, as their historian notes, the unit had only taken over positions on the island from the Poles the day before the attack began. As Dandy recalled, the Wasps would

> take a run at the thing and the tracks would just spin. I figured if I could get one up, I could tow the others up. ...... maybe I can blow that damn tank off [the back of the carrier] with hand grenades. I backed the carrier up by this canal, pulled the pin out of the hand grenade, and put it near the brackets and walked away. And it just dented the metal. So I couldn't get the carriers up.[32]

Leaving the useless vehicles behind, Dandy's men advanced west along the dyke top towards Lambert's A Company.

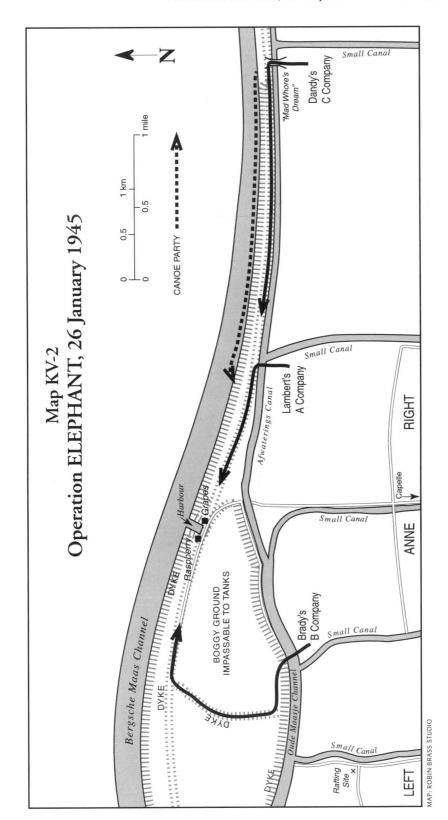

Map KV-2
Operation ELEPHANT, 26 January 1945

N

1 mile
0   0.5   0.5   1 km

CANOE PARTY

Bergsche Maas Channel

DYKE

DYKE

DYKE

DYKE

Harbour
Raspberry
Grapes
"Mad Whore's Dream"

Dandy's C Company

Small Canal

Lambert's A Company

Afwaterings Canal

Small Canal

RIGHT

Capelle

Small Canal

ANNE

BOGGY GROUND IMPASSABLE TO TANKS

Brady's B Company

Small Canal

Oude Maasje Channel

Small Canal

Rafting Site ×

LEFT

MAP: ROBIN BRASS STUDIO

334 ✎ FIGHTING FOR CANADA

Lambert's men, transported with two Wasps to the Veer by amphibious vehicles, had lost one carrier crossing the Oude Maasje. The second vehicle made it safely but couldn't climb onto the dyke. At that moment A Company came under accurate and heavy enemy mortar fire from the north bank but Lambert decided to press on and his men, choking in the harsh acrid fumes of the chemical smoke, moved west along the dyke top toward the two houses code-named GRAPES and RASPBERRY.[33]

The sixty-man canoe party reached the island by way of the "Mad Whore's Dream." When they attempted to launch their craft into the main river channel, however, they discovered that there was an inch of ice on the surface – a fact that had been reported at 5 A.M. by the Algonquin Regiment, who were monitoring river conditions. The party was forced to haul their canoes over this crust of ice to reach open water and by the time they embarked and moved downstream both the men and their weapons were soaked.[34]

Unfortunately, the canoeists' troubles were just beginning. The ice along the north bank of the island forced them to move farther out into the main channel of the Maas where the smoke was less thick, and as they paddled their fragile craft furiously toward the harbour they came under accurate fire from the north bank of the river. Matters were not helped when the wind began to shift, thinning out their smoke cover even more. Lieutenant Lloyd Grose of the Argylls, whose platoon was on the eastern spit of the Veer to hold a "firm base" for the sappers at the bridge, watched horrified through windows in the smoke screen as the men in the canoes were "picked off by the machine guns from the far side of the river."[35] Several of the craft were sunk and the party was forced to land on the north side of the Veer near where Lambert's A Company had reached the island. They were now about halfway to their objective but only about fifteen were still on their feet. As soon as they moved on top of the dyke, they came under heavy fire from German machine guns firing along fixed lines through the smoke. When they tried to return this fire, the canoeists discovered that their weapons, thoroughly soaked during their short but perilous voyage, were frozen solid and would not work. The survivors withdrew to the mainland.[36]

Lambert meanwhile had advanced toward the centre of the German position. His company was within thirty yards of GRAPES when the Germans opened up with every weapon they could bring to bear. The volume of fire brought his advance to a standstill, five of the six officers in his company being killed or wounded. Lambert was last seen walking up the dyke by himself, swearing and cursing "a blue streak," until he disappeared in the smoke.[37] He did not return.

Attempts to flush out the defenders with the portable flamethrowers proved useless as most of the men carrying them were cut down as soon as they started their flames. One Lincs officer commented on the difficulties of these weapons:

I had lifebuoy flamethrowers. I think I had ten. Lost every goddamn man; every one of them was killed. You can imagine what it was like. I think they weighed about 60 pounds. He's got army boots on with metal cleats on the heels filled with snow. He's walking on an angle and carrying the goddamned thing; trying to manoeuvre is almost impossible. And the minute they shot any flames they were a target and every one of them got it. I always felt really badly about that [because] we asked for volunteers. I didn't want to take them in the first place, but they felt that's what we had to have so we took them. And I never used them again.[38]

By 9.45 A.M. the survivors of Lambert's A Company had fallen back and were beginning to dig in along the dyke, a few hundred yards short of the objective. At that moment the Germans brought down a heavy and accurate mortar barrage from the north bank of the river and then counterattacked, driving the remnants of the company back on Dandy's C Company coming behind them. Dandy tried to rally A Company and resume the advance but this movement became confused when he and all his C Company officers became casualties.[39]

The attack on the right was over and the remnants of Dandy and Lambert's men were withdrawn through Grose's Argyll platoon at the bridging site, a movement that caused Grose some problems:

They had lost their weapons and so on, and they started to congregate around our platoon, where we were on the dikes. And I said "Move on or you'll draw fire." So the next thing I knew, we were getting mortar fire ourselves 'cause they were observed from the far shore when they had stopped.[40]

In contrast, progress on the left, or western, side of the island was initially good. Major Ed Brady's B Company of the Lincs crossed to the island in Buffalos and then moved steadily east along the dyke toward RASPBERRY, the westernmost of the two houses. Then they ran into trouble – as Corporal Howard Loughlin remembered: "You couldn't see in front of you and the phosphorus [smoke] got into your lungs," the German slit trenches " were all covered with snow" and "you couldn't tell where their fire was coming from" and "talk about cold."[41] "All of a sudden," Loughlin continued, this guy yelled and here these grenades coming over the dyke. Where are you going to go in seven seconds? That was the third grenade that I had thrown at me, and the other two didn't go off ... but this one sure as hell did. I just covered my head up ... I waited for the damn thing to go off, it seemed like an eternity. It just felt like somebody had punched me ... And then I went to stand up and I couldn't.

Brady's company tried to push forward but, as he remembered it, "they opened up on us both with mortars and machine guns" and he "started losing men hand over fist."[42] With his soldiers "going down like ten pins," and realizing that he "would just lose more and more men," Brady decided to pull back and dig in at the junction of the main dyke and a smaller dyke that ran north from his crossing spot. The Germans immediately began to infiltrate around his position using the dykes as cover, snipers became active, and his situation was very shaky.[43]

By noon it was obvious that the assault on the Kapelsche Veer was a total failure. So much for the element of surprise.

The South Alberta Regiment had taken little part in the morning's battle. Lieutenant Smith Bowick's troop from A Squadron had provided indirect fire on call for the Lincoln and Welland Regiment and some echelon personnel had been detailed to help with the smoke screen. Among them was Trooper George Armstrong, who remembered that he and Trooper Jack Spillet "went up after dark [on 25 January] and here was some 10 Brigade people and they were going to make a kayak [canoe] attack in there and that's what these smudge pots [smoke generators] were for." The two men placed the generators as directed in weather so cold they had to use socks for mitts. Just before first light on 26 January, Armstrong and Spillet lit the generators and the Lincs "were pleased with the smoke cover they gave." "Later," George continued, "they brought up a kitchen truck and Jack and I were getting something to eat when we heard that all of those kayak fellows were lost. They said that there was no smoke as apparently the wind blew it down the wrong way. I mind that we never finished our meal, we were just sick."[44]

During the morning a large audience had gathered in the South Alberta Regimental Headquarters at nearby Kaatsheuvel to follow the course of the fighting on the radio but the "news coming in was very meagre." A few minutes later the crowd thinned out after a German artillery shell demolished a building across the street and "a large piece of shrapnel rocketed through the orderly room bringing dust and plaster down on the heads of the assembled multitude." Things were then quiet until 3 P.M. when an order came down from brigade headquarters to send officers out to recce tank routes to the Kapelsche Veer.[45]

If he hadn't suspected it before, it was by now clear to Brigadier Jim Jefferson that taking the island would require a slow and deliberate set-piece operation and it was going to be a thoroughly nasty business. His revised plan was to push on the central German position from both sides – the Lincs from the left and the Argylls from the right – with South Alberta tanks supporting both units (see Map KV-2). Getting armoured vehicles onto the Veer was not going to be easy. The "Mad Whore's Dream" might be capable of supporting tanks but, as the Germans held the centre of the island, a raft would be needed to get them onto the west end. An alert therefore went out to 9 Field Squadron of the RCE which began to assemble materials to build a Class 40 raft on the bank of a subsidiary canal about 450 feet directly south of the Oude Maasje channel.[46]

January days in northern Europe are short and the sun set at 4.30 P.M., several hours before the first South Alberta tanks, two light Stuarts commanded by Sergeant Vaughan Stevenson and Corporal Matthew McSherry of Recce Troop, crossed the "Dream" to the island. They had no problems but as soon as they managed to climb onto the dyke and move forward they found that "there was not one good road to work on" and the slippery surface of the dyke was so narrow they could not turn around but "had to proceed in reverse all the way when we moved back."[47] Stevenson consolidated with the Argylls, who were under heavy mortar fire from the north bank of the Maas. For the next two days,

South Alberta trooper wearing his "Zoot Suit"

Tank crew member of the 29th Armoured Reconnaissance Regiment (South Alberta Regiment) which fought on the Kapelsche Veer wearing the Canadian-designed and manufactured tank suit issued to units of the Canadian Armoured Corps in the autumn of 1944. It was a practical and warm garment much liked by those who received it and it was called a "zoot suit" after the nattily-dressed social phenomenon making headlines back home. (Painting by Ron Volstad, courtesy, Department of National Defence)

South Alberta Recce Troop Stuarts on the Veer
The first South Alberta tanks to reach the island were two light Stuart VI tanks. Unfortunately, the vehicle in the background bogged badly, blocking the dyke top and all attempts to either move it or blow it up proved futile so the sappers were forced to spend eighteen hours to construct a diversion around it. (Courtesy, Argyll & Sutherland Highlanders of Canada)

until relieved by other crews, he and McSherry provided direct fire support, evacuated wounded and brought up ammunition and supplies to the infantry's forward positions.

The wartime radio code-name for the Royal Canadian Engineers was HOLDFAST. It is a good handle for these practical soldiers and at no time did the sappers live up to it more than on the cold night of 26/27 January 1945 when they constructed the raft at the Veer. They began to unload the heavy components – pontoons, piers, stringers and flooring – about midnight and then spent eight terrible hours assembling them:

> The trap doors on the pontoons were all frozen tight and had to be chopped and prised open with picks. When this was accomplished it was found that the drain plug-holes were frozen solid with ice and mud. Most of the ice was chopped away with a bayonet, and that in the threads thawed out by inserting fingers in the hole. The next job was getting the piers joined. Since the canal was full of cracked ice from 2" to 5" thick it was extremely difficult to keep the square ends clear to hook them up. Incidentally the square ends were not square, as they were covered with lumps of ice and frozen mud, as were the connecting hooks. To add to the unpleasantness of the situation a

German patrol sallied forth from the VEER and shot the site up for a while before being driven back by the Lincoln and Welland Regt. Then a severe snow storm came along to impair even further the miserable working conditions. In spite of this by 0830 hours next morning [27 January] the raft was ready and a ramp constructed by a section of 3 Troop 9 Field [Squadron].[48]

What the author of this account does not say is that it was impossible to build that raft without some of the sappers standing waist deep in water almost at freezing point.

That night B Company of the Lincs tried to recover some of their wounded who had been left on the dyke when it had pulled back that morning. Major Ed Brady took a party forward under cover of dark but they hadn't moved more than a hundred yards, he remembered, when the Germans "went right down both sides of us with machine gun fire. I still don't know why they didn't get us, but they didn't."[49] Realizing that any movement would simply cost him more losses, Brady had to abandon the attempt.

Casualty evacuation and treatment was to remain a serious problem throughout the fighting on the Veer. Brady recalled the efforts he made during the night of 26 January to help one of his men:

> One of the fellows had his arm blown off. And they gave us these morphine syrettes ... and of course it's pitch black and you're on the side of the bloody dyke and you couldn't see what you were doing. ... They'd got the blood stopped. We put a tourniquet on the upper part of his arm ... and I knew we had to get him out of there as quick as possible, but he was in terrible pain. ... So I fumble around and my fingers are so frozen ... All you were supposed to do was jab him in the chest and break [the syrette and] squeeze it. Well, I can't tell you whether I ever jabbed him. I knew I jabbed him in the chest with something. ... What a helpless feeling when your fingers are so damn cold that you can't feel a damn thing. You can't see anything and a guy is suffering and you're trying to do something for him. ... But he lived. ... We got him out that night.[50]

Those wounded who could be removed safely were taken to the Regimental Aid Post established on the main land. Here they were stripped of their white snow suits, which were thrown on a pile outside, and treated. As the fighting on the Kapelsche Veer continued, that pile of blood-soaked snow suits was to grow higher, day by day.[51]

By first light at about 7.30 A.M. on Saturday, 27 January 1945, the tired sappers had finally finished their raft. They waved forward Lieutenant Ken Little, who had been waiting patiently with three Shermans of his troop from A Squadron of the South Albertas. Little's driver gently nosed his Sherman down the ramp onto the raft but,

> Unfortunately, the tide had gone down and the approaches to the raft were impossible. Rubble, wood, anything was thrown down to allow the t[an]k to get on the raft. The feat was accomplished but in doing so, the raft buckled in the centre and settled on the bottom of the river. So with some difficulty, the Sherman was backed off and had to wait until the raft could be strengthened and the tide was higher.[52]

The sappers looked at the thing, scratched their heads and reported that there would be a long delay.

The Kapelsche Veer was not a good place to be that cold Saturday. Neither the Argylls nor the Lincs had much luck closing in on the German position, which could only be approached along the dyke tops under enemy observation and fire. The width of the tops, about thirty feet, restricted the number of men that could be used for an attack to platoon size – about twenty to twenty-five men – and German automatic weapons fire soon sent them to cover. What it amounted to was an attack over open ground in platoon strength against an entrenched and reinforced German company generously supplied with machine guns and with plentiful mortar fire on call from the north bank of the river. All the weight of artillery and tactical air (when it was available) was useless; what was needed were flamethrowers or direct fire from tanks at close range. But the Wasps had all bogged down and, knowing the fate of the men who had used them on the first day, nobody wanted to carry the life-buoy flamethrowers. Tanks it would have to be but, as will be seen, the Kapelsche Veer was probably the worst ground in Europe on which to operate armoured vehicles.

During the morning, the Lincs made three separate attempts to take RASP-BERRY but the closest they got was 300 yards and their position was in constant danger of being cut off by Germans infiltrating along the north side of the dyke behind them. On the right the Argylls had farther to go but managed with the help of the Browning .30 calibre machine guns of Stevenson and McSherry's Stuarts to get within a thousand yards of GRAPES before they too were pinned down. Unable to move in any direction the infantry huddled in shallow water-

On the Veer, January 1945

This sketch by an officer of 15 Field shows the forward position of the Lincoln & Welland Regiment looking east toward RASPBERRY and GRAPES, the German strongpoints, whose locations are marked by a pile of smoking rubble. In the background can be seen the church spires of villages on the north side of the Maas. Note the casualties, the artillery FOO with his radio and the tank (lower left corner) positioned well forward to support the infantry. Reproduced from Spencer's *Fifteen Canadian Field Regiment* by permission of 15 Field, RCA)

logged slit trenches hastily scraped in the ground, cold, wet and hungry because it was difficult to get food up to them. It also proved impossible to recover the dead, and the scattered corpses, clad in their white snow suits, lay where they had fallen. The only succour for the men on the island was the occasional issue of service rum, which one veteran of the action remembered as "a very good stimulant for morale and health in this type of weather and operation."[53]

Suffering constant casualties from heavy and accurate German 81 and 120 mm mortar fire, the frustrated infantry called down artillery "stonks" using the Forward Observation Officers (FOOs) from 15 Field Regiment who shared their advanced positions.[54] Lieutenant Bowick's South Alberta troop fired throughout the day, at one point shooting HE (High Explosive) for thirty minutes at the request of the Lincs. The Germans replied by mortaring Bowick's position and his crews were forced to close their hatches. By mid-afternoon three of Bowick's own crew were overcome by carbon monoxide fumes from the Homelite motor in the turret, which they had to keep running to keep their batteries charged, while all of his crews, having spent more than twenty-four hours in their unheated vehicles, were suffering from exposure. At 5 P.M., they were relieved in their tanks by Lieutenant Earle Johnston's troop.[55]

Throughout the day the German mortar fire never let up and the FOOs had a busy time as they tried to locate and bring down fire on the enemy artillery positions and break up persistent enemy attempts to cross the Maas in rubber rafts to reinforce the garrison. The German mortars, well camouflaged and frequently moved, were difficult to pinpoint despite the efforts of 1st Canadian Radar Battery which had recently been created for just such a task.[56] Towards evening, one FOO party on the island decided they had earned the bottle of rum they had thoughtfully brought with them and someone was just reaching for it when a mortar bomb burst on the edge of their trench. After digging dirt out of their eyes, the horrified gunners discovered "that not only had the shell cut off

Gun position, 15 Field Regiment, 1945

For five days, the gunners of 15 Field struggled hour after hour in wet and muddy gun positions to deliver artillery support to their infantry comrades fighting on the Veer. Their fire was directed by Forward Observation Officers on the island itself but all the weight of fire brought down on the defenders seemed to make little difference. (From Spenser's *History of Fifteen Canadian Field Regiment*)

the aerial [of their radio], but it had neatly decapitated the bottle, which was now quite empty."[57] Curses rang out on the Kapelsche Veer.

Conditions, of course, were no better for the Germans, who had to suffer heavier shelling and the attentions of a squadron of Spitfires which strafed the harbour area during the day. Canadian artillery frustrated numerous enemy attempts to reinforce the garrison but some specialists from the engineer and anti-tank companies of *Fallschirmjägerregiment* 17 did succeed in crossing the Maas. Their job was to assist the garrison to defend against tank attack, because the Germans fully expected the Canadians would use armour – the Poles, who were monitoring German radio traffic, passed on the information that the paratroopers on the Veer had been warned to "check their anti-tank weapons."[58]

The weary sappers of 8 and 9 Field Squadrons, RCE, worked all through that Saturday to repair the raft and improve the ramp to the launching site. They were hampered by the fact that the river level was low (the Maas is tidal at this point) and the weather so cold that ice kept forming on the bank. Four amphibious Buffaloes had to be kept in constant motion nearby to prevent it freezing solid as the sappers dragged the damaged end of the raft onto land, jacked it up and began mending the damage caused by Little's tank. This chore was done by midday but work in the afternoon was interrupted by enemy mortar fire that frequently drove the sappers to shelter. Nearby, the crews of Little's three Shermans waited patiently for the sappers to finish their hammering, as until the raft was finished, their tanks were going nowhere.[59]

Concern over the need to get Shermans, with their 75 mm HE weapons, onto the Veer led to Lieutenant Wilfred Kennedy of A Squadron of the South Albertas being ordered at 3 P.M. to take two tanks from his troop over to the island. Kennedy was a good choice for this assignment because, unlike most South Albertas (a regiment raised in the Prairie), he was no stranger to water, boats and islands, having served briefly as an officer in the Royal Canadian Navy before becoming a diesel engineer on an ocean tug working out of Vancouver. Kennedy and his second tank, commanded by Corporal Sidney "Rizzy" Risdale, therefore headed for the "Mad Whore's Dream."

The "Dream" was nominally a Class 18 bridge (a structure able to support eighteen long tons of weight or 40,320 lb.) while, fully loaded for combat, a Sherman weighed nearly thirty-five short tons (70,000 lb.). Even worse, as Kennedy's tank approached the rickety structure, the watching engineers realized to their horror that the extra tracks welded on every available surface for additional protection increased its weight by several tons. On paper it was impossible for a Sherman to cross the "Dream" and onlookers probably closed their eyes as Kennedy's driver, with seatbelt unfastened for a quick exit, eased the tank onto the bridge, which went down under its weight – but held – and then slowly, very slowly, guided the vehicle across the narrow, icy span until it reached the other side. Risdale also got over without mishap and there were now Shermans on the Kapelsche Veer. Their arrival, one Argyll officer remembered, "a considerable achievement in itself, gave the riflemen new heart."[60]

It took Kennedy some time to move along the icy and treacherous dyke top to the forward Argyll position, where he picked up Lieutenant Alan Earp and a small detachment from that battalion's pioneer platoon. Kennedy's job was to protect Earp and three of his men while they cleared the dyke top of mines so that the South Alberta tanks could advance the next morning. It was now about 10.30 P.M. and quite dark as the combined group moved east but they immediately came under fire. Kennedy's tanks were unable to reply because his Sherman, which was in the lead, could not use its weapons for fear of hitting the mine-clearing party, while Risdale behind him could not bring any guns to bear. Earp and one of his men did their best "to cover the two [up ahead] with [the mine] detectors, with small-arms fire." "Seeing this," he remembered, Kennedy let him fire "his .50 calibre [turret] Browning machine gun," and "we blazed away with this and were able to test a fair amount of track before having to withdraw, quite pleased with what we were able to accomplish."[61]

The two tanks backed up slowly to the forward Argyll position, followed by Earp's men. When it appeared they were out of harm's way, Kennedy raised his hatch, Earp recalled, "thanked us for our help and made us a present of the Browning."[62] Unfortunately, as Kennedy "was standing in the turret taking down our names, he himself was hit and the tank withdrew." For Earp and his men, the "exhilaration of what had seemed a successful skirmish was quickly dissipated" but they proudly bore the Browning on their jeep for the duration of the war. Kennedy had been shot through the head but the wound was so clean his crew were "at first doubtful as whether he was actually hit" or had simply fainted.[63] He was evacuated with great difficulty but died sixteen hours later.

At about the same time that Earp and Kennedy were clearing the dyke on the right, the engineers managed to raft Lieutenant Ken Little's three tanks across on the left or western end of the Veer. Little went first and his journey – by raft, in a bitter winter night under a fall of snow, up a small canal, and then into the Oude Maasje and across to the island – was an epic:

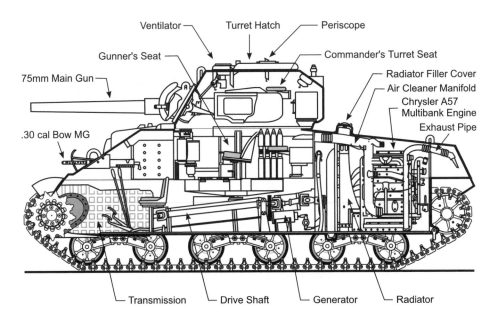

The Sherman V, workhorse of the South Alberta Regiment, 1945

Thanks to the almost herculean efforts of the sappers, the South Albertas were able to get eight of these tanks onto the island by rafts or bridges. Armed with a 75 mm gun and two .30 calibre machine guns, they provided the direct fire support necessary to blast the defenders out of their positions. (Drawing by Chris Johnson, courtesy of the artist)

The weather was very cold and the ice floes began to freeze together, there being a solid mass across the water at the time. After a long struggle with the shifting tide and the monstrous ramp the tank was loaded. The far side of the canal [actually the Oude Maasje] 450' away could not be seen for the falling snow. The four petters [raft engines] roared at full throttle and the raft moved slowly away from the shore with an acre of icepack frozen to it. All the crew chopped, pushed and pulled at the thick blocks of ice jammed between the frail pontoons and piling up around the propellers. Each time a L.V.T. passed it was hailed to come and circle the raft thus loosening up the pack. About 10 to 15 feet was gained each time. Then perhaps the tide would shift and loosen the pack and a few more feet would be gained, all the while the 4 petters roaring at top speed and the crew fighting the ice with boathooks and oars. Then an L.V.T ran into the raft in the darkness and snow and shifted one pontoon 3 feet under the raft and tank. Miraculously it held together though everyone had reconciled themselves to an icy grave. By turning the propellers alternately to the left and right a few more feet were gained against the ice now piling up against the far bank. No one thought it even remotely possible to reach the far bank [the Kapelsche Veer] and unload the tank, it was just a matter of time before a pontoon would give in to the relentless pressure of the ice and sink the whole issue. Three hours from the far shore the raft was close enough so that a passing L.V.T could be hooked on, on the shore and the raft pulled up so the tank could be disembarked through 3 feet of packed ice. It wasn't possible, the crew nearly fainted. For once seeing was not believing.[64]

Having got Little over, the sappers then spent the rest of the night bringing over his other two tanks. With Shermans available on both flanks there was now hope that the business could be finished on the following day.[65]

At about 9 A.M., on Sunday, 28 January 1945, the Argylls and Lincs renewed the attack. On the left, Little led his three Shermans east along the dyke but the temperature had risen and, instead of ice, thick glutinous mud now became the obstacle to movement. When Little's second tank bogged badly, blocking the third vehicle behind it, he ordered them to remain where they were and support him with fire as he moved forward with the Lincs against RASP-BERRY. On the right, Lieutenant Ernest Hill, who had come up to replace Kennedy, advanced with his two Shermans and two Stuarts. As they inched their way forward along the treacherous dyke tops Little and Hill laid down heavy speculative fire on possible enemy positions. By 9.40, Hill was almost at GRAPES but heavy automatic weapons fire and mortaring had driven the Argylls to ground behind him and he had no infantry support. As his ammunition was running low, he reluctantly backed up to where the infantry were taking cover, intending to resupply and start forward again. On the left, Little had a similar experience; he came close to RASPBERRY but the infantry, which had been forced by German fire to go to ground behind him, became disorganized when their officers were killed or wounded. Despite heavy Canadian artillery fire brought down on the north bank of the river, German mortar bombs continued to fall thick and heavy along the dyke tops. At this point the infantry's communications failed on both flanks and operations came to a halt in the late morning until the flat feet could get themselves sorted out.[66]

When this was done, they started back along the dykes at about 2 P.M. On the right, the Argylls managed to get a Wasp on top of the dyke and it moved forward but due to some confusion, "instead of stopping at the inf[antry] pos[itio]n the driver speeded up and made for the objective at GRAPES."[67] Hill had been having trouble communicating with his other crews and the infantry by radio and had left his tank to work on foot. Without hesitation his gunner, Trooper Albert Broadbent, assumed command of Hill's vehicles and immediately moved them up the dyke to provide covering fire for this brave but unplanned assault by the Wasp crew. The Wasp bogged in the mud short of GRAPES but managed to get off a few shots with its flamethrower – one onlooker later reported with awe that he saw "four Germans flamed in a slit trench," who, "after they had beaten out the flames, continued to fight until they were killed."[68] A very stalwart bunch, these paratroopers, but the advancing Argylls managed to grab nine prisoners and by late afternoon were in possession of GRAPES.[69]

Trooper Broadbent made this success possible and his actions came as a surprise, for nobody thought Albert Broadbent capable of commanding a tank, let alone a troop of four tanks engaged in one of the worst battles the South Alberta Regiment had yet experienced. Corporal John Galipeau, a member of Broadbent's troop, knew the man as well as anybody:

> He was one of those people who never seem to be concerned about his appearance. He always looked rumpled even in a uniform which he appeared to have pressed with a waffle iron. He was quiet and was quite happy to remain in the background. Whereas some of the glamour boys would be surrounded with friends, Albert had only one or two that he palled around with. He was friends with everybody in the troop but not that talkative. He would voice an opinion in a group discussion but he was never argumentative. He carried out orders without complaint and did his job well but he never showed any signs of being a leader.[70]

Albert Broadbent became a leader on the Kapelsche Veer when he took over command of the tanks on the right after Hill was evacuated with frostbitten feet. There were more senior men in the troop but Broadbent's tank was in the lead and had the only working radio.

Broadbent manoeuvred his tank into "position in a small bend in the dyke from where it could depress its guns sufficiently to rake the north slope of the dyke with m.g. fire."[71] That sector of the defences was held by a platoon of *Fallschirmjägerregiment* 17, about twenty-five strong, under the command of *Stabsfeldwebel* (Sergeant Major) Heinrich Fischer. Fischer, a veteran of combat in Russia and Italy and "an old soldier who described himself as a fox," warned his men not to move or expose themselves. Unfortunately, most of his paratroopers

The face of the enemy

Although the Allies were poised on the borders of Germany, the German soldier remained a tough and skilled opponent who was prepared to fight desperately in defence of his homeland. On the Kapelsche Veer, a single company of German paratroopers resisted the efforts of two Canadian infantry battalions and an armoured regiment, supported by 300 pieces of artillery, to get them out of their defences. (Author's collection)

were "betrayed by their own carelessness" and attempted to shift at some point during the day only to be "picked off one by one" by what Fischer described as "sniper accuracy." Broadbent was no stranger to this kind of shooting – it was the same as potting gophers with a .22 calibre rifle near his home town of Leedale, Alberta – and hunting was in his blood for Albert Broadbent was a warrior of the Cree people. He did the spotting from his turret but most of the shooting was done by Trooper C.D. "Slim" Tilsley, an artistic man who liked to decorate the white interior of his Sherman with cartoons when he had a spare moment.[72] At one point Fischer actually caught a fleeting glimpse of Broadbent "searching the ground with binoculars but the slightest attempt to leave a slit trench brought down an immediate burst of m.g. fire."[73] The German estimated that Broadbent and Tilsley killed seventeen of his men and wounded five. Despite these losses, Fischer was so filled with "a soldier's admiration of a good job well done" that, at his prisoner of war interrogation, he felt compelled to single out for praise the unknown (to him) Canadian tank commander who had wiped out his platoon – his testimonial resulted in Broadbent receiving the Distinguished Conduct Medal.

Broadbent's accurate fire kept the Germans down and permitted the Argylls to move along the dyke and get possession of GRAPES. Things did not go so well on the left, as Little had only his own Sherman to support the Lincs' attack on RASPBERRY. However, he could see the tanks on the right working west along the dyke and it looked like this thing would shortly be over. With Broadbent's help, the Lincs secured RASPBERRY by mid-afternoon but not very securely, because the Germans kept popping up in the rear of the infantry from positions they had constructed in the dyke. This caused such confusion that, at 4 P.M., the infantry fell back a few hundred yards to regroup, leaving Little by himself. He remained in his position, trying to support the Argylls whom he could see fighting around GRAPES but was forced to back down the dyke to re-ammunition. As his driver's vision to the rear was extremely limited, Little opened his hatch to guide the man and was killed instantly when a German sniper shot him in the head.[74]

By the last light on 28 January the situation appeared to be good, if some-what uncertain. The Argylls had GRAPES, although they were still having trouble clearing the area around the house, which was a warren of trenches and tunnels. On the left the Lincs had secured RASPBERRY but were experiencing problems with German infiltration into their rear. To prevent this happening, the 8th Polish Infantry Battalion and 41 Royal Marine Commando were later moved onto the island west of the Lincoln position.[75] The Lincs also had no tank support as, shortly after Little's crew brought his body back to where the other tanks were stuck, they too bogged in the mud, blocking the dyke top to vehicle traffic.[76]

After three days Major General Chris Vokes was anxious to finish the job. The heavy fighting on the Kapelsche Veer, coming at a quiet time in the war af-ter the German offensive in the Ardennes had nearly ended but before the Allied offensives into Germany had begun, attracted considerable media attention. When the name of the island began to crop up in the nightly Wehrmacht high command communiqués broadcast from Berlin as a shining example of the ob-stinacy of the German soldier defending his *Vaterland,* war correspondents de-scended on 4th Canadian Armoured Division like crows flapping down on road kill.[77] This attention was not welcome as Vokes was involved in a slugging match over which he really had no control and there was little he could do except to urge subordinates to greater efforts.

The general's tension became apparent when Lieutenant David Wiens from the divisional intelligence staff was called forward to interrogate the prisoners captured that afternoon. When Wiens got up to the front, he found four Ger-mans in the yard of a tavern where Vokes "had ordered them stripped to their shorts and had the guard pour pails of ice-cold water over them, apparently in an attempt to soften them up."[78] Wiens, an experienced interrogator, "could have told him, that procedure had proved counter-productive" when dealing with prisoners from elite units and, although the paratroopers "were near collapse, teeth chattering and bodies turning blue," they were not talking.

Wiens tried a more subtle approach:

> I don't know what Vokes expected of me but, against his objections, I had one of the prisoners brought inside, gave him a blanket and a shot of schnapps to warm him up and only then attempted to get him to talk. Some interrogation – with the General shouting questions and hurling curses at the man. Vokes was really in a rage at his attack being stalled for so long, and his impatience did not make my job any easier. It may have been the alcohol or my promise that the sooner he talked the sooner would his pals outside be allowed to get warm that broke his silence. Eventually I was able to get enough details on the strengths and locations of the German defences to satisfy the General. The prisoners were then given back their uniforms and taken back to the PW [Prisoner of War] cage.[79]

Wiens was disgusted with Vokes's behaviour, not so much by his treatment of the prisoners because war is a tough business, but by the man's lack of self-control.

That night *Fallschirmjägerregiment* 17 gave everyone an object lesson in toughness. Although the Lincs and the Argylls were on GRAPES and RASPBERRY, the Germans were still present in strength, hiding in their extensive network of tunnels. The paratroopers waited until dark when the South Alberta tanks would be unable to provide accurate fire support and then, at 10 P.M., emerged, beside and behind the Canadian positions, to launch a vicious surprise counterattack that forced the two units to withdraw about five hundred yards back down the dyke on their respective sides of the harbour. The hard-won gains of the day were lost and the Germans still owned the Veer.[80]

During the bitterly cold night of 28 January 1945, fresh crews from C Squadron of the South Albertas relieved the A Squadron men who had been fighting for the last forty-eight hours. Lieutenant Orlando Bodley replaced Lieutenant Earle Johnston's men at the direct fire support position, code-named ANNE; Lieutenant Ken Wigg's crews took over from Albert Broadbent's crews on the right; and Sergeant Arthur "Duke" Sands and fresh men took over the vehicles on the left. The two Stuart crews from Recce Troop were also relieved at the same time.[81]

Corporal Jake Wiebe of C Squadron remembered how replacements were found for the crews on the island:

We were all sitting around and we heard that there were some tanks on the island. The sergeant-major came around and said: "We want four volunteers for a tank." I asked my crew but none of them were foolish enough to volunteer and I certainly didn't volunteer. The sergeant-major could have said, "You, you and you" but he did the right thing and said, "Boys, draw straws." I was unlucky and I drew a short straw and two of my crew drew short and, of course, this tank needed five men so they got two from another crew.[82]

Trooper Art Baker, one of Broadbent's men, was sent back along the dyke to guide the relief crews up to the tanks. Baker was "half asleep and doddling along and they were yelling and hollering at me to get down and, all of a sudden, 'shewww, shewww' – there were sniper rounds going by my head and I got down fast."[83] When Wiebe got into the Sherman he was to take over, he found "four inches of ice inside it" – his comment: "What a place to die."[84]

Trooper Ed Hyatt was with the crews that relieved Johnston's men at ANNE. A few minutes after they took over, Hyatt got a funny feeling:

We were standing at the back of the tank and we had the Homelite going to keep the batteries charged up and suddenly I said to the fellows "Duck" and we jumped into the canal and a mortar shell hit right where we had been standing. I don't know why I said "duck." Fortunately for us it was so cold that the canal was frozen and we didn't get wet.[85]

A similar procedure took place with the infantry companies and artillery FOOs on the island – it was impossible to keep men in the waterlogged, shallow trenches, exposed to constant shelling and sniping for more than twenty-four hours and, as it was, many had to be evacuated with frostbite. Corporal Ken Hippel was with a Lincoln and Welland Regiment reinforcement party, most of whom had no combat experience, sent onto the island:

So we found our way up there, nobody volunteered to show us the way: "just keep going, you'll find it." So we got up there and I reported to [Major Jim Swayze] and told him I had the reinforcements for C Company. "Well," he says, "things have been bad. Take them out there and you'll find some slit trenches and put them in and hold that section up there … So there's six inches of snow on the ground and colder than hell. So we get up there. We got one blanket. So we get in the slit trenches … But then it was real hell, because of the cold, and all those guys with no battle experience. The only time you could be fed was at night. In the day time, if you stuck your head out, it was "Goodbye, Charlie."[86]

The Kapelsche Veer was a battle in which personal leadership was important at the lower level but it was hard for junior officers and NCOs to demonstrate enthusiasm for such an apparently senseless operation. A platoon commander who fought on the island put it this way: "My men came to me and said they were cold and I gave them clothes, they said they were hungry and I tried to give them food, they told me they were scared and I told them we were all scared."[87]

Dawn on Monday, 29 January 1945, revealed dyke tops strewn with the bodies of Canadian and German dead – to Lieutenant Ken Wigg of the South Albertas the island "looked like a 1914-1918 battlefield."[88] Trooper Joe Strathearn, a gunner in one of Sands's crews had a similar reaction: "The thing I remember most were the bodies. We even ran over German and Canadian bodies, what can you do?"[89] One Argyll private never forgot the terrible sight of the Veer covered with

Men and parts of men, in muddy uniforms of grey, blue-grey, and khaki … scattered across the face of the rising ground that had been fought for so bitterly and so long. Men with rifles still clutched in claw-like frozen hands that refused to let them go; men with bucket helmets; men with round helmets and men with neither; men with white, bare feet that told of the desperation of winter warfare and men frozen face-down in the mud where they had fallen.[90]

At first light, the tempo of the German mortar fire from the north bank, which had been intermittent through the night, began to pick up. The Canadian artillery responded and the daily duel between the two banks of the Maas got under way again. The FOOs of 15 Field, who shared the wretched conditions on the dykes with the infantry, directed the fire and, conscious "of the desperate conditions in the forward areas," the 25-pdr. detachments, struggling in wet, muddy gun pits, "worked their hearts out striving to get accurate fire away at top

Tank crew, South Alberta Regiment, 1945

For five days the men of the South Albertas did their best to support their infantry comrades on the Veer, fighting in what was possibly the worst tank country in Europe. This photograph, taken a few weeks after the battle ended, shows some of the tankers who fought on the island. From left to right: Trooper Elmer Stewart, Corporal Lyle Levers, and Troopers Cliff Allen and Dave Clendenning. (Courtesy, Cliff Allen)

speed."[91] Before the operation was over, 15 Field would fire 14,000 rounds, twice its original planned allotment; the other field, medium and heavy units, the twenty-four 4.2 inch mortars of the mortar support group and the tank guns, of not only the South Albertas but also the British Columbia Regiment, expended a similar rate of ammunition. Although tactical aircraft were available from 84 Group, RAF, they could not be used against the island for fear of hitting friendly troops, so close were the positions of the opposing forces, and were directed instead to targets on the north bank of the Maas.

The heavy artillery bombardment didn't seem to have had any effect when the attack was resumed at 7 A.M. German mortar fire and machine-gun fire was as heavy and accurate as ever and the infantry were soon forced to ground. By this time, the snow on the Veer had disappeared, melted by the sun as 29 January proved to be a warmer day and churned by the constant explosions, and the infantry realized that their white snow suits, far from providing camouflage, made them obvious targets against the grey-brown earth of the dyke tops. The attack got nowhere because on both flanks the South Albertas had trouble with the viscous mud caused by the day's thaw. Sergeant Sands's tank, the only mobile Sherman of the three on the left, bogged as it moved forward leaving the Lincoln and Welland Regiment without armour support. On the right, one of the Stuarts got badly stuck in a position that blocked all vehicle traffic behind Wigg's two Shermans. Wigg tried five times without luck to push it and even fired HE at it to try and dislodge it, but that Stuart would not budge. Orders therefore went out to the sappers to bring a bulldozer over the "Dream" and construct a detour around it, a difficult job that took them nearly eighteen hours to complete.[92]

The Argylls got going again in the late morning. By 12.45 P.M., with the help of fire from Wigg's two Shermans, they had retaken GRAPES but could not reach RASPBERRY – although they made a number of attempts throughout the day – due to the perpetual problem of German machine gun fire pinning the infantry down. For their part, the Lincs were unable to approach from the left because none of Sands's tanks were moving and the best he could do was to render long-range fire support. The good news was that a prisoner reported that only seventy paratroopers – half starved and drinking melted snow because they could not get water – were still alive and twenty of these were wounded. Not much happened during the rest of the day because bogged tanks hampered operations on both flanks.[93]

By last light on 29 January the German-controlled part of the island had been compressed to the few hundred square yards around the wreckage of the house at RASPBERRY and the west side of the harbour. But the paratroopers were still obstinately resisting despite the fact that Bodley's four tanks had fired at them all afternoon while two South Alberta Crusader AA tanks, which had come up under the command of Lieutenant Jack Summers of Recce Troop, had laced their positions with 20 mm Oerlikon fire. This was in addition to the direct support fire from Wigg's and Sands's tanks on the island and the massive indirect fire support provided by the British Columbia Regiment's Shermans and the heavy, medium and field regiments that could be brought down without hitting friendly troops. So ferocious and close was the artillery fire poured onto the German positions in the centre of the Veer that the Lincs complained their trenches were being hit and hastily deployed recognition panels.[94]

That night was a busy one. On the right the engineers managed to finish the detour around the Stuart while on the left a fourth Sherman under Sergeant

Argyll forward position on the Veer, January 1945

This position of C Company of the Argylls is typical of the shallow trenches the infantry had to scrape as they advanced, almost foot by foot, over a period of five days, toward the central German position. (Courtesy, Argyll & Sutherland Highlanders of Canada)

William McKie was rafted over to join Sands. McKie was supposed to support a mine-clearing operation by the Lincs on the dyke but was unable to reach the island in time so Sands, who had managed to get his tank unstuck after hours of labour, went forward in his place. He had only moved a few feet when he again fell victim to the mud and, despite every effort, was unable to move. The Germans were also active and boats were seen crossing the Maas, either reinforcing or withdrawing the garrison on the island, which brought calls for artillery fire to prevent the movement. On the right Wigg's two crews made foot patrols from GRAPES towards RASPBERRY to recce the route they planned to use in the morning.[95]

The Argylls were determined to make an attempt at RASPBERRY under the cover of darkness. At about 1 A.M., Lieutenant Norman Perkins's 15 Platoon of C Company left their slit trenches and crawled as quietly as possible through "a churned ruin of bricks, mud and melted snow" toward the German strongpoint. Private Robert Mason remembered the attack as being "a nightmare of close-in hide and seek, bursting grenades, flashing 'Verey lights' and machine-gun fire" that lasted about an hour. Perkins and Mason were the only two men to reach the objective and crawled into one room of the cellar of RASPBERRY only to find that there were Germans in an adjoining room. In the resulting firefight, one German was killed but the two Argylls withdrew when the remainder of their platoon "found it impossible to get through the German machine-gun fire covering the house."[96] Private Sidney Webb of the Argylls recalled that, when Mason returned, he had an amazing sight to show his comrades: "a bullet lodged right in his chest, it was half in and half out."[97] The projectile had gone through Mason's tunic and shirt and "was just sitting there" but Mason was not evacuated as a casualty – "they just put a patch on it."

At first light on Tuesday, 30 January 1945, Wigg's two Shermans at GRAPES opened fire on the ruins of the house at RASPBERRY. A problem immediately became apparent: the Browning machine guns of these tanks, which Kennedy had originally brought over to the island three days before, had fired so much that both the original and replacement barrels were worn smooth and had neither range nor accuracy.[98]

Operations were delayed until new weapons could be rushed over to the Veer and it was not until 11.15 A.M. that the Argylls began to move west along the 100 yards of dyke that separated GRAPES from RASPBERRY, supported closely by Wigg's tanks and every weapon that could be brought to bear. Despite the terrific covering fire, the infantry were again forced to ground by German automatic weapons and, once they were stationary, mortared from the north bank of the river. The Argylls pulled back but at 3 P.M. gave it another try. Again they were beaten back and this time they had to leave some of their wounded. The paratroopers may have been tough opponents but they fought a clean war – at 3:30 they held their fire while stretcher parties went out under the Red Cross flag to pick up the men on the dyke. That done, everyone opened up again.[99]

In the late afternoon the Argylls made a third attempt to cross those one hundred terrible yards. By this time Major Bert Coffin, the commanding officer of the South Albertas, had moved onto the island and was controlling the tank battle from the Argylls' command post on the right. Corporal Wiebe remembered Coffin coming up to his tank and saying, "Let's get this damn show over, take this place" and "then he buggered off – I would have done the same in his place."[100] Coffin reinforced Wigg with two more Shermans, which made it over the shaky "Dream" and around the perilous detour by the bogged Stuart, and Wigg had four tanks in column when the Argylls pushed west at 4.30 P.M. Progress was measured almost in inches and the German fire was heavy, but

Wigg's Shermans blanketed the entire area with HE and .30 calibre until the paratroopers called down smoke from the north bank which obscured the crews' vision. The Argylls got into RASPBERRY, however, which was "a mass of rubble," and "started to dig into the ruins for the tunnel that was known to be there."[101] They couldn't find it so threw demolition charges into every hole they could see.[102]

Now all that remained was to move along a short stretch of dyke to the west and join up with the Lincs. That unit had been unable to take a greater part in the fighting of the day because three of Sands's four Shermans on their side of the island were stuck in the mud and the fourth could not get around them. As the infantry knew well by now, any attempt to advance along those awful dyke tops without tank support was doomed to failure so the final push would have to be made by the Argylls moving west from RASPBERRY. Sands's four tanks did what they could to support the Argylls with fire. Trooper Strathearn remembered shooting off a lot of HE but his crew "couldn't get our guns low enough." There was no enemy artillery but "the odd bazooka and lots of rifle fire" and Corporal Walter Fengler, Strathearn's crew commander "couldn't stick his head out, he had the two flaps [of the turret hatch] open and there were bullets zinging off them."[103]

An Argyll platoon started out toward the Lincs but immediately came under heavy mortar and machine-gun fire from the north bank. Wigg opened fire across the river but "it was impossible to pinpoint the German positions."[104] The Argylls fell back to RASPBERRY and there was a delay while the tanks re-ammunitioned from a supply brought forward by the one mobile Stuart. At about 4.30 P.M., just as the light was beginning to fail, another attempt was made with Corporal Mike Nichol's Sherman going in front of the infantry while the other tanks covered him from their positions. Nichol stopped in front of a large crater on the dyke and at that moment was hit by a Panzerfaust. The South Alberta War Diarist recorded the fate of the crew:

> This t[an]k was the only one in the Regt that was fitted with the new all-round vision cupola and because of this the turret cupola flaps were down [i.e. the turret was "buttoned up"]. When the projectile hit it wounded the co-driver Tpr LaPrade, L, M45749, and set his compartment on fire. The driver Tpr Noble G.W., M45582, was quick to grab an extinguisher and put the fire out. He leapt out of his driver's hatch to find that the [turret] crew were unable to lift [open] their hatch. He pulled it open allowing the boys to bail out and upon returning to the front of the t[an]k, found Tpr LaPrade

German MG 42 machine gun in action

The main weapon of the German defenders on the Veer, the MG 42 (called the Spandau or "zipper" by Allied troops) could fire 1,000 rounds per minute and made it impossible for the Canadian infantry to move on the dyke tops without tank support. (Author's collection)

struggling to get out of his compartment. He jumped up on the hull and started to pull LaPrade out when a burst of MG fire cut LaPrade's head off. Noble was also hit in the head, staggered and fell on the NORTH side of the dyke.[105]

"No further attempts," noted the South Alberta War Diarist, "were made to go forward until the following day."

Things were quieter that night. There being concern that the Germans might use Nichol's knocked-out tank as a pillbox, Sergeant George Penney on the left, who had managed to get himself unstuck, moved his Sherman within sixty yards of it and stayed there without infantry protection throughout the hours of darkness, using his Brownings to beat off a couple of German attempts to enter the vehicle. The tank crews on the Veer remained on alert throughout the night, shivering in the unheated interiors of their vehicles. In Trooper Cliff Allen's tank, the cold wasn't the only problem. For twenty-four hours, all the crew had eaten were "boiled eggs and hard tack and this made quite an odour in the tank and everybody blamed everybody else."[106]

Shortly after dawn on Wednesday, 31 January 1945, Lieutenant Robert Crawford of the South Albertas, who had brought over fresh crews to replace Wigg's men, supported the Argylls as they moved over the last few hundred yards and joined up with the Lincoln and Welland Regiment at about 9 A.M. There was no sign of the Germans except a few dazed prisoners and the occasional mortar bomb from the north bank. Most of the garrison had been evacuated during the previous night – and for that everyone was truly thankful.[107]

The men knew it was over for sure when reporters were escorted onto the island to talk to real frontline soldiers. By this time in the war, these same soldiers had learned that you had to be careful with the press because they were prone to sensationalize things. The best way to handle them was to be as reticent as possible – but to make sure they got your name and home town right – lest they exaggerate some chance remark into a heroic feat that your buddies would never let you forget. Lieutenant Earp of the Argylls was somewhat startled when he read the account of his mine-clearing operation published in the *Toronto Star*. "Earp was with three pioneers when the Germans opened fire. He reached for his Sten but it jammed, so he pulled out a revolver. When it jammed also, he climbed into the nearest tank, got a machine gun and fired 1,000 rounds which finally dispersed the enemy."[108]

Troopers Cliff Allen and Elmer Stewart of the South Albertas got it just right. When a reporter questioned them about the fight, with "the tankmen boldly going on top of the dyke, silhouetted against the sky," to get possession of GRAPES they let an Argyll sergeant do the initial running.[109] "A Jerry with a bazooka could have nailed them, but they came up here," he enthused, "they've been wonderful those guys in the tanks." By the time the reporter got around to Allen, he didn't have to add much but only modestly ventured: "We sort of gave them a little help, I guess." Not that the boys didn't like some press attention. Corporal Wiebe and his co-driver had their hatches open when a reporter approached to talk to them. The turret crew, who had their hatch closed, were unaware of what was going on and when the drivers' picture later appeared in the papers, they were annoyed with Wiebe for not alerting them to the photo opportunity.[110]

A light rain began to fall during the afternoon, which was spent removing the dead from the island. The South Alberta war diarist noted somewhat sardonically that, although the "cold and exposure had very bad effects," the "freezing of the dead was beneficial in the removal of them."[111] It was a grim business; Private Donald Stark of the Argylls remembered stacking the corpses in a truck "like they were pieces of wood – you looked at it and you just walked away."[112] There were so many Canadian dead that they were buried in a single mass grave dug by an engineer bulldozer following a service presided over by the chaplains of all the units involved in the operation. In later years most of the Canadians who fell at the Kapelsche Veer were transferred to individual graves at the Commonwealth War Graves Commission cemetery at Holten.[113]

Casualties had been heavy on both sides. When 10 Brigade headquarters asked for a German body count, "the estimated figure submitted by all units concerned was some 150" but this was later revised downward to 64 paratroopers killed and wounded, and 34 taken prisoner, although some of the German wounded had been earlier evacuated.[114] The actual number of Germans killed on the island may have been higher as, during the fighting, the paratroopers, having no place to bury their dead, had simply dumped them in the Maas.[115] Plocher, the commander of *Fallschirmjägerdivision* 6, later estimated that "to hold this isolated bridge-head" from mid-December to 31 January cost him "between 300 to 400 serious casualties, while another 100 men suffered severely from second-degree frost bite."[116] On the Canadian side, the Lincoln and Welland Regiment lost 89 officers and men killed and 143 wounded; the Argylls lost 15 dead and 35 wounded and the South Alberta Regiment 4 dead and 5 wounded for a brigade total of 291 casualties. When this figure is added to the 231 casualties incurred by the Poles and Royal Marines in the previous attempts to take the Veer, the total cost to get possession of what the Canadian Army historian, quoting Shakespeare, called "a little patch of ground" that "hath in it no profit but the name," was 522 killed or wounded.[117]

General Harry Crerar, the commander of First Canadian Army, complimented "all ranks on a difficult task well done" but nobody in 10 Brigade was in the mood for cheering.[118] Jefferson submitted a post-battle report which stated that the initial assault had no chance of taking the Germans by surprise, the extravagant use of smoke was almost useless, and the operation should have been "conducted at a very slow pace" with tank support from the outset.[119] Vokes was forced to agree with these criticisms of his own plan but defended the use of the ill-fated waterborne force, which he felt would have succeeded if the wind had not shifted the smoke screen, a full moon on the night before the attack had made preparations visible to the Germans, and there had not been "severe icing conditions."[120] Since all of these factors were observable and thus predictable before the initial assault went in, the Lincoln and Welland historian has the matter entirely right when he concludes that "the tactics of the first day were the result of some very serious misconceptions which developed from an increasingly urgent need to capture a stubborn German stronghold of questionable military value." The result was a tragedy as "the initial tactics employed were inappropriately based on surprise and speed, rather than the less spectacular, though tested principles which eventually led to the island's capture after five long days."[121]

The Lincoln and Welland Regiment, which had borne the brunt of the fighting, took a long time to recover from the Veer. As Major James Swayze, their commanding officer during the battle, commented, it "was a turning point in that we had so many casualties. It was a different Regiment afterwards."[122] Vokes relieved Swayze of command at the end of the action and, on 1 February 1945, visited the unit and spoke to its surviving officers (sixteen having been killed, wounded or injured during the five days the battle lasted). As one recalled, the

general was not complimentary about the unit's performance on the Kapelsche Veer but it was also clear from his words that Vokes, a veteran of Italy, "had never spent five days on the top of a dyke."[123] Swayze, however, received a personal note of congratulations from Crocker and was assigned to head the 4th Division armoured training school.

The Lincs were not the only soldiers in 4th Division dissatisfied with their commanding general as Vokes's handling of the operation caused bad feelings throughout his formation. His quartermaster, Lieutenant Colonel John Proctor, who had faithfully served three previous divisional commanders, was so disgusted that he went to Lieutenant General Guy Simonds, the commander of 2nd Canadian Corps, and asked for a transfer to get away from Vokes, saying "I have backed him up but I can't serve him any more."[124] Proctor was transferred and promoted. Jefferson of 10 Brigade was also very upset – Lieutenant Colonel Gordon Wotherspoon, the commanding officer of the South Albertas, complained that after the Veer Jefferson

The face of the Kapelsche Veer

"I was that which others did not want to be. I went where others failed to go, and did what others failed to do ... I am a soldier." Private Carl Montage of the Argylls and Sutherland Highlanders leans against a South Alberta tank on 31 January 1945, the day it was all over. (Courtesy, Argyll and Sutherland Highlanders of Canada)

Gone to perish on the polder, 1945

This cartoon by Private J.W. Mackay of the Lincoln and Welland Regiment, attached to the regimental war diary for February 1945, sums up the lower ranks' view of the Veer battle — lacking the wisdom of their generals, they could see no purpose to the business.

always tried to keep as far away from Vokes as possible and often pitched tents beside Wotherspoon's own headquarters, which "was a bloody nuisance."[125]

To the men who fought on that wretched little island, Operation ELEPHANT always remained an enigma. Lieutenant Gordon Irving of the South Albertas recalled that the "way we understood it is that someone said that we want everything clear to the other side of the Maas River and those guys are on this side and we want them out."[126] What disturbed Private Robert Mason of the Argylls (who would receive the Military Medal for his part in the action) was the belief that the war "wasn't all over with yet and that this would happen again and again."[127] On the Kapelsche Veer, Mason felt, men had been killed "in a terrible way ...... yet how much more horrible if possibly they had died for nothing." Why so many lives were apparently wasted for such a useless piece of real estate was a complete mystery to the men of 10 Canadian Infantry Brigade who could not fathom the motives of their senior officers. "If only we had the wisdom of our generals," Corporal Jake Wiebe of the South Albertas remembered his comrades saying after the Veer battle had ended, "if only we had the wisdom of our generals."[128]

The Kapelsche Veer Today

To visit the Kapelsche Veer, from Amsterdam take Motorway A-2 to 's-Hertogenbosch and A-59 to Waspik; from Antwerp take Motorways A-1, A-58, A-27 and A-59 to the same destination. Follow the main street out of Waspik east in the direction of Waalwijk. About a mile and a half out of Waspik, turn left or north on a small side road marked with a ferry sign which will bring you onto the island by way of a small postwar bridge over the Oude Maasje. As soon as you reach the Veer, the road will make a turn to the left and at that point you will see a number of plaques commemorating the action placed by Polish and Canadian units. Park the car close by and climb on top of the dyke behind the plaques and you will be very close to the ferry harbour. Today there are no people on the Veer and there are no buildings – GRAPES and RASPBERRY were not rebuilt although parts of their foundations can still be seen.

You are now standing right in the middle of what was the German position in January 1945 and two aspects of the Veer will be clearly evident. The first is the fine field of fire in all directions – the distant ground around the island is dead flat, except from some nearby postwar tree plantations, and is only occasionally relieved by the church spires of villages on both sides of the Maas while the immediate ground, the dyke tops of the Veer, offers no cover for troops approaching this position.

The Kapelsche Veer today
This photograph shows the island today. Note the high, steeply sloped sides of the dyke. Cows now occupy the Veer and they are welcome to it. (Photograph by Dianne Graves)

The second thing that will strike you is that the Kapelsche Veer is one soggy piece of real estate. When the author visited it in April 1997, during the worst drought in Europe in nearly half a century, the dyke tops were wet, black and soft. If you go to the Veer, you would be well advised to take rubber boots with you, no matter what the time of year or state of weather.

Except that the present garrison is composed of grazing cows from nearby farms, very little on the island has changed since the war. It does not take much imagination to stand on the dyke top and visualize this midden in the winter days of late January 1945, shrouded in thick, oily chemical smoke and dotted with the mushrooms of explosions. If you pause there long enough you will hear the whine and wail of artillery shells and the buzzing sounds of mortar bombs descending, the tap-tap-tap of the Brens and the ripping noise of German MG 42 machine guns responding, the clatter of tracks and the gunning of powerful engines as tanks push through the mud … and the shouts, the screams and the moans.

The Kapelsche Veer is a miserable place. Leave it, go somewhere, have a good lunch, and forget it – but never forget the young men who fought and died there in January 1945.

Orders of Battle and Strengths, Opposing Forces, Ticonderoga, 8 July 1758

BRITISH FORCES

Commanding General:	Major General James Abercromby
Second in Command:	Brigadier General Thomas Gage*
Naval and Flotilla Commander:	Captain Joshua Loring, RN

ARMY STAFF

Aides to General Abercromby:	Captain James Abercrombie, 42nd Foot
	Captain James Delancey, 60th Foot
	Captain James Cunningham, 45th Foot
Brigade Majors:	Captain John Spital, 47th Foot
	Captain Alexander Monypenny, 55th Foot
Commander, Royal Artillery:	Captain Thomas Ord, RA
Commander, Royal Engineers:	Lieutenant Matthew Clerk, 27th Foot+
Deputy Quarter Master General:	Lieutenant Colonel John Bradstreet, 60th Foot
Assistant Deputy Quarter Master Generals:	Captain Gabriel Christie, 46th Foot
	Ensign George Coventry, 55th Foot
Commissary of Stores:	Mr. Washington
Commissary of Provisions:	Mr. Lyme
Provost Marshal:	Sergeant William Martin, 44th Foot
Chief Surgeon:	Dr. John Munro
Chaplain:	Reverend John Ogilvie, 60th Foot

BRITISH REGULARS (est. 6,261 all ranks)

Brigaded Grenadier Companies:	Lieutenant Colonel Frederick Haldimand,* 60th Foot
Brigaded Light Infantry Picquets & Marksmen:	Major John Proby,+ 55th Foot

---

* = wounded in action

+ = killed in action or died of wounds

Army Troops (965)
80th Foot (359)   Colonel Thomas Gage*
Rogers' Rangers (416)[1]   Major Robert Rogers

Right Brigade (est. 2,096)
Commander: Lieutenant Colonel William Haviland,
                                                        27th Foot
27th Foot (664)   Major Eyre Massey
1st Battalion, 60th Foot (6 companies, 560)   Major John Tullikens*
4th Battalion, 60th Foot (932)   Major John Rutherford[+]

Centre Brigade (est. 1,539)
Commander: Lieutenant Colonel John Donaldson,[+]
                                                        55th Foot
44th Foot (888)   Major William Eyre*
55th Foot (651)   Lieutenant Colonel John Donaldson[+]

Left Brigade (1,633)
Commander: Lieutenant Colonel Francis Grant,*
                                                        42nd Foot
42nd Foot (1,000)   Major Duncan Campbell[+]
46th Foot (633)   Lieutenant Colonel Samuel Bever[+]

Artillery (190)[2]   Captain-Lieutenant James Stephens
24th Company, Second Battalion, RA

   Guns
   2 x brass 24-pdr.
   4 x iron 18-pdr.
   6 x brass 12-pdr.
   6 x brass 6-pdr.

   Howitzers
   4 x 8-inch brass
   5 x 8-inch iron
   4 x 5.5-inch brass

   Mortars
   1 x 13-inch iron
   2 x 10-inch brass
   2 x 8-inch brass
   8 x 5.5-inch brass (Royals)

AMERICAN PROVINCIALS (est. 9,829 all ranks)

Right Wing (est. 5,345)
Commander: Colonel Jedidiah Preble, Massachusetts

   Massachusetts Units (est. 4,054)
   Colonel Jonathan Bagley's Regiment (est. 446)
   Colonel Thomas Doty's Regiment (772)
   Colonel Jedidiah Preble's Regiment (525)
   Colonel Ebenezer Nicol's Regiment (est. 475)

Colonel Timothy Ruggles's Regiment (377)
Colonel William Williams's Regiment (471)
Colonel Oliver Partridge's Battalion of Light Infantry (989)

New York Units (est. 1,291)
Colonel Oliver DeLancey's Regiment (1,291)

1st Battalion	Lieutenant Colonel Bartholomew Leroux
2nd Battalion	Lieutenant Colonel Melancthon Woolsey
3rd Battalion	Lieutenant Colonel Beamsley Glasier

Left Wing (est. 3,944)

Commander:	Major General Phineas Lyman, Connecticut
Brigade Major:	Lieutenant John Stoughton, Independent Coy.

Connecticut Units (est. 1,949)

1st Connecticut Regiment (est. 500)	Major General Phineas Lyman
2nd Connecticut Regiment (est. 475)	Colonel Nathaniel Whiting
3rd Connecticut Regiment (est. 424)	Colonel David Wooster
4th Connecticut Regiment (est. 475)	Colonel Eleazer Fitch
Connecticut Rangers (est. 75)	Major Israel Putnam

Other Units (est. 1,995)

New Hampshire Regiment (est. 610)	Colonel John Hart
New Hampshire Rangers (est. 90)	Captain Lovell
New Jersey Regiment (615)	Colonel John Johnston
Rhode Island Regiment (680)	Colonel Henry Babcock

PROVINCIAL AUXILIARIES (est. 2,000 all ranks)

Bradstreet's "Battoemen" (est. 1,600)
Sir William Johnson's Mohawk warriors (est. 400)

RECAPITULATION

British regulars:	6,261 all ranks
American provincials:	9,289 all ranks
Provincial auxiliaries:	2,000 all ranks
Total:	17,550 all ranks

FRENCH FORCES

Commanding General:	Louis-Joseph de Montcalm, Marquis de Montcalm, *maréchal de camp*

ARMY STAFF

Aides to Montcalm:	Jean-Nicolas de Desandrouins, *capitaine*
	Louis-Antoine de Bougainville,* *aide-maréchal de logis*

Adjutant-General:	Pierre-A. Gohin, Chevalier de Montreuil, *aide-major general*
Chief Engineer:	Nicolas Sarrebource de Pontleroy, *capitaine*
Chief of Artillery:	Chevalier François-Marc-Antoine Le Mercier, *capitaine*
Assistant:	M. de Jacau de Fiedmont, *capitaine*

BRIGADE OF LA REINE, OR RIGHT BRIGADE (1,245 all ranks)

Commander:	Chevalier François de Lévis, *brigadier*
2nd Battalion, Régiment de la Reine (365)	M. de Rocquemaure, *lieutenant-colonel*
2nd Battalion, Régiment de Béarn (410)	Jean Dalquier, *lieutenant-colonel*
2nd Battalion, Régiment de Guyenne (470)	M. de Fontbonne, *lieutenant-colonel*

BRIGADE OF ROYAL-ROUSSILLON, OR CENTRE BRIGADE (980)

Commander:	Louis de Montcalm, *maréchal de camp*
2nd Battalion, Régiment de Royal-Roussillon (480)	M. le Chevalier de Bernetz, *lieutenant-colonel*
2nd Battalion, Régiment de Berry (450)	M. de Trivio, *lieutenant-colonel*
Grenadier coy., 3rd Battalion,[3] Régiment de Berry[4] (50)	M. de Fouilihac, *capitaine de grenadiers*

BRIGADE OF LA SARRE, OR LEFT BRIGADE (886)

Commander:	François-Charles de Bourlamaque,* *colonel d'infanterie*
2nd Battalion, Régiment de la Sarre (460)	Etienne-Guillaume de Senezergues de La Rodde, *lieutenant-colonel*
2nd Battalion, Régiment de Languedoc (426)	M. de Privat, *lieutenant-colonel*

OTHER UNITS

Troupes de la marine (8 companies, 400)	M. Florimond de Raymond, *capitaine de la colonie*
Troupes de la marine artillery (1 company, 50)	Chevalier de Mercier, *capitaine*
Canadien militia (250)	
Outaouais (Ottawa) warriors (15)	

ORDNANCE IN FORT CARILLON

Guns
12 x 18-pdr. iron
1 x 16-pdr. iron
15 x 12-pdr. iron
4 x 9 pdr. iron
4 x 6 pdr. iron
1 x 4 pdr. iron

Howitzers
1 x 8 in. iron

Mortars
2 x 13 in. iron
1 x 6 _ in. iron

ORDNANCE AT THE ENTRENCHMENTS

14 x swivel guns ("pierrettes" or "patteraroes")

RECAPITULATION

Troupes de terre:	4231
Troupes de la marine:	450
Canadien militia:	250
Ottawa warriors:	15
Total	4946

SOURCES

British

NAC, MG 11, vol 50, CO 5, folios 174-175, Return of the Present State of His Majesty's Forces … at Lake George, July 29th 1758; Alexander Monypenny Orderly Books contained in the *Bulletin of the Fort Ticonderoga Museum*, 12; *Army Lists*, 1758, 1759; Stanley Pargellis, *Military Affairs … 1748-1765* (New York, 1969); John Knox, *A Historical Journal* …, eds., Doughty & Parmalee, (3 vols.), Toronto, 1914-1916; *Dictionary of Canadian Biography*, vols 3 and 4.

French

The American Journals of Louis-Antoine de Bougainville, 1756-1760, trans., E.P. Hamilton (Norman, 1964); Pouchot, *Memoirs on the Late War in North America Between France & England* (Youngstown, 1994); "French Regimental Officers Lists," *Le bulletin des recherches historiques*, 51 (1945); E.B. O'Callaghan, *Documents Relative to the Colonial History of the State of New York* (15 vols, Albany, 1865-1877); *Dictionary of Canadian Biography*, 3.

NOTES

1. According to Rogers' memoirs and the account of a light infantry officer, Rogers' Rangers were increased in strength to 600 with drafts of volunteers from the provincials just one week prior to the departure from Lake George.

2. Abercromby complained bitterly before and after the battle that he didn't have enough gunners to man his artillery, having lost Captain Webdell's company to the Louisbourg expedition in May 1758. In June he tasked all the regular British infantry regiments to provide a total of 63 infantrymen to join the artillery as "additional gunners."

3. The number of the battalions of the various regiments of the *troupes de terre* bears some comment. Most accounts of the battle, contemporary or modern, refer to the 1st and 2nd Battalions of the Régiment de Berry. In fact, they were the 2nd and 3rd Battalions of that unit. All of Montcalm's other battalions were, in fact, the second battalions of their respective regiments, the other battalions campaigning in Europe.

4. The battalion companies of the 3rd Battalion of the Régiment de Berry (400 men) under the command of Lieutenant Colonel Sieur de Trecesson, while not directly engaged in fighting the British from the entrenchments, were active participants in the defence. After the battle, Bougainville commended the men of the battalion for their crucial logistical support in bringing up ammunition to the firing line "as well as refreshments so necessary in such a long fight."

Orders of Battle and Strengths, Opposing Forces, Queenston Heights, 13 October 1812

AMERICAN FORCES ON THE NIAGARA

Commander:	Major General Stephen Van Rensselaer, NY Militia
Quartermaster General:	Brigadier General Peter B. Porter, NY Militia
Aide and Secretary:	Major John Lovett, NY Militia
Adjutant General:	Lieutenant Colonel Solomon Van Rensselaer, NY Militia

Sixth Brigade, New York Militia

Commander:	Brigadier General Daniel Miller, NY Militia

Seventh Brigade, New York Militia

Commander:	Brigadier General William Wadsworth, NY Militia

Brigade, United States Army

Commander:	Brigadier General Alexander Smyth, USA

FORCE THAT CROSSED INTO CANADA, 13 OCTOBER 1812

Regular Army (est. 700)

First US Artillery Regiment (est. 40)	Commander: Lieutenant John Gansevoort
Regiment of Light Artillery (est. 150)	Commander: Lieutenant Colonel John R. Fenwick
Sixth US Infantry Regiment (est. 70)	Commander: Captain John Machesnay,
Thirteenth US Infantry Regiment (est. 300)	Commander: Lieutenant Colonel John Chrystie
Twenty-Third US Infantry Regiment (est 140)	Commander: Major James Mullany

New York Militia (est. 500)

Sixth and Seventh Brigades, NY Militia	Commander: Brigadier General William Wadsworth, NY Militia
Sixteenth Regiment:	Lieutenant Colonel Farrand Stranahan, NY Militia
Seventeenth Regiment:	Lieutenant Colonel Thompson Mead, NY Militia
Eighteenth Regiment:	Lieutenant Colonel Hugh W. Dobbin, NY Militia
Nineteenth Regiment:	Lieutenant Colonel Henry Bloom, NY Militia
Twentieth Regiment:	Lieutenant Colonel Peter Allen, NY Militia

Artillery in Action

Fort Gray
2 x iron 18-pdr. guns, 1 x iron mortar   Major John Lovett, NY Militia

Near embarkation point
2 x light 6-pdr. guns   Captain Nathan Towson, Second Artillery, USA

Queenston Heights
1 x iron 6-pdr. gun   Captain James Gibson, Light Artillery

RECAPITULATION OF AMERICAN FORCE THAT CROSSED INTO CANADA

Regular Army

First Artillery:	40
Light Artillery:	150
Sixth Infantry:	70
Thirteenth Infantry:	300
Twenty-Third Infantry:	140
New York Militia:	est. 500
Total:	1,200 men with 6 artillery pieces firing in support

BRITISH ARMY IN NORTH AMERICA

Commander, Upper Canada:	Major General Isaac Brock
Second-in- Command:	Major General Roger Hale Sheaffe
Aides to Major General Brock:	Captain John Glegg
	Captain John Macdonell
Brigade Major:	Major Thomas Evans
Assistant Deputy Quartermaster General:	Lieutenant George Fowler
Engineer:	Captain Henry M. Vigoureux
Commander, Lincoln Militia at Fort Erie and Chippawa:	
	Lieutenant Colonel Thomas Clark
Commander, Lincoln Militia at Queenston and Fort George:	
	Lieutenant Colonel William Claus

FORCE AT QUEENSTON (est. 325)

Grenadier Company, 49th Foot (est. 80)	Captain James Dennis
Royal Artillery (est. 10)	
Light Company, 49th Foot (est. 80)	Captain John Williams
5th Lincoln Militia Regiment	
1st Flank Company (est. 50)	Captain Samuel Hatt
2nd Flank Company (est. 50)	Captain James Durand
1st Lincoln Artillery Company (est. 30)	Lieutenant John Ball
2nd York Militia Regiment	
1st Flank Company (est. 25)	Captain John Chisholm

FORCE FROM BROWN'S POINT (est. 50)

3rd York Militia Regiment	
1st Flank Company (est. 25)	Captain Duncan Cameron
2nd Flank Company (est. 25)	Captain Stephen Heward

FORCE FROM FORT GEORGE (est. 535)

Light Company, 41st Foot (est. 100)	Captain William Derenzy
Royal Artillery Regiment (est. 30)	Captain William Holcroft
Grand River Warriors (80)	Captain John Norton
Cayugas (est. 20)	
Two Battalion Company, 41st Foot (140)	Lieutenant Angus McIntyre
1st Lincoln Militia Regiment	
1st Flank Company (est. 25)	Captain James Crooks
2nd Flank Company (est. 25)	Captain John McEwan
4th Lincoln Militia Regiment	
1st Flank Company (est. 25)	Lieutenant Thomas Butler
2nd Flank Company (est. 25)	Lieutenant Henry Nelles
1st York Militia Regiment	
1st Flank Company (est. 25)	Lieutenant Barnet Vanderburgh
Niagara Light Dragoons (est. 10)	Major Thomas Merritt
Miscellaneous Regulars and Militia (est. 30)	William Martin

FORCE FROM CHIPPAWA (est. 250)

Two Companies, 41st Foot (est. 150)	Captain Richard Bullock
2nd Lincoln Militia Regiment	
Two Flank Companies (est. 100)	Captain John Rowe
	Captain Robert Hamilton

RECAPITULATION

Regulars		Militia		Native Warriors	
41st Foot	390	Lincoln	300	Norton's party	80
49th Foot	160	York	100	Cayugas	20
Royal Artillery	40	Dragoons	10		
		Coloured & Misc.	30		
Totals	590		440		100

NOTES ON AMERICAN UNITS AND STRENGTHS

No one record provides the exact strength of the American force that actively participated in the action but the official British tally of prisoners of war shows 436 regulars and 489 militia captured, for a total of 925, of which about 120 were wounded. Given the American estimate that between 60 and 100 men were killed and that about 80 regular gunners were deployed on the American side, a number of wounded were evacuated before the surrender while others deserted back to their own shore, it is estimated that 1,300 officers and men fought in the action of whom about 700 regulars and 500 militia landed in Canada (out of more than 5,000 American troops stationed along the Niagara River). Major General Roger Sheaffe estimated that the American force numbered between 1,300 and 1,400 men.

On the strengths of the American regular units, a return dated 12 October shows that Chrystie had about 350 men in the Thirteenth Infantry and Fenwick commanded 550 regulars at Fort Niagara, for a total of 900 men. Anecdotal evidence strongly supports the idea that 300 men of the Thirteenth Infantry and 40 of the First Artillery embarked but which units contributed to the remaining 360 regulars who entered action is uncertain. Casualty reports, which listed officers only, show that the Sixth Infantry (1 company, estimated at 70 strong) and the Twenty-Third Infantry (described as being 140 strong) fought in Canada. The remaining 150 appear to have been drawn from the Light Artillery Regiment (which had four officers captured or fatally wounded).

The same return of 12 October shows more than 2,300 New York militia in and around Lewiston. Lieutenant Colonel Mead's account of the action states that 100 men of his regiment, the Seventeenth New York, and 100 of Lieutenant Colonel Farrand Stranahan's Sixteenth New York crossed the river. Twenty officers of these two units were listed among the prisoners and casualties. Major John Morrison, Eighteenth New York Regiment, was supposed to have led a force of 300 men drawn from Dobbin's Eighteenth, Bloom's Nineteenth and Allen's Twentieth New York Regiments but Morrison grew too ill to fight and it is uncertain how many men of this force actually landed in Canada. The casualty returns show that the Twentieth Regiment was present in numbers, but that the Eighteenth and Nineteenth Regiments suffered little.

An examination of the muster and pay rolls of the New York militia for October 1812 reveals as many as 2,500 men were on duty at Lewiston and that the order of involvement of the units ranged from the Sixteenth (greatest) down through the Eighteenth, Seventeenth, Twentieth to the Nineteenth which had the least involvement. These records show 310 officers and men specifically noted as having been involved in the action – other sources confirm involvement by individuals who were not so indicated in these records.

NOTES ON BRITISH AND CANADIAN UNITS AND STRENGTHS

There is no single record that provides precise information on the number of British regulars and Canadian militia who fought at Queenston. Estimates of the regulars and militia deployed by Major-General Sheaffe during the final stage of the battle vary between 800 and 900. Given that a number of men were left with the Royal Artillery on the north of the village, that about 80 casualties had been suffered to that time, that some militia had deserted, that 20 had been captured and that more parties of regulars and militia had gone to Fort George with prisoners, it is likely that between 1,100 and 1,200 were involved in this battle (out of more than 2,000 troops along the Niagara River defence line). They were mainly infantry, with a small troop of dragoons and some gunners.

Anecdotal accounts indicate the size of two units: two companies, 140, of the 41st Foot with Lieutenant McIntyre; and two companies one of which was the grenadier company, 150 total, of the 41st with Captain Bullock. Returns of the regular troops before and after the battle indicate that there were about 485 officers and men of the 49th Foot in the Niagara Peninsula. Brock mentioned that he had six companies of the 49th, which suggests that there were about 80 men in each of the grenadier and light companies. There were seven companies and about 700 of the 41st Foot on the peninsula, suggesting that Captain Derenzy's light company had about 100 men. There were about 80 Royal Artillery officers and gunners in the province at the time and Captain William Holcroft commanded about 40 of them at Fort George.

The camp of native warriors near the town of Niagara contained about 300 warriors of which Captain John Norton led 80 into battle, joined later in the day by a small number of Cayugas.

Ascertaining the numbers of the Canadian militia who participated in the battle is very difficult. Captain Crooks noted that he led 130 militia from five units to Queenston. He explained that, although there were about 75 men in each flank company, on

13 October about one third of the men were at the batteries along the lake or at the fort while another third were having their routine one-day-in-three off duty. Crooks did not refer to the 2nd Flank Company of the 4th Lincoln Regiment specifically. His brother, William, was captain in that unit and Crooks mentioned that they debated who should lead the detachment, implying that the 2nd Flank Company was part of Crooks's detachment. Crooks also indicates that Captain John Burn of the 1st Flank Company of the 1st Durham Regiment was present at the battle, though no other connection can be found between that unit and the battle.

A party of miscellaneous regulars and militia left Fort George to fight at Queenston, and probably included the Company of Colour which was mentioned in a couple of accounts. This was a small unit of skilled artificers that was not officially embodied until 24 October 1812 under the command of Captain Robert Runchey, a lieutenant in the 2nd Flank Company of the 1st Lincoln at the time of the battle.

Musters show that in July the 1st and 2nd Flank Companies of the 5th Lincoln Regiment (numbering about 70 each) were attached to the 49th Foot at Queenston as was the 1st Flank of the 2nd York Regiment (about 40). Lieutenant John Ball's 1st Lincoln Artillery had only 14 officers and men. An assumption is made here that the off-duty routine, described by Crooks, was followed on 13 October, giving those companies about two thirds of their men on duty during the battle.

The York militia companies appear to have been smaller in size than the Lincoln companies, so it is assumed that the 1st and 2nd Flank Companies of the 3rd York Regiment, situated at Brown's Point had about fifty men each, and anecdotal evidence suggests that they did not all go to Queenston.

The two flank companies of the 2nd Lincoln Regiment were stationed at Chippawa. Like the other companies it is assumed that two-thirds of their normal 75 men marched with Captain Bullock's companies.

The Provincial Light Dragoons, commanded by Major Thomas Merritt, served as dispatch riders on 13 October, although one officer, Captain Alexander Hamilton, was injured and volunteered at Holcroft's artillery battery.

The three batteries at Queenston were manned by a small detachment of Royal Artillery gunners and the 1st Lincoln Artillery under Lieutenant John Ball. The best available evidence suggests the strengths of these batteries were:

Redan Battery or "Mountain Battery"
　1 x iron 18-pdr. gun on garrison carriage
　1 x 8-inch mortar
Queenston – village
　1 x iron 9-pdr. gun on garrison carriage
　1 x brass 6-pdr. gun on garrison carriage
Vrooman's Point
　1 x iron 12-pdr. gun on garrison carriage

Captain William Holcroft rode from Fort George with three, possibly four, pieces of field artillery: two brass 6-pdr. guns and one 5.5-inch howitzer for certain, and possibly a second howitzer was employed. Lieutenant Walter Crowther brought up two 3-pdr. guns from Fort George.

SOURCES

American

Geneva Historical Society, Dobbin Family Papers; Ontario County Historical Society, Dox Family Papers.

United States National Archives, RG 94: Boxes 126-9, Volunteer Organizations and State Militia, War of 1812, Office of the Adjutant General; *DHC*, vol. 4: 68, Troops under Major General S. Van Rensselaer, 12 Oct 1812; 73, Sheaffe to Prevost, 14 Oct 1812; 74, Return of Killed, Wounded and Prisoners, by Evans, 15 Oct 1812; 76, List of American officers killed, wounded or taken prisoners; 79, Van Rensselaer to Eustis, 14 Oct 1812; 90, Statement by Lieutenant-Colonel Stranahan Mead; 95, Chrystie to Cushing, 22 Feb. 1813; 118, Unattributed account, *The War*, 31 Oct 1812; 125, Unattributed account, the *Aurora*, Philadelphia, 29 Oct 1812; 126, Unattributed account, *Poulson's American Daily Advertiser*, 24 Nov 1812; 127, Unattributed account, the *Aurora*, Philadelphia, 4 Nov 1812; 155, Wool to Van Rensselaer, 23 Oct 1812; 158, Van Rensselaer to Tompkins, 23 Oct 1812; 159, Smyth to Dearborn, 24 Oct 1812; 162, Lovett to Alexander, 25 Oct 1812; 166, List of captured officers, *Buffalo Gazette*, 27 Oct 1812; Catharina V. R. Bonney, *Legacy of Historical Gleanings* (Albany, 1875); Solomon Van Rensselaer, *A Narrative of the Affair at Queenstown: In the War of 1812* (New York, 1836); "Narrative of Robert Walcot," *The Philadelphia Times*, 22 Nov 1880; Ludwig Kosche, "Relics of Brock: An Investigation," *Archivaria*, 9, (1979-80), 33-103, Willson to Stewart, 9 Nov 1812; "A Rifleman of Queenston," *Publications of the Buffalo Historical Society*, Vol. IX, 1906, 373-76; Mary Roach Archer, "The Journal of Isaac Roach, 1812-1814," *Pennsylvania Magazine of History and Biography* 17 (1893), 131-43.

British: General

NAC, RG 8 1: vol 1707, Return of the Troops in the Montreal District, 4 July 1812; Return of Troops in Upper Canada under Brock, 30 July 1812; Distribution of the Forces in Canada, 12 Nov 1812; Monthly Distribution of Troops in Upper Canada, 25 Nov 1812; Distribution of the Troops in Canada, 21 Dec 1812.

Campaigns of 1812-1814, Niagara Historical Society, #9 (1902): 8-10, "Personal Narrative," W.H. Merritt; 23-5; William Claus, "An Account of the Operations . . . 1812-13,; 43-5, Norton to Goulburn, 29 Jan. 1816.; Niagara Historical Society, #23 (1911), 35-7, E. A. Cruikshank, "Col. Daniel McDougal and Valuable Documents," A. McLean to A. McNab, 22 July 1860; *Family History and Reminiscences of Early Settlers*, Niagara Historical Society, #28 (1916): 28-41, "Recollections of the War of 1812," Narrative by James Crooks; 51-2, Biographical Sketch of Adam Vrooman and ancestors; Ernest A. Cruikshank, ed., *Documentary History of the Campaigns upon the Niagara, 1812-1814* [hereafter: *DHC*], vol 3 (Welland, 1903): 76, District General Order by Clark, 27 June 1812; 283, DGO by Evans, 20 Sept 1812; Vol 4:18, Return of Fifth Lincoln Militia, 3 July 1812; 18, State of the Fourth Division (Fort George); 19, State of the Third Division (Queenston), 7 July 1812; 71, Sheaffe to Prevost, 13 Oct 1812; 175, Sheaffe to Prevost, 3 Nov 1812; 77, Woodruff to Thorburn, 29 July 1840; 103, Account by John Beverley Robinson, 14 Oct. 1812; 108,

Evans to ?, 15 Oct 1812; 114, Letter from Brown's Point (by Archibald McLean), 15 Oct 1812, in *Quebec Mercury*, 27 Oct 1812; 117, Letter from Fort George (probably by William Holcroft), 14 Oct 1812, in *Quebec Mercury*, 27 Oct 1812; 207, DGO by Evans, 13 Nov 1812. Carl F. Klinck and James J.Talman, eds, *The Journal of Major John Norton, 1816* (Toronto, 1970), 304-10; William Wood, ed., *Select British Documents of the Canadian War of 1812* (Toronto,1920-1928, 3 vols.), 3:556-63 "Merritt's Journal"; Carl Benn, *The Iroquois in the War of 1812* (Toronto, 1998); E. A. Cruikshank, "Record of the Services of the Canadian Regiments in the War of 1812. Part IX – The Lincoln Militia," *Selected Papers from the Canadian Military Institute, No. 13* (Welland, 1904); William Gray, *Soldiers of the King: The Upper Canadian Militia, 1812-1815* (Erin, 1995); L. Homfray Irving, *Officers of the British forces in Canada during the War of 1812-15* (Welland, 1909).

Sources on Numbers and Calibres of British Artillery

NAC, RG 8, I: 1707, Return of Brass and Iron Ordnance ... In Lower and Upper Canada, 15 December 1812; Return of Brass and Iron Ordnance ... between York and Fort Erie, 19 Dec 1812; vol 387, Bruyeres to Prevost, 13 Feb 1813. *DHC*, 4: 71, Sheaffe to Prevost, 13 Oct 1812; 117, Letter from Fort George (probably by William Holcroft), 14 Oct 1812, in *Quebec Mercury*, 27 Oct 1812.

Orders of Battle, Opposing Forces, Ridgeway, 2 June 1866

In describing operations involving units of three nations, but with officers and men with remarkably similar names, words have been used for the Fenian numbered units, e.g. the Seventh IRA Regiment. British and Canadian units are listed either by title – the Dunnville Naval Brigade and the Queen's Own Rifles – or their numerical designation – the 47th Foot and the 13th Battalion. In the latter case "Foot" designates a British unit.

IRISH REPUBLICAN ARMY (FENIANS)

Centre Wing (Buffalo Column) (embarked strength est. 600, see Note 1 below)

Commander:	Lieutenant Colonel John O'Neill
Staff	Captain Rodolph Fitzpatrick
	Medical Officer: Dr. Eamonn Donnelly
	Chaplain: Father John McMahon
Seventh IRA Regiment (Buffalo, N.Y.) (est. 165)	Lieutenant Colonel John Hoy
Thirteenth IRA Regiment (Nashville, Tenn.) (est. 85)	Lieutenant Colonel John O'Neill (also force commander)
Seventeenth IRA Regiment (Louisville, Ken.) (est. 110)	Lieutenant Colonel Owen Starr
Eighteenth IRA Regiment (Cleveland, Ohio) (est. 165)	Lieutenant Colonel John Grace
Independent Company (Terre Haute, Ind.) (est. 75)	Captain Hugh Haggerty
Troop of Scouts (See Note 2 below)	Commanding Officer unknown

BRITISH AND CANADIAN FORCES (See Note 3 below)

Chippawa Column

Commander:	Lieutenant Colonel George Peacocke

Governor General's Body Guard (cavalry) (See Note 4 below)

Commanding Officer:	Major George T. Denison

D Battery, 4th Brigade, Royal Artillery (six Armstrong guns)

Battery Commander:	Lieutenant Colonel Dixon Edward Hoste

16th Foot, Right Wing (four companies, 200 officers and men)

Commanding Officer:	Major Charles Coote Grant

47th Foot (five companies, 16 officers and 350 men)

Commanding Officer:	Lieutenant Colonel Charles C. Villiers

10th Royal Grenadiers (eight companies, 27 officers and 390 men)

Acting Commanding Officer:	Major James Boxall
Regimental Headquarters and Staff:	Major James Worthington
	Adjutant: Captain C.H. Connon
	Quartermaster: Captain Rufus Skinner
	Surgeon: Dr. J.H. Richardson
	Assistant Surgeon: Dr. James Newcombe
No. 1 Company	Captain George McMurrich, Lieutenant John Paterson
No 2. Company	Captain George R. Hamilton, Lieutenant Fred Richardson, Ensign Alexander Macdonald
No. 3 Company	Lieutenant H.J. Browne, Ensign Walter H. Barrett
No. 4 Company	Captain William A. Stollery, Lieutenant Arthur Coleman, Ensign W.D. Rogers
No. 5 Company	Captain George W. Musson, Lieutenant Charles S. Musson, Ensign J. Widmer Rolph
No. 6 Company	Captain J.W. Laurence, Lieutenant C.J.H. Winstanley, Ensign Hayward
No. 7 Company	Captain J.W. Hetherington, Lieutenant G. Brunel
No. 8 Company	Lieutenant T. Brunel, Ensign L. Sherwood

19th Battalion (five companies, 225 officers and men) (See Note 5 below)

Commanding Officer:	Lieutenant Colonel James G. Currie
Regimental Headquarters and Staff	Major John Powell
	Major T.L. Helliwell
	Adjutant: Captain Silas Spillett
	Quartermaster: Captain William McGhie
	Surgeon: Dr. Edwin Goodman, M.D.
No. 1 Company	Captain Edward Thompson, Lieutenant Johnson Clench
No. 2 Company (attached from 20th Battalion)	Captain Fred W. Macdonald, Lieutenant F. Benson
No. 3 Company	Captain William Kew, Lieutenant James K. Osborne, Ensign Kew
No. 4 Company	Captain Mathias Konkle, Lieutenant G. Walker, Ensign Delos Wolverton
No. 8 Company	Captain Henry Carlisle, Lieutenant Edwin I. Parnell, Ensign Josiah G.Holmes

St. Catharines Battery of Garrison Artillery (See Note 6 below)

	Captain George Stoker, Lieutenant James Wilson

Port Colborne Column

Commander:	Lieutenant Colonel Alfred Booker

Queen's Own Rifles (ten companies, 450 officers and men)

Commanding Officer:	Major Charles T. Gillmor

Regimental Headquarters and Staff:	Adjutant: Captain William D. Otter Quartermaster: Captain James Jackson Staff Paymaster: Captain W.H. Harris Surgeon: James Thorburn, M.D. Assistant Surgeon: Samuel P. May, M.D. Chaplain: Reverend David Inglis Chaplain: Reverend Mr. Burwash
No. 1 Company	Captain John Brown, Lieutenant Joseph Davids, Ensign William Fahey
No. 2 Company	Captain Fred E. Dixon, Lieutenant Farquhar Morrison, Ensign James Benett
No. 3 Company	Captain J.H. Boustead, Lieutenant James H. Beavan; Ensign William Wharin
No. 4 Company	Captain John Douglas, Lieutenant William Arthurs, Ensign John H. Davis
No. 5 Company	Captain John Edwards, Lieutenant Alexander G. Lee, Ensign Malcom McEachran
No. 6 Company	Captain G.M. Adam, Lieutenant William C. Campbell, Ensign T.A. McLean
No. 7 Company	Captain A. Macpherson, Lieutenant John G.R. Stinson, Ensign Smith
No. 8 Company	Captain L.P. Sherwood, Lieutenant John O'Reilly
No. 9 (Trinity College) Company	Acting Captain George Y. Whitney
No. 10 (Highland) Company	Captain John Gardner, Lieutenant Robert H. Ramsay, Ensign Donald Gibson

13th Battalion (six companies, 16 officers and 249 men)

Acting Commanding Officer:	Major James A. Skinner
Colour Party:	Ensigns Charles Armstrong and Hugh C. Baker
Regimental Headquarters and Staff	Major Stephen T. Cattley Adjutant: Captain John Henery Medical Officer: Dr Isaac Ryall
No. 1 Company	Captain Robert Grant; Lieutenant John M. Gibson, Ensign Joseph M. McKenzie
No. 2 Company	Captain John H. Watson, Lieutenant Charles R.M. Sewell
No. 3 Company	Lieutenant John W. Ferguson
No. 4 Company	Lieutenant Percy G. Routh, Ensign John B. Young
No. 5 Company	Captain Alexander H. Askin, Lieutenant Frederick E. Ritchie
No. 6 Company	Ensign W. Roy
Caledonia Rifle Company (circa 4 officers, 44 men)	Captain William Jackson, Lieutenant Robert Thornton, Ensign Chrystal, Ensign Ronald McKinnon (attached)
York Rifle Company (circa 3 officers and 44 men)	Captain Robert H. Davis, Lieutenant Davis, Ensign Jeffrey Hill

Dennis Expedition (embarked on the steam tug *W.T. Robb* at Port Colborne)

Commander:	Lieutenant Colonel J. Stoughton Dennis
Staff	Captain Charles S. Akers, Royal Engineers
Welland Canal Field Battery (3 officers and 59 men)	Captain Richard S. King, Lieutenant A.K. Schofield, Lieutenant Charles Nimmo
Dunnville Naval Brigade (3 officers and 43 men)	Captain Lachlan McCallum, Lieutenant Walter T. Robb, Second-Lieutenant Angus Macdonald

NOTES

Fenian Units and Strength

1. The Fenian strength is taken from O'Neill's report of 27 June 1866 in which he states that the size of the force assembled in Buffalo was 800, of which 600 actually crossed into Canada. The breakdown by regiments is based on his reported strength of the Thirteenth and Seventeenth IRA Regiments and the Independent Company (total 359 all ranks). This figure was subtracted from 800 and the result apportioned equally between the two remaining regiments. The figures given, those that crossed the river, are distributed equally across the army, a dubious assumption, but the best that can be done given the available information. As a result, the figures for each unit can only be considered as an estimate.

   As these figures are considerably lower than Canadian estimates of Fenian strength which ranged from 700 to 2,000, we should attempt to find corroborating evidence. Fortunately such evidence exists. A Fenian veteran of Ridgeway, Captain John S. Mullen estimated the Canadian strength at about 1,200, "or nearly three times our number." In the late afternoon of 1 June two Canadian government officials visited the Fenian camp at Newbigging's farm. Richard Graham, the collector of customs at Fort Erie estimated the Fenian strength as a maximum of 400 while Canadian government intelligence agent "detective" Charles Clarke, who had reported that 1,500 Fenians had landed on the morning of 1 June, put their strength at 450. It is possible that the Seventh Regiment was deployed at Black Creek at this time, but the total Fenian strength could not have exceeded 600. At about midday on 2 June Captain Charles Akers, the British officer who had accompanied Lieutenant Colonel J.S. Dennis on his ill-conceived expedition to Fort Erie, inspected the abandoned campsite. He later testified under oath that the Fenian camp was in a small field, under an acre in size, which points to a smaller, rather than a larger, force. (An acre is roughly 70 yards by 70 yards.) According to the 1885 edition of William Otter's *The Guide, a Manual for the Canadian Militia (Infantry)*, an infantry battalion of eight companies each of 60 men required an area of 160 yards by 246 yards for a formal camp. A late-Victorian infantry battalion of approximately 850 officers and men without its transport and using shelters instead of tents – which seemed to have been the case for the Fenians – occupied an area that measured 75 yards by 105 yards, or 1.5 acres) Finally Colonel O'Neill reported that 317 officers and men were taken into custody by the USS *Harrison* when they attempted to return to Buffalo. This leaves at the least 283 Fenians who crossed into Canada unaccounted for. Given the numbers of prisoners taken by the British and Canadian forces and after making due allowance for casualties, roughly 150 officers and men are still unaccounted for. O'Neill reluctantly acknowledged there were a large number of deserters and the force had shrunk to 500 before the march to Ridgeway began in the evening of 1 June. He also wrote that a number of officers and men deserted after the Fenians returned to Fort Erie on 2 June. A number of Fenians were captured in and around Fort Erie after O'Neill had left Canada and local legend has it that at least one Canadian farmer near Ridgeway employed a Fenian straggler as an unpaid farm hand after the invasion. The figure of a maximum of 600 invaders, therefore, seems correct.

2. The Fenians formed a small body of mounted scouts using horses requisitioned from the local Canadian population. One source claims that up to 50 horses were seized, but some of these were used to draw transport wagons and as officers' mounts. Perhaps 20-25 men operated as mounted scouts.

British/Canadian Units and Strengths

3. The 1863 *Volunteer Militia Act* authorized an infantry company establishment of three officers, six non-commissioned officers, a bugler and 48 privates.

4. The unit was called out late in the afternoon of 1 June and joined the Chippawa Column at New Germany at 4 P.M. the next day.

5. Two companies were detached to guard the suspension bridge at Niagara Falls and one company was detached to Port Colborne to guard the entrance to the Welland Canal. The estimated strength is of the five companies with the column on 2 June.

6. The St. Catharines Battery of Garrison Artillery was originally left at Chippawa on the morning of 2 June to guard the bridges but was ordered forward to join Peacocke during the day.

SOURCES

Fenian

National Archives of Canada: MG 29 E 74, Stephen Beatty Manuscript; RG 9 IC 8, Vol 6, Inquiry to Investigate the Case of Lieut-Col. J. Stoughton Dennis, 8 November 1866, Testimony of Captain Charles Akers; John O'Neill, "Official Report of the Battle of Ridgeway, Canada West, Fought June 2nd, 1866," (Republished, Nashville, Tennessee, 1966); David Owen, *The Year of the Fenians*, (Buffalo, 1900); George Denison, *Soldiering in Canada*, (Toronto, 1900); Brereton Greenhous, *Semper Paratus: The History of the Royal Hamilton Light Infantry (Wentworth Regiment) 1862-1977*, (Hamilton, 1977); Beverly Jewson, *The Battle of Limeridge*, (Ridgeway, 1976).

British and Canadian

Directorate of History and Heritage, DND, Ottawa: DHH, 000.8 D51, Imperial Officers serving in Canada at the time of the Fenian Raids; John Macdonald, *Troublesome Times in Canada: A History of the Fenian Raids of 1866 and 1870*, (Toronto, 1910); Ernest Cruikshank, *The Original and Official History of the Thirteenth Battalion of Infantry*, (Hamilton, 1899); Thomas Champion, *History of the 10th Royals and of the Royal Grenadiers from the formation of the Regiment until 1896*, (Toronto, 1896); R. Rogers, *History of the Lincoln and Welland Regiment*, 2nd ed., (St. Catharines, 1979).bb

---

APPENDIX D

Orders of Battle and Strengths, Opposing Forces, Leliefontein, 7 November 1900

BOER FORCES

Overall Commander:	Assistant-General Joachim Christoffel Fourie
Carolina Commando (est. 300) Commander:	Commandant Hendrik Frederik Prinsloo
Ermelo Commando (est. 100) Commander:	Commandant Johannes Nicolaas Hendrik Grobler
Middelburg Commando (est. 100) Commander:	(rank unknown) Louis Steyn

BRITISH AND CANADIAN FORCES

Flying Column, Belfast Garrison
Commander: Major General Horace L. Smith-Dorrien

British Units
D Squadron, 5th Lancers (100)[1]

84 Battery, Royal Field Artillery   Major Guiness
    4 x 15-pdr. guns

S Section, Vickers-Maxims, RFA
    2 x 1-pdr. pom-poms

Section, 14 Company, Southern Division, Royal Garrison Artillery
    2 x 5-inch guns

X Division Ammunition Column, Royal Artillery

Section Royal Engineers

Wing, 1st Battalion, The Suffolk Regiment   Major Lloyd
    4 companies, (300 men)

2nd Battalion, The King's Shropshire Light Infantry   Lieutenant Colonel James Spens
    8 companies, (600 men)

Detachment, 43 Company, Army Service Corps

19 Brigade Bearer Company, Royal Army Medical Corps

Canadian Units
The Royal Canadian Dragoons (90)   Lieutenant Colonel François Lessard
Adjutant: Lieutenant James Elmsley
Regimental Scouts   Sergeant Robert Ryan
    1 Troop, A Squadron   Lieutenant Francis Sutton
    2 Troop, A Squadron   Lieutenant Hampden Cockburn
    2 Troop, B Squadron   Lieutenant Richard Turner
    Machine Gun Section   Sergeant Edward Holland
1 x .303 Colt Machine Gun

Composite Squadron, Canadian Mounted Rifles   Lieutenant Colonel Thomas D.B. Evans
    2 Troop, A Squadron   Lieutenant J.V. Begin
    3 Troop, A Squadron   Lieutenant T.A. Wroughton
    2 Troop, B Squadron   Sergeant C.R. Tryon

Left Section, D Battery, Royal Canadian Field Artillery   Lieutenant Edward W.B. Morrison
    2 x 12-pdr. guns

SOURCES

Boer

Hugh Robertson, "The Royal Canadian Dragoons and the Anglo-Boer War, 1900," Unpublished MA Thesis, University of Ottawa, 1982; Ian Uys, *South African Military Who's Who, 1452-1992* (Germiston, 1992).

British-Canadian

History of the War in South-Africa 1899-1902, Vol 3, (London, 1908); Department of Militia and Defence, *Canadians in Khaki, South Africa 1899-1900, Official Correspondence, Nominal Roll, Casualties Etc.,* (reprint, Ottawa, 1994); Brian Reid, *Our Little Army in the Field; The Canadians in South Africa 1899-1902* (St. Catharines, 1996); Horace Smith-Dorrien, *Memories of Forty-Eight Years Service* (London, 1925).

NOTE

1. Strengths given are for mounted men only and do not include members of organizations such as the regimental scout and machine gun sections or men employed in supporting roles such as medical, supply and transport.

Orders of Battle, Opposing Forces, Moreuil Wood, 30 March 1918

ALLIED FORCES

2ND BRITISH CAVALRY DIVISION

Commander:	Major General T.T. Pitman

Canadian Cavalry Brigade (est. 750)

Commander:	Brigadier-General J.E.B. Seely
Brigade-Major:	Major C. Connolly

The Royal Canadian Dragoons (est. 250)	Lieutenant-Colonel C.T. van Straubenzie
A Squadron	Captain R. Nordheimer
B Squadron	Major R.S. Timmis
C Squadron	Captain T.R.G. Newcomen

Lord Strathcona's Horse (Royal Canadians) (est. 250)	Lieutenant Colonel D.J. MacDonald
A Squadron	Major J.G. Tatlow
B Squadron	Captain J.B. Trotter
C Squadron	Lieutenant G.M. Flowerdew

The Fort Garry Horse (est. 250)	Lieutenant Colonel R.W. Paterson
A Squadron	Captain F.C. Thomson
B Squadron	Captain R.G. Hutchinson
C Squadron	Captain R.W. Allen

Canadian Cavalry Brigade Machine-Gun Squadron	Major J.H. Boulter
6 x .303 Vickers Machine Guns	

3rd British Cavalry Brigade

Commander	Brigadier General J.A. Bell-Smyth
The 4th (The Queen's Own) Hussars	Lieutenant Colonel J.E.C. Darley (KIA 31 Mar 1918)
The 5th (Royal Irish) Lancers	Lieutenant Colonel G.F.H. Brooke
The 16th (The Queen's) Lancers	

GERMAN FORCES

23. *(Sachsen) Infanterie-Division*
Grenadiere-Regiment 101

243. *(Württembergische) Infanterie-Division*
Fusilier-Regiment 122
Infanterie-Regiment 479
Feldartillerie-Regiment 238
Pionier-Bataillon 306
Pionierkompanie 253

SOURCES

Allied

J.R. Grodzinski, *The Battle of Moreuil Wood* (1993); A.F. Becke, *History of the Great War: Order of Battle of Divisions – Part I —The Regular Divisions* (London, 1935), 10; *Canada in the Great War, Vol 6, Special Services, Heroic Deeds, etc.* (Toronto, 1921), 354.

German

D.H. Gramm, *Das Fusilier-Regiment Kaiser Franz Joseph von Osterreich, König von Ungarn, Nr. 122 in Weltkrieg 1914-1918* (Stuttgart, 1921); Alfred Meyer, *Das Rgl. Gescht. 2 Grenadier-Regiment Number 101 'Kaiser Wilhelm, König von Preussen'* (Dresden, 1924); K. Storz, *Das Württemberg Feld-Artillerie-Regt Nr. 238 im Weltkrieg 1914-1918,* (Stuttgart, 1921); *Histories of the Two Hundred and Fifty-One Divisions of the German Army which participated in the War (1914-1918)* (Washington, 1919).

APPENDIX F

Orders of Battle, Opposing Forces, Le Mesnil-Patry, 11 June 1944

CANADIAN FORCES

2 CANADIAN ARMOURED BRIGADE

Commander: Brigadier R.A. Wyman

First Hussars

Regimental Headquarters
Commanding Officer: Lieutenant Colonel R.J. Colwell
Second-in-Command: Major F.E. White
Adjutant: Captain R.G. Rogers
Intelligence Officer: Lieutenant E.D.L. Miller
Padre: Honorary Captain H.C. Creelman

A Squadron
Officer Commanding: Major W.D. Brooks

B Squadron
Officer Commanding: Captain R.H. Harrison
Second in Command: Captain H.L. Smuck
Battle Captain: Catpain R. Wildgoose
1st Troop Leader: Lieutenant H.A. Mills

2nd Troop Leader:	Lieutenant W.J. Martin
3rd Troop Leader:	Lieutenant L.S.J. Dunn
4th Troop Leader:	Lieutenant R.F. Seaman
5th Troop Leader:	Lieutenant C.E. Harwood
Supernumerary Officer:	Lieutenant B.M. Deans

C Squadron

Officer Commanding:	Major D.A. Marks
Second in Command:	Captain O.G. Stoner
1st Troop Leader:	Lieutenant G.W. Gordon
2nd Troop Leader:	Lieutenant W.F. McCormick
3rd Troop Leader:	Lieutenant G.K. Henry
4th Troop Leader:	Lieutenant F.B. Allen
5th Troop Leader:	Unknown

Attached to the First Hussars

The Queens Own Rifles of Canada

Mortar Platoon

Officer Commanding	Lieutenant B. Dunkelman

D Company

Officer Commanding:	Major J.N. Gordon
Second in Command:	Captain R.W. Sawyer
Company Sergeant Major:	Warrant Officer II J. Forbes
16 Platoon Commander:	Lieutenant R.W. Barker
17 Platoon Commander:	Lieutenant H.G.W. Bean
18 Platoon Commander:	Lieutenant R. Fleming

Royal Canadian Artillery

Forward Observation Officer:	Captain C. Rivaz

GERMAN FORCES

12. SS-Panzerdivision Hitlerjugend

SS-Panzerregiment 12

Commanding Officer:	*Obersturmbannführer* M. Wunsche

  2nd Battalion

Commanding Officer:	*Sturmbannführer* K.-H. Prinz
5 Kompanie	*Obersturmführer* H. Bando
6 Kompanie	*Hauptsturmführer* L. Ruckdeschel
7 Kompanie	*Hauptsturmführer* H. Bracker
8 Kompanie	*Obersturmführer* H. Siegel
9 Kompanie	*Hauptsturmführer* Buettner

SS-Panzerjägerabteilung 12

SS-Panzergrenadierregiment 26

Commanding Officer:	*Obersturmbannführer* W. Mohnke

  2nd Battalion

Commanding Officer:	*Sturmbannführer* B. Siebken
5 Kompanie	*Obersturmführer* K. Gotthard
6 Kompanie	*Obersturmführer* Schmolke
7 Kompanie	*Obersturmführer* A. Henne
8 Kompanie	*Hauptsturmführer* Fasching

SS-Panzerpionierbataillon 12
Commanding Officer: *Sturmbannführer* S. Muller
  1 Kompanie   *Oberleutnant* O. Toll
  2 Kompanie   *Obersturmführer* P. Kuret
  3 Kompanie   *Hauptsturmführer* Tiedke
  4 Kompanie   *Obersturmführer* Bischof
  Machine Gun Platoon   *Untersturmführer* W. Stremme
  Mortar Platoon   Unknown

SOURCES

Unless otherwise noted, the sources for the Canadian units above are the War Diaries of the 3rd Canadian Infantry Division, 2 Canadian Armoured Brigade, 7 Canadian Infantry Brigade and the 6th Canadian Armoured Regiment (First Hussars) located in Record Group 24 of the National Archives of Canada, Ottawa. Organization and strength of the German units from Hubert Meyer, *The History of the 12. SS-Panzerdivision Hitlerjugend*, (Winnipeg, 1994).

APPENDIX G

Order of Battle, The Kapelsche Veer, 26-31 January 1945

ALLIED FORCES

ON THE KAPELSCHE VEER

10 Canadian Infantry Brigade

The Lincoln and Welland Regiment
  A, B, C and D Rifle Companies
  Anti-Tank Platoon
  Carrier Platoon (dismounted)

The Argyll and Sutherland Highlanders of Canada
  A, B, C and D Rifle Companies

29th Canadian Armoured Reconnaissance Regiment (The South Alberta Regiment)
  A Squadron
    1 Troop (4 x Sherman V tanks with 75 mm guns)
    2 Troop (2 x Sherman V tanks with 75 mm guns)
    3 Troop (2 x Sherman V tanks with 75 mm guns)
  C Squadron (crews only)
  Recce Troop (2 Stuart VI light tanks with 37 mm guns)

10th Independent Machine Gun Company (The New Brunswick Rangers)
  Vickers .303 Heavy Machine Gun Platoon

Other Units
8th Polish Infantry Battalion
41 Royal Marine Commando

IN IMMEDIATE SUPPORT

Control of Rear Areas
The Algonquin Regiment

Armoured Units Firing as Artillery
29th Canadian Armoured Reconnaissance Regiment (The South Alberta Regiment)
    One troop (3 x Sherman V tanks with 75 mm guns)
    detachment, AA Troop (2 x Crusader III AA tanks each with 2 x 20 mm guns)
28th Canadian Armoured Regiment (The British Columbia Regiment)
    36 x Sherman V tanks for fire support (75 mm guns)

Heavy Mortar Group
Mortar Company, The Toronto Scottish Regiment (Machine-Gun)
    16 x 4.2 mortars
Mortar Platoon, 10th Independent Machine Gun Company (New Brunswick Rangers)
    4 x 4.2 mortars
Mortar Platoon, 1st Polish Armoured Division Independent Heavy Squadron
    4 x 4.2 mortars

Engineers
8th Field Squadron, Royal Canadian Engineers
9th Field Squadron, Royal Canadian Engineers
803 Pioneer Company, Royal Engineers

ARTILLERY AND AIR SUPPORTING UNITS

4th Army Group, Royal Artillery
Four medium regiments
    64 x 4.5 or 5.5 inch guns
Two heavy batteries
    16 x 155 mm or 8-in. guns

First Canadian Army
1st Radar Battery

2nd Army Group, Royal Canadian Artillery
19 Army Field Regiment (Self-Propelled), Royal Canadian Artillery
    24 x 25-pdr. gun/howitzers

4th Canadian Armoured Division
15 Field Regiment, Royal Canadian Artillery
    24 x 25-pdr. gun/howitzers
23 Field Regiment (Self-Propelled), Royal Canadian Artillery
    24 x 25-pdr. gun/howitzers

1st Polish Armoured Division Artillery
1st Motorized Artillery Regiment (Self-Propelled)
   24 x 25-pdr. gun/howitzers
2nd Motorized Artillery Regiment (Towed)
   24 x 25-pdr. gun/howitzers
90 Field Regiment, Royal Artillery (under command)
   24 x 25-pdr. gun/howitzers

Second Tactical Air Force
84 Group, Royal Air Force
   elements of 24 squadrons of Spitfire IX fighter and Typhoon ground-attack aircraft

GERMAN FORCES

ON THE KAPELSCHE VEER

Fallschirmjägerregiment 17
10 *Kompanie*
elements, 12 *Kompanie* (medium machine guns)
elements, 14 *Kompanie* (88 mm Panzerschreck a/t weapons)
elements, 15 *Kompanie* (engineers, with anti-tank and anti-personnel mines)

IN IMMEDIATE SUPPORT

Fallschirmjägerregiment 17
8 *Kompanie*, 7-8 x 80 mm mortars
12 *Kompanie*, 6 x 120 mm mortars

Fallschirmjägerregiment 16
8 *Kompanie*, 7-8 x 80 mm mortars

elements, *Fallschirmjägerartillerieregiment* 6
est. 4-6 105 mm howitzers

elements, *Fallschirmjägergranatwerferbataillon* 6
est. 4-6 120 mm mortars

RECAPITULATION OF OPPOSING ARTILLERY

	Allied	*German*
20 mm guns	4	–
81 mm mortars	–	est. 14-16
4.2 (106 mm) mortars	24	–
120 mm mortars	–	est. 10-12
75 mm guns (Shermans)	47	–
105 mm howitzers	–	est. 4-6
25-pdr. (85 mm) gun-howitzers	144	–
4.5 or 5.5 in. medium guns	64	–
155 mm or 8 in. heavy guns	16	–
Totals	299	28-34

SOURCES

Allied

NAC, RG 24, War Diaries: 4th Canadian Armoured Division; 10 Canadian Infantry Brigade; South Alberta Regiment; Lincoln and Welland Regiment; Argyll and Sutherland Highlanders; Public Record Office, War Establishment II/240/1; Hubert Fairlie Wood, "Operation ELEPHANT: The Battle for Kapelsche Veer," *Canadian Army Journal* (September 1949), 8-12.

German

1st Canadian Army Intelligence Summary No. 225, 10 February 1944, Appendices A and B.

APPENDIX H

The Military Heritage of the Units in *Fighting for Canada*

TICONDEROGA, 1758

Period Title	*Fate or Modern Title*
BRITISH	
Captain W. Martin's Company, RA	Disbanded 1871
27th Regiment of Foot	The Royal Irish Regiment
42nd Regiment of Foot	The Black Watch (Royal Highland) Regiment
44th Regiment of Foot	The Royal Anglian Regiment
50th Regiment of Foot	The Princess of Wales's Royal Regiment (Queen's and Royal Hampshires)
55th Regiment of Foot	The King's Own Royal Border Regiment
60th Regiment of Foot	The Royal Green Jackets
80th Regiment of Foot	The Staffordshire Regiment (The Prince of Wales's)
NORTH AMERICAN	
Rogers' Rangers	Disbanded 1762, traditional link claimed by 75th US Army Ranger Regiment
Bradstreet's "Battoemen"	Disbanded 1759
1st Connecticut Regiment	Disbanded 1759
2nd Connecticut Regiment	Disbanded 1759
3rd Connecticut Regiment	Disbanded 1759
4th Connecticut Regiment	Disbanded 1759
Connecticut Rangers	Disbanded 1759
Massachusetts Units	
Bagley's Regiment	Disbanded 1759

Doty's Regiment	Disbanded 1759
Preble's Regiment	Disbanded 1759
Nicol's Regiment	Disbanded 1759
Ruggles's Regiment	Disbanded 1759
Williams's Regiment	Disbanded 1759
Partridge's Battalion of Light Infantry	Disbanded 1759
New Hampshire Regiment	Disbanded 1759
New Hampshire Rangers	Disbanded 1759
New Jersey Regiment	Disbanded 1759
DeLancey's New York Regiment	Disbanded 1759
Rhode Island Regiment	Disbanded 1759

FRENCH

Régiment de Béarn	Disbanded 1762
Régiment de Berry	35e Régiment d'Infanterie
Régiment de Guyenne	Disbanded as 29e Régiment d'Infanterie, 1940
Régiment de Languedoc	Disbanded as 67e Régiment d'Infanterie, 1998
Régiment de la Reine	Disbanded as 41e Régiment d'Infanterie, 1999
Régiment de Royal-Roussillon	Disbanded as 54e Régiment d'Infanterie, 1997
Régiment de la Sarre	51e Régiment d'Infanterie/ 31e Groupement de Camp
Troupes de la Marine	Troupes de Marine (modern French marines)
Milice *Canadien*	Various Quebec militia units of the Canadian Forces

QUEENSTON HEIGHTS, 1812

AMERICAN

Regular Units

Regiment of Artillerists	Corps of Artillery in 1814
Regiment of Light Artillery	Retained in service, 1815
Second Artillery Regiment	Corps of Artillery in 1814
Sixth U.S. Infantry Regiment	Second Infantry in 1815
Thirteenth U.S. Infantry Regiment	Fifth Infantry in 1815
Twenty-Third U.S. Infantry Regiment	Second Infantry in 1815

New York Militia Units

Sixteenth Regiment	Perpetuated by elements of the 42nd Division, New York Army Reserve National Guard
Seventeenth Regiment	Perpetuated by elements of the 42nd Division, New York Army Reserve National Guard
Eighteenth Regiment	Perpetuated by elements of the 42nd Division, New York Army Reserve National Guard

Nineteenth Regiment — Perpetuated by elements of the 42nd Division, New York Army Reserve National Guard

Twentieth Regiment — Perpetuated by elements of the 42nd Division, New York Army Reserve National Guard

BRITISH

Royal Regiment of Artillery — Royal Regiment of Artillery
41st Regiment of Foot — The Royal Regiment of Wales
49th Regiment of Foot — The Royal Gloucestershire, Berkshire and Wiltshire Regiment

Canadian

1st Lincoln Artillery Company — Disbanded 1815, traditional link with 56 Field Regiment, RCA

Niagara Light Dragoons — Disbanded, 1815
Lincoln Militia units — The Lincoln and Welland Regiment
York Militia units — Disbanded 1815
Coloured Company — Disbanded, 1815

RIDGEWAY, 1866

BRITISH

D Battery, 4th Brigade, RA — 17 (Corunna) Battery, Royal Artillery
16th Regiment of Foot — The Royal Anglian Regiment
47th Regiment of Foot — The Queen's Lancashire Regiment

CANADIAN

Governor General's Body Guard for Upper Canada — The Governor General's Horse Guards
St. Catharines Garrison Battery — Disbanded prior to 1892
Welland Canal Field Battery — 56 Field Regiment, Royal Canadian Artillery

Queen's Own Rifles of Toronto — The Queen's Own Rifles of Canada
10th Battalion, or Royal Regiment of Toronto Volunteers — The Royal Regiment of Canada

13th Battalion Volunteer Militia — The Royal Hamilton Light Infantry
19th Battalion Volunteer Militia (Infantry), Canada — The Lincoln and Welland Regiment
20th Battalion Volunteer Militia (Infantry), Canada — The Lincoln and Welland Regiment
York and Caledonia Rifle Companies — 56 Field Regiment, Royal Canadian Artillery

Dunnville Naval Brigade — Disbanded 1867

FENIAN

Seventh Infantry Regiment — Disbanded, c. 1866-1870
Thirteenth Infantry Regiment — Disbanded, c. 1866-1870
Seventeenth Infantry Regiment — Disbanded, c. 1866-1870
Eighteenth Infantry Regiment — Disbanded, c. 1866-1870
Independent Company — Disbanded, c. 1866-1870

LELIEFONTEIN, 1900

BOER[1]

Carolina Commando	Carolina Commando, South African Defence Force
Ermelo Commando	Ermelo Commando, South African Defence Force
Middleburg Commando	Middelburg Commando, South African Defence Force

BRITISH

The 5th (Royal Irish) Lancers	The Queen's Royal Lancers
84 Battery, Royal Field Artillery	Disbanded 1962 as 166 HAA Battery
14 Company, Royal Garrison Artillery	92 LAA Battery, Royal Artillery
The Suffolk Regiment	The Royal Anglian Regiment
The King's (Shropshire) Light Infantry	The Light Infantry

CANADIAN

The Royal Canadian Dragoons	The Royal Canadian Dragoons
1st Battalion, Canadian Mounted Rifles	The Royal Canadian Dragoons
D Battery, Royal Canadian Field Artillery	2nd Field Battery, 30 Field Regiment, Royal Canadian Artillery; D Battery, 2 Regiment of Royal Canadian Horse Artillery

MOREUIL WOOD, 1918

BRITISH

The 4th, (The Queen's Own) Hussars	The King's Own Hussars
The 16th, (The Queen's) Lancers	The Queen's Royal Lancers

CANADIAN

The Royal Canadian Dragoons	The Royal Canadian Dragoons
Lord Strathcona's Horse (Royal Canadians)	Lord Strathcona's Horse (Royal Canadians)
The Fort Garry Horse	The Fort Garry Horse
Canadian Motor Machine Gun Brigade	The Royal Canadian Hussars

GERMAN

23. *(Sachsen) Infanterie-Division* *Grenadier-Regiment* 101	Disbanded, 1918 Disbanded, 1945 as II. *Bataillon, Panzergrenadierregiment* 10
243. *(Württembergische) Infanterie-Division* *Fusilier-Regiment* 122	Disbanded, 1918 Disbanded, 1945 as I. *Bataillon, Füsilierregiment* 34
Infanterie-Regiment 479	Disbanded, 1945 as II. *Bataillon, Gebirgsjägerregiment* 13
Feldartillerie-Regiment 238	Disbanded, 1945 as III. *Bataillon, Artillerieregiment (Motoriziert)* 25
Pionier-Bataillon 306 *Pionierkompanie* 253	Disbanded, 1918 Disbanded, 1918

LE MESNIL-PATRY, 1944

CANADIAN

6th Canadian Armoured Regiment (1st Hussars)   The First Hussars Regiment
The Queen's Own Rifles of Canada   The Queen's Own Rifles of Canada

GERMAN

SS-Panzerregiment 12   Disbanded, 1945
SS-Panzergrenadierregiment 12   Disbanded, 1945
SS-Panzerpionierbataillon 12   Disbanded, 1945
SS-Panzerjägerabteilung 12   Disbanded, 1945

KAPELSCHE VEER, 1945

CANADIAN

29th Canadian Armoured Reconaissance Regiment   The South Alberta Light Horse
   (South Alberta Regiment)
8 Field Squadron, Royal Canadian Engineers   Supplementary Order of Battle, 1970
9 Field Squadron, Royal Canadian Engineers   9e Escadron de Genie de Campagne
15 Field Regiment, Royal Canadian Artillery   15 Field Regiment, RCA
The Lincoln and Welland Regiment   The Lincoln and Welland Regiment
The Argyll and Sutherland Highlanders of Canada   The Argyll and Sutherland Highlanders
   of Canada (Princess Louise's)

10th Independent Machine Gun Company   1st Battalion, The Royal New Brunswick
   (New Brunswick Rangers)Regiment   (Carleton and York)

GERMAN

Fallschirmjägerregiment 17   Disbanded, 1945

SOURCES

Commandant Adolenko, *Récueil d'historiques de l'infanterie française*, (Paris, 1949); John M. Hitsman, *The Incredible War of 1812: A Military History*. Updated by *Donald E. Graves* (Toronto, 1999); Arthur Swinson, ed., *A Register of the Regiments and Corps of the British Army* (London, 1972); M.E.S. Laws, *Battery Records of the Royal Artillery, 1716-1859* (Woolwich, 1952).

The following individuals contributed specialised information: Colonel J.-F. Bacherot, Defence Attaché, Ambassade de France, Ottawa; Mr. Simon Bendall, London, UK: *Oberstleutnant* Dr. W. Heinemann, *Militärgeschichtlicheforschungsamt*, Berlin; Lieutenant-Colonel F. Guelton, *Service historique de l'armée de terre*, Paris; Major Paul Lansey, Directorate of History and Heritage, DND, Ottawa; Colonel AUS (Ret) Leonid Kondratiuk, Massachusetts National Guard, Military Museum & Archives, Worcester, Mass.; Colonel Charles Nutting, British Defence Liaison Staff, Ottawa; Major General (Retd.) Michael Reynolds, Eastbourne, UK; and Lieutenant-Colonel (Retd.) Joseph Whitehorne, USA, Front Royal, Virginia.

NOTE

1. With the Boer surrender on 31 May 1902, the commandos turned in their arms and were disbanded. After a discreet interval, the commando system was reintroduced to provide a locally-based force to deal with any civil or military emergency until the regular army could be deployed. With the introduction of universal military training in the post Second World War period, young men served one and then two years on active duty and then became a member of their local commando until they reached the age of 65. After the 1994 election, universal military service was abolished and service in the commandos became voluntary, although their role as a local militia force was retained. Thus descendants of the Boers that fought so bravely and well at Leliefontein may still be found in the ranks of the Carolina, Ermelo and Middelburg Commandos.

Battle Honours, Awards and Decorations Resulting from the Military Actions in *Fighting for Canada*

BATTLE HONOURS

QUEENSTON HEIGHTS, 1812

Battle Honour, "Queenstown," awarded to the 41st and 49th Regiments of Foot and held today by their respective successors, The Royal Regiment of Wales and The Royal Gloucestershire, Berkshire and Wiltshire Regiments of the British army.

RIDGEWAY, 1866

Perhaps understandably, no Battle Honour was ever granted for Ridgeway. In 1923, however, the Queen's Own Rifles made a determined effort to get such an honour, Colonel A.J.E. Kirkpatrick of that regiment, in reviewing the documentation on the action, noted that

> great stress is made upon the stupid bungle made by Colonel Booker in withdrawing the Queen's Own from a successful skirmish action at the time when they were steadily driving the Fenians back, fighting in the way which their natrual instincts would teach them to fight, and having gained complete superiority over the Fenians.
>
> Colonel Booker knew, or should have known, from the information gained, which was common knowledge in the hands of our Staff, that the Fenians had no Cavalry, no reports of Cavalry having travelled across the river, nor was it ever suggested that they were in possession of any Cavalry, after all, at their rendezvous. Despite this fact, on the approach of several

mounted farmers, bringing in information, Colonel Booker, not the Commanding Officer of the Queen's Own, admits that he recalled this brave skirmishing line of untried troops, who were fighting a winning action against the veterans of the World's greatest war, and ordered them to stand out in the open field in a square to be shot down like cattle.

> These men were intelligent, educated young men who understood, from their reading something of the nature of Military operations, of the conduct of war, and the palpable error and stupidity of a Commander, whom they knew not, would break up the morale of even the most highly trained troops. Had he had a regiment of ignorant peasants, unable to make an intelligent appreciation of the situation, you might have excused such men from not knowing enough to remove themselves ...

This was a most remarkable piece of creative writing but it went for nought as the Rifles' application was refused and the regiment was told in no uncertain terms never to raise the matter again.[1]

LELIEFONTEIN, 1900

A specific Honour was not awarded for Leliefontein but a broadcast Honour, "South Africa 1900," incorporates this action. It is borne on the guidon of the the Royal Canadian Mounted Police, which perpetuate the Honours of the 2nd Battalion, Canadian Mounted Rifles.

MOREUIL WOOD, 1918

A specific Honour was not awarded for Moreuil Wood but a broadcast Honour, "France and Flanders, 1915-1918," incorporates this action. It is borne on the guidons of The Royal Canadian Dragoons, Lord Strathcona's Horse and The Fort Garry Horse.

LE MESNIL-PATRY, 1944

A Battle Honour, "Le Mesnil-Patry," was awarded and is held today by The First Hussars of London, Ontario, and The Queen's Own Rifles of Canada.

KAPELSCHE VEER, 1945

A Battle Honour, "Kapelsche Veer," was awarded and is held today by The South Alberta Light Horse, The Queen's Own Rifles of Canada, The Argyll and Sutherland Highlanders of Canada and the 1st Battalion, The Royal New Brunswick Regiment (Carleton and York).

AWARDS AND DECORATIONS

Action and Award or Decoration	Recipient	Unit
Leliefontein, 1900		
Victoria Cross	Lieutenant Hampden Cockburn	The Royal Canadian Dragoons
Victoria Cross	Lieutenant Richard Turner	,,
Victoria Cross	Sergeant Edward Holland	,,
Distinguished Service Order	Lieutenant Edward Morrison	Royal Canadian Field Artillery
Distinguished Conduct Medal	Private William A. Knisley	The Royal Canadian Dragoons
Moreuil Wood, 1918		
Victoria Cross	Lieutenant Gordon Flowerdew	Lord Strathcona's Horse
Le Mesnil-Patry, 1944		
Distinguished Service Order	Lieutenant Colonel R. Colwell	The First Hussars
Military Cross	Lieutenant George Bean	The Queen's Own Rifles
Military Medal	Sergeant Samuel Scrutton	,,
Kapelsche Veer, 1945		
Distinguished Service Order	Captain Edward J. Brady	The Lincoln and Welland Regiment
Distinguished Conduct Medal	Trooper Albert Broadbent	South Alberta Regiment
Military Medal	Warrant Officer I Peter C. McGinley	The Argyll & Sutherland Highlanders of Canada
Military Medal	Sergeant L.C. Stewart	The Lincoln and Welland Regiment
Military Medal	Corporal John M. McEachern	,,
Military Medal	Private Robert Mason	The Argyll and Sutherland Highlanders
Order of Bronze Lion, Netherlands	Corporal W.E. Firlotte	The Lincoln and Welland Regiment
Order of Bronze Lion, Netherlands	Corporal Thomas Craigen	,,
Bronze Cross, Netherlands	Sergeant R.R. Nethery	,,
Bronze Cross, Netherlands	Sergeant G.W. Penney	South Alberta Regiment

NOTE

1 .DHH 325.009 (D123) Battle Honours – Canadian Militia, Letter from Colonel A.J.E. Kirkpatrick, 10 Nov 1923.

Endnotes

Abbreviations

Due to the great number of endnotes in *Fighting for Canada*, considerable use has been made of the following abbreviations throughout the notes section.

AB	Abercromby Papers, Huntingdon Library
ASH	Argyll & Sutherland Highlanders of Canada
BFTM	*Bulletin of the Fort Ticonderoga Museum*
BP	Bradstreet Papers
CAB	Canadian Armoured Brigade
CAR	Canadian Armoured Regiment
CHR	*Canadian Historical Review*
CIB	Canadian Infantry Brigade
CID	Canadian Infantry Division
CMH	*Canadian Military History*
CMR	Canadian Mounted Rifles
CO	Colonial Office
DAB	*Dictionary of American Biography*
DCB	*Dictionary of Canadian Biography*
DCHNY	*Documents Relative to the Colonial History of the State of New York*
DHC	E.A. Cruikshank, ed., *The Documentary History of the Campaign upon the Niagara Frontier* (9 vols., Welland, 1896-1905
DHH	Directorate of History and Heritage, Department of National Defence Headquarters
HL	Huntingdon Library
JSAHR	*Journal of the Society for Army Historical Research*
LdSH	Lord Strathcona's Horse
LO	Loudon Papers, Huntingdon Library
MG	Manuscript Group
NAC	National Archives of Canada
Ops Log	Operations Log
PRO	Public Record Office
QOR	Queen's Own Rifles of Canada
RCD	Royal Canadian Dragoons
RFCA	Royal Canadian Field Artillery
RG	Record Group
SAR	South Alberta Regiment
SHAEF	Supreme Headquarters, Allied Expeditionary Force
USNA	United States National Archives
WD	War Diary
WO	War Office

Introduction

1. Definition of the strategical level of war adapted from *Canada's Army: We Stand on Guard for Thee* (Ottawa, 1998), 79.

2. Definition of the operational level of war extracted from *Canada's Army: We Stand on Guard for Thee* (Ottawa, 1998), 80.

3. *NATO Glossary of Terms and Definitions (English and French)* (Brussels, 1995), 2-T-1.

4. This summary of the events surrounding the attack on Tilly-la-Campagne on the night of 1/2 August 1944 is extracted from the editor's book, *South Albertas: A Canadian Regiment at War* (Toronto, 1998), 105-106.

5. Ian Hamilton, *A Staff Officer's Scrap-Book during the Russo-Japanese War*, (2 vols., London, 1906), I, v.

6. Robert Rhodes James, "Thoughts on Writing Military History," *RUSI Journal* (May 1966), 100.

7. Colonel (Retd.) Robert Cook, US Army, to Lieutenant Colonel (Retd.) Joseph Whitehorne, 1986. Colonel Cook was a tank officer in Europe in 1944-1945.

8. Dominick Graham and Shelford Bidwell, *Tug of War, The Battle for Italy, 1943-1945*, (New York, 1986), 274.

9. Much of what is called Canadian military history actually consists of studies of diplomacy and international relations; defence policy, strategy, procurement and construction; veterans' postwar re-adjustment and benefits;

war memorials and commemorations; industrial-military relations; leadership (except in battle); intelligence; civil-military relations; officer education and career profiles; gender, race and ethnicity in the services; medicine; war art; prisoners of war; and on and on. The variety is endless but there have been notably few serious investigations into what actually happens when Canadians go into battle.

10. John Keegan, *Face of Battle* (New York, 1976) 30-31. Among the popular historians, the many books of Daniel Dancocks and Tony Foster's *Meeting of Generals* are far superior to the remainder of the pack.

11. Of the nineteen men and one woman who have held the office of prime minister since 1867, two were newspaper editors, two can only be charitably termed political hacks, one was a doctor, one a diplomat and (inevitably) fourteen were lawyers.

12. Keegan, *Face of Battle*, 36-38.

1. Ticonderoga

The author acknowledges his gratitude to his friend, historian Nicholas Westbrook, Director of the Fort Ticonderoga Museum and pre-eminent North American scholar on the 1758 campaign, for being the sounding-board and critic for this study. The best compilation of primary sources on the battle of Ticonderoga is contained in Nick's article, "Like Roaring Lions Breaking from their Chains:" The Highland Regiment at Ticonderoga," *BFTM*, 16 (1998), 17-91.

1. Song, "La carillon de la Nouvelle-France," attributed to Father Etienne Marchand, 1707-1774. The song is a play on words as "carillon" is not only the sound of bells ringing to celebrate a victory, it was also the French word for Ticonderoga. The fort was named because the falls on the nearby La Chute River had a musical sound. An English translation would be:

> You have encountered the different sounds
> Of our many varied bells.
> To distinguish each sound,
> You had to come a little closer!
> But you were unable to advance
> After a certain point   .
> When you perceived the beginning of
> The Carillon! The Carillon!
> The Carillon de la Nouvelle-France!

2. On Abercromby, see *DCB*, 4, 4-5.; and Stanley M. Pargellis, *Military Affairs in North America, 1748-1765*, (New Haven, 1969 reprint), 235.

3. George Augustus,, Lord Viscount Howe, eldest son of Sir Edward Scrope, second Lord Viscount Howe, was born in 1724 and succeeded to the title in 1735. In the forepart of 1757, he was ordered to America, being then colonel commandant of the 3rd Battalion, 60th Foot (Royal Americans), and arrived at Halifax in July 1757. On 28 Sep. 1757, he was appointed colonel of the 55th foot, and on 29 Dec. 1757, Brigadier-General in America. Killed in an ambush on 6 July prior to the Battle of Ticonderoga, Howe's corpse was escorted to Albany for interment by Philip Schuyler, a young officer of DeLancey's New Yorkers and was buried in St. Peter's Church. Massachusetts erected a monument to his memory in Westminster Abbey at an expense of £250. Lord Howe was a member of Parliament for Nottingham at the time of his death. See *DCHNY*, 10, 735.

4 William Pitt to Lord Grenville, 22 Aug 1758, in Francis Parkman, *Montcalm and Wolfe*, vol. 2, (London, 1899), 94. Unidentified Massachusetts officer letter dated 12 June 1758, in *New Hampshire Gazette*. The same letter appeared in the *Boston Evening Post* and the *Boston News Letter*.

5. HL, LO 5837, Richard Huck to Loudoun, 29 May 1758.

6. Monypenny, "Orderly Book," *BFTM*, 12 (1969), 336-37.

7. The Royal Americans were raised in 1755 after Braddock's defeat as a response to the shortage of troops. It was a unique regiment of four battalions, originally to have been recruited among the Swiss and German settlers in the North American colonies. Many officers and non-commissioned officers of German, Swiss and Dutch service were enrolled in Europe in anticipation of the new regiment's soldiery but recruiting amongst the settlers of Pennsylvania and New England fell far short of expectations. Shortfalls had to be filled with drafts sent over from British battalions on the Irish establishment. The 80th Foot stood apart from the brigades as specialist army troops, much like Rogers' Rangers. Nicknamed the "Leathercaps" because of

their particular type of headdress, the regiment was the brainchild of Colonel Thomas Gage but the unit was so new it still awaited the King's approval and pleasure. The 80th was the result of a perceived need for more regular light infantry. Numbering only five companies for a total of 400 men, the "Leathercaps'" roles and duties essentially matched those of the Rangers, though the former were deemed to be more disciplined and reliable troops. For more information on these regiments read Ian McCulloch, "'Within Ourselves': The Development of British Light Infantry in North America During the Seven Years' War," *CMH*, 7, (1998), 41-55.

8. This Mohican father and son were probably the real life inspiration for James Fenimore Cooper's Chingachcook (John Mohegan) and son, Uncas, who appear in his popular novel *Last of the Mohicans*.

9. Charles Lee, "Narrative," accompanying letter dated 16 September 1758 to his sister, Sydney Lee, *Fort Ticonderoga Museum Manuscript Collection*, 10, (1858), 729.

Lee was an adopted warrior of the Seneca nation. A native of Wales and son of a colonel in the British service, Lee entered the army early in life; was commissioned captain in the 44th foot, 11 June 1756; major in the 103rd, or Volunteer Hunters, 28 Oct. 1761, and in 1762 served, with the local rank of colonel in the auxiliary British force sent to Portugal where he distinguished himself. He went on half pay at the peace and entered the Polish service; became a brevet lieutenant colonel in May 1772, and came to America in 1773 and settled in Virginia. He resigned his commission in 1775, when he was appointed by Congress a major general in the Continental Army. He served until 1780 when, in consequence of disobeying Washington's orders, he resigned his commission to avoid court-martial. He returned to his plantation in Virginia and then removed to Philadelphia, where he died in 1782.

10. *Pennsylvania Gazette*, 17 Aug 1758, provides a list of 40 pieces of artillery and 200 rounds for each weapon being carried north while Captain Hugh Arnot's "Journal," in Westbrook's "Lions," 33-34, lists 44 guns of various calibres adding two brass 24-pdrs.

and two 8-inch brass mortars. Another return of the British artillery train is found in Dr. James Searing, "The Battle of Ticonderoga," New-York Historical Society *Proceedings*, 5 (1847), 113.

11. Loudoun to Cumberland, in Pargellis, *Military Affairs*, 227-28; Monypenny, "Orderly Book," 349.

12. In a fairly self-serving letter written after the battle, William Eyre reported that Abercromby had insisted he make a choice between his field command and his engineer's role before the campaign, as Eyre could not perform both. Eyre had taken the field command, "as there was no other field Officer to the regt but myself" and, because he was hoping for promotion to lieutenant colonel as there were "but three Majors in America older than Me." That the army as a whole could have benefited from his rather extensive engineering expertise was not part of the equation as far as Eyre was concerned. However, pension considerations were probably part of the decision as Eyre was not on the Ordnance Board list of authorized engineers in North America. Abercromby could not compel Eyre to serve as he did not hold such power over the Ordnance Board, and Eyre may have been very reluctant to serve unless he was allowed to keep his infantry status in case of being wounded and no longer capable of service. With a career-threatening wound, Eyre as an infantry major could go on half-pay where as an unauthorized engineer he would receive nothing.

William Eyre was promoted major in the 44th Foot, 7 Jan. 1756; in which year he built Fort William Henry, at the head of Lake George; in Jan. 1758, he was commissioned engineer-in-ordinary, and on 17 July was advanced to the rank of lieutenant colonel in the army with the 55th Foot. In July 1759, during Amherst's campaign, Eyre was appointed chief engineer to the army, and soon after laid out the ground for a new fort at Ticonderoga. In Oct 1759, he became lieutenant colonel of the 44th Foot and accompanied Amherst from Oswego to Montreal in 1760, and remained in America until 1764 when he was unfortunately drowned, in the prime of his life, on his passage to Ireland.

See Eyre to Napier, 10 July 1758, in

Pargellis, *Military Affairs*, 420; James Montresor, "The Journals of Colonel James Montresor," *Collections of the New-York Historical Society*, 14, (1882), 63; W. Porter, *History of the Corps of Engineers*, 1 (London, 1889) 186; *DCHNY*, 10, 729.

13. Beckles Willson, *The Life and Letters of James Wolfe*, (London, 1909), 369.

14. Monypenny, "Orderly Book," 436-37.

15. Arnot, "Journal," 28.

16. Captain Henry Pringle wrote of the Rangers that they "were created Indians, many of them Irish – They shoot amazingly well, and mostly with riffled barrels." See NAC, MG 18/18, reel H-1954, Henry Pringle's Entrybook, 17 Dec 1757. The 1000-man regiments (42nd, 46th and 4/60th) were to form 100-man companies, the 700-man battalions, 80-man companies, and the 1/60th, a 60-man company, see Stanley Pargellis, *Lord Loudoun in North America*, (New Haven, 1933), 305; Monypenny, "Orderly Book," 348.

17. Abercromby also had howitzers which were short-barrelled weapons used to fire explosive shells at a higher trajectory than guns and used for firing over the heads of friendly troops or enemy earthworks. Mortars were large calibre, short stubby pieces resembling upturned buckets, suitable only for very high-trajectory fire to drop shells inside defensive positions which could not be damaged with direct fire. Mortars were essentially a siege weapon.

18. W.J. Eccles, "The French Forces in North America during the Seven Years' War," *DCB*, 3, xx.

19. French regular infantry battalions had arrived in New France in 1755, the first contingent comprising the 2nd Battalions of the Languedoc, Guyenne, Béarn and La Reine regiments under the command of Dieskau. These went to in Montreal while the battalions of the Artois and Bourgogne regiments were sent to Louisbourg. The following year, Montcalm landed at Quebec, bringing with him the 2nd Battalions of the Royal-Roussillon and La Sarre regiments. In 1757, the 2nd and 3rd Battalions of the Berry Régiment, which had been in convoy to India, were re-routed to Quebec. On arrival, they were found to be under strength and three quarters of their rank and file to be mere boys.

Each battalion had an establishment of officers consisting of a lieutenant colonel in command, an adjutant (aide-major), and a surgeon major; a captain, a lieutenant, and a sub-lieutenant (sous lieutenant) of grenadiers; 12 fusilier captains, 12 lieutenants and two ensigns. The authorized strength of a battalion was 525 all ranks. See Eccles, "French Forces,", 3, xx.

20. Eccles, "French Forces," xx.

21. On Montreuil, see *DCB*, 4, 307-8.

22. Montcalm quoted in Ian McCulloch, "'The King Must be Obeyed:' Montcalm's Army at Quebec," *The Beaver*, (October/November 1992), 11.

23. Eccles, "French Forces," xix.

24. *Pennsylvania Gazette*, 27 Jul 1758.

25. Robert Rogers, *Journals of Robert Rogers*, F.B. Hough, ed., (Albany, 1883), 111.

26. Captain Peter Dubois of Colonel DeLancey's New Yorkers wrote that their arrival at the northern end of Lake George at dawn of the 6 July "extreamly surprised" the French "as they imagined our Halt at Sabbath-day Point would have been continued till Morning," see *Pennsylvania Journal*, 27 July 1758.

27. Lee, "Narrative," 6.

28. Arnot, "Journal," 36.

29. HL, AB, 445, Abercromby to DeLancey, 18 July 1758.

30. Rogers, *Journals*, 118a.

31. 44th Foot officer, quoted in John Knox, *Journal of the Campaigns in North America 1757-1760*, A.G. Doughty, ed., (Toronto, 1914), I, 190.

32. Rogers, *Journals*, 118a.

33. Alexander Monypenny letter, quoted in S.B. Pell, *Fort Ticonderoga*, (Fort Ticonderoga, reprint 1994), 29.

34. Arnot, "Journal," 38.

35. "Diary of the Reverend John Cleaveland," *BFTM*, 10, (1959), 198; Arnot, "Journal," 38.

36. "Journal of Archelaeus Fuller – May-Nov. 1758," *BFTM*, 13, (1970), 10.

37. HL, AB 445, Abercromby.

38. Major William Eyre in Pargellis, *Military Affairs*, 419.

39. Major William Eyre in Pargellis, *Military Affairs*, 419.

40. Major William Eyre in Pargellis, *Military Affairs*, 419; Garrett Albertson, "Montcalm's Victory," *BFTM*, 4, (1936), 45.

41. HL, AB 445, Abercromby.

42. On Bourlamaque, see *DCB*, 3, 84-86; J-N. Desandrouins, *Le Maréchal de Camp Desandrouins 1729-1792: Guerre du Canada 1756-1760*, Abbé Gabriel, ed. (Verdun, 1887), 160-61.

43. Pierre Pouchot, *Memoirs Upon the Late War in North America Between the French and English 1755-1760*, Brian Dunnigan, ed., (Youngstown, 1994), 142.

44. Desandrouins, *Memoirs*, 160-61.

45. "Memoir on Fort Carillon by M. de Pont le Roy," in *DCHNY*, 10, 720.

46. "Rélations de la victoire remportée sur les Anglais le 8 juillet 1758 par l'armée du Roi commandé par le marquis de Montcalm" in *Guerre du Canada – Rélations et Journaux de différentes expéditions faites durant les années 1755-1760*, Abbé Casgrain, ed., (Quebec, 1859), 154. Though this statement is commonly attributed to Montcalm, it was most probably from the writings of chevalier de la Pause, his principal staff officer responsible for reports. An almost word-for-word description of the officers' behaviour also appears in Louis-Antoine de Bougainville's account translated as *Adventures in the Wilderness*, by E.P. Hamilton, ed. (Norman, 1964), 229. By contrast, Desandrouins, who was actually on site supervising the work firsthand, says the officers were slack and idle: "Mais dans les plus pressantes occasions, la plupart des officiers sont d'une indolence inconcevable sur les travaux." See Desandrouins, *Memoirs*, 166.

47. Le Comte de Maurès de Malartic, *Journal des Campagnes au Canada de 1755-1760*, Paul Gafferel, ed. (Paris, 1890), 182.

48. De la Pause, *Report*, 155; Desandrouins, *Memoirs*, 166.

49. Desandrouins, *Memoirs*, 166.

50. Bougainville, *Journals*, 230.

51. Private Abel Spicer, "Journal of Abel Spicer," *Chronicles of Lake George*, Russell Bellico, ed., (Fleischmanns, 1995), 101; Caleb Rea, "The Journal of Dr. Caleb Rea," *Essex Institute Historical Collection*, 18, Fabius Maximus Rea, ed., (Salem, 1881), 25; Rogers, *Journals*, 119n.

52. John Shy, in his "James Abercromby and the Campaign of 1758," (unpublished MA thesis, University of Vermont, 1957), 115, is at a loss to explain Gage's absence or his blatant omission from any contemporary accounts of the battle. Bradstreet in explaining his leadership role to his agent Charles Gould makes no mention of Gage's whereabouts during the battle, see NAC, MG 40/K2, Bradstreet Papers, reel A-1659, Bradstreet to Gould, 21 Sep 1758.

53. On Bradstreet, see *DCB*, 4, 83-6. Wolfe was one senior British officer who had a high opinion of Bradstreet, see Willson, *Life and Letters of James Wolfe*, 369, Wolfe to Sackville, 24 May 1758.

54. NAC, Chatham MSS, Bundle 96/98, Loring to Pitt, 19 Aug 1758.

55. Benjamin Glasier, "French and Indian War Diary," *Essex Institute, Historical Collections*, 86 (1950), 76.

56. This unidentified Highland officer was most probably Captain James Abercrombie, erstwhile engineer and scout himself. See "Eyewitnesses Accounts of the British Regulars at Ticonderoga," *CHR*, 2, (1921), 360-63.

57. Eyre, in Pargellis, *Military Affairs*, 420; Captain William Hervey, 8 July 1758, in *Journals of the Honourable William Hervey in North America and Europe, from 1755 to 1814*, (Bury St. Edmunds, 1906), 50.

58. It is no wonder that one of the regular officers bitterly claimed after the battle that they had been assured that the enemy were still "making a breastwork which we might easily get to and push down with our shoulders." Indeed, the moment that the regulars encountered the actual main position in all surviving accounts is depicted as being one of complete surprise and dismay! Thus Bradstreet's somewhat cursory engineering reconnaissance conducted at ground level on the morning of 8 July became the basis for the plan of attack, but he would not have to worry about Abercromby censuring him for negligence. What little of the General's reputation remained after the disastrous battle was contingent on the dynamic Bradstreet's success in capturing Fort Frontenac a month later. As a result, Abercromby, in his letters and reports home, was unwilling to implicate the officer whose actions under his command would be the only ray of light in an otherwise dismal campaign. The dead Clerk was a more convenient scapegoat and, in order to leave

the impression that it was Clerk alone who was responsible for the bad intelligence, Abercromby remained deliberately silent on Clerk's actual whereabouts and doings on the final day of battle. This explicable silence is why historians have failed to pick up on the enfilade battery plan that came to nought under the guns of the French fort. All have accepted at face value the French participants' perception that the advance of gun rafts towed by whaleboats down the river at 1 P.M., in conjunction with the premature general assault, was a daring but ill-judged amphibious assault to turn the French left flank. Instead, they were the well-thought out, but poorly supported, efforts of a dynamic young professional officer who never had a chance to show his talent, nor was able at the end of the day, to defend his actions. See, Searing "Narrative," 116; Rea, "Journal," 27.

59. Searing, "Narrative," 115.

60. Glasier, "Diary," 76.

61. Fuller, "Journal," 10; Albertson, "Narrative," 45.

62. Oliver Partridge to his wife, 12 July 1758, in Parkman, *Montcalm and Wolfe*, 105.

63. Pouchot, *Memoirs*, 138.

64. Chevalier de la Pause, "Dispositions de Carillon," *Rapport de l'Archiviste de la Province de Québec pour 1932-1933*, 1933, 353-54.

65. Pouchot, *Memoirs*, 143-44; Malartic, *Journal*, 183-5.

66. Bougainville, *Journals*, 232.

67. Malartic, *Journal*, 183; Desandrouins, *Memoirs*, 173.

68. Glasier, "Diary," 76; Unidentified 1/60th Foot (Royal Americans) Officer, most likely Major John Tullikens, to Lieutenant Colonel Henri Bouquet, 14 July 1758, in "Ticonderoga 1758," *JSAHR*, 1 (1921), 12. Another translated version appears in *DCHNY*, 10, 736. The original letter, which was written in French to Bouquet, the Swiss commanding officer of the 60th, was first published in the *Pennsylvania Archives: First Series*, 3, 472-5. Major John Tullikens was acting commanding officer of the six companies of the 1st/60th Foot that participated in the Ticonderoga campaign, as Bouquet was serving as a brigade commander on the southern expedition against Fort Duquesne under General Forbes. This letter has every appearance of the acting commanding officer making a report to his superior on the state of the unit after the battle.

69. Spicer, "Journal," 102.

70. HL, AB 445, General Abercromby.

71. HL: AB 445, Abercromby; AB 447, "General Orders for the Attack on Ticonderoga."

72. Monypenny, "Orderly Book,", 460-1; various Provincial Orderly Books, 8 July 1758, in private collection.

73. Dubois letter to *Pennsylvania Journal*, 27 July 1758.

74. Eyre in Pargellis, *Military Affairs*, 420.

75. Rogers, *Journals*, 119-120; de la Pause, *Report*, 156; Malartic, *Journals*, 184.

76. Dubois letter in *Pennsylvania Journal*, 27 July 1758.

77. James Abercrombie to Erskine, 10 July 1758, in Westbrook, "Lions," 68-9.

78. Rogers, *Journals*, 120.

79. Rogers, *Journals*, 120.

80. Arnot, "Journal," 41.

81. Abercrombie to Erskine, 10 July 1758, in Westbrook, "Lions," 69.

82. Eyre in Pargellis, *Military Affairs*, 420-21.

83. Chevalier de Lévis, *Journal de campagne de 1756 à 1760 en Canada* (Montreal, 1889), 137.

84. Tullikens, "Report," 12; "J.B." to Clerk family, 25 Aug 1758, in Westbrook, "Lions,"

85. Westbrook is of the opinion that the writer of this letter is Jacob Bryant, Secretary to the Board of Ordnance, who was not at the battle but had heard of the circumstances from General Abercromby's senior aide-de-camp, Captain James Cunningham, who had been sent back to make the rounds of the key ministries and report on the defeat. See *BFTM*, 16 (1998), 229n., for further discussion.

85. Private John Bremner, "Extracts from the Journal of John Bremner, 55th Foot," typescript in Fort Ticonderoga Museum Manuscript Collection.

86. Colonel Henry Babcock, letter dated 10 July 1758, in C. Chapin, *Rhode Island in the Colonial Wars*, (Providence, 1918), 13; Spicer, "Diary," 101.

87. Lieutenant William Grant, "Copy of a letter from North America," *Scots Magazine*, 20, 698-99.

88. NAC, RG 8, I, vol 187, 9-10, Memorial of Private Thomas Busby.

89. Grant, "Copy of a Letter," *Scots Magazine,* 20, 698-699.

90. Grant, "Copy of a Letter," *Scots Magazine,* 20, 698-699; Captain Allan Campbell to John Campbell, 11 July 1758, in Westbrook, "Lions," 52.

91. Bougainville, *Journals,* 232.

92. Dubois letter in *Pennsyvlania Journal,* 27 July 1758; Hervey, *Journals,* 50.

93. Fuller, "Journal," 10; Captain David Perry, *Recollections of an Old Soldier: The Life of Captain David Perry,* (Windsor, 1822) reprinted in *BFTM,* 14, (1981), 5-6.

94. "Plan du Fort de Carillon et ses Environs avec L'attaque des Retranchements faite Par une Armée Anglaise de 25000 Hommes aux ordres de Mylord Abercrombie. Le 8e Juillet 1758." The original map is in the William L. Clements Library and a copy is in the NAC, National Map Collection, NAC-13277. The map legend indicates "point E. Rocher ou etoit G""A"" pendant le combat." (the rocky outcrop where General Abercromby was during the combat.)

95. Monypenny, "Orderly Book," 460-1; Provincial Orderly Books, 8 July 1758, in private collection.

96. Searing, "Narrative," 116.

97. De la Pause, *Report,* 156.

98. Bougainville, *Journals,* 233; Searing, "Narrative," 116.

99. Tullikens, "Report," 12.

100. Tullikens, "Report," 12.

101. Eyre, in Pargellis, *Military Affairs,* 421;.

102. Lee, "Narrative."

103. Lee, "Narrative."

104. Eyre in Pargellis, *Military Affairs,* 421; Fuller, "Journal," 10.

105. Perry, *Recollections,* 6.

106. Henry Babcock in Chapin, *Rhode Island,* 13.

107 Letter from Lake George, 26 July 1758, in Parkman, *Montcalm and Wolfe,* 112-13.

108. Albertson, *Narrative,* 45-6.

109. Perry, *Recollections,* 6.

110. Captain James Murray to John Murray, 19 July 1758, in Westbrook, "Lions," 48.

111. Unidentified 55th Foot officer in *Scots Magazine,* Aug 1758, 438-9; Bougainville, *Journals,* 233.

112. De la Pause, *Report,* 157.

113. Bougainville, *Journals,* 233; Grant, "Letter," 698-699.

114. Desandrouins, *Memoirs,* 180-181.

115. Captain Dubois, 10 July 1758, in *Gentleman's Magazine,* (28), 446; Pouchot, *Memoir,* 147-48.

116. Pouchot, *Memoir,* 148; Dubois, 446; Bremner, "Journal."

117. Desandrouins, *Memoirs,* 181.

118. Bougainville, *Journals,* 233. The Highland officer was Captain-Lieutenant John Campbell, one of the two Highland privates who had performed sword drill for King George II at Whitehall in 1743 to be rewarded with a gold sovereign. Campbell had been given a battlefield promotion for gallantry at Fontenoy. An account in the *Scots Magazine* (1759), 213, claims that a total of twenty Highlanders got over the walls with Captain Campbell of which seven were given quarter.

119. Captain Salah Barnard, 8 July 1758, quoted in Westbrook, "Lions," 18.

120. In the American Civil War, one regiment, the 1st Minnesota sustained an 82 per cent casualty rate at Gettysburg but the battle was fought over three days and the entire regiment was not engaged. The 1st Minnesota had 47 killed and 168 wounded for a total of 215 casualties out of 262 men engaged. The 9th Illinois at Shiloh fought over two days and lost 61 killed, 300 wounded and five missing for a total of 63 per cent casualties. See "Regimental Losses in the American Civil War, 1861-1865," cited in Frederick B. Richards, *The Black Watch at Ticonderoga,* (Fort Ticonderoga Museum Library, [n.d.]), 43-44.

121. Rogers, *Journals,* 120; Lévis, *Journal,* 137-38.

122. Perry, *Recollections,* 6. Private Jesse Parsons of Wooster's Connecticut Regiment, reported that Lieutenant John Small of the 42nd Foot, commanding a post-battle truce party trying to recover the wounded some weeks later, discovered that the French had dispatched all the British wounded for whom they could not provide care. See Jesse Parsons's journal in Fort Ticonderoga Museum Manuscript Collection.

123. General Abercromby to James Abercromby, 19 Aug 1758, in Westbrook, "Lions," 76.

124. General Abercromby to James Abercromby, 19 Aug 1758, in Westbrook,

"Lions," 76; Henry Babcock in Chapin, *Rhode Island*, 13.

125. Bougainville, *Journals*, 234-35.

126. Tullikens, "Report," 13; Lee, "Narrative."

127. NAC, Bradstreet Papers, Bradstreet to Charles Gould, 21 Sep 1758.

128. Dubois letter, 10 July 1758, in *Gentleman's Magazine*, (1758), 446.

129. Marquis de Montcalm to Doreuil, quoted in Parkman, *Montcalm and Wolfe*, 116; *DCB*, 3, 462.

130. Montcalm to Minister of War, 28 July 1758, see *DCB*, 3, 463.

131. Archives Nationales de France, C11A, vol. 103, folio 144, Marquis de Vaudreuil to Minister of the Navy, 4 Aug 1758.

132. Bougainville to wife, Apr. 1759, quoted in Parkman, *Montcalm and Wolfe*, 186.

Interlude – "A Mere Matter of Marching:" Defending Canada, 1758 to 1812

1. Montcalm quoted in Ian K. Steele, *Guerillas and Grenadiers* (Toronto, 1969), 109.

2. Vaudreuil, quoted in Steel, *Guerillas and Grenadiers*, 109.

3. W.J. Eccles, *The Canadian Frontier, 1534-1760* (Albuquerque, 1974), 185.

4. NAC, CO 42, vol 34, Carleton to Dartmouth, 7 June 1775.

5. CO 42, vol 35, Carleton to Sackville-Germain, 28 Sep 1776.

6. John Elting, *Amateurs to Arms! A Military History of the War of 1812* (Chapel Hill, 1991), 1.

7. NAC, CO 42, vol 23, Prince Regent's Instructions to Prevost, 11 Dec 1811.

2. Queenston Heights

1. Van Rensselaer to Dearborn, 8 Oct. 1812, *DHC*, 4:41.

2. "Come all, ye bold Canadians" is a ballad that dates from the late summer of 1812, see R.I. Warner, "The Bold Canadian: A Ballad of the War of 1812," in Morris Zaslow, ed., *The Defended Border: Upper Canada and the War of 1812* (Toronto, 1964), 303-305.

3. Jacques Redway, "General Van Rensselaer and the Niagara Frontier," *Proceedings of the N.Y. State Historical Association* 8 (1909), 15. For a biography of Stephen Van Rensselaer, see *DAB*, 10:211-12; and Carol Whitfield, "The Battle of Queenston Heights," *Occa-sional Papers in Archaeology and History*, #11 (Ottawa, 1974), 42-48.

4. Tompkins's choice of Van Rensselaer is discussed in Catharina V. R. Bonney, *Legacy of Historical Gleanings* (2 vols, Albany, 1875), 1:194; and Whitfield, "Queenston Heights," 44.

5. Lovett's correspondence makes up a large part of Chapters 10 through 14 of Bonney, *Historical Gleanings*. For a biography of Solomon Van Rensselaer, see *DAB*, 10: 210-11 and Whitfield, Queenston Heights," 40-2. To differentiate in these notes between the two Van Rensselaers all references to Solomon Van Rensselaer will include his first name.

6. General Order by Lamb, 13 Aug. 1812, *DHC*, 3:177; unattributed letter, 17 Aug. 1812, *New York Statesman*, 15 Aug. 1812, *DHC*, 3:187; Van Rensselaer to Dearborn, 18 Aug. 1812, *DHC* 3:189; Van Rensselaer to Myers, 18 Aug. 1812, *DHC* 3:189; Van Rensselaer to Tompkins, 19 Aug. 1812, *DHC* 3:191; Van Rensselaer to Dearborn, 28 Aug. 1812, *DHC* 3: 218; Lovett to Alexander, 14 Aug. 1812, in Bonney, *Gleanings*, 1:205; Lovett's "Journal of the Campaign," in Bonney, *Gleanings*, 1:209; General Orders by Solomon Van Rensselaer, 13, 16, 18, 19, 22 Aug. 1812, in Solomon Van Rensselaer, *A Narrative of the Affair at Queenstown: In the War of 1812* (Boston, 1836), 82-6. *DHC* is used as the main source although many of its documents may also be found in Bonney, *Gleanings* and Solomon Van Rensselaer, *Narrative*.

7. Dearborn to Van Rensselaer, 25 Aug. 1812, *DHC*, 3:205; Van Rensselaer to Tompkins and Dearborn, 1 Sep. 1812, *DHC*, 3:228; Dearborn to Van Rensselaer, 2 Sep. 1812, *DHC* 3:232; Fenwick to Van Rensselaer, 3 Sep. 1812, *DHC*, 3:235; Van Rensselaer to Brock, 4 Sep. 1812, *DHC*, 3:236; Solomon Van Rensselaer to Van Vechten, 5 Sep. 1812, *DHC*, 3:237.

8. Solomon Van Rensselaer to Porter, 14 Sep. 1812, *DHC*, 3:261; Solomon Van Rensselaer to Van Vechten, 5 Sep. 1812, *DHC*, 3:237; General Orders by Solomon Van Rensselaer, 15, 30 Sep. 1812; *DHC*, 3:263, 304; Tompkins to Van Rensselaer, 9 Sep. 1812, *DHC* 3:247.

9. Van Rensselaer to Dearborn, 17 Sep. 1812, *DHC*, 3:270; Tompkins to Magher, 11 Sep. 1812, *DHC*, 3:255; Lovett to Alexander, 22 Sep. 1812, *DHC*, 3:288; *Buffalo Gazette*, 29 Sep. 1812, *DHC*, 3:301; General Orders by Solomon Van Rensselaer, 17, 19 Sep. 1812, *DHC*, 3:275, 282; Van Rensselaer to Tompkins, 22 Sep. 1812, *DHC*, 3:286; Brock to Prevost, 13 Sep. 1812, *DHC*, 3:258.

10. Dearborn to Van Rensselaer, 27 Sep. 1812, *DHC*, 3:297.

11. Troops under Major General Van Rensselaer, 12 Oct 1812, *DHC*, 4:68; Lovett to Van Vechten, 8 Sep. 1812, *DHC*, 3:244.

12. Van Rensselaer to Dearborn, 8 Oct. 1812, *DHC*, 4:40.

13. Smyth to Van Rensselaer, 29 Sep. 1812, *DHC*, 3:300; Van Rensselaer to Smyth, 30 Sep. 1812, *DHC*, 3:305; Smyth to Van Rensselaer, 2 Oct. 1812, *DHC*, 4:28; Van Rensselaer to Smyth, 5, 6, 10, 11 Oct. 1812, *DHC*, 4:34, 38, 59, 66; Van Rensselaer to Dearborn, 8 Oct. 1812, *DHC*, 4:40; Van Rensselaer to Eustis, 14 Oct. 1812, *DHC* 4:80.

14. Van Rensselaer to Eustis, 14 Oct 1812, *DHC*, 4:80.

15. Van Rensselaer to Eustis, 14 Oct. 1812, *DHC*, 4:80.

16. Van Rensselaer to Eustis, 14 Oct. 1812, *DHC*, 4:80.

17. Smyth to Van Rensselaer, 12 Oct 1812, *DHC*, 4:68; Van Rensselaer to Smyth, 12 Oct 1812, *DHC*, 4:68.

18. Brock to Prevost, 11 Oct. 1812, with postscript 12 Oct., *DHC*, 4:63; Elliott to Hamilton, 9, 10 Oct. 1812, *DHC* 4:45, 47; Towson to Elliott, 6 July 1843, *DHC*, 4:50.

19. Brock to Savery Brock, 18 Sep. 1812, *DHC*, 3:278; Brock to Prevost, 18 Sep. 1812, *DHC*, 3:276; Prevost to Brock, 7, 10 July, 2 Aug. 1812, *DHC*, 3:113, 120, 160; Brock to Prevost, 11 Oct. 1812, *DHC*, 4:63.

20. Brock to Irving Brock, 10 Jan. 1811, Ferdinand Brock Tupper, *Life and Correspondence of Major-General Sir Isaac Brock, K. B.* (London, 1845), 70. For a biography of Brock, see *DCB*, 5:109. See also section on Brock in Whitfield, "Queenston Heights," 19-30. Brock was knighted on 9 Oct. 1812 for his victory at Detroit but news of the honour did not reach Canada until months after his death.

21. Prevost to Brock, 31 July 1812, *DHC*, 3:154. For a biography of Sheaffe, see *DCB*, 8:793; and Whitfield, "Queenston Heights," 31-7.

22. Evans to unknown recipient, 15 Oct. 1812, *DHC*, 4:110.

23. Ernest Green, "The Niagara Portage Road," *Ontario History*, 22 (1926), 260-311. Descriptions of Queenston during this time are found in William W. Campbell, *The Life and Writings of De Witt Clinton* (New York, 1849), and H. F. Gardiner, "The Hamiltons of Queenston, Kingston and Hamilton," *Ontario History*, 8 (1907), 24-33.

24. The Militia Law of March 1812 was discussed in detail by the anti-Republican newspaper, the *New York Evening Post*, on 27 Aug. 1812.

25. This order of battle is derived from several sources, the most precise being Solomon Van Rensselaer, *Narrative*, 24-5. The deployment of Scott's guns is described in Mary Roach Archer, "The Journal of Major Isaac Roach, 1812-1824," *Pennsylvania Magazine of History and Biography*, 17 (1893), 131-43.

26. Times noted by the participants vary by up to two hours. The British generally felt the action began shortly after 3.00 A.M. while the Americans cited 4.00 A.M.. The latter time was taken as the standard for this study since it concurs more closely with the normal 13 October sunrise (at 6.30 A.M., daylight saving time exempted) and sunset (at 5.40 P.M.) in the area.

27. Lovett to Alexander, 14 Oct. 1812, *DHC*, 4:86.

28. Brock to Savery Brock, 18 Sep. 1812, *DHC*, 3:278.

29. Solomon Van Rensselaer, *Narrative*, 25.

30. Solomon Van Rensselaer, *Narrative*, 25. Details about Van Rensselaer's wounds in a letter to his wife, 14 Oct. 1812, *Gleanings*, 1:268.

31. Lovett to Alexander, 14 Oct. 1812, *DHC*, 4:86.

32. Chrystie to Cushing, 22 Feb. 1813, *DHC*, 4:97.

33. Robinson to unknown recipient, 14 Oct. 1812, *DHC*, 5:12. This account, abbreviated, is also in *DHC*, 4:103. Other reports of damage to the American boats is found in *Poulson's American Daily*, 24 Nov. 1812, *DHC*, 4:126, and a memoir by John Clark in

DHC, 5:8. Fenwick's capture is mentioned by Chrystie, *DHC*, 4:95.

34. Chrystie to Cushing, 22 Feb. 1813, *DHC*, 4:98.

35. Chrystie to Cushing, 22 Feb. 1813, *DHC*, 5:98.

36. James Crooks manuscript, "Reflections of the War of 1812," *Family History and Reminiscences of Early Settlers*, Niagara Historical Society, 28, (1916), 32. "Nor did we hear the report of the guns … so strong was the gale off the Lake," Crooks noted in his manuscript, 33. A similar observation was made by John Norton, Klinck and Talman, *Journal*, 304.

37. Evans, *DHC*, 4:111. Brock's horse may have been the legendary Alfred – "ten years old, but being a high bred horse, and latterly but very little worked, he may be considered as still perfectly fresh" – given to him by Sir James Craig when he returned to England, leaving Brock to make arrangements for Alfred's transportation to Upper Canada, which, it has long been assumed, Brock did. See Baynes to Brock, 4 Mar. 1811, in Tupper, *Brock*, 85.

38. McLean to McNab, 22 July 1860, Janet Carnochan, "Col. Daniel MacDougal and Valuable Documents," *Niagara Historical Society*, #23, 1912, 35. Lieutenant Colonel Ralph Bruyeres twice noted the four batteries and five pieces of ordnance (1 12-pdr. and 2 9-pdr. long guns and 2 18-pdr. carronades) between Fort George and Queenston, see NAC, RG 8I, vol 1707, 82, Return of Ordnance … 19 Dec. 1812, and vol 387, 71, Bruyeres to Prevost, 13 Feb. 1813. The sites of three of the batteries are implied in a district general order by Evans, 19 Nov. 1812 (*DHC*, 4:223) that shows officers on grand rounds responsible for inspecting from McFarland House to Two-Mile Hut and from Brown's Point to Two-Mile Hut. It is assumed that the fourth battery was at Vrooman's Point.

39. Robinson, *DHC*, 5:12. For a biography of Robinson, see *DCB*, 9:668. Casualties based on Return of British Casualties at Queenston, 13 Oct. 1812, *DHC*, 4:73 and an unattributed letter (probably by William Holcroft, RA), 14 Oct. 1812, *Quebec Mercury*, 27 Oct. 1812, *DHC*, 4:117. See also

McLean to McNab, 22 July 1860, Carnochan, "Valuable Documents," 36.

40. For a biography of Wool, see *DAB*, 10:513. A controversy arose when Captain Peter Ogilvie was identified in Solomon Van Rensselaer's report to Dearborn as the officer in charge. Wool described his actions, supported by others and confirmed by Ogilvie in a series of correspondence: Wool to Solomon Van Rensselaer, 23 Oct. 1812, *DHC*, 4:155; Randolph to Wool, 11 Nov. 1812, *DHC*, 4:156; Chrystie to Wool, 21 Dec. 1812, *DHC*, 4:156; Solomon Van Rensselaer to Wool, 24 Dec. 1812, *DHC*, 4:157; and Ogilvie to Wool, 27 Dec. 1812, *DHC*, 4:157.

41. William Hamilton Merritt, "Personal Narrative," *Campaigns of 1812-14*, Niagara Historical Society, #9, (1902), 10. This appears to be an earlier version of Merritt's "Journal of Events Principally on the Detroit and Niagara Frontiers," published in 1863, and contained in William Wood, ed., *Select British Documents of the Canadian War of 1812* (4 vols, Toronto, 1920-28), 3:543-648. The latter features a condensed version of Merritt's description of the action in 3:559. For a biography of Merritt, see *DCB*, 9:544. A Royal Artillery sergeant, bombardier and gunner were mentioned as being at the redan battery in an unattributed letter (probably by William Holcroft, RA), 14 Oct. 1812, in *Quebec Mercury*, 27 Oct. 1812, and contained in *DHC*, 4:117.

42. Robinson, *DHC*, 5:12. The second quote is from the Jarvis account, undated, *DHC*, 4:116. For a biography of Jarvis, see *DCB*, 10:379.

43. Jarvis, *DHC*, 4:116.

44. Walcot's narrative is in Ludwig Kosche, "Relics of Brock: An Investigation," *Archivaria*, 9 (1979-80) 101. A problem with this account is that it was given in 1880 when Walcot, then aged 100, was attempting to prove his claim to a thirty-year-old account in a Philadelphia bank, and demonstrated the strength of his memory by reciting events unrelated to the issue under debate.

45. Jarvis, *DHC*, 4:116.

46. Glegg to W. Brock, 14 Oct. 1812, *DHC*, 4:83. For a biography of Macdonell, see Whitfield, "Queenston Heights," 38-9.

47. Robinson, *DHC*, 5:12-13. McLean to unknown recipient, 15 Oct. 1812, *DHC*, 4:114-16. Also, McLean to McNab, 22 July 1860, "Col. Daniel MacDougal and Valuable Documents," *Niagara Historical Society* No. 23 (1911-12), 37. For a biography of McLean, see *DCB*, 9:512.

48. Robinson, *DHC*, 5:13

49. Robinson, *DHC*, 5:13.

50. A preliminary examination of muster and pay rolls for most of the New York militia regiments reveals that 310 officers and men were identified as having been involved in the Queenston affair, United States National Archives, RG 94, Office of the Adjutant General, Volunteer Organizations and State Militia War of 1812, Boxes 126-9. Estimates from participants suggest the number was closer to 500.

51. Chrystie noted that the gun was spiked by "one of our own artillerists," (*DHC*, 4:100) as did Solomon Van Rensselaer: "one of the number in a fit of over-zealous patriotism . . . spik[ed] the cannon as soon as captured" (*Narrative*, 28).

52. Norton, *Journal*, 304. Carl Benn, *The Iroquois in the War of 1812* (Toronto, 1998), 10-66. For a biography of Norton, see *DCB*, 6:550.

53. Evans to unknown, 15 Oct. 1812, *DHC*, 4:110.

54. Norton, *Journal*, 305.

55. Norton, *Journal*, 306.

56. Willson to Stewart, 9 Nov. 1812, "A Rifleman of Queenston," *Publications of the Buffalo Historical Society*, 9 (1906), 374.

57. Winfield Scott, *Memoirs of Lieut.-General Scott, LL.D.* (2 vols, New York, 1864), 1:59.

58. Unattributed (probably Holcroft), *Quebec Mercury*, *DHC*, 4:118.

59. Norton, *Journal*, 306.

60. Chrystie, *DHC*, 4:101.

61. Chrystie, *DHC*, 4:101.

62. Willson, "Rifleman," 374.

63. Brock to his brothers, 3 Sep. 1812, *DHC*, 3:235. Brief quotes from Brock to Green, 8 Feb. 1804, in Whitfield, "Queenston Heights," 48.

64. Crooks, "Reflections," 34.

65. Crooks, "Reflections," 35.

66. Chrystie, *DHC*, 4:102.

67. Mead, *DHC*, 4:92.

68. Scott, *Memoirs*, 1:60.

69. Crooks, "Reflections," 36.

70. Crooks, "Reflections," 36.

71. Crooks, "Reflections," 36.

72. Woodruff to Thorburn, 29 July 1840, *DHC*, 4:78.

73. Lovett, *DHC*, 4:87.

74. Crooks, "Reflections," 37.

75. Walcot, in Kosche, *Relics*, 101.

76. McLean to McNab, 22 July 1860, "Col. Daniel MacDougal and Valuable Documents," *Niagara Historical Society* No. 23 (1911-12), 37.

77. Van Rensselaer to Dearborn, 20 Oct. 1812, *DHC*, 4:143. Lovett to Alexander, 25 Oct. 1812, *DHC*, 4:162. The unofficial tabulation was printed in Lieutenant Colonel J. Heaton, *Returns of the Killed and Wounded of American Troops ... from the Year 1790, to the close of the War with Mexico, in 1848*, 1850-1851.

78. Return of prisoners of war, 15 Oct. 1812, *DHC*, 4:74. List of Americans killed and wounded or taken prisoner, no date, *DHC*, 4:76; *Buffalo Gazette*, 27 Oct. 1812, *DHC*, 4:166; Agreement for the Exchange of Prisoners, by Winder and Evans, undated, *DHC*, 4:90.

79. Return of British Casualties, 15 Oct. 1812, *DHC*, 4:73. Names of Indians killed at Queenston, no date, *DHC* 4:76; Return of Casualties in 3rd York, 5 Jan. 1813, *DHC*, 4:124.

80. Return of Ordnance, etc., Captured, 1 Dec. 1812, *DHC*, 4:74. One participant mentioned that 1,600 muskets were originally seized, Ridout to Ridout, 21 Oct. 1812, *DHC*, 4:146. The 6-pdr. had probably been equipped with fifty-four fixed rounds of round shot and seventeen fixed rounds of canister, see Donald E. Graves, "American Ordnance of the War of 1812," *Arms Collecting*, 31 (1993), 113.

81. Van Rensselaer to Dearborn, 20 Oct. 1812, *DHC*, 4:143.

82. Mead, *DHC*, 4:92, 93.

83. Solomon Van Rensselaer, *Narrative*, 28-9.

84. Willson, "Rifleman," 374-5.

85. *New York Evening Post*, 22 Oct. 1812.

86. Prevost to Bathurst, 21 Oct. 1812, *DHC*, 4:148; General Order by Baynes, 21 Oct. 1812, *DHC*, 4:149. For Sheaffe's biography, *DCB*, 8:793.

Interlude – Undefended Borders, Valiant Militia and Other Myths: Defending Canada, 1812 to 1866

1. An Exhortation pronounced after the Sermon, York, 22 Dec 1812, in *Report of the Loyal and Patriotic Society of Upper Canada* (Montreal, 1817).

2. PRO, WO 17, Monthly Returns of the Army in North America, 25 June 1812 to Dec 1814.

   In the attention given during the war to the exploits of the militia, the fact that Canadians served in British regular or near-regular units is often overlooked. The 104th Regiment of Foot was recruited in North America as were the Nova Scotia, Newfoundland, New Brunswick, Canadian and Glengarry Light Infantry Fencible Regiments. There were also a number of effective near-regular units such as the Voltigeurs Canadian of Lower Canada, the Incorporated Militia Battalion of Upper Canada and the six battalions of Select Embodied Militia of Lower Canada which served for long periods under the command of regular officers. These units and other smaller corps of gunners, cavalry, artillery, and boatmen made an outstanding contribution to the defence of their country.

3. Toronto *Globe*, 18 June 1862, quoted in J.M. Hitsman, *Safeguarding Canada, 1763-1871* (Toronto, 1968), 176.

4. Williams to Secretary of State for War, 13 June 1864, quoted in Hitsman, *Safeguarding Canada*, 187.

3. Ridgeway

1. Fenian drinking song sung to the tune of "The Wearing of the Green," circa 1865

2. David Owen, *The Year of the Fenians*, (Buffalo, 1990), 54.

3. Owen, *Fenians*, 45-48; Hereward Senior, *The Last Invasion of Canada*, (Toronto, 1991), 19-20.

4. Owen, *Fenians*, 57.

5. George Denison, *Soldiering in Canada*, (Toronto, 1900), 59-62.

6. John Macdonald, *Troublesome Times in Canada: A History of the Fenian Raids of 1866 and 1870* (Toronto, 1910), 5.

7. Owen, *Fenians*, 57; David Meyler, "To the Glory of Our Country," *Command Magazine* 15 (1992), 58.

8. Owen, *Fenians*, 57-59; Senior, *Last Invasion*, 40-41.

9. This was the first recorded appearance of that title.

10. Owen, *Fenians*, 59-60; Senior, *Last Invasion*, 62.

11. Owen, *Fenians*, 59; Macdonald, *Troublesome Times*, 11-13.

12. Owen, *Fenians*, 65; Senior, *Last Invasion*, 42.

13. Owen, *Fenians*, 65; Macdonald, *Troublesome Times*, 16-17, 21-23.

14. Senior, *Last Invasion*, 55-56.

15. Owen, *Fenians*, 63, 66; Macdonald, *Troublesome Times*, 23-24.

16. Owen, *Fenians*, 67.

17. Of a Canadian population of 3,485,761 enumerated in the 1871 census, the top four ethnic origins were 1,082,940 French, 846,414 Irish, 706,369 English and 549,946 Scottish. 1871 Census cited in Government of Canada, *Sixty Years of Canadian Progress 1867-1927*, (Ottawa, 1927), 39.

18. Owen, *Fenians*, 60; Tom Brosnahan, *Central America* (Hawthorne, 1994), 186-187.

19. Peter Toner, "The Military Organization of the "Canadian" Fenians 1866-1870," *The Irish Sword* 38 (1971), 27; Owen, *Fenians*, 59-60, 62; Meyler, "Glory," 61.

20. Owen, *Fenians*, 67; Macdonald, *Troublesome Times*, 24-25; Meyler, "Glory," 61-62.

21. Senior, *Last Invasion*, 61.

22. Senior, *Last Invasion*, 61.

23. Senior, *Last Invasion*, 61; Denison, *Soldiering*, 87.

24. Senior, *Last Invasion*, 61.

25. Senior, *Last Invasion*, 67; Meyler, *Glory*, 61-62.

26. John O'Neill, "Official Report of the Battle of Ridgeway, Canada West, Fought June 2d, 1866," (republished, Nashville, 1966), 37.

27. Owen, *Fenians*, 67.

28. O'Neill, "Report," 37; Owen, *Fenians*, 67; Senior, *Last Invasion*, 66.

29. Owen, *Fenians*, 67.

30. O'Neill, "Report," 37; Owen, *Fenians*, 67.

31. Senior states the men were formed into companies of fifty, but O'Neill wrote that the men were distributed in squads. I have accepted the latter, see O'Neill, "Report," 37; Senior, *Last Invasion*, 61, 68.

32. Senior, *Last Invasion*, 67-68.

33. O'Neill, "Report," 37.

34. O'Neill, "Report," 37; Owen, *Fenians*, 67.

35. Owen, *Fenians*, 68; Senior, *Last Invasion*, 67; Meyler, "Glory," 62.

36. O'Neill, "Report," 37.

37. Owen, *Fenians*, 68-69.

38. O'Neill, "Report," 38.

39. Denison puts the number at Fenians in Buffalo in early June as 5,000 or 6,000. Macdonald wrote that 5,166 Fenians signed parole papers on 15 June 1866 and returned to their homes from Buffalo. However Beatty includes a published list of the destinations of the men paroled on 15 June that totals 1,566. Macdonald's transposed figures have been accepted by historians for nearly a century. See Denison, *Soldiering*, 115; Macdonald, *Troublesome Times*, 93; Stephen Beatty, *Fenian Raid, 1866* (St. Catharines, 1910), 35.

40. Owen, *Fenians*, 69; Senior, *Last Invasion*, 68; Macdonald, *Troublesome Times*, 27.

41. This description is based on the map in Denison and Owen's description as well as personal reconnaissance. Denison, *Soldiering*, 96; Owen, *Fenians*, 69.

42. Owen, *Fenians*, 69.

43. Beatty, *Raid*, 10-11.

44. R. Rogers, *History of the Lincoln and Welland Regiment*, (2nd ed., St. Catherines, 1979), 24.

45. DHH, 000.8 D51, Imperial Officers serving in Canada at time of Fenian Raids, 5, 11, 16, 18. This undated list includes Royal Navy officers.

46. Senior, *Last Invasion*, 68-69.

47. O'Neill, "Report," 38.

48. O'Neill, "Report," 38; Owen, *Fenians*, 69; Senior, *Last Invasion*, 69.

49. O'Neill, "Report," 38; Owen, *Fenians*, 69-70.

50. O'Neill, "Report," 38.

51. Senior, *Last Invasion*, 62.

52. Owen, *Fenians*, 70.

53. The Fenians had remedied the lack of maps before embarkation. Owen, *Fenians*, 70.

54. NAC, RG 9 IC8, Vol 6, Inquiry to Investigate the Case of Lieut-Col. J. Stoughton Dennis, 8 November 1866, Testimony of Richard Graham, 257 (hereafter Dennis Inquiry followed by name of witness); Senior, *Last Invasion*, 76.

55. NAC, MG 29, E 73, Official Reports, Report by Peacocke, 1 (hereafter Official Reports followed by the name of the officer who made the report); Senior, *Last Invasion*, 70.

56. O'Neill, "Report," 38.

57. Macdonald, *Troublesome Times*, 34-36.

58. Owen, *Fenians*, 72; Senior, *Last Invasion*, 72.

59. Owen, *Fenians*, 72; Senior, *Last Invasion*, 74.

60. NAC, Official Reports, Lowry, 7,8.

61. NAC, Official Reports, Peacocke, 1.

62. Senior, *Last Invasion*, 76.

63. Denison, *Soldiering*, 92-94.

64. Senior, *Last Invasion*, 75.

65. NAC, Official Reports, Peacocke, 1.

66. NAC, Official Reports, Peacocke, 1.

67. NAC, Official Reports, Peacocke, 1.

68. NAC, Official Reports, Peacocke, 1; Ernest Cruikshank, *The Original and Official History of the Thirteenth Battalion of Infantry*, (Hamilton, 1899), 46.

69. O'Neill, "Report," 38; Owen, *Fenians*, 71.

70. The logic is also summarized by Owen in *Fenians*, 71; and Macdonald, *Troublesome Times*, 31.

71. O'Neill, "Report," 38.

72. O'Neill, "Report," 38.

73. O'Neill, "Report," 39.

74. Senior places the Fenian Camp at Black Creek at this time. However the testimony of Akers and Graham at the Dennis Inquiry, when read with O'Neill's report, indicates that the Fenians remained in camp at Newbigging's farm. See Senior, *Last Invasion*, 76; NAC, Dennis Inquiry, Akers, 221; Graham, 257; O'Neill, "Report," 38.

75. O'Neill, "Report," 39.

76. Brereton Greenhous, *Semper Paratus The History of The Royal Hamilton Light Infantry (Wentworth Regiment) 1862-1977*, (Hamilton, 1977), 49.

77. Other rifles were found in the river. NAC, Dennis Inquiry, Akers, 221-222; Macdonald, *Troublesome Times*, 31.

78. O'Neill, "Report," 39.

79. Owen, *Fenians*, 9, 77.

80. Greenhous, *Semper Paratus*, 58.

81. O'Neill, "Report," 39; Owen, *Fenians*, 77.

82. NAC, Official Reports, Peacocke, 1-2.

83. Rogers, *Lincoln*, 26.

84. Macdonald, *Troublesome Times*, 40, 44.

85. Macdonald, *Troublesome Times*, 40.

86. NAC, Official Reports, Dennis, 11.

87. Macdonald, *Troublesome Times*, 34-35; Beatty, *Raid*, 18-19.

88. Macdonald, Macdonald, *Troublesome Times*, Appendix, Inquiry to Report on the Late Engagement at Lime Ridge, 3 July 1866, Evidence of Lieutenant Colonel Booker, 200 (Hereafter *TT – Booker Inquiry* followed by the name of the witness).

89. NAC, Official Reports, Dennis, 13.

90. Denison, *Soldiering*, 98-99.

91. NAC, Official Reports, Peacocke, 2.

92. NAC, Official Reports, Peacocke, 2; Macdonald, *TT – Booker Inquiry*, Booker, 200.

93. Macdonald, *Troublesome Times*, 38.

94. NAC, Official Report, Dennis, 11.

95. NAC, Official Report, Dennis, 11-12.

96. NAC, MG 29, E 108, Recollections of Sergeant McIntosh, 3 (hereafter McIntosh).

97. Macdonald, *TT – Booker Inquiry*, Gillmor, 223.

98. NAC, Official Reports, Dennis, 12.

99. This source contains material that does not appear in Beatty's published work on the raid. NAC, MG 29 E 74, Stephen Beatty Manuscript, 19.

100. Denison, *Soldiering*, 88-90.

101. NAC, Dennis Inquiry, Roote, 256.

102. NAC, Dennis Inquiry, Graham, 257.

103. Senior, *Last Invasion*, 77.

104. NAC, Official Report, Dennis, 13.

105. NAC, Beatty ms, 19.

106. NAC, Official Reports, Peacocke, 3.

107. Macdonald, *TT – Booker Inquiry*, Booker, 200.

108. Macdonald, *TT – Booker Inquiry*, Booker, 200.

109. NAC, Official Reports, Akers, 18.

110. Macdonald, *TT – Booker Inquiry*, Booker, 200-201.

111. Akers wrote Peacocke here in his report, but obviously meant Booker. NAC, Official Reports, Akers, 18.

112. NAC, Official Reports, Akers, 18-19.

113. NAC, Official Reports, Akers, 19.

114. Peacocke made reference to the telegram of 3 A.M. that outlined the proposed plan. NAC, Official Reports, Akers, 19; Macdonald, *TT – Booker Inquiry*, Booker, 201.

115. Macdonald, *Troublesome Times*, 43.

116. Macdonald, *TT – Booker Inquiry*, Booker, 201.

117. Owen, *Fenians*, 76.

118. NAC, Official Reports, Peacocke, 3.

119. NAC, Official Reports, Akers, 18.

120. NAC, Dennis Inquiry, Akers, 216-217.

121. Macdonald, *TT – Booker Inquiry*, Booker, 201.

122. NAC, RG 9 IC 8, vol 8, Official Report by Major Gillmor.

123. Macdonald, *TT – Booker Inquiry*, Booker, 199.

124. Macdonald, *TT -Booker Inquiry*, Booker, 204.

125. Macdonald, *TT -Booker Inquiry*, Clarke, 211.

126. Macdonald, *TT – Booker Inquiry*, Booker, 202.

127. Macdonald, *TT – Booker Inquiry*, Clarke, 211.

128. This analysis is based on the author's personal observation, examination of the works of Fenian war artist Alexander Van Ericksen in the Fort Erie Museum, and study of David Owen's work. Owen, *Fenians*, 77 and illustrations 12-15, 75, 79.

129. Most Canadian accounts place the Fenian skirmishers too far north. The report of the battle with accompanying map prepared in June 1866 by Lieutenant Colonel William Durie, the Assistant Adjutant-General, indicates that the Fenian skirmishers deployed very close to, if not behind the fences on the north side of the Garrison Road. See Macdonald, *Troublesome Times*, 47-49; NAC, RG 9, IC 8, vol 8, Durie to MacDougall, 30 June 1866; Owen, *Fenians*, 77.

130. George Welch, "The Fenian Foray into Canada," *The Irish Defence Journal* 18 (1958) 287.

131. Macdonald, *TT – Booker Inquiry*, Clarke, 212; Senior, *Last Invasion*, 69.

132. Macdonald, *TT – Booker Inquiry*, Booker, 202.

133. Owen, *Fenians*, 76.

134. Macdonald, *TT-Booker Inquiry*, Booker, 202, 204; Inglis, 239.

135. Steven Harris, *Canadian Brass, The Making of a Professional Army 1860-1939*, (Toronto, 1980), 6.

136. Both Peacocke and Denison demonstrate that these deficiencies were not confined to

the Port Colborne column. See NAC, Official Reports, Peacocke, 2; Macdonald, *Troublesome Times*, 41; Denison, *Soldiering*, 98-99.

137. Macdonald, *TT-Booker Inquiry*, Booker, 202.

138 Macdonald, *TT-Booker Inquiry*, Gillmor, 223-234; Henery, 226.

139. Greenhous, *Semper Paratus*, 8, 30-33.

140. Owen, *Fenians*, 77; Macdonald, *Troublesome Times*, 46; Macdonald, *TT-Booker Inquiry*, Booker, 203.

141. Macdonald, *TT- Booker Inquiry*, Booker, 203.

142. Macdonald, *TT-Booker Inquiry*, Booker, 202-203.

143. Macdonald, *TT-Booker Inquiry*, Booker, 203.

144. NAC, McIntosh, 3.

145. Macdonald, *TT-Booker Inquiry*, Booker, 203.

146. NAC, McIntosh, 3; Macdonald, *TT-Booker Inquiry*, Booker, 203; Muir, 215.

147. Macdonald, *TT-Booker Inquiry*, Booker, 203.

148. Macdonald, *Troublesome Times*, 47.

149. NAC, Official Reports, Booker, 6; NAC, McIntosh, 3; Macdonald, *Troublesome Times*, 47.

150. NAC, McIntosh, 4.

151. NAC, Official Reports, Booker, 6.

152. Macdonald, *TT-Booker Inquiry*, Booker, 203.

153. NAC, McIntosh, 4; Macdonald, *Troublesome Times*, 47.

154. NAC, McIntosh, 3.

155. Greenhous, *Semper Paratus*, 60.

156. O'Neill, "Report," 39.

157. NAC, McIntosh, 4.

158. Macdonald, *TT- Booker Inquiry*, Booker, 203.

159. Macdonald, *TT-Booker Inquiry*, Inglis, 239.

160. Macdonald, *TT-Booker Inquiry*, Booker, 203.

161. Macdonald, *TT-Booker Inquiry*, Skinner, 227.

162. Macdonald, *TT-Booker Inquiry*, Booker, 204.

163. Macdonald, *TT-Booker Inquiry*, Booker, 204.

164. NAC, RG 9 IC 8, vol 8, Report of Major Gillmor.

165. NAC, Official Reports, Booker, 6.

166. This layout is based on the testimony of witnesses at the Booker inquiry as well as Macdonald's narrative. An educated guess, it actually closely matches the casualties suffered during the battle. See Macdonald, *Troublesome Times*, 50-51; Macdonald, *TT-Booker Inquiry*, Booker, 203; Gillmor, 209; Muir, 216; Skinner, 227-228; Ferguson, 231; Davis, 233; Gardner, 235-236; Maclean, 237-238; Inglis, 240.

167. Macdonald, *TT-Booker Inquiry*, Davis, 233.

168. NAC, Official Reports, Booker, 6.

169. NAC, Gillmor; Macdonald, *TT-Booker Inquiry*, Maux, 221; Gillmor, 223.

170. NAC, Official Reports, Booker, 6; NAC, Gillmor; Macdonald, *TT-Booker Inquiry*, Booker, 205; Gillmor, 209; Ferguson, 231-232.

171. Macdonald, *TT-Booker Inquiry*, Booker, 205; Clarke, 212; Muir, 216-217; Ferguson, 232; Gardner, 236; Maclean, 238.

172. Macdonald, *TT-Booker Inquiry*, Gardner, 236.

173. NAC, McIntosh, 5.

174. Casualty data supplied by the regiment.

175. NAC, RG 9 IC 8, vol 8, Drurie to Macdougall, 30 June 1866.

176. Casualty data supplied by the QOR; Cruikshank, *Thirteenth Battalion*, 53; Macdonald, *Troublesome Times*, 52-53.

177. O'Neill, "Report," 39.

178. Macdonald, *Troublesome Times*, 50; Macdonald, *TT-Booker Inquiry*, Booker, 205; Clarke, 211-212; Muir, 216-217; Maun, 222-223; Skinner, 228-229; Davis, 233; Greenhous, *Semper Paratus*, 63-64.

179. Macdonald, *TT-Booker Inquiry*, Skinner, 229.

180. Owen, *Fenians*, 80.

181. Greenhous, *Semper Paratus*, 64-65; Beverly Jewson, *The Battle of Limeridge*, (Ridgeway, 1976), 17.

182. Macdonald, *Troublesome Times*, 53.

183. O'Neill, "Report," 40.

184. O'Neill, "Report," 40.

185. NAC, Beatty ms, 21.

186. NAC, Dennis Inquiry, Akers, 221-222; Owen, *Fenians*, 80.

187. NAC, Beatty ms, 21-22.

188. NAC, Dennis Inquiry, McCracken testimony, 7; Macdonald, *Troublesome Times*, 66-67.

189. Macdonald, *Troublesome Times*, 67.

190. NAC, Dennis Inquiry: McCracken, 9; Graybird, 22.

191. Macdonald, *Troublesome Times*, 68-70.

192. Denison, *Soldiering*, 100-101.

193. NAC, Official Reports, Akers, 20.

194. O'Neill, "Report," 40.

195. Owen, *Fenians*, 82.

196. O'Neill, "Report," 40-41.

197. NAC, Official Reports, Peacocke, 3-4.

198. Denison, *Soldiering*, 99.

199. NAC, Official Reports, Peacocke, 4.

200. NAC, Official Reports, Peacocke, 4.

201. Denison, *Soldiering*, 95-96; NAC, Official Reports, Peacocke, 4.

202. The efforts of O'Neill and his men came to nought when the invasion by General Spears's Right Wing managed only to make a small incursion near St. Armands, Quebec on 4 June. When the expected reinforcements did not arrive Spears returned to the United States on 9 June.

203. Denison, *Soldiering*, 117-118.

204. Owen, *Fenians*, 74.

205. Denison, *Soldiering*, 108, 117.

206. Owen, *Fenians*, 68.

Interlude – The Creation of a Canadian Army, 1866-1899

1. Bruce Tascona and Eric Wells, *Little Black Devils. A History of the Royal Winnipeg Rifles* (Winnipeg, 1983), 23.

4. Leliefontein

1. Major General W.A. Griesbach, who served in South Africa as a private in the Canadian Mounted Rifles, claimed this anonymous poem appeared in the *San Francisco Call* towards the end of 1899. See William Griesbach, *I Remember*, (Toronto, 1946) 227; William Hart-McHarg, *From Quebec to Pretoria with the Royal Canadian Regiment*, (Toronto, 1902) 263. *Rooi-baatje* (red coats) was the Boer's name for British soldiers.

2. Brian A. Reid, *Our Little Army in the Field* (St. Catharines, 1996), 21.

3. Reid, *Little Army*, 22-23.

4. Reid, *Little Army*, 32.

5. Reid, *Little Army*, 32, 97.

6. Reid, *Little Army*, 33.

7. Reid, *Little Army*, 33-34.

8. The personnel data are from the personnel files in NAC, RG 38 1.A series in the NAC supplemented by *Toronto Globe*, 10 Apr 1899, for Ault; Griesbach, *I Remember*, 230-

231; Griesbach, Albert Hilder, "Sentimental Journey," *The Springbok*, (1946-1947), 24-25.

9. Hugh Robertson, "The Royal Canadian Dragoons and the Anglo-Boer War, 1900," unpublished MA Thesis, University of Ottawa, 1982, 12, 33; Royal Canadian Dragoon Archives, Letters, Anderson to father, 17 Mar 1900, and to "Edith and all," 9 Apr 1900.

10. Robertson, "Dragoons," 82-84, 92-93.

11. Anonymous, "Mounted Rifles and Mounted Infantry," *The Cavalry Journal*, 1 (1906), 29.

12. Robertson, "Dragoons," 132.

13. Reid, *Little Army*, 18-19.

14. Reid, *Little Army*, 34-35.

15. Reid, *Little Army*, 18; Robertson, "Dragoons," 93.

16. Griesbach, *I Remember*, 265.

17. Griesbach, *I Remember*, 256-258.

18. Edward Morrison, *With the Guns in South Africa*, (Hamilton, 1901), 216.

19. *South African Field Force Casualty List 1899-1902*, 21 March to 31 July 1900, 137-138.

20. Robertson, "Dragoons," 84.

21. NAC, RG 9 II, A 3, vol 33, CMR Staff Diary 29 May 1900.

22. Reid, *Little Army*, 116.

23. NAC, RG 9 II, A 3, vol 32, RCD Staff Diary 16 Oct 1900.

24. Morrison, *Guns*, 216.

25. NAC, Sessional Paper 35a, *Canadian Forces in South Africa*, (Ottawa, 1901), 98 (hereafter SP 35a).

26. RCD Archives, Letter, Howard to anonymous, 30 July 1900.

27. "Obituary," *Canadian Cavalry Association Journal*, (1927), 77.

28. Reid, *Little Army*, 83.

29. Diary, CMR , 3 Apr 1900.

30. Reid, *Little Army*, 83.

31. Reid, *Little Army*, 106-107.

32. David Bercuson and Jack Granatstein, *Dictionary of Canadian Military History*, (Toronto, 1992), 72; Government of Canada, *The Quarterly Militia List of the Dominion of Canada 1 January 1904*, (Ottawa, 1904), 23.

33. Bliss had left a string of unpaid bills across South Africa, a habit he had also displayed in the Yukon. Evans had relieved him from command of a troop after the troop non-commissioned officers had lodged a formal complaint about him, a highly unusual oc-

currence. Spud is identified as an Irish Terrier in Brereton Greenhous's book on the Yukon Field Force. See NAC, MG 27 II, B 1, vol 16, Hutton to Minto, 30 Oct 1900; Diary, CMR, 13-14 Oct 1900; Brereton Greenhous, *Guarding the Goldfields*, (Toronto, 1987), 69; Morrison, *Guns*, 300.

34. A six-gun battery commanded by a major was divided into three two-gun sections called the right, centre and left sections.

35. Morrison, *Guns*, 188.

36. Morrison, *Guns*, 198.

37. While the author's 12-pounder manual is dated 1905, the data are generally correct for earlier editions. See *Handbook for the 12-Pr. B.L. 6 CWT. Gun 1905 (Marks I-IV and Iva) and Carriages, Marks I*, I**, and II. (Horse Artillery)*, 70-1; Reid, *Little Army*, 17.

38. Morrison, *Guns*, 266.

39. Morrison, *Guns*, 159.

40. Reid, *Little Army*, 17.

41. Greenhill Gardyne, *The Life of a Regiment, The History of the Gordon Highlanders. Vol III From 1898 to 1914*, (London, 1972), 279. *Gordons*).

42. Robertson, "Dragoons," 133.

43. Gardyne, *Gordons*, 279.

44. Gardyne, *Gordons*, 279.

45. Gardyne, *Gordons*, 279.

46. O'Moore Creagh and E.M. Humphris, *The VC and DSO, The Distinguished Service Order*, (London, 1924), 8; Ian Uys, *South African Military Who's Who, 1452-1992*, (Germiston, RSA, 1992), 220; Horace Smith-Dorrien, *Memories of Forty-Eight Years Service*, (London, 1925), 246-247.

47. Ron Bester, *Boer Rifles and Carbines of the Anglo-Boer War*, (Bloemfontein, 1994), 9-10.

48. Morrison, *Guns*, 222.

49. Basil Williams, *The Times History of the War in South Africa 1899-1902*, vol IV, (London, 1906), 513.

50. Robertson, "Dragoons," 186.

51. Bester, *Rifles*, 16.

52. Uys, *Military*, 82.

53. Uys, *Military*, 189.

54. Smith-Dorrien, *Memories*, 252.

55. While the name "cow" is said to be an acronym for Coventry Ordnance Works, the manufacturer, it is likely that most troops used the term because the guns were drawn by oxen.

56. Smith-Dorrien, *Memories*, 252; Morrison, *Guns*, 249-50.

57. Smith-Dorrien, *Memories*, 252; Morrison, *Guns*, 250.

58. NAC, SP 35a, 93; Morrison, *Guns*, 251.

59. Morrison, *Guns*, 252.

60. 57. NAC, Diary, CMR, 3 Nov 1900; Smith-Dorrien, *Memories*, 253.

61. Lieutenant "Gat" Howard, the machine gun officer, was on leave during the first week in November.

62. NAC, RCD diary, 2 Nov; NAC SP 35a, 93; Gardyne, *Gordons*, 280; Morrison, *Guns*, 252.

63. NAC, SP 35a; Gardyne, *Gordons*, 282.

64. Reid, *Little Army*, 128.

65. Smith-Dorrien, *Memories*, 256.

66. Morrison, *Guns*, 258-259.

67. Smith-Dorrien, *Memories*, 256; NAC, SP 35a 94; Morrison, *Guns*, 259-260.

68. NAC, Diary, CMR, 6 Nov 1900.

69. Robertson, "Dragoons," 182-183.

70. Reid, *Little Army*, 130.

71. Morrison, *Guns*, 260-261.

72. Morrison, *Guns*, 261-262; Smith-Dorrien, *Memories*, 256.

73. Smith-Dorrien, *Memories*, 256; Morrison, *Guns*, 262.

74. Robertson, "Dragoons," 184.

75. Smith-Dorrien, *Memories*, 256-257.

76. Smith-Dorrien, *Memories*, 257.

77. Robertson, "Dragoons," 186.

78. Morrison, *Guns*, 264.

79. Morrison, *Guns*, 264.

80. Robertson, "Dragoons," 190.

81. Reid, *Little Army*, 133.

82. Robertson, "Dragoons," 187-189.

83. Smith-Dorrien, *Memories*, 257.

84. NAC, Diary, CMR, 7 Nov 1900.

85. Morrison, *Guns*, 265.

86. Smith-Dorrien, *Memories*, 257.

87. Morrison, *Guns*, 265-266.

88. Morrison, *Guns*, 266.

89. Robertson, "Dragoons," 191; Morrison, *Guns*, 266.

90. NAC, Diary, CMR, 7 Nov 1900.

91. Robertson, "Dragoons," 190.

92. Morrison, *Guns*, 266-267.

93. The guns in a battery were numbered 1 through 6 from the right, thus the two guns in the left section were numbers 5 and 6.

94. NAC, RG 9 II, A3, vol 33, Diary, Left Section D Battery, 7 Nov 1900.

95. Morrison, *Guns*, 267-268.
96. NAC, Diary, Left Section, 7 Nov 1900.
97. Robertson, "Dragoons," 192-193.
98. Robertson, "Dragoons," 192-193.
99. NAC, Diary, RCD, 7 Nov 1900, Statement by Cpl Price.
100. NAC, Diary, Left Section, 7 Nov 1900.
101. Brereton Greenhous, *Dragoon: The Centennial History of the Royal Canadian Dragoons, 1883-1983*, (Ottawa, 1983) 129.
102. Greenhous, *Dragoon*, 129; NAC, Reel M 300, Turner Diary, 7 Nov 1900.
103. Robertson, "Dragoons," 197.
104. Reid, *Little Army*, 134.
105. RCD Archives, Anderson, letter to "Edith and all," 9 Nov 1900.
106. Information supplied to author by Mr. Hannes Von Rensberg, Middelburg, South Africa.
107. Reid, *Little Army*, 134-135.
108. Greenhous, *Dragoon*, 131-132.
109. NAC, Turner diary, 7 Nov 1900
110. This sequence of events is based upon the report and other correspondence written by Morrison on his return to Belfast and Turner's narrative in his diary. Both officers agree in their sequence of events, but vary somewhat from Private Hilder's narrative which was written some time after his return to Canada.
111. NAC, Diary, Left Section, 7 Nov 1900.
112. NAC, Diary, CMR, 7 Nov 1900.
113. Morrison, *Guns*, 270.
114. Morrison, *Guns*, 270.
115. Robertson, *Dragoons*, 198; Smith-Dorrien, *Memories*, 258.
116. Smith-Dorrien, *Memories*, 259.
117. NAC, SP 35a, 95.
118. Morrison, *Guns*, 270-271.
119. *South African War Honours and Awards 1899-1902*, (London, 1971), 82-87, 118.
120. Smith-Dorrien, *Memories*, 234.

Interlude – From the Veld to the Fields of Flanders, 1900 to 1918

1. Stephen Leacock, *Canada: The Foundations of Its Future* (Montreal, 1941), 222.
2. G.R. Stevens, quoted in W.D. Mathieson, *My Grandfather's War. Canadians Remember the First World War 1914-1918* (Toronto, 1981), 4.
3. D.J. Goodspeed, *The Armed Forces of Canada, 1867-1967*, (Ottawa, 1967), 26.
4. Canadian War Records Office, *Canada in Khaki 1918* (London, 1918), 17-18.

5. Moreuil Wood

1. "Roses of Picardy," one of the great hit songs of the First World War, sounds best sung around a piano by a male chorus who have ingested entirely too much cheap, red wine.
2. LdSH Archives, Calgary, Unpublished Manuscript History of the Canadian Cavalry Brigade; G.W.L. Nicholson, *Canadian Expeditionary Force, 1914-1919: The Official History of the Canadian Army in the First World War* (Ottawa, 1962), 29, 35, 39-40.
3. On British cavalry swords, see John Latham, *British Military Swords* (New York, 1967), 34.
4. Information on cavalry training, equipment, saddlery, weaponry taken from: D. Tylden, *Horses and Saddlery: An Account of the Animals Used by the British and Commonwealth Armies from the Seventeenth Century to the Present Day with a Description of Their Equipment* (London, 1965), 38-44; *Cavalry Training, 1904*; and Mike Chappel, *British Army Cavalry Equipments, 1800-1941* (London, 1996), 17-22. Information on cavalry doctrine and tactics from *Cavalry Training 1904*; *Field Service Regulations. Part I (Operations) 1909 (Reprinted 1914)*; and *Field Service Regulations. Part II (Organization and Administration 1909 (Reprinted 1913)*, various sections.
5. The more popularly known rank of trooper did not take legal effect until 1923. See General Order 138, 1 September 1923.
6. *Cavalry Training 1904*, 136-139.
7. The description of equipment and saddlery comes from Tylden, *Horses and Saddlery*, 38–44, 155, 156, 157; *Cavalry Training 1904*; and Chappel, *British Army Cavalry Equipments*, 17-22. Sources for doctrinal practice are from *Cavalry Training 1904*; *Field Service Regulations Part I (Operations) 1909* (Reprinted 1914) and *Field Service Regulations Part II (Organization and Administration) 1909* (Reprinted 1913), various sections.
8. John Grodzinski, *The Battle of Moreuil Wood* (LdSH, 1993), 5.
9. Grodzinski, *Moreuil Wood*, 6.
10. Background of Operation MICHAEL is

based on Martin Middlebrook, *The Kaiser's Battle. 21 March 1918: The First Day of the German Spring Offensive* (Harmondsworth, 1983), 26-34; Grodzinski, *Moreuil Wood*, 4.

11. Grodzinski, *Moreuil Wood*, 7.

12. Summary of the events and operations, 21-29 Mar 1918, taken from: NAC RG 24, WD, CCB, Mar 1918, Appendix D, Lessons Drawn from the Operations Carried out by the 1st, 2nd, 3rd Cavalry Divisions from March 21st 1918 to 5 April 1918; NAC, RG 24: WD, CCB, 21-29 Mar 1918; WD, FGH, 21-29 Mar 1918; S.H. Williams, *Stand to Your Horses* (Winnipeg, 1961), 191-201; R. Cunniffe, *The Story of a Regiment* (n.p., 1995), 137-140.

13. J.E.B. Seely, *Adventure*, (London, 1930), 299.

14. Seely, *Adventure*, 299.

15. *Cavalry Training, 1904*, 32-34, 136, 141.

16. Alex Lynch, *Dad, the Motors and the Fifth Army Show*, (Kingston, 1978), no pagination.

17. Brereton Greenhous, *Dragoon. The Centennial History of the Royal Canadian Dragoons. 1883-1983* (The Regiment, 1983), 229.

18. Ludwig Uhland, *Die 243. württ. Infanterie-Divison im Weltkriege 1917-1918* (Stuttgart, 1926).

19. Greenhous, *Dragoon*, 225.

20. Thomas T. Pitman, "The Operations of the Second Cavalry Brigade (with the Canadian Cavalry Brigade Attached) in the Defence of Amiens, March 30 – April 1, 1918," *The Cavalry Journal*, 13 (1923).

21. Connolly later commanded the Strathconas from 1924 to 1929. Biographical material from R. Cunniffe, *The Story of a Regiment* (Lord Strathcona's Horse (Royal Canadians), 1995), 117 – 118.

22. Orléans was a member of the French royal family and forbidden from military service, but he managed to obtain a commission in the Royal Canadian Dragoons in December 1916. He was cited for bravery at Moreuil Wood and later won a Military Cross. Prince Antoine died from injuries suffered in an aircraft crash on 29 November 1918. See John Gardam, "The Case of the Missing Dragoon," *Canadian Defence Quarterly*, Spring 1988, 49.

23. J.E.B. Seely, *Adventure*, (London, 1930), 302. The orderlies for the brigade commander and each unit commanding officer carried a pennant or flag to distinguish the unit from a distance. The Canadian Cavalry Brigade Pennant was red in colour with a white star in the centre. The letter "C" was superimposed on the star. From "Miscellaneous Notes on the History of the Canadian Cavalry Brigade," the Regimental Museum of Lord Strathcona's Horse (Royal Canadians), Museum of the Regiments, Calgary, Alberta.

24. Charles E. Connolly, "The Action at of the Canadian Cavalry Brigade at Moreuil Wood and Rifle Wood – March and April, 1918," *Canadian Defence Quarterly* (October, 1925).

25. Connolly, "The Action."

26. 7. K. Storz, *Das Württemberg Feld-Artillerie-Regiment Nr. 238 im Weltkrieg 1914-1918*, (Stuttgart, 1921), 66.

27. Brereton Greenhous, "The Position was Desperate if Not Fatal," *Canadian Defence Quarterly*, (Spring, 1988), 46.

28. Anonymous, "Notes: Action of B Squadron, Royal Canadian Dragoons, At Bois de Moreuille, March 30,' *The Cavalry Journal*, 14 (1924), 355.

29. NAC, RG 24, vol 1834, file G.A.Q. 9-10, Lieutenant Colonel C.E. Connolly to H.H. Matthews, editor, *Canadian Defence Quarterly*, 23 Mar 1928.

30. Victor Nordheimer was a cousin of Roy Nordheimer, the commander of A Squadron.

31. Greenhous, *Dragoon*, 225.

32. Helmut Gnamm, *Das Füsilier-Regiment Kaiser Franz Joseph von Österreich, König von Ungarn (4. württ.) Nr. 122 in Weltkrieg 1914-1918*, (Stuttgart, 1921), 240.

33. Connolly, "The Action."

34. Seely, *Adventure*, 303.

35. S.H. Williams, *Stand To Your Horses, Through the First World War 1914 – 1918 with Lord Strathcona's Horse (Royal Canadians)*, (Altona, 1961), 204.

36. Albert Dale, "A Letter to the Editors of the Ottawa 'Journal'," *The Strathconian*, (May 1954), 16.

37. Williams, *Stand to Your Horses*, 208.

38. Williams, *Stand To Your Horses*, 206.

39. Williams, *Stand to Your Horses*, 209-210.

40. Alfred Meyer and Georg Reyher, *Kgl. Sächs. 2. Grenadier-Regiment Nr. 101, "Kaiser Wilhelm, König von Preussen"*, (Dresden, 1924), 131, 132.

41. Williams, *Stand to Your Horses*, 208.

42. Williams, *Stand To Your Horses*, 206.

43. Paddy Griffith, ed., *Battle Tactics of the Western Front. The British Army's Art of Attack, 1916-1918*, (New Haven: 1996), 140.

44. French, Barker, and Barker, eds, *History of the Canadian Army Veterinary Corps … 1914-1919*, 2, 96, 277.

45. Greenhous, "The Position was Desperate."

46. Connolly, "The Action," .

47. Williams, *Stand To Your Horses*, 212.

48. Williams, *Stand to Your Horses*, 212.

49. James Lunt, *16th/5th Lancers The Queen's Royal Lancers*, (London, 1973), 57.

50. Lunt, *16th/5th Lancers*, 57.

51. Pitman, "Operations."

52. Connolly, "The Action," Williams, *Stand to Your Horse*, 209-210.

53. Geoffrey Brooke, *The Brotherhood of Arms*, (London, 1941), 106.

54. *Histories of Two Hundred and Fifty-One Divisions of the German Army which participated in the War (1914-1918)*, (Washington, 1919).

55. Cunniffe, *Story of a Regiment*, 141.

56. Grodzinski, *Moreuil Wood*, 19-20.

57. LdSH Archives, Brigadier General A.H. Bell to District Officer Commanding, Military District 13, 5 Feb 1931, in Minutes of a Meeting of a Committee for Selecting a List of Honours to be Borne on the Regimental Guidon, Lord Strathcona's Horse, n.d.

58. LdSH Archives, Lieutenant Colonel C.E. Connolly to Officer Commanding, A Squadron, 23 June 1926.

59. For a discussion of these claims, see Edward Green, "The Last Great Cavalry Charge," *Cavalier Magazine*, (February 1961); N.G. Thwaites, "Is this the Man Who Won the World War?"; and information in the Archives of the Regimental Museum, Lord Strathcona's Horse (Royal Canadians).

60. Brooke, *Brotherhood of Arms*, 104.

61. Norm Christie, *For King and Empire: The Canadians at Cambrai*, (Ottawa, 1997), 72.

Interlude – From the Western Front to Normandy, 1918 to 1944

1. W.W. Murray, *The History of the 2nd Canadian Battalion (East. Ontario Regiment) Canadian Expeditionary Force, in the Great War, 1914-1919*, (Ottawa, 1947), 330.

2. Goodspeed, *Armed Forces of Canada*, 67.

3. Editor's interview with Lieutenant Gerald Adams of the South Alberta Regiment, 22 Nov. 1995.

6. Le Mesnil Patry

Unless otherwise noted, the sources for this action are the War Diaries of the 3rd Canadian Infantry Division, 2 Canadian Armoured Brigade, 7 Canadian Infantry Brigade and the 6th Canadian Armoured Regiment (First Hussars) located in Record Group 24 of the National Archives of Canada, Ottawa.

1. Words by Trooper Joe Beef of the First Hussars, 1939, sung to the tune of the regimental march, "Bonnie Dundee".

2. C.P. Stacey, *The Victory Campaign* (Ottawa, 1960), 650, Appendix B.

3. A.B. Conron, ed., *A History of the First Hussars: 1856-1980* (London, 1981), 64-67.

4. NAC, RG 24, WD 1H, 6-10 June 1944.

5. Stacey, *Victory Campaign*, 139. The left arm of the pincer was the 51st (Highland) Division to the east of the Canadians; the right arm was the 7th (British) Armoured Division to their west. Between the 7th Armoured and the Canadian right flank was the 50th (British) Division, which was to provide a diversion to keep the Germans from shifting forces to defend against the main attack.

6. L.F. Ellis, *Victory in the West* (vol 1, London, 1962), 253.

7. Conran, *First Hussars*, 68; DHH 145. 202011(4) Special Report by Lt. R. Rae, QOR, Action at Le Mesnil-Patry, 11 Jun 1944.

8. NAC, RG 24, WD 1H, June 1944, Appendix, Account of Personal Experience in Action on Sunday Jun 11 – 44.

9. Donald E. Graves, *South Albertas: A Canadian Regiment at War* (Toronto, 1998), 104, 129.

10. NAC, RG 24, WD 1H, June 1944, A.O. Dodds, Account of Personal Experiences in Action on Sunday, Jun 11 – 44.

11. Stacey, *Victory Campaign*, 650, Appendix B; DHH, File 145.2Q2011 (4), Special Report Lt. Rae, Intelligence Officer, QOR, Action at Le Mesnil-Patry, 11 June 44; NAC, RG 24, vol 10986, File 265C8.011-01, Interview with Major J.N. Gordon, QOR, 12 July 1944.

12. In French, *mesnil* means a human habitation, of any size from two houses to a town

while Patry was the name of the leading family in the area when the community was founded.

13. DHH. File 145.202011 (4), Special Report by Lieutenant R. Rae, QOR, Action at Le Mesnil-Patry, 11 June 1944; NAC, RG 24, 3rd Canadian Infantry Division, Intelligence Summary No. 3, 23:59 Hours, 10 June 1944.

14. Information on Captain Rivaz from Mr. Ian Barker to author, 16 Aug 99.

15. Ben Dunkelman, *Dual Allegiance*, (Toronto, 1976), 92.

16. DHH, File 145.2Q2011 (4), Special Report Lt. Rae, Intelligence Officer, QOR, Action at Le Mesnil-Patry, 11 June 44; NAC, RG 24: vol 10986, File 265C8.011-01, Interview with Major J.N. Gordon, QOR, 12 July 1944; WD, 2 CAB, 11 June 1944; WD, 1H, June 1944, Appendix, Trooper A.O. Dodds, Account of Personal Experiences in Action on Sunday, June 11, 1944.

17. Author's interview with Lieutenant Colonel (Retd) William McCormick, 13 July 1993.

18. NAC, RG 24, WD, 2 CAB, 11 June 1944.

19. Conron, *First Hussars*, 69.

20. Ben Dunkelman, *Dual Allegiance*, 92; NAC, RG 24, WDs, 2 CAB and 1H, 11 June 1944.

21. Alexander McKee, *Caen: Anvil of Victory*, (London, 1964), 90.

22. The best source on the 12th SS Panzer Division and the best study of the German side of the Normandy campaign in English is Hubert Meyer, *The History of the 12. SS-Panzerdivision "Hitlerjugend"*, (Winnipeg, 1994).

23. Meyer, *History*, 67.

24. Author's interview with Miller

25. Conron, *First Hussars*, 69.

26. NAC, RG 24, vol 10986, File 265C8.011-01, Interview with Major J.N. Gordon, Queen's Own Rifles, 8 Brigade, 3rd Canadian Infantry Division.

27. Author's interview with O.G. Stoner, July 1992.

28. Meyer, *History*, 68; Mr. H. Siegel to author, 22 Aug 1994.

29. NAC, RG 24, WD 1H, June 1944, Appendix, Account of Personal Experiences in Action on Sunday, June 11, 1944; McKeen, *Anvil of Victory*, 92.

30. NAC, RG 24, WD, 2 CAB, 11 June 1944; Conron, *First Hussars*, 69.

31. Meyer, *History*, 67-68.

32. NAC, RG 24, WD, 1H, June 1944, Appendix, Account written by P 1109 Sgt Gariepy.

33. NAC, RG 24, WD 1H, June 1944, Appendix, Account of Personal Experiences in Action on Sun. Jun 11-44 by B 19502 Tpr Dodds, A.O., 6 CAR (1H).

34. Conron, *First Hussars*, 69; Meyer, *History*, 68-69; DHH, Citation Files, Northwest Europe, Military Cross, Lieutenant Harvey George Willmott Bean, Queen's Own Rifles of Canada, 15 Jun 1944.

35. Meyer, *History*, 69; Mr. H. Siegel to author, 22 Aug 1994; NAC, RG 25, WD 1H, June 1944, Appendix, Account of Personal Experiences in Action on Sun. Jun 11-44 by B 19502 Tpr Dodds, A.O., 6 CAR (1H).NAC, RG 24, WD 1H, June 1944.

36. Letter from Mr. W. Simpson to author, 13 Sep 1993.

37. Author's interview with Brigadier J.N. Gordon, 30 Apr 1993.

38. Meyer, *History*, 67.

39. Meyer, *History*, 68.

40. NAC, RG 25, WD 1H, June 1944, Appendix, Account of Personal Experiences in Action on Sun. Jun 11-44 by B 19502 Tpr Dodds, A.O., 6 CAR (1H).

41. Meyer, *History*, 68.

42. NAC, RG 24, WD, 1H, June 1944, Appendix, Account of Personal Experiences in Action on Sun. Jun 11-44 by B 19502 Tpr Dodds, A.O., 6 CAR (1H).

43. Mr. H. Siegel to author, 22 Aug 1994.

44. Meyer, *History*, 68.

45. Mr. H. Siegel to author, 22 Aug 1994; Meyer, *History*, 68-69.

46. Mr. H. Siegel to author, 22 Aug 1994.

47. Mr. H. Siegel to author, 22 Aug 1994.

48. DHH, Citation Files, Northwest Europe, Military Cross, Lieutenant Harvey George Willmott Bean, Queen's Own Rifles of Canada, 15 Jun 1944.

49. DHH, Citation File, Northwest Europe, Distinguished Service Medal, Sergeant Samuel Thomas Scrutton, QOR, 15 Jun 1944.

50. NAC, WD 1H, June 1944, Appendix, Account written by P 1109 Sgt Gariepy.

51. J. Simpson to author, 8 July 1993.

52. Meyer, *History*, 68-69; Mr. H. Siegel to author, 22 Aug 1994.

53. Conron, *First Hussars*, 70; Author's inter-

view with Lieutenant Colonel (Retd) W.F. McCormick, 13 July 1993.

54. Conron, *First Hussars*, 70.

55. Conron, *First Hussars*, 69-70; author's interview with O.G. Stoner, July 1992.

56. Letter to author by Mr. Jack Martin, n.d., c. Oct 1993.

57. Author's interview with O.G. Stoner, July 1992.

58. Mr. J. Martin to author, c. Oct 1993; Conron, *First Hussars*, 76.

59. Ronald Morton, *Vanguard: The Fort Garry Horse in The Second World War*, (Doetinchen, 1945), 128.

60. NAC, RG 24, WD 2 CAB, 11 June 1944; Conron, *First Hussars*, 70.

61. Letter to author from Mr. J. Martin, n.d., c. Oct 1993.

62. Letter to author from Mr. J. Martin, n.d., c. Oct 1993.

63. Conron, *First Hussars*, 70.

64. NAC, RG 24, WDs, 2 CAB, 7 CIB, 1H, 11 June 1944; Conron, *First Hussars*, 70.

65. NAC, RG 24, WD 1H, June 1944, Appendix, Tpr. A.O. Dodds, Account of Personal Experiences in Action on Sunday, Jun 11 -44.

66. NAC. RG 24, WD 1H, June 1944; Conron, *First Hussars*, 76.

67. DND, Judge Advocate General's Library, NDHQ, Ottawa, Canadian War Crimes Investigation, SHAEF Court of Inquiry: Mouen Case, 1945.

68. Author's interview with Mrs. M.J. (Cranfield) Stonehouse, 29 Jan 1994.

69. Letters to author from Mr. L.W. Soroke, 27 Sep 1993; and L. Allen, Sep 1993.

70. Meyer, *History*, 69.

71. Letter to author from Mr. J. Simpson, 8 July 1993.

72. McKee, *Caen*, 95.

73. NAC, RG 24, WDs, 1H, QOR, 11 June 1944.

74. The most recent examination of the murder of Canadian soldiers in Normandy by members of the 12th SS Panzer Division is Howard Margolian, *Conduct Unbecoming: The Story of the Murder of Canadian Prisoners in Normandy* (Toronto, 1998). See also Ian Sayer and Douglas Batting, *Hitler's Last General: The Case Against Wilhelm Mohnke* (London, 1989).

75. Meyer, *History*, 69.

76. Conron, *First Hussars*, 74.

77. DHH, DG Hist File 260C11. (D7) 21 Army Group Miscellaneous Memoranda on Infantry and Tank Cooperation.

7. Kapelsche Veer

An earlier version of this study appeared as Chapter 14 of the author's book, *South Albertas: A Canadian Regiment at War* (Robin Brass Studio, 1998), and he wishes to thank the South Alberta Veterans Association for permission to rework it for inclusion in *Fighting for Canada*.

1. Canadian soldiers' song from the last years of the Second World War sung to the tune of "What a Friend We Have in Jesus."

2. C.P. Stacey, *The Victory Campaign* (Ottawa, 1960), 444-450.

3. DHH, Interrogation Report of *General* Eugen-Felix Schwalbe, n.d.

4. Stacey, *Victory Campaign*, 450.

5. K. Jamar, *With the Tanks of the 1st Polish Division* (Hengelo, 1946), 279.

6. Jamar, *With the Tanks*, 279.

7. H.F. Wood, "Operation ELEPHANT. The Battle for Kapelsche Veer," *CAJ* (Sep 1949), 9.

8. Wood, "Operation ELEPHANT," 9.

9. DHH, First Canadian Army Daily Intelligence Summaries, 2-9 January 1945.

10. Wood, "Operation ELEPHANT," 9.

11. The 4th Division was called the Green Patch Division from the colour of its square cloth shoulder badge.

12. NAC, MG 24, WD, 4th Canadian Armoured Division, 14 Jan 1945.

13. Training and Operational Reports, 4th Canadian Armoured Division, 14 Jan 1945, quoted in Geoffrey Hayes, *The Lincs: A History of the Lincoln and Welland Regiment at War* (Stratford, 1986), 91.

14. Wood, "Operation ELEPHANT," 9.

15. R.A. Paterson, *A History of the 10th Canadian Infantry Brigade* (n.p., 1945), 53. The ammunition scales for the supporting artillery in Op ELEPHANT provided for a total of 56,220 rounds of HE and 33,500 rounds of smoke calibres ranging from 4.2 inch mortars to 5.5 inch guns, see Wood, "Op ELEPHANT," 10.

16. NAC, RG 24, WD 10 Brigade, 17 Jan 1945.

17. Wood, "Op ELEPHANT," 10.

18. Hayes, *Lincs*, 77-78.

19. Vokes interview, c. 1979, in David Kaufman, ed., *A Liberation Album. Canadians in the Netherlands, 1944-1945* (Toronto, 1980), 69.

20. Vokes, in Kaufman, ed., *Liberation Album*, 69-70.

21. Hayes, *Lincs*, 91.

22. National Film Archives, Ottawa, Canadian Army Newsreel 59, c. Feb 1945.

23. Hayes, *Lincs*, 78.

24. M.O. Rollefson, ed, *Green Route Up: 4th Canadian Armoured Division* (Holland, 1945), 64-65.

25. DHH, Interrogation Report of *Generalleutnant* Hermann Plocher, 13 Sep 1946.

26. DHH, 1st Canadian Army Intelligence Summary, 24 Jan 1945, Report of Officer Cadet Hartkampf, 10 Company, to Medical Officer, 3rd Battalion, 17th Parachute Regiment.

27. NAC, RG 24, WD 10 Brigade, 24 Jan 1945.

28. Douglas Amaron, "Kapelscheveer Raid No Minor Operation," Canadian Press, 7 Feb 45.

29. Amaron, "Kapelscheveer."

30. Rollefson, *Green Route*, 66.

31. Amaron, "Kapelscheveer." Also NAC, RG 24, Ops Log, 10 Brigade, 26 Jan 1945.

32. Hayes, *Lincs*, 79.

33. Hayes, *Lincs*, 79; NAC, RG 24, Ops Log, 10 Brigade, 26 Jan 1945.

34. Hayes, *Lincs*, 82-83.

35. Robert Fraser, ed., *Black Yesterdays. The Argylls' War* (Hamilton, 1996), 349.

36. Hayes, *Lincs*, 83.

37. Hayes, *Lincs*, 83.

38. Hayes, *Lincs*, 81.

39. NAC, RG 24, Ops Log, 10 Brigade, 26 Jan 1945.

40. Fraser, *Black Yesterdays*, 349.

41. Hayes, *Lincs*, 83.

42. Hayes, *Lincs*, 83-84.

43. NAC, RG 24, WD, 10 Brigade, 26 Jan 1945.

44. Author's interview with George Armstrong, 18 Aug 1996; NAC, RG 24, WD SAR, 26 Jan 1945.

45. NAC, RG 24, WD, SAR, 26 Jan 1945.

46. Rollefson, *Green Route Up*, 66.

47. NAC, RG 24, WD SAR, Feb 1945, Appendix, Report of Sergeant V.L. Stephenson.

48. Rollefson, *Green Route Up*, 66.

49. Hayes, *Lincs*, 84.

50. Hayes, *Lincs*, 84.

51. R.L. Rogers, *History of the Lincoln and Welland Regiment* (St. Catharines, 1954), 228.

52. Rollefson, *Green Route Up*, 66-67.

53. Author's interview with G.L. Irving, 3 Jan 1996. Also, NAC, RG 24, WD 10 Brigade, 27 Jan 1945; WD SAR, 27 Jan 1945; Ops Log, 10 Brigade, 27 Jan 1945.

54. An artillery "stonk" was a short, abbreviated bombardment by all available barrels on a limited target.

55. Hayes, *Lincs*, 83-84; Robert Spencer, *History of the Fifteenth Canadian Field Regiment* (Amsterdam, 1945), 203-204; NAC, RG 24, WD and Ops Log, 10 Brigade, 27 Jan 1945.

56. G.W.L. Nicholson, *The Gunners of Canada*, Volume II (Toronto, 1967), 396-397.

57. Spencer, *Fifteenth Field*, 204.

58. NAC, RG 24, Ops Log, 10 Brigade, 27 Jan 1945.

59. Rollefson, *Green Route UP*, 65.

60. A. Earp to author, n.d. (c. Oct 1995); also Rollefson, *Green Route Up*, 66.

61. A. Earp to author, n.d. (c. Oct 1995).

62. A. Earp to author, n.d. (c. Oct 1995).

63. NAC, RG 24, WD SAR, 28 Jan 1945.

64. Rollefson, *Green Route Up*, 67.

65. NAC, RG 24, WD SAR, 27 Jan 1945.

66. NAC, RG 24: WD SAR, 28 Jan 1945; Ops Log, 10 Brigade, 28 Jan 1945.

67. NAC, RG 24, WD ASH, 28 Jan 1945.

68. Paterson, *10 Brigade*, 56.

69. NAC, RG 24, WDs SAR and ASH, 28 Jan 1945; Ops Log, 10 Brigade, 28 Jan 1945.

70. John Galipeau, "Pee Wees on Parade," unpublished, c. 1996.

71. NAC, RG 24, WD SAR, Feb 1945, Appendix, PW Statement of *Stabsfeldwebel* Heinrich Fischer, 30 Jan 1945.

72. Gallipeau, "Pee Wees," 159.

73. NAC, RG 24, WD SAR, Feb 1945, Appendix, PW Statement of *Stabsfeldwebel* Heinrich Fischer.

74. NAC, RG 24, WD SAR, 30 Jan 1945.

75. Rogers, *Lincoln and Welland Regiment*, 227.

76. NAC, RG 24, WD SAR, 28 Jan 1945.

77. DHH, Interrogation Report of *Generalleutnant* Felix-Eugen Schwalbe.

78. David Wiens, "Intelligence Officer," unpublished memoir, c. 1990.

79. Wiens, "Intelligence Officer."

80. Amaron, "Kapelscheveer"; NAC, RG 24, WD ASH, 28 Jan 1945; Ops Log, 10 Brigade, 28 Jan 1945.

81. NAC, RG 24, WD SAR, 29 Jan 1945.

82. Author's interview with J. Wiebe, 24 Sep 1995.

83. Author's interview with A. Baker, 25 Nov 1995.

84. Author's interview with J. Wiebe, 24 Sep 1995.

85. Author's interview with E. Hyatt, 26 Aug 1996.

86. Hayes, *Lincs*, 87-88.

87. Author's interview with G. Irving, 23 Sep 1995.

88. NAC, RG 24, WD SAR, Feb 1945, Appendix, Report of Lt. K. Wigg.

89. Author's interview with Joe Strathearn, 19 Sep 1996.

90. Fraser, *Black Yesterdays*, 352.

91. Spencer, *Fifteenth Field*, 207.

92. NAC, RG 24, WD SAR, 29 Jan 1945; WD SAR, Feb 1945, Appendix, Report of Lt. K. Wigg; Ops Log, 10 Brigade.

93. NAC, RG 24: WD SAR, 29 Jan 1945; WD 10 Brigade, 29 Jan 1945; Ops Log, 10 Brigade, 29 Jan 1945; and account in the *Toronto Star*, 1 Feb 1945.

94. NAC, RG 24, WD SAR, 29 Jan 1945; WD 10 Brigade, 29 Jan 1945; Ops Log, 10 Brigade, 29 Jan 1945.

95. Author's interview with A.E. Coffin, 27 Aug 1995; NAC, RG 24, WD SAR, 29 Jan 1945.

96. Fraser, *Black Yesterdays*, 351.

97. Fraser, *Black Yesterdays*, 352.

98. NAC, RG 24, WD SAR, 30 Jan 1945.

99. NAC, RG 24, WD SAR, 30 Jan 1945; WD ASH, 30 Jan 1945; WD 10 Brigade, 30 Jan 1945; Ops Log, 10 Brigade, 30 Jan 1945.

100. Author's interview with J. Wiebe, 24 Sep 1995.

101. NAC, RG 24, WD ASH, 30 January 1945.

102. NAC, RG 24, WD SAR, 30 Jan 1945; Ops Log, 10 Brigade, 30 Jan 1945.

103. Joseph Strathearn, unpublished memoir, c. 1996.

104. NAC, RG 24, WD SAR, 30 Jan 1945.

105. NAC, RG 24, WD SAR, 30 Jan 1945.

106. Author's interview with C. Allen, 22 Aug 1995; NAC, RG 24, WD SAR, 30 Jan 1945.

107. NAC, RG 24, WD SAR 30 Jan 1945; Ops Log, 10 Brigade, 30 Jan 1945.

108. Report in *Toronto Star*, 1 Feb 1945.

109. Report in *Toronto Star*, 1 Feb 1945.

110. Author's interview with J. Wiebe, 24 Sep 1995.

111. NAC, RG 24, WD SAR, 31 Jan 1945.

112. Fraser, *Black Yesterdays*, 351.

113. NAC, RG 24, WD ASH, 31 Jan 1945.

114. Paterson, *10 Brigade*, 56.

115. Rogers, *Lincoln and Welland*, 228.

116. DHH, Interrogation Report of *Generalleutnant* Hermann Plocher, 13 Sep 1946.

117. Stacey, *Victory Campaign*, 454. The quote is from Hamlet, Act IV, Scene 4, in which the captain of troops sent on a campaign in Poland states that "Truly to speak, and with no addition, We go to gain a little patch of ground, That hath no profit in it but the name. To pay five ducats, five, I would not farm it ..."

118. NAC, RG 24, WD SAR, 31 Jan 1945.

119. Hayes, *Lincs*, 93.

120. Hayes, *Lincs*, 93.

121. Hayes, *Lincs*, 93-94.

122. Hayes, *Lincs*, 95.

123. Rogers, *Lincoln and Welland*, 95.

124. Tony Foster, *Meeting of Generals* (Toronto, 1986), 429.

125. Interview of G. Wotherspoon by W. Wiley, 1986.

126. Author's interview with G. Irving, 23 Sep 1995.

127. Fraser, *Black Yesterdays*, 352.

128. Author's interview with J. Wiebe, 24 Sep 1995.

Acknowledgements

The authors of *Fighting for Canada* owe a debt of gratitude to the many individuals and institutions who contributed to the writing of this book.

First and foremost, we must pay heartfelt tribute to our wives and sweethearts (may they never meet), who, with the best of grace, tolerated our obsession with military history and put some of us on diets which will supposedly extend our life spans.

Second, all the authors wish to particularly single out Chris Johnson for his good humour, unending patience and skilful map work.

Our thanks overall must go to Dianne Graves of Almonte and Stuart Sutherland of Toronto for editing all of the studies in this book; René Chartrand of Hull for his invaluable knowledge of sources and illustrations (and good advice); Michael J. Whitby of Carleton Place for unpaid courier services; Professor Joseph Whitehorne of Front Royal, Virginia, *Oberstleutnant* Dr. Winfried Heinemann of Berlin, Major General (Retd.) Michael Reynolds and Simon Bendall of Britain for assistance in establishing unit lineages; Jim Crawford of Almonte for technical assistance with computer problems; and the staff of both the National Archives of Canada and the Directorate of History and Heritage, DND, Ottawa

The author of the Ticonderoga study gratefully acknowledges the invaluable advice, assistance and generosity of Nicholas Westbrook, Executive Director of Fort Ticonderoga, Chris Fox, and Anthony D. Pell, Curator of Collections, Fort Ticonderoga Museum; J. Robert Maguire; René Chartrand; Brian L. Dunnigan; Tim Dubé of the National Archives of Canada, Dr. Yves Tremblay of the Directorate of History and Heritage, DND; and The Black Watch of Canada Museum.

The author of the Queenston Heights study acknowledges his gratitude to John Burtniak and Lynn Prunskus of the Special Collections at Brock University; the staff of Parks Canada, Ontario Region, and Fort George National Historic Site for assistance with illustrations and military research; Erika Alexander and the Friends of Fort George for support on an earlier study of this battle; A. T. Holden for his information on British militia units; and the staffs of the following institutions: the Niagara-on-the-Lake Public Library, the Weir Gallery in Queenston, the Mills Library at McMaster University, the Baldwin Room at the Toronto Reference Library, the Archives of Ontario, the United States National Archives in Washington, D.C., the Geneva Historical Society, and the Ontario County Historical Society in Canadaigua, New York.

The Ridgeway study was made possible through the assistance of the members and staff of the Fort Erie Historical Museum Board; Ted and Bev Jewson; David Owen, local historian extraordinaire; The Queen's Own Rifles Museum; The Royal Hamilton Light Infantry Museum; and the National Army Museum, London.

The Leliefontein study benefited from the help of the Commanding Officer and Regimental Archives staff of The Royal Canadian Dragoons; Meurig Jones, chairman of the Victorian Military Society and South African war enthusiast; and Hannes Von Rensburg of Middelburg, South Africa.

The authors of the Moreuil Wood study would like to acknowledge the assistance of the Commanding Officer and Regimental Archives staff of Lord Strathcona's Horse (Royal Canadians) and the staff of the Army Library at Fort Frontenac, Kingston; Noreen Young of Almonte for the loan of her player piano and collection of music rolls; and the late Colonel (Retd.) John Elting of Cornwall-on-the-Hudson, N.Y., for information on cavalry matters.

The author of the Le Mesnil-Patry study wishes to acknowledge the assistance of Dr. Jean-Pierre Benamou, Director of the Museé de la Bataille de Normandie in Bayeux, France; and former officers and men of the 1st Hussars, The Queen's Own Rifles of Canada and the 12th Waffen SS Panzer Division who consented to be interviewed on their part in the action or to answer written queries.

The author of the Kapelsche Veer study acknowledges his gratitude to Helga Grodzinski of Kingston for advice on Shakespearean literature; Colonel Alan Earp for information on the battle; Major Brian Doucet of The Lincoln and Welland Regiment; Robert Fraser, historian of The Argyll and Sutherland Highlanders of Canada; and the South Alberta Regiment Veterans Association for permission to use copyright material.

Suggested Books for Further Reading

Canadian Military History in General

Bernier, Serge. *Canadian Military History. Volume III*. Montreal: Art Global, 2000

Chartrand, René. *Canadian Military Heritage. Volume I*. Montreal: Art Global, 1994.

————. *Canadian Military Heritage. Volume II*. Montreal: Art Global, 1995.

Cooke, Owen. *The Canadian Military Experience 1867-1945: A Bibliography*. Ottawa, DND, 1997

Goodspeed, Donald J. *The Armed Forces of Canada, 1867-1967. A Century of Achievement*. Ottawa: Directorate of History, 1967.

Harris, Stephen J. *Canadian Brass. The Making of a Professional Army, 1860-1939*. Toronto: University of Toronto, 1988

Hitsman, John M. *Safeguarding Canada, 1763-1871*. Toronto: University of Toronto Press, 1968.

Marteinson, John, ed. *We Stand on Guard: An Illustrated History of the Canadian Army*. Montreal: Ovale, 1992.

Morton, Desmond. *A Military History of Canada*. Edmonton: Hurtig, 1985.

Stanley, George F. *Canada's Soldiers: The Military History of an Unmilitary People*. Toronto: Macmillan, 1974.

Combat and the Experience of Soldiers in Combat

Baynes, J. *Morale, a Study of Men and Courage*. London: Cassel, 1967

Bourke, Joanna. *An Intimate History of Killing*. London: Granta, 1999.

Copp, Terry and Bill McAndrew. *Battle Exhaustion: Soldiers and Psychiatrists in the Canadian Army, 1939-1945*. Montreal: McGill-Queen's University Press, 1990.

Dixon, Norman F. *On the Psychology of Military Incompetence*. London: Jonathan Cape, 1976.

Fussell, Paul. *The Great War and Modern Memory*. New York: Oxford, 1989.

————. *Wartime: Understanding and Behaviour in the Second World War*. New York: Oxford, 1989.

Holmes, Richard. *Acts of War: The Behavior of Men in Battle*. New York: Free Press, 1985.

Hynes, Samuel L., ed. *The Soldiers' Tale: Bearing Witness to Modern War*. New York: Penguin, 1998.

Keegan, John. *The Face of Battle*. New York: Viking, 1976.

Kellet, Anthony. *Combat Motivation*. Boston: Kluwer-Nijhoff, 1982.

Linderman, Gerald. *Embattled Courage: The Experience of Combat in the American Civil War*. New York: Free Press, 1987.

Marshall, S.L.A. *Men Against Fire*. New York: William Morrow, 1947.

Moran, Lord. *The Anatomy of Courage*. London: Constable, 1966.

Muir, Rory. *Tactics and the Experience of Battle in the Age of Napoleon*. New Haven: Yale, 1998.

Tactics and Weaponry, 1700-1945

Bidwell, Shelford and Dominick Graham. *Fire-Power: British Army Weapons and Theories of War, 1904-1945*. Boston: George Allen & Unwin, 1982.

English, John A., and Bruce Gudmusson. *On Infantry*. Westport: Praeger, rev. ed., 1994.

Griffith, Paddy. *Battle Tactics of the Civil War*. New Haven: Yale University Press, 1989.

———. *Forward into Battle. Fighting Tactics from Waterloo to the Near Future*. 2nd edition, Swindon: Crowood Press, 1990.

——— ed. *British Fighting Methods in the Great War*. Portland: International Specialty Book Service, 1996

———. *Battle Tactics of the Western Front. The British Army's Art of Attack, 1916-1918*. New Haven: Yale, 1996.

Gudmusson, Bruce. *Stormtrooper Tactics*. Westport: Praeger, 1995.

Hughes, B.P. *Firepower. Weapons Effectiveness on the Battlefield, 1630-1850*. London: Arms & Armour Press, 1974.

Johnson, Hubert C. *Break-Through! Tactics, Technology and the Search for Victory on the Western Front in World War I*. Novato: Presidio Press, 1994.

Lupfer, Timothy. *The Dynamics of Doctrine: The Changes in German Tactical Doctrine During the First World War*. Fort Leavenworth: U.S. Army Command and General Staff College, 1981.

Muir, Rory. *Tactics and the Experience of Battle in the Age of Napoleon*. New Haven: Yale, 1998.

Nosworthy, Brent. *The Anatomy of Victory: Battle Tactics, 1689- 1763*. London: Constable, 1993.

———. *Battle Tactics of Napoleon and His Enemies*. London: Constable, 1995.

Rawling, Bill. *Surviving Trench Warfare: Technology and the Canadian Corps, 1914-1918*. Toronto: University of Toronto, 1992.

Ross, Steven. *From Flintlock to Rifle, Infantry Tactics 1740-1866*. New York: Frank Cass & Co, 1995, reprint of 1979 title.

Rothenberg. Gunther E. *The Art of Warfare in the Age of Napoleon*. Bloomington: Indiana University Press, 1978.

Travers, Timothy. *The Killing Ground: The British Army, the Western Front and the Emergence of Modern Warfare, 1900-1918*. London: Allen and Unwin, 1987.

The Seven Years' War, the Battle of Ticonderoga and the American Revolutionary War

Bellico, Russell P. *Sails and Steam. A Maritime and Military History of Lake George and Lake Champlain*. Fleischmanns: Purple Mountain Press, 1992.

Chartrand, René. *Québec 1759*. Oxford: Osprey and Ravelin, 1999.

———. *Ticonderoga 1758*. Oxford: Osprey, 2000.

————. *Louisbourg, 1758*. Oxford: Osprey, 2000.

Duffy, Christopher. *The Military Experience in the Age of Reason*. New York: Macmillan, 1987.

Eccles, William J. *The Canadian Frontier, 1534-1760*. Albuquerque: University of New Mexico, 1969.

Frégault, Guy. *La Guerre de la Conquête*. Montreal: Fides, 1966.

Hamilton, E.P. *Ticonderoga – Key to a Continent*. Boston: Little, Brown & Co., 1964

Hatch, Robert M. *Thrust for Canada: The American Attempt on Quebec in 1775-1776*. Boston: Houghton, Mifflin, 1979.

McLennan, J.S. *Louisbourg from its Foundation to its Fall*. Sydney: Fortress Press, 1969, reprint 1918 edn.

Moore, Christopher. *Louisbourg Portraits. Five Dramatic True Tales of People Who Lived in an Eighteenth Century Garrison Town*. Toronto: Macmillan, 1982.

Parkman, Francis. *Montcalm and Wolfe. The French and Indian War*. New York: Da Capo, 1995, reprint of 1884 edn.

Stacey, Charles P. *Quebec, 1759: The Siege and the Battle*. Toronto: Macmillan, 1959.

Stanley, George F.G. *New France: the Last Phase 1744-1760*. Toronto: McClelland and Stewart, 1969.

————. *Canada Invaded, 1775-1776*. Toronto: Hakkert, 1973.

Steele, Ian K. *Guerillas and Grenadiers*. Toronto: Ryerson, 1969.

Trudel, Marcel. *Introduction to New France*. Toronto: Holt, Rinehart and Winston, 1968.

The War of 1812 and Queenston Heights

Benn, Carl. *The Iroquois in the War of 1812*. Toronto: University of Toronto Press, 1998.

Elting, John R. *Amateurs to Arms: A Military History of the War of 1812*. Chapel Hill: Algonquin Press, 1991.

Gray, William. *Soldiers of the King: The Upper Canadian Militia, 1812-1815*. Erin, Ont.: Boston Mills, 1995.

Graves, Donald E. *Field of Glory: The Battle of Crysler's Farm, 1813*. Toronto: Robin Brass Studio, 1999.

————. *Where Right and Glory Lead! The Battle of Lundy's Lane, 1814*. Toronto: Robin Brass Studio, 1997.

————. *Red Coats and Grey Jackets: The Battle of Chippawa, 1814*. Toronto: Dundurn, 1994.

Haythornewaite, Philip J. *The Napoleonic Source Book*. New York: 1990

Hitsman, J. Mackay. *The Incredible War of 1812: A Military History*. Updated by Donald E. Graves. Toronto: Robin Brass Studio, 1999

Malcomson, Robert. *Lords of the Lake: The Naval War on Lake Ontario, 1812-1814*. Toronto: Robin Brass Studio, 1998

The Fenian Raids, 1866-1871, and Ridgeway

Owen, David. *The Year of the Fenians.* Buffalo: Western New York Heritage Press, 1990.

Greenhous, Brereton. *Semper Paratus: The History of the Royal Hamilton Light Infantry (Wentworth Regiment) 1862-1977.* Hamilton: The Regiment, 1977.

Senior, Hereward. *The Last Invasion of Canada.* Toronto: Dundurn, 1991.

The Boer War, 1899-1902, and Leliefontein

Greenhous, Brereton. *Dragoon: The Centennial History of The Royal Canadian Dragoons.* Ottawa: The Guild of The Royal Canadian Dragoons, 1983.

Griesbach, W.A. *I Remember.* Toronto: Ryerson, 1946.

Miller, Carmen. *Painting the Map Red: Canada and the South African War.* Montreal; McGill-Queen's University Press, 1993.

Morrison, Edward. *With the Guns in South Africa.* Hamilton: Hamilton Spectator, 1901.

Pakenham, Thomas. *The Boer War.* London: Weidenfeld and Nicolson, 1979.

Reid, Brian A. *Our Little Army in the Field: Canadians in South Africa, 1899-1902.* St. Catharines: Vanwell, 1996.

The First World War and Moreuil Wood

Cunniffe, R. *The Story of a Regiment. Lord Strathcona's Horse (Royal Canadians).* N.P.: Regimental Society, 1995

Dancocks, Daniel. *Legacy of Valour; the Canadians at Passchendaele.* Edmonton: Hurtig Publishers, 1986.

———. *Spearhead to Victory; Canada and the Great War.* Edmonton: Hurtig, 1987.

———. *Welcome to Flanders Fields; the First Canadian Battle of the Great War: Ypres, 1915.* Toronto: McClelland and Stewart, 1988.

French, Cecil, C.A.V. Barker and Ian K. Barker, eds. *A History of the Canadian Army Veterinary Corps in the Great World War, 1914-1919.* Guelph: Crest Books, 1999.

Goodspeed, Donald J. *The Road Past Vimy: The Canadian Corps 1914-1918.* Toronto: Macmillan, 1969.

Granatstein, J.L., and Desmond Morton. *Marching to Armageddon: Canadians and the Great War 1914-1919.* Toronto: Lester & Orpen Dennys, 1989.

Graves, Dianne. *A Crown of Life: The World of John McCrae.* St. Catharines: Vanwell, 1997.

Greenhous, Brereton. *Dragoon: The Centennial History of The Royal Canadian Dragoons.* Ottawa: The Guild of The Royal Canadian Dragoons, 1983.

———, and Stephen Harris. *Canada and the Battle of Vimy Ridge.* Montreal: Art Global, 1992.

Grodzinski, John R. *The Battle of Moreuil Wood.* N.P.: The Regimental Association of Lord Strathcona's Horse (Royal Canadians), 1993.

Mathieson, W.D. *My Grandfather's War: Canadians Remember the First World War 1914-1918.* Toronto: Macmillan, 1981.

Middlebrook, Martin. *The Kaiser's Battle: 21 March 1918: The First Day of the German Spring Offensive.* Middlesex: Penguin, 1983.

Nicholson, G.W.L. *Canadian Expeditionary Force 1914–1919: The Official History of the Canadian Army in the First World War*. Ottawa: Queen's Printer, 1962.

———. *The Gunners of Canada: The History of the Royal Regiment of Canadian Artillery, Volume I: 1534 – 1919*. Toronto: McClelland and Stewart, 1967.

Seely, J.E.B. *Adventure*. London: Heinemman, 1930.

———. *My Horse Warrior*. London: Hodder & Stoughton Limited, 1934.

Service, G.T. and J.K. Marteinson. *The Gate: A History of The Fort Garry Horse*. Calgary: privately printed, 1971.

Williams, S.H. *Stand to Your Horses: Through the First World War, 1914 – 1918, With the Lord Strathcona's Horse (Royal Canadians)*. Winnipeg, n.p., 1961.

The Second World War, Le Mesnil-Patry and the Kapelsche Veer

Barnard, W.T. *The Queen's Own Rifles of Canada 1860-1960*. Don Mills: 1960.

Blackburn, George. *The Guns of Normandy: A Soldier's Eye View, France, 1944*. Toronto: McClelland and Stewart, 1997.

———. *The Guns of Victory: A Soldier's Eye View, Belgium, Holland, and Germany, 1944-1945*. Toronto: McClelland and Stewart, 1998.

Conron, A.B. ed. *A History of the First Hussars Regiment. 1856-1980*. London: The Regiment, 1986.

Copp, Terry and Robert Vogel. *Maple Leaf Route: Caen*. Alma: Maple Leaf Route, 1983.

———. *Maple Leaf Route: Falaise*. Alma: Maple Leaf Route, 1983.

———. *Maple Leaf Route: Antwerp*. Alma: Maple Leaf Route, 1984.

———. *Maple Leaf Route: Scheldt*. Alma: Maple Leaf Route, 1985.

———. *Maple Leaf Route: Victory*. Alma: Maple Leaf Route, 1988.

Dancocks, Daniel. *The D-Day Dodgers. The Canadians in Italy, 1943-1945*. Toronto: McClelland and Stewart, 1991.

English, John A. *The Canadian Army and the Normandy Campaign. A Study of Failure in High Command*. Westport: Praeger, 1991.

Foster, Tony. *Meeting of Generals*. Toronto: Methuen, 1986.

Fraser, Robert, ed. *Black Yesterdays: The Argylls' War*. Hamilton: The Regiment, 1996.

Granatstein, J.L., and Desmond Morton. *A Nation Forged in Fire; Canadians and the Second World War 1939-1945*. Toronto: Lester & Orpen Dennys, 1989.

———. *Bloody Victory; Canadians and the D-Day Campaign 1944*. Toronto: Lester & Orpen Dennys, 1984.

Graves, Donald E. *South Albertas: A Canadian Regiment at War*. Toronto: Robin Brass Studio, 1998.

———, W.J. McAndrew and Michael J. Whitby. *Normandy 1944. The Canadian Summer*. Montreal: Art Global, 1994.

Greenhous, Brereton. *Dieppe, Dieppe*. Montreal: Art Global, 1992.

Hayes, Geoffrey. *The Lincs: A History of the Lincoln and Welland Regiment at War*. Alma: Maple Leaf Route, 1986.

McAndrew, W.J. *Canadians and the Italian Campaign, 1943-1945*. Montreal: Art Global, 1996

————, Bill Rawling and Michael Whitby. *Liberation: The Canadians in Europe*. Montreal: Art Global, 1995.

McKee, Alexander. *Caen: Anvil of Victory*. London: Souvenir Press, 1960.

Meyer, Hubert. *The History of the 12. SS-Panzerdivision Hitlerjugend*. Winnipeg: J.J. Fedorowicz, 1994.

Moulton, J.L. *Battle for Antwerp*. New York: Hippocrene, 1978.

Nicholson, G.W.L. *Official History of the Canadian Army in the Second World War. Vol. II. The Canadians In Italy, 1943-1945*. Ottawa: Queen's Printer, 1957.

————. *The Gunners of Canada. The History of the Royal Regiment of Artillery. Volume II: 1919-1967*. Toronto: McClelland and Stewart, 1967.

Reader's Digest. *The Canadians at War. 1939/1945*. 2 vols, Montreal: Readers Digest, 1969.

Roy, Reginald. *1944. The Canadians in Normandy*. Ottawa: Macmillan, 1984.

Stacey, Charles P. *Official History of the Canadian Army in the Second World War. Vol III. The Victory Campaign. The Operations in North-West Europe, 1944-1945*. Ottawa: Queen's Printer, 1960.

Whitaker, Dennis and Shelagh. *Tug of War: The Canadian Victory that Opened Antwerp*. Toronto: Stoddart, 1984.

Index

THE CONTRIBUTORS TO *FIGHTING FOR CANADA*

Donald E. Graves

Donald E. Graves, editor of *Fighting for Canada* and author of the study on the battle for the Kapelsche Veer, has been called "Canada's most reliable and readable military historian" and the "master of the battlefield narrative." A graduate in history of the University of Saskatchewan, he has written, co-written or edited more than a dozen books and served as an historical consultant for the Canadian Broadcasting Corporation's "People's History of Canada." He is also editor of the sequel to this book, *More Fighting for Canada: Five Battles, 1760-1944.*

As a military historian, Don Graves is perhaps best known for his popular series *Forgotten Soldiers: The War of 1812 in the North* (*Field of Glory: The Battle of Crysler's Farm, 1813*, and *Where Right and Glory Lead: The Battle of Lundy's Lane, 1814*, with a third volume forthcoming) but he is also the author of *South Albertas: A Canadian Regiment at War*, regarded by many as one of the best unit histories of the Canadian army in the Second World War. His most recent book is *Century of Service: The History of the South Alberta Light Horse,* the centennial history of Alberta's senior militia regiment.

Don Graves is the managing director of Ensign Heritage, a consulting firm with interest in historic sites, museums and publishing. He is in demand as a battlefield tour guide for both military units and commercial organizations. He resides with his author wife, Dianne, near Ottawa.

John R. Grodzinski

John Grodzinski, co-author of the study on Moreuil Wood, is a native of Hamilton, Ontario. He graduated from McMaster University in 1983 with a degree in political science and was commissioned in the Canadian Forces. After a year as a field engineer, he transferred to the armoured corps and has served two tours with his regiment, Lord Strathcona's Horse, in Calgary, and in staff positions in Winnipeg, Halifax and Kingston. Major Grodzinski has also held the appointments of museum officer for his regiment; director of public relations and historian at the Museum of the Regiments in Calgary; and executive secretary of the Canadian Army Museum in Halifax. He is author of *The Battle of Moreuil Wood* (1993) and *The Operational Handbook on the First Canadian Army* (1996) and has contributed articles to a number of journals. He is also a contributor to *More Fighting for Canada* (Robin Brass Studio, 2004). His interests include 18th and 19th century North American warfare; formation and unit organization and tactics; and the evolution and application of tactical doctrine from 1800 to the present. He also leads military tours of musket-period battlefield sites. John and his wife, Helga, enjoy music, any product of the grape, canoeing, hiking and spending time with their three children, Sylvia, Karl and Natasha.

Christopher Johnson

The cartographer and illustration artist for this book, Christopher Johnson graduated in history from Queen's University in Kingston. A serving officer of the Ontario Provincial Police for more than twenty-five years, Christopher Johnson has long had a fascination with armoured fighting vehicles and Canadian military history. These interests have led him into the field of computer-generated graphic art including maps and scale drawings of vehicles and weapons. He has contributed maps to Michael Green's *Patton and the Battle of the Bulge,* and maps and illustrations for Donald Graves's *Century of Service: The History of the South Alberta Light Horse* as well as many other books by that author. He also prepared maps and drawings for the histories of the Royal Canadian Armoured Corps, the Governor General's Horse Guards, Lord Strathcona's Horse and The Lake Superior Regiment. Chris resides with his wife, Debi, and children, Amanda and Michael, in Newcastle, Ontario.

Robert Malcomson

Robert Malcomson, author of the study of Queenston Heights, is an historian who specializes in the War of 1812 and has published many articles on that subject in such journals as *The Beaver, Freshwater, Naval History, Military History, The American Neptune, Inland Seas* and *The Mariner's Mirror.* He has also written monographs on the Battle of Queenston Heights and Brock's Monuments, contributed the section on operations on the Great Lakes to *The Naval War of 1812* (1998), co-authored (with his brother, Thomas) *HMS Detroit: The Battle for Lake Erie* (1991), and edited *Sailors of 1812: Memoirs and Letters of Naval Officers on Lake Ontario* (1997). His most recent book is *A Very Brilliant Affair: The Battle of Queenston Heights, 1812* (Robin

Brass Studio, 2003). His earlier work, *Lords of the Lake: The Naval War on Lake Ontario, 1812-1814* (RBS, 1998), described by one reviewer as an "outstanding book, beautifully produced" that "should be read by anyone interested in the War of 1812," received the John Lyman Award of the North American Society for Ocean History as the best work of Canadian naval and maritime history of 1998. Robert Malcomson resides with his wife, Janet, in the Niagara Peninsula, and is writing a book on the attack and burning of York during the War of 1812.

Ian M. McCulloch

The author of the study on Ticonderoga, Ian McCulloch is a native of Halifax, Nova Scotia. Educated in Scotland and Switzerland, he received an honours degree in journalism from Carleton University before being commissioned in the Canadian Forces in 1977 and serving with the Royal Canadian Regiment. In 1981-1983, he was an exchange officer with the 1st Battalion of the Royal Regiment of Fusiliers, part of the British Army of the Rhine. On his return to Canada, he again served with his regiment as a company commander before holding a series of appointments at army headquarters in St. Hubert, Quebec. Promoted to lieutenant colonel in 1993, he assumed command of the Black Watch (Royal Highland Regiment) of Canada. On completion of a Master's Degree in War Studies at the Royal Military College of Canada in 1997, Lieutenant Colonel McCulloch assumed his present appointment as deputy director of history and heritage, Ottawa. An avid student of military history, he is the author of a number of articles published in *The Beaver, Canadian Military History, Atlantic Advocate, The Journal of the Canadian Medical Association*, the *Canadian Infantry Journal* and *Civil War Magazine*. He is also a contributor to *More Fighting for Canada* (RBS, 2004). He was editor (with Timoth J. Todish) of *Through So Many Dangers: The Memoirs and Adventures of Robert Kirk, Late of the Royal Highland Regiment* (Purple Mountain Press and Robin Brass Studio, 2004). He has also been an historical consultant for "Civil War Journal" on the Arts & Entertainment Channel and the Canadian Broadcasting Corporation's forthcoming "Millenium History" project.

Michael R. McNorgan

Major Michael McNorgan, author of the study on Le Mesnil-Patry and co-author of the study on Moreuil Wood, is a native of London, Ontario, and holds a Master's Degree in History from Carleton University. A former member of the First Hussars, he served in the Canadian Forces for more than thirty years, most recently with the Directorate of History and Heritage in Ottawa. A lifelong student of mounted warfare, Mike McNorgan is the co-author of *The Royal Canadian Armoured Corps: An Illustrated History* (Robin Brass Studio, 2000) and a contributor to *More Fighting for Canada* (RBS, 2004).

Brian A. Reid

Lieutenant Colonel (Retd.) Brian Reid, author of the studies on Ridgeway and Leliefontein, was born in Fort Erie, Ontario, and attended school at Ridgeway. He joined the Canadian Army (Regular) as a gunner in 1957 and was commissioned through the Officer Candidate Programme in 1961. During a military career that spanned thirty-seven years, Brian Reid served in regimental, staff and liaison appointments in Canada, Europe and the United States. His last appointment, prior to his retirement in 1994, was in the Joint Plans and Operations Staff at National Defence Headquarters in Ottawa. Brian Reid is the author of *No Holding Back: Operation Totalize, Normandy, August 1944* (Robin Brass Studio, 2005), a detailed study of the first major operation fought by Canadians as an army in Normandy in the Second World War. He is also author of *Our Little Army: The Canadians in South Africa*, co-author of *RCHA – Right of the Line*, and has contributed a number of magazine articles on military history subjects. He is also a contributor to *More Fighting for Canada* (RBS, 2004). He is a member of the Victorian Military Society and the Royal Flashman Society of Upper Canada. Brian Reid resides with his wife, Patricia, near Ottawa and his interests include military history and travel.

ALSO PUBLISHED BY ROBIN BRASS STUDIO, THE COMPANION VOLUME
TO *FIGHTING FOR CANADA*

More Fighting for Canada: Five Battles, 1760–1944

Edited by Donald E. Graves

Don't miss the sequel to *Fighting for Canada: Seven Battles, 1758-1945* – five more fascinating battles fought by Canadians or on Canadian soil. The actions examined in detail are:

- **Sillery, 1760:** Eight months after the British victory at the Plains of Abraham, a bigger, more hard-fought and bloodier battle is fought on almost the same ground, and this time the outcome is different. – *by Ian M. McCulloch*

- **Cut Knife Hill, 1885:** During the Riel Rebellion, a Canadian force moves to surprise the Cree nation under Chief Poundmaker, only to be in turn surprised by the aboriginal peoples. This is the most detailed study ever published on this controversial encounter. – *by Robert H. Caldwell*

- **Paardeberg, 1900:** In February 1900 the Royal Canadian Regiment attacks an entrenched enemy across open ground swept by rifle fire – an act of incredible bravery or incredible stupidity? Paardeberg was Canada's first major overseas battle. – *by Brian A. Reid*

- **Iwuy, 1918:** A mixed force of Canadian cavalry and armour encounters a stubborn German rearguard position near the little village of Iwuy. The battle included Canada's last cavalry charge and the only occasion during the First World War when Canadians fought German armour. – *by Michael R. McNorgan*

- **Melfa Crossing, 1944:** As part of the Allied offensive in the Liri Valley, Canadian regiments make a surprise crossing of the heavily-defended Melfa River, winning a VC in the process. The strategic plan to destroy an entire German army hinged on the actions of a handful of Canadian soldiers with three small armoured vehicles. – *by John R. Grodzinski*

368 pages • 6.75 x 9.75 inches • about 120 pictures and maps • hardcover 1-896941-36-2 • paperback 1-896941-37-0

No Holding Back: Operation Totalize, Normandy, August 1944

Brian A. Reid

A major work in Canadian military history – the first detailed study of this key Canadian operation to appear in many years. Whether Totalize was a success or failure has been the subject of controversy for sixty years, and there was much to criticize. Brian Reid looks at all aspects of the operation, and in addition he has uncovered evidence that throws new light on the death of the "Black Baron," *SS-Hauptsturmführer* Michael Wittman, the top-scoring German tank ace of the war.

"With so much information so well presented, *No Holding Back* will probably remain the best book on this subject for many years. Highly recommended and likely to emerge as one of the best new WWII books of the year." *Stone & Stone Second World War Books*

500 pages • 6 x 9 inches • about 85 photographs, maps, diagrams • hardcover 1-896941-40-0

A Very Brilliant Affair: The Battle of Queenston Heights, 1812

by Robert Malcomson

The full story of the famous engagement, when American forces invaded across the Niagara River. The British defeated the intruders but their revered General Isaac Brock was killed. This is the first full-length study of this well known battle.

352 pages • 6 x 9 inches • about 60 pictures and maps • hardcover 1-896941-33-8 • (Published in U.S.A. by Naval Institute Press)

South Albertas: A Canadian Regiment at War

by Donald E. Graves

The gripping account of a Canadian World War II regiment, born on the Prairies, that forged a splendid record at the Battle of the Falaise Gap and in the Allied advance across northwest Europe.

"Without a doubt *South Albertas* is one of the finest unit histories ever published and in fact transcends that genre to rate as a truly great history of Canada at war." Christopher Evans, *Canadian Military History*

Revised edition • 408 pages • 8.5 x 11 inches • about 300 pictures • 19 maps • 8 pages of colour photos • hardcover 1-896941-39-7

The Incredible War of 1812: A Military History

by J. M. Hitsman, updated by Donald E. Graves

Widely regarded as the best one-volume history of the War of 1812, this book is available in a handsome paperback edition with additional maps and illustrations and extensive new appendices and notes.

"A good book, lavishly illustrated, and its author is pleasantly unimpressed by conventional wisdom." *The Times Literary Supplement* on the 1st edition.

432 pages • 6 x 9 inches • about 75 pictures and maps • paperback 1-896941-13-3